"Madeleine Blais, one of my favorite all-time ~~~~~~, ~~~~~~~ ~~~~~~~
Marble back to life in all of her splendid contradictions, breaking through
the mythology to restore the too-often overlooked tennis great to her rightful
place in the history of women in sports."
                              —**David Maraniss, Pulitzer Prize–winning author of**
                                    Path Lit by Lightning: The Life of Jim Thorpe

"Alice Marble took up tennis on public park courts in California and became
an international champion, known in her time as 'the girl who has everything,' and 'the first woman who plays tennis like a man.' Hers was a charm
school-era life of sporting success, stardust celebrity, public conscience,
private discontent, and lonely prevarication. The great victory of Madeleine
Blais's careful, moving biography is her sensitive understanding of a formidable competitor whose greatest rival was herself."
                              —**Nicholas Dawidoff author of *The Catcher Was A Spy***
                                          and *The Other Side of Prospect*

"Alice Marble was a dazzling beauty who played like a man, a clothing
designer who won Wimbledon in shorts, a writer, singer, and Hollywood
hobnobber, an activist whose words broke the color barrier in tennis. Her
personal life was full of mystery and myth . . . and she wanted it that way.
This extraordinarily researched book chases down every strand of Marble's
tangled life. Alice would have loved it, resented it, disputed it, refuted it . . .
and that only makes her more fascinating."
                              —**Mary Carillo, sportscaster/commentator on**
                                          NBC Sports and HBO Sports

"As the nation's current-day fascination with women's sports builds by the year,
best-selling author Madeleine Blais takes us back to another place and time,
to the thrilling and wonderfully entertaining life of 1930s tennis legend Alice
Marble. Never heard of her? Blais takes care of that, bringing this enchanting
icon of the twentieth century to life in riveting and rich detail in her meticu-
lously researched new book, *Queen of the Court*."   —**Christine Brennan,**
          ***USA Today* columnist; CNN, ABC News, and PBS NewsHour**
                              commentator; author of the best-selling *Inside Edge*

"This deeply researched biography offers an illuminating look at a major star
of her era—but it also portrays a woman whose later life was marked increasingly by loneliness, economic hardship, and perhaps some self-delusion . . .
Full of indelible scenes of just how lively and unconventional a person
[Marble] could be."   —***Daily Hampshire Gazette***

Queen
of the
Court

Also by Madeleine Blais

To the New Owners: A Martha's Vineyard Memoir

In These Girls, Hope Is a Muscle: A True Story of
Hoop Dreams and One Very Special Team

Uphill Walkers: A Memoir of a Family

The Heart Is an Instrument: Portraits in Journalism

Queen
of the
Court

The Many Lives of
Tennis Legend
Alice Marble

Madeleine Blais

Grove Press
New York

Published simultaneously in Canada
Printed in the United States of America

First Grove Atlantic hardcover edition: August 2023
First Grove Atlantic paperback edition: August 2024

Library of Congress Cataloging-in-Publication data is available for this title.

ISBN 978-0-8021-6345-5
eISBN 978-0-8021-6574-9

Grove Press
an imprint of Grove Atlantic
154 West 14th Street
New York, NY 10011

Distributed by Publishers Group West

groveatlantic.com

24 25 26 27   10 9 8 7 6 5 4 3 2 1

For Maureen Shea Blais
1913–2006

CONTENTS

Preface: Sixty Steps   ix

PART ONE: 1913–1931

CHAPTER 1   The Little White House on the Hill   3

CHAPTER 2   "Atta Boy, Alice"   15

CHAPTER 3   Where It Is Always June   26

CHAPTER 4   High Hat   32

CHAPTER 5   Three Crisp Twenty-Dollar Bills   40

CHAPTER 6   "Teach"   46

CHAPTER 7   Precarious   54

PART TWO: 1932–1934

CHAPTER 8   Cannonball   63

CHAPTER 9   A Little Hideaway   72

CHAPTER 10   Heat Wave   83

CHAPTER 11   Hello, Venus   90

CHAPTER 12   "You Don't Know Me, But . . ."   100

PART THREE: 1935–1939

CHAPTER 13   Starry Nights   111

CHAPTER 14   And Then . . . She Kissed It   121

CHAPTER 15   The Heart of Their Universe   130

CHAPTER 16   Debut Tonight!   151

CHAPTER 17   July 8, 1939   159

CHAPTER 18   Swing High, Swing Low   168

PART FOUR: 1940–1945

CHAPTER 19 $100,000 on the Table   179

CHAPTER 20   Sixty-One Stops   192

CHAPTER 21   Wonder Woman   215

PART FIVE: 1946–1966

CHAPTER 22   A Good Address   231

CHAPTER 23   A Vital Issue   249

CHAPTER 24   This Is Your Life   258

CHAPTER 25   The Homestretch   269

PART SIX: 1966–1990

CHAPTER 26   Once A Champion   287

CHAPTER 27   Queen Alice   295

CHAPTER 28   Taking a Chance on Love   303

CHAPTER 29   Lullaby at Night   313

CHAPTER 30   Iron Lady   324

CHAPTER 31   Game, Set, Match . . . And Questions   332

Acknowledgments   349

Appendix   353

Photo Credits   356

Notes   357

Selected Bibliography   397

Index   403

PREFACE

Sixty Steps

ALICE MARBLE PASSED in front of the grandstand, a short-sleeved blue cardigan resting on her shoulders. At five feet seven inches, her face filled with a kind of prairie openness, Marble appeared statuesque and accessible at the same time. There were seats on either side of the umpire's chair for spare rackets and towels, where she and her opponent, Britain's favored native daughter Kay Stammers, could rest for a few seconds during game changeovers. Good manners reigned, with gently spoken commands of "more balls, please" on the court, and praise, from announcers and spectators alike, intoned ever so softly: "Lovely shot, lovely shot, lovely shot."

On July 8, 1939, the women's singles final championship was contested at Wimbledon in the London suburbs.

Spectators stood in line all night to guarantee a place in the stands, a degree of ardor Marble had never witnessed in the United States. Rain had fallen on and off, and the air smelled of grass and diesel. "Lorry-loads of roses and geraniums"[1] enlivened the grounds. If Marble looked toward the press box, she could see a cluster of reporters, most of whom had ranked her as the favorite to win the tournament but also as tennis's number-one eyeful.

The crowd was on edge, less about the matches (the entire Wimbledon fortnight was considered a soggy letdown that season, and the men's singles final had been so lackluster that fans filed out before the finish in disgust) than about Germany. Hitler's forces had just seized Bulgaria. Poland could not be far behind.

Providing a dose of dignity and celebrity, the seventy-two-year-old queen mother perched in the royal box, "a large enclosure, seating fifty persons, with armchairs in the front row."[2] Alice Marble and her opponent stood side by side and performed, in unison, a bow, in the style of a page boy, in the queen's direction. Among her guests were Joseph Kennedy Sr., the ambassador from the United States to the Court of St. James's, bespectacled, with a ready grin and a bouncing gait, and his wife, Rose, the youthful dark-haired mother of nine.

Marble's measured manner as she traveled to Centre Court contrasted with her headlong dash as a child toward the public courts at Golden Gate Park in San Francisco, not far from her house. After playing for hours, she would return to her home "at the center of two very high hills"[3] in the Sunset District. Sixty steps took her from the bottom of the yard to the lofty eleva-tion of the front door. How often she had bounded up and down, two steps at a time, especially when she had forgotten something—her baseball mitt, her beanie, her kid brother, Tim, at one point almost a permanent appendage.

Now at the height of her powers as one of the most decorated athletes of her day, Alice Marble carried herself like a movie star: gorgeous outfits, a love of the spotlight, a side job as a torch singer. More than one person has observed that she was the human equivalent of Seabiscuit, the racehorse that won the hearts of so many Americans in the same era. Her ups and downs during the Great Depression fed the public's need for color in a world that was all too black and white. Newspapers in the most remote sections of the country ran wire-service stories extolling her accomplishments. In both 1939 and 1940, the Associated Press named her female athlete of the year.

She was called "the girl who has everything" in a book by Charlotte Himber, *Famous in Their Twenties*: "If the tennis champion had never played a game in her life Alice Marble would nevertheless have been included in one of those lists that organizations draw up annually of famous people. First of all, she is good to look at, with her golden crown of hair cut in the latest vagabond style, her large green-tinted eyes with the slightly overhanging lids, her pert nose, and her husky, endearing voice. She speaks like a delighted child breaking often into a wide, warm smile that makes one cheek dimple. She has a crisp, tingling quality."[4] Magazines predicted a glorious future in film: "A Tennis Tumble Bug Becomes a Hollywood Oomph Girl."[5] In the bloated language of a promotional brochure for a tour, she was hailed as a combination of "Joan D'Arc, Victoria Regina and Helen of Troy."[6]

An early avatar of the pressures and rewards attached to the public woman, she was a female with the gall and ability to make a name for herself, such that she could ride the gale force of her celebrity even after her ath-letic star faded into various new roles: pundit, fashion maven, book author, columnist, and sought-after public speaker. If Marble felt any misgivings or bitterness about having donated some essential component of her selfhood to her admirers as a form of entertainment, she rarely expressed it.

BORN IN 1913 on an isolated farm, Marble spent her early years on the frontier before moving to San Francisco, a city then in rapid transition. Her young womanhood in her twenties reflected America between the wars and the extremes of wealth in that time. Tennis offered her temporary membership in the upper class via transcontinental rail travel, ocean crossings, big band dinner dances, and impeccable service at grand hotels. After the Second World War put an end to her tennis career, she enjoyed a freedom of expression and movement not experienced by many women before her time.

Marble had her share of secrets, including the exact details about her relationship with her mentor and coach, Eleanor "Teach" Tennant, whose hold over her protégée verged on a kind of ownership. Questions abound about her friendship with the patron who saw to it that Marble would never sink into poverty for as long as he lived and beyond. Details of her biography spin out in unexpected directions. Two major events, a romance and a heroic mission, may have been fantasies. Smaller, less consequential contradictions weave in and out. She liked to embellish, and the question is not so much in what ways she gilded the lily but why.

The brilliance of Marble's tennis at her peak has never been in doubt. Martina Navratilova called her "a pioneer" and "the first woman to serve and volley well." Althea Gibson said, "She was my idol."[7] In her 1990 obituary, the New York Times quoted Jack Kramer, the United States champion in 1946 and 1947, winner of men's singles at Wimbledon in 1947, known above all for establishing the open era in American tennis for men: "She was the lady who most changed the style of play for women. She introduced the aggressive and athletic style that has led down to the female stars of today like Billie Jean King, Martina Navratilova and Steffi Graf."

Billie Jean King, Marble's most famous pupil, admired her on many levels, calling her, in the same obituary, a "picture of unrestrained athleticism. She is remembered as one of the greatest women to play the game because of her pioneering style in power tennis. I also admired her tremendously because she always helped others."[8]

Marble changed the game of women's tennis, turning it from a baseline-clinging endeavor into an all-court spectacle, but perhaps her greatest contribution was as a leader in civil rights. Marble influenced the future of tennis when she wrote an editorial in *American Lawn Tennis* magazine in 1950 (see appendix for full text), successfully urging integration, welcoming Althea Gibson first and foremost. A statue of Gibson has greeted visitors to the US Open in Forest Hills, Queens, New York, since 2019. During its unveiling, older fans shared stories of how thrilling it had been to see Gibson play.

Alice Marble faded from view long before her death, in 1990, at the age of seventy-seven, replaced by younger players with their own signature shots and their own compelling personalities, yet her story, if anything, has become more intriguing, not less, over the years.

QUEEN OF
THE COURT

PART ONE

1913–1931

CHAPTER 1

THE LITTLE WHITE HOUSE
ON THE HILL

FARM LIFE AND STOICISM go hand in hand, so when the Marble family decided in 1919 to leave its ranch in the Sierra Nevada mountain range, six-year-old Alice never forgot the way her parents transformed before her young eyes into people not quite recognizable: less reined in, more openly emotional. Her task-driven mother wept in happiness at the prospect of returning to her hometown in a less isolated part of the world. On the day of the move, Alice observed her father, thinking he was alone, kneeling on the floor of the soon-to-be-vacant house. The image was so beseeching, so penitential, it appeared out of character for a man who could, in her view, accomplish anything. Alice began to cry. Her father comforted her, hoisting her high on his shoulders. They headed outdoors to the horse and cart that would take them to the train station, then on to San Francisco and to a new vista.

Before he met his wife, Harry Marble had worked as a high climber in the logging industry in a task fit for either the brave or the foolish. Alice's first memoir, *The Road to Wimbledon,*[1] a slim, 166-page volume that provides a useful blueprint to the athlete's earliest years, documented his superhuman skills. Using his arms and the spikes of his shoes to get to the "dizzy height where the slight young branches begin," he would sway, "hundreds of feet above the ground." Securing himself with a leather belt that he flung around the tree and attached to iron rings in his belt and then jabbing the steel spikes on his "heavy leather-laced boots" into the trunk of the tree, he would lean "back precariously against the belt" and saw through the wood.

"As it begins to sway and crack," Marble wrote, "he calls a warning to the logging crew at the base of the tree. With a surging sound like the sea, the treetop falls, crashing its way to earth. The high climber sways with the lashing, vibrating shaft, keeping his balance by a sixth sense and the grace of God. Not until he feels a steadying quiet in the tree does he make a move—this aerialist who has no net. Then with a nonchalant ease and catlike agility, he climbs down spike by spike to the dull, unadventurous earth."[2]

In early 1905, closing in on forty, Harry met Jessie Wood. Suffering from hay fever, he had made an appointment with her brother-in-law, throat specialist Dr. George Gere, for whom she worked as a nurse. In Alice's telling, romance blossomed instantly: "The door was opened by a nurse in a trim white uniform, her white cap perched on her auburn curls. She was short, with the pleasantest curves. He looked down his lanky six feet at an oval face, with wide, very blue eyes."[3]

Harry manufactured reasons to hang around the city during his recovery to win the favor of Jessie, who had longed for a career as a singer in lounges and concert halls. Her family cautioned that such a pursuit would sully her good name, but she could perform in as many churches as she wished. Jessie, twenty-eight, dismissed another suitor before she consented to marry Harry, who had purchased a cattle farm, proof of his desire to settle down.

In the months between meeting his wife-to-be and their December 1905 wedding, Harry Marble and his brother Mel built a two-story house for the couple in the mountains near Beckwourth, in Plumas County, to which Harry's father had migrated from Maine years earlier in search of gold. The house's most distinguishing feature was the veranda on all four sides. Jessie Marble turned her back on the ninth-largest city in America and the largest city in California for a quieter life in the country.

The town to which they moved had been founded by and named after James Beckwourth, one of the few African American mountain men in the western frontier.[4] Alice Marble's version of her early years charts the nonstop activity associated with farm life. Every moment was accounted for: "Our day began at four in the morning and ended at eight at night. . . . I must have been a healthy, well-cared-for scrap of humanity, . . . for every one of us, big or little, had a definite place in the daily routine."[5] Alice's special charge, supervising her younger brother, Tim, started in earnest at the farm and continued throughout their childhood. She much preferred hardy tasks, especially in the company of her father. Her first memory, drenched in sodden detail, is of milking a cow at the age of four, incorrectly and, much to the amusement of the farmhands who watched as she fell flat on her back, splattered in fluid. She thought it was hilarious—anything to be outdoors, roaming free; anything to escape the domestic tasks that her mother performed with such seeming cheer.

Depending on the season, Jessie Marble, short but strong at four feet ten inches, got out "big kettles and made jellies and jams from fruit grown on the farm, and in odd hours she fixed kegs of pickled beets and salted down cabbage to make sauerkraut, and then marinate fish caught from the stream that crossed our land."[6] It was a full house. Although Alice's parents had married late in life by the standards of their era, the children arrived quickly and often, five in all. Dan came first, in 1906, George in 1908, followed by Hazel in 1910, then Alice in 1913, and baby Tim three years later. With seven family members and six farmhands, Jessie Marble prepared meals three times a day for up to thirteen people at a time, of "beef and lamb, pork, wild game, ducks and geese, and the freshest of vegetables from the garden." She did all the housekeeping, and she sewed most of the family's clothing by hand. In the evening, Alice and Hazel would sometimes huddle at her side, poring over the catalog from Montgomery Ward, a paraffin lamp lighting its pages while they chose fabrics. Alice always treasured the noisy memory of Jessie at a "rickety sewing machine. It clattered and banged and jammed and stuck, but mother managed it with the patience and the skill of a bronco buster."[7]

Not just the family but also neighbors benefited from Jessie's sense of industry. Alice remembered how her mother's forays outside the home combined charity and efficiency; she would help "Mrs. Jones when the baby came, or lend a hand when sickness struck, or take a home-made gift to a child on a birthday. The busiest woman I have ever known, yet she always seemed to have plenty of time."[8]

Harry Marble, for whom self-reliance was an art form, concerned himself with infrastructure and crops and animal husbandry. His daughter saw him as a problem-solving wizard, the "handiest man in the world." Stoves, wheelbarrows, lamps—he could, she boasted, fix anything. When he wasn't applying his ingenuity to home repair, he applied it to creating products from scratch. Alice recalled how he would take cattle hides, tanned and pliant, and make shoes for the family, after first tracing everyone's foot on a piece of cardboard. She watched while "he cut the leather sole, punched holes with an awl along the edge, and sewed the top on with the narrowest strips of leather. Our boots were laced up with buckskin lacings and fitted so well we never knew we had them on." Among his inventions was a washing machine "operated by a horse, going around it in a circle." The children would ride the horse, and as it moved, the wash would get done.[9] He had, in effect, joined whimsy with practicality in the form of a carousel with a work ethic.

The farm had no plumbing, but it featured a bathtub that Harry Marble carved inside the trunk of a redwood tree, piping water into it from nearby sulfur springs. The warmth of the healing waters attracted arthritis sufferers, leading him to construct cabins on the family's property that he rented out to augment income. Families with invalids arrived routinely. The Sacones from Spain, numbering eighteen family members, were the first foreigners Alice had ever seen. They claimed to be Romani, which deepened their allure. Only the patriarch spoke English, explaining that "his *senora* was molested most terribly with pains in the joints," and the family had traveled many miles after hearing about the "miraculous power in the bubbling, boiling and pain-killing springs." Alice remembered being thrilled by "their black curly heads, ruddy dark faces, and their gay endless chatter in rippling soft speech, though not a word could I understand." She was entranced by the way they cooked over an open fire, and the food itself intrigued, especially *ajo* (garlic), which Jessie disdained and young Alice devoured. Thanks to the Sacones, Alice saw her first toy—a wondrous device—a top of many colors. The family stayed for a couple of years, the older children going to school with Alice's older siblings and helping with the chores.[10]

A "banner day," in Alice's ebullient memory, meant a trip to town, presumably Beckwourth, riding on the buckboard, a four-wheeled wagon hitched to a horse or another large animal. These excursions combined a sense of adventure with the more practical purpose of provisioning the household. Town provided the few staples the farm could not generate, including "sugar and salt, pepper and spices, tea, and coffee in the bean." Harry Marble traditionally treated the children to "a bag of white, round peppermint sweets," Alice remembered, "the only sweets I knew."[11]

At Christmas, the high point of the year, as recorded by Marble in *The Road to Wimbledon*, the Marble family decorated a tree with garlands of popcorn and "sugar apples," pared slices of fruit coated in hot red syrup, dried out, and then strung as ornaments. Alice recalled that each child received "a single gift, a useful thing." One year it was a gun for Dan, a skunk trap for George, new dresses for Hazel and Alice, and a knitted cap for Tim. In her 1946 memoir, Alice recalled how holiday tradition called for a pig to be roasted on a spit in the open fireplace in the kitchen. Neighbors—the nearest four miles distant, most ten or more—arrived with their own contributions. As a prelude to the celebration, there might be a few treats, cookies with a wholesome pedigree, such as oatmeal or molasses. The crowning glory was a "chocolate cream cake with chocolate frosting and thick whipped cream on top." As the festivities wound down at twilight, Jessie Marble would play carols and hymns on her pride and joy, the only upright piano in the valley. "Father had sent it from San Francisco," Alice wrote, "and brought it over in the wagon from Oroville [a distance of sixty-eight miles]." Sometimes Jessie Marble soloed in her low register—the songs filled with swollen avowals of lasting love set to classical rhythms, old parlor-room favorites such as "Beautiful Dreamer," "Drink to Me Only with Thine Eyes," and "Ah! Sweet Mystery of Life." Years later, the memory of those songs prompted an older Alice to try her hand at the public singing career denied to Jessie.

The Marbles spent thirteen years on their cattle farm in the mountains, sequestered from the larger world. Major global events appear to have had little impact on the family. World War I was "fought and won without appreciably touching our lives, until one day after the Armistice, word came which greatly excited my mother,"[12] recalled Alice, who was five at the time. From the initial move in 1906 to November 1918, Jessie Marble had not seen a single one of her relatives. When her two nephews, fresh from the battlefield, showed up, she became overwhelmed with feelings of homesickness. The duo guaranteed that the Marble children would hold them in high regard forever by slipping each of them a silver dollar. Their effect on the family's destiny was even more profound. Jessie Marble started talking with greater and greater longing about the city she had left behind. Acceding to her wishes, her husband took an unusual week off from the farm and went to San Francisco on his own to look for work and a place to live. An announcement soon followed: Harry Marble had found a job with a lumber company, and instead of living five miles from the nearest tiny town, the family would be moving to the big city. Alice's parents enumerated the selling points: neighbors, right next door; modern marvels such as tall buildings, some as high as twenty stories; schools nearby; the ocean.

Jessie Marble would be returning to a city markedly different from the one she had left. While the family had been away, the city's population had risen from four hundred thousand to more than a half million residents. The most defining event in their absence had been the earthquake that struck at five in the morning on April 18, 1906, leaving, in the official estimate, 375 dead.[13]

There was brief talk of taking time to slowly rebuild, to create "Paris, but with hills," a sophisticated city with monuments and vistas galore, but such a prospect would take patience. San Francisco was a young city moving at a fast pace. By the Sunday after the earthquake, hundreds of workers had already descended on it to restore order and remove debris. As one report claims, "At the gutted door of a ruined building, appeared a firm order: 'Don't Talk Earthquake. Talk Business.'"[14]

As the city rebuilt, it endured corruption, jailed politicians, and a violent (thanks to professional union busters) streetcar strike in May 1907 that left twenty-five passengers and about a half dozen workers dead. Nonetheless, with thousands of new structures and its harbor and the trade it brought in, the city was soon revived. Using the opening of the Panama Canal as a pretext to celebrate its rebirth, San Francisco mounted the Panama–Pacific International Exhibition, from February 20 to December 4, 1915. The enticements included an early steam locomotive, the Liberty Bell, on tour from Philadelphia, an auto race in which one vehicle reached a speed of fifty-six miles per hour, and perhaps most thrilling, a telephone line through which people from New York City, three thousand miles away, could listen to the roar of the Pacific Ocean.[15]

The influenza epidemic of 1918 might have caused the family to think twice before relocating to such a populous area. San Francisco was hit hard that fall, despite advance warning about deaths on the East Coast starting in the previous spring. As the flu spread, Dr. William Hassler, the city's health officer, ordered streetcars to be disinfected. He issued instructions to use handkerchiefs, clean contaminated utensils, and avoid anyone in the "habit of coughing, sneezing or spitting promiscuously."[16] Soon the board of health ordered churches, schools, and "all amusement and public gathering places" to close. Forbidden diversions included merry-go-rounds, penny arcades, dances at cabarets and cafés, movies, community singing, and "all social gatherings of whatsoever nature and kind."[17] The Red Cross organized the city into nine districts, supervised by a captain who sent nurses and aides to homes.

San Francisco led the way in the early and widespread use of masks—sold for ten cents at Red Cross booths downtown—as a way to "prevent the spread of the dread malady."[18] Dr. Hassler issued cleaning instructions: plunge the mask in alcohol or boil for five minutes.[19] Masks soon became mandatory for everyone from baseball umpires and barbers to "hotel and rooming house employees, bank tellers, druggists, store clerks, and any other person serving the public." When the supply of gauze masks dwindled, newspapers ran articles encouraging resourceful alternatives, such as chiffon or linen for women and children or the creation of "nosebags, from the Turkish-inspired muslin *yashmak* veil."[20]

On October 25, 1918, the *San Francisco Chronicle* ran a banner headline across the front page: "Wear Your Mask! Commands Drastic New Ordinance." The preferred fabric was four-ply gauze, five inches wide, seven inches long. Those who did not conform were labeled slackers and subjected to scornful stares, fines of $5 to $100, and/or jail sentences.[21]

Dr. Hassler stayed upbeat: "We can keep the influenza within bounds . . . and we will with the co-operation of everyone."[22] Funeral services were limited to fifteen minutes, dance halls were shuttered, and travel during rush hour was discouraged. Streetcar conductors had specific instructions to "keep the windows of their cars open in all but rainy weather."[23]

On November 21, 1918, bells, sirens, and whistles proclaimed the repeal of the mask law.[24] Soon after, schools reopened, with a shortened Christmas vacation and an extended term, and the public libraries provided a place for students to study, maskless. A feeling of optimism prevailed.[25]

The joy was premature. By January 17, the mask law was reinstated. Afterward, cases begin to decline, a downward trend that "continued unbroken until the epidemic sank below the threshold of public attention."[26]

Unfortunately, some citizens remained vulnerable to the infection, including members of the Marble family. Since Alice always reported her age as six at the time of the family's move, the relocation would appear to have occurred sometime after her birthday, September 28, in 1919. In her record of the trip, Alice recounted that the family first traveled to Oroville, the biggest city she had ever seen. Her father pointed out various wonders: a bank, a post office, and "places called restaurants where people could go have dinner." In Oroville, she met a Black person for the first time, a porter who helped the family board the train. In the dining car, the fare was not up to her standards. The milk, not fresh off the farm, made her gag. The bread had a nebulous taste, "like straw."[27]

Traveling overnight by train, the Marbles arrived after breakfast to a city now featuring automobiles chugging up and down the streets alongside cable cars, thanks to Henry Ford's invention of the Model T. Alice was proud that her Uncle Mel owned such a wondrous vehicle. With leather seats and interior brass trim, the Model T sold for $500 in 1918, down from the original price of $825 in 1909, the year after its invention.[28] Driving a Model T was not easy. There was no gas pedal; the accelerator was on the steering wheel, on the right, echoing the position of the whip in a horse and buggy. At its fastest, the car could go forty to forty-five miles per hour ("downhill, with the wind behind you," as one driver has attested).[29]

The family stopped first at Jessie Marble's sister's grand house, where Jessie and Harry Marble had met fourteen years earlier. It was four stories high, with "black shiny floors and a beautiful piano,"[30] and Aunt Jo lived there with her husband, Dr. George Gere. After lunch, the Marbles boarded a trolley and rode west to the Sunset District, once known as the "outside lands," a humbler neighborhood than Aunt Jo's, famous for its ominous geography. "The coldest winter I ever spent was summer in San Francisco," Mark Twain is alleged to have said, a witticism that applies above all to the Sunset, bordering the Pacific, where ocean breezes clashing with warm land guarantee a frequent glum combination of wind, fog, and cold temperatures, especially in summer.

Jessie Marble pointed out their new home: "The little white house on the hill, that's ours, children." Harry Marble was already there, waiting at the top of the sixty steps. "From the tiny front porch we could see all of San Francisco and the bay," Alice observed—on the days that were free from fog.[31]

The exterior staircase at the house on the hill figured in a rare photograph of Alice Marble's entire family, taken just after the move. Harry Marble, even-featured and rugged, is next to Jessie, dressed in what looks like a bibbed apron, as if she could not afford to pause for long from her household duties. Crowded onto a single step, the offspring sit in birth order, oldest to youngest, left to right. Dan at thirteen years, dark-haired, smiling, is next to George, head down, squinting. They are dressed in jackets and ties and short pants, hats on their laps, removed for the sake of the shot. Hazel sits next to Alice, the girls twinned in white dresses, their hands folded. Hazel's smile is, if anything, even bigger than her sister's. Alice, whose hair is fashioned in a bowl cut, already conveys the spark-plug hardiness that she would eventually put to good use in a variety of youthful athletic endeavors. Tim, at the age of three, in shorts, stares quizzically in the direction of the camera. His mother's left arm grips his chest, likely guarding against a break for freedom.

The poignancy of the photograph lies in the knowledge of what was to come. The family on the staircase would have been spared so much sorrow and so many struggles had someone said to Harry, on a day not so far off, "Don't get in that car with your brother."

NOT TOO LONG before the Marbles settled in the Sunset District, it had been a landscape of sand dunes, some a hundred feet high. The fog was "not just unappealing," a history of the area claims, "it could be homicidal." One cautionary tale, reported in an 1897 newspaper article, documented the death of a woman who lived in a nearby almshouse that catered to luckless prospectors who landed penniless in the city after their dreams of easy riches evaporated when they failed to strike either gold or silver. A female resident of the charitable institution became disoriented in the dunes. Footprints revealed that she had traveled in an endless circle before she died, "overcome by exhaustion and cold."[32]

At the beginning of the twentieth century, the Sunset District was nicknamed "Carville" because squatters lived there in abandoned vehicles on the dunes. Jackrabbits and squirrels were sufficiently plentiful that residents could count on them for supper. In 1917, the city fathers reclaimed some of the land, and as a result small homes, such as the one the Marbles moved to, sprang up. They were among the first wave of new residents. Just a few blocks from the family's address, dunes still beckoned, and Alice remembered picking strawberries and wildflowers. Wealthier citizens of the city sometimes dismissed the houses in the Sunset as cookie-cutter: too similar, too simple. Such snobbery did not factor in the economic reality of the new homeowners. Many had been living in cramped apartments. A house in the Sunset represented entrée into the American dream, with more spacious and more sanitary dwellings.[33]

The Marbles' house had two bedrooms, one each for the parents and the boys. Hazel and Alice slept in the living room. The single bathroom had a washbasin and a bona fide bathtub, not one carved into a tree trunk. The first telephone Alice remembered seeing was the one in the hallway. The kitchen spilled onto the back porch with a gas stove and an icebox.[34] Like most children, Alice and her brothers could turn anything into a toy, including the coal stove in the kitchen, seeing who could hit it with their spit from farthest away.[35] Her family called her Miss Perpetual Motion because of the way she played a rudimentary form of basketball indoors. She would perch a garbage can on top of two chairs and from across the room try to throw balled-up paper or rubbish into it.[36] Best of all, there was a family next door with eleven children, a ready and constant source of playmates.

In those first hopeful days at her new residence, Alice enjoyed going to a real grocery store, where she was most entranced, of all the enticements that might have caught her fancy, by the packaging. Never had she seen such a plethora of boxes and bottles. She accompanied her father on errands and listened as he, pleased to share his expertise with the butcher, discussed cuts of meat.[37] A brother and a sister in the neighborhood taught Alice how to fly a kite. The children played in the dunes, pretending to be members of the French Foreign Legion as they chased each other and rolled down the sand. Their play coincided with the pleadings of the rags and bottles and sacks man as the bells in his horse-drawn cart jangled.

Generous with his rides, Harry's brother Mel took the Marbles on a tour in his Model T. Alice was impressed by the steep hills that made the streets appear limber, almost double-jointed. The family was poised to tread a solid path to a decent future when, after only a few short months in the new setting, the four older children, arriving home from school, were ushered into the kitchen by their mother, her eyes swollen.

Their father had been in an accident in Uncle Mel's car and was recovering from a broken shoulder and a crushed back. He required solitude, strict bed rest, and a quiet household. After days of whispers and tiptoes, his health improved, and the doctor pronounced him on the mend, but the recovery was short-lived.

Then Hazel contracted pneumonia, and the three boys in the family came down with the flu, as did thousands of other San Franciscans, during what Marble called the "epidemic."[38] Only Alice and her mother were spared. In his weakened condition, Harry Marble succumbed to bronchial pneumonia, at age fifty-three, on January 1, 1920. An atmosphere of "gloom and great silence" filled the house.

"I had never seen death before, so I didn't really understand," Alice wrote later. "The only reason I knew that something terrible had happened was that there were no presents, no tree and no Christmas carols."[39] Time compressed in her young mind. For the rest of her life, Alice reported her father's death as having occurred on Christmas Eve, despite the date recorded on the death certificate. In the surge of grief, there was one mercy: The other family members all recovered, including Hazel, the hardest hit.

Compounding the sorrow over her father's death was the death of a playmate soon after. Describing San Francisco as "one big playground for a kid from the backwoods," Marble was thrilled when she acquired her first pair of roller skates, calling them "my automobile, my locomotive, my sailing ship." She and a pal she called Billy (never providing a last name), while out wheeling around the neighborhood, raced each other home at dusk. They came to a wide street. Alice crossed without incident, but Billy wasn't as quick. "I had just skipped over the streetcar tracks when I heard the car's warning bell, the screech of locked brakes on metal tracks, and the startled cries of passengers thrown from their seats," she recounted. "Looking back, I saw Billy stumble on the tracks and fall screaming under the trolley's wheels. I will take that memory to my grave." Among the repercussions of losing her father and her friend in such a short interval was that she "never again attended a funeral after Billy's."[40]

WITH HARRY GONE, the family's financial prospects plummeted. The house was "only half paid for," and "there were many doctor's bills . . . no insurance."[41] Jessie Marble found work cleaning offices that began at four in the morning. Hazel helped run the house. Alice continued to care for Tim. Dan dropped out of school at age thirteen and worked as a hardwood-floor apprentice. George, eleven, followed suit two years later. Jessie ceded most of the parental authority to her oldest son.

Alice recalled: "Dan selected our clothes, told us when to go to bed, gave us the devil when our school grades were not up to par. He took complete charge of the family budget, and I went with him once a week to buy large quantities of food."[42] Young Alice took to calling him the "papa of the family" and even "dictator."

Alice missed her father: "It was always to him I went with my little problems to sit on his lap and to dog his footsteps." She liked her public school, and she tolerated Sunday school at the Congregational church, where she and Hazel often accompanied their mother, who sang in the choir. Sing-alongs at home, a common low-cost amusement, provided entertainment: "Music was very important in our family. All of us could sing. My mom had a nice contralto voice, and my brother Dan a baritone. My sis and all of us, that's what we did for fun. We'd sit around the piano. And my mother was such a ham that she'd say, 'Children, what time is it?' And we'd say, 'Oh, mother, it's only 8:00.' It would be ten, but she didn't know the difference because she loved to play and sing."[43]

While the two older boys were often off playing in the park, Alice and Tim enjoyed classic amusements such as "top spinning and jacks." Hazel was a homebody, but the rest of the family was a talented lot, as their many future athletic accomplishments would make clear, especially Dan's in handball and Tim's in baseball. Even Jessie Marble earned respect as one of the fastest moms on the block during nighttime games of kick the can.

At that time, Alice discovered the movies. The one way she could get her mother to rest was to entice her to attend a double feature from time to time, and sometimes Dan accompanied her as well. Alice fancied herself an expert on film from an early age and often spouted movie trivia to prove the point.

The movies became a lifelong love of supreme entertainment for Alice: "When I was a child, ten cents let me into that magic world. I saw every movie that came to town, and—thanks to my photographic memory—had a wealth of knowledge about all the actors and actresses, even the bit ones. Movie stars were a breed apart to me, untouchable and wonderful."[44]

CHAPTER 2

"ATTA BOY, ALICE"

B IG MAN. FALSE TEETH. Worked long hours. Not above offering the occasional bribe.

Alice's recollection of her mother's unmarried brother Arthur Wood, who moved into the already well-populated Marble household shortly after Harry's death, included all of the above. The addition of Uncle Woodie did not interrupt the family routine so much as enhance it, inserting the authority of an older male into the household.

He would introduce young Alice to her first, and perhaps most lasting, athletic love. Uncle Woodie enjoyed several sporting instincts of his own, especially betting on the horses. He taught his niece about racing forms and how to organize his wagers for him. "I learned the names of horses and owners by heart, their handicaps, the best jockeys, and the names of famous races and racetracks," she recalled.[1] On the rare day of a big win, he would give her a quarter, which she spent on groceries for the family; in 1924, twenty-five cents could purchase a dozen eggs or three pounds of macaroni or three heads of lettuce.[2]

Uncle Woodie's job as the gripman on the cable car that went up California Street was nerve-racking,[3] as he had to control the massive brake line on the steep hills. Given the responsibilities it entailed, the job earned city-wide prestige and admiration. His shift ended at one a.m., and if the children stayed quiet, and he managed to sleep in for the whole week, he rewarded them with a dime on Saturday mornings.

A former semiprofessional baseball player, their uncle often took Alice and Tim to watch a Pacific Coast League game and cheer for the home team, the San Francisco Seals, at Recreation Park. Located in the Mission District, the ballpark had wooden stands and could seat fifteen thousand fans. A new world opened for Alice, a place where she could go after school and on weekends. For children like her and young Tim, hanging out at the park when the team was practicing hit the perfect price point: it was free.

Uncle Woodie also took Alice and Tim to a vacant corner lot near their house and played baseball with them. On Sundays, Uncle Woodie took them to Golden Gate Park, where they would watch "all the boys gathered to have their morning and afternoon games," Alice recalled. "Uncle brought us gloves and a bat and ball. During the time between the two big games, he played with us, and then we sat watching the final game between the two teams."[4] On occasion, Uncle Woodie, though older than fifty, would be asked to play in the outfield, which pleased him and his young charges. The two competing teams economized on verbiage by sharing the same name, the Park Bums.

Alice and Tim made good use of their weekly allowance from Uncle Woodie. On the way to the park, they would stop at a bakery for a ten-cent square of lead cake, a thrifty treat that came into vogue during World War I, when the motto was, "Use it up, wear it out, make it do, or do without." Concocted of whatever was available in kitchens often lacking milk, eggs, and sugar, lead cake was so dense it took both Marble children to carry their purchase to the park, where, in a spirit of enterprise, they sold pieces for two cents each. With the profit, they would buy a bottle of milk to wash down their own portions.

Alice's freedom to roam had one hitch—the need to keep an eye on Tim: "Mother had made it very clear that I had to look after my younger brother at all times. I didn't mind him too much, but I resented mother's concern for him. When I fell off a building or got a nail in my foot or skinned my knee, mother said, 'Put some iodine on it.' But when Tim scratched himself, mother rushed him to the doctor."[5]

Even so, Alice could see that her baby brother had the makings of a stellar athlete. After dinner on weeknights, while Uncle Woodie was at work, Alice often practiced with Tim in the corner lot. She could see that he was better at baseball than most of the boys her age. "We had a special routine," she wrote. "First, I practiced my curves and fastballs, while Tim caught. Then Tim's turn would come. We stood about twenty feet apart while I bunted balls for Tim's in-fielding practice."[6] Tim had his eyes on shortstop.

Try as she might, Alice was not always the most effective custodian of Tim. One day she threw a fastball when he was expecting a curve. The ball smashed into the catcher's mask, causing Tim to fall over backward. The wire front of the mask embedded in his skin and, even with a half dozen kids trying to pry it off, would not budge. Money was always a consideration for Alice, but in that moment, she forgot about the twenty-five cents that the mask cost and found a hardware man willing to "file it off," removing it and the skin beneath it in strips.[7]

Afterward, Alice invested several of her own pennies on a jawbreaker for Tim, hoping it would make him feel better. The peace offering backfired when he drank some water with the candy in his mouth and aspirated, almost choking to death. She hit him on the back, twice, with as much force as she could summon. The candy flew out of his mouth, straight into a soda-fountain mirror, managing to break it. Alice delivered the details of this series of events in a tone of evenhanded amusement in *The Road to Wimbledon*, yet surely in the moment her brother's possible disfigurement and threatened suffocation, and the accidental vandalism, were in some way terrifying.

As often as possible, Alice and Tim attended Seals games at Recreation Park. The stadium was rickety, with wooden seats; the lower deck was covered by an upper deck open to the elements. Tim and Alice occupied the left-field bleachers, where seats cost ten cents. Alice could earn a dollar a day stocking groceries, and she also made money pitching pennies. On Fridays, children were admitted free. If a Seals outfielder managed to catch the last out of the game, tradition dictated that "kids would pour out of the bleachers, climb on to the top of the inner left field wall, hang by their arms, and drop down into the outfield," one chronicle of the times recounts. "They would surround the outfielder who caught the fly ball and he would throw it into the air for a wild scramble for the cherished souvenir."[8] Despite that idyllic moment, it was often a rough scene, in part owing to the "booze cage." In this section, only fifteen feet from the baseline and closed off by chicken wire, a seat cost seventy-five cents and included a choice of a shot of whiskey, two bottles of beer, or a ham and cheese sandwich.

"You know, ballgames for us kids were such an inexpensive hobby," Alice recalled. "We were poor, so naturally we picked a hobby that was cheap."[9] She could not get enough: "Why, baseball almost made a bum out of me. I went every day that the club was home."[10]

At Seals practices, Alice caught fly balls, outshining her peers. Dan was not as sold on baseball, however. He had another sport in mind for her, one he thought was more refined, in which his sister had already made a bit of a splash. On October 16, 1926, a Saturday, at Golden Gate Park, Alice, then thirteen, had played competitive tennis for the first time successfully: "A. Marble d. [defeats] R. Rosenbach 6–0, 6–0," the *San Francisco Examiner* reported.[11] She had played in the park before but not in a formal competition until that moment. On November 20, she played in the handicap singles in a tournament. She was assessed at "plus 15," meaning that she needed only three points instead of four to win. In those early efforts, Alice was armed mainly with her enthusiasm. She told one interviewer she played with a borrowed racket: "It was a little on the dead side and weighed fifteen ounces—like playing with a screen door."[12] One of Alice's many interviewers summed up the system of who got to play when: "You had to be good to get a chance to do a decent amount of playing, because, when you applied for a court, you were put on a list. If you had finished and lost your first set, you were placed at the bottom of the list and had to wait two hours to play again. If you won you stayed on the court and took on the next person on this list."[13]

Determined to get his sister to love the game, when Dan found out that the dazzling French tennis star Suzanne Lenglen, the top-ranked woman that year, was on a four-month pro tour that would take her from Boston to Miami to Cuba to Canada to California, he invested in tickets to an exhibition match on December 7, 1926, at the Civic Auditorium in San Francisco.

Lenglen and *legend*: the two words sound alike, as well they should.[14] From 1914 to 1926, Lenglen won thirty-one major championships. Like many great athletes, beyond muscle and cunning she possessed a knack for attracting a narrative around her exploits. One story told of a time in 1921 when she had to default an exhibition match against the Norwegian-born American champ Molla Bjurstedt Mallory at the US National Championships (renamed the US Open in 1968) in Forest Hills, New York, suffering from a genuine bout of whooping cough, which the crowd took as fake. The spectators' jeers of disapproval caused "La Divine," as she was known in her country, to burst into tears. Lenglen took on Mallory twice subsequently, defeating her decisively. After the victorious second match, Lenglen shook Mallory's hand and then, in a delicious taunt, emitted a couple of gentle fake coughs to punctuate the moment.

Lenglen's grace, as she swooped and bent and bowed and stood on tiptoe on the court, echoed the liquidity of her last name. The early tennis costumes for women were unappealing and cumbersome—bulky, corseted dresses—but eventually those outfits gave way to more comfortable alternatives, a trend Lenglen led.[15] She favored one-piece flowing frocks designed by a French couturier and a modern bobbed hairdo. Even Alan Little, the one-man encyclopedia of tennis, who until his death in 2017 presided over the library at Wimbledon with a sense of formality, an ironclad commitment to midafternoon tea, and a penchant for understatement (when asked about the bombing of Wimbledon's Centre Court during World War II, he said, "Oh, that . . ."), rhapsodized over Lenglen's couture: "Her dresses always appeared uncreased as she never sat, once dressed for tennis. The soft hat was replaced by what became known as the 'Lenglen bandeau,' several yards of georgette, varying in color from heliotrope to lemon, swathed around her hair. Later, Suzanne chose multi-colored silk chiffon for the bandeau, which was usually held in place by a diamond arrow. With every match she changed the color of her bandeau and matching cardigan. She scarcely ever wore jewelry."[16]

Lenglen's dresses ended at mid-calf, shockingly short at the time. She bared her arms, another affront to contemporary standards. She sometimes wore a white fur coat to matches. Encouraged to take up the game as a child to control her asthma, between sets she often sucked on sugar cubes dipped in brandy or cognac. She did not mince her words: if she thought she was going to win, she said so. Rather than clinging to the baseline, she favored a more masculine style of play, a harbinger of Alice's future approach. Both women would be known for claiming the entire court as their rightful kingdom.

Lenglen's US tour was organized by C. C. Pyle, nicknamed "Cash and Carry." Lenglen had turned professional in August 1926, the first woman to do so. There had been pro tournaments before, but this was the first traveling pro exhibition series in tennis history. Fans in San Francisco hoped she would square off against local star Helen Wills, a three-time US champion, who had played, and lost to, Lenglen in the so-called Match of the Century in Cannes the previous February.[17] Instead, American player Mary K. Browne said she too was going pro and would join Lenglen. Pyle also hired four male players, after being turned down by Bill Tilden and Billy Johnston: Vincent Richards, Paul Féret, Howard Kinsey, and Harvey Snodgrass.

Lenglen postured in interviews, exhibiting Gallic impatience with Prohibition, dismissing it as American idiocy: "There is one thing you should do to improve your country. Get rid of prohibition. How do I like it? I hate it. Since I was a little girl, I have had wine with my meals. Here your law says I can't."[18]

The French star showed the same superior attitude when the subject involved the hypocrisy about being a good sport: "How can a good sport not care if he loses? To want to win, that makes the good sport. Myself, I would not be a good loser—it is not expected of me."[19]

Lenglen's love of beautiful clothes, on the court and off, was well established, and the high-end San Francisco store I. Magnin and Company took out a full-page newspaper ad welcoming Lenglen and telling its discerning customers that the store's fourth floor and its display windows were featuring "original models as well as a collection of exact replicas" of Lenglen's fashions, designed by the "famous French couturier" Jean Patou.

When Lenglen arrived in San Francisco, she met with the press at the elegant Palace Hotel. The *Examiner* reported that she spoke in a "soft voice whose musical quality hasn't been sufficiently noted in the past." Lenglen was enjoying America and said, "If I ever come to this country to live, I shall choose the West, I promise you."[20]

The morning of the match, December 7, 1926, the *Examiner* proclaimed that one thousand tickets, costing a dollar each, would go on sale that evening—"a pleasing announcement to a great many devotees of the sport."[21] Marble never specified whether her brother had purchased tickets in advance or had been able to take advantage of the bargain.

In the crowd at the stately Civic Auditorium, built for the 1915 Panama–Pacific International Exposition, the *San Francisco Examiner* reported the presence of the regal Helen Wills.[22]

The four matches started at 8:30 p.m.: men's singles, women's singles, men's doubles, and mixed doubles. When Lenglen and Browne made their entrance, "they were applauded roundly by the gathering, which included many of the elite of the bay cities." At one point, after a "strenuous battle," fans were "applauding in almost frenzied fashion." Helen Wills, the *Examiner* observed, was democratic with her enthusiasm, joining in "when either player made great shots."[23]

The outcome was the same as it would be throughout the tour. "Possessing the cool brain and steady hand of the master strategist and the nimble feet of the ballet dancer, the famous French titlist defeated Miss Mary K. Browne," the *Examiner* reported. The game's "greatest strategist" won in "straight, but hard fought, sets, 8–6, 6–2." A crowd of some fifty-five hundred witnessed Lenglen's triumph, and many went away "marveling at her technique, her clever placements and her unexpected coolness under fire."[24] The enthusiasts did not include thirteen-year-old Alice Marble, who, perhaps influenced by the combination of a seat with an obstructed view and the start time, late on a school night, fell asleep and missed the entire spectacle.

As for Lenglen, the tour was a financial success. With her share of box office receipts, she earned $100,000, and suddenly a woman and her earnings were spoken of in the same tone of admiration as Babe Ruth, whose three-year contract with the Yankees amounted to $210,000.

AT THE TIME of Lenglen's appearance in San Francisco, Alice was in the eighth grade. It was not clear which pursuit would win her heart: tennis, at which she had only rudimentary training, or baseball, at which she had no prospects. Even when she was ostensibly dedicating herself to other pursuits, baseball managed to insert itself. For instance, on Sundays, Alice and Tim sometimes teamed up with Dan and George for an all-day hike on the Dipsea Trail in Marin County. (Hazel stayed behind.) After awakening at five a.m. and digging into a breakfast of "hotcakes, eggs, bacon and coffee," the children traveled by tram to the Ferry Building, crossed the bay, and took a train to Mill Valley, then a rustic way station. Next, they trekked seven and half miles over the hills, with their moss-covered trees and clear streams and ravines, all the way to Stinson Beach, the first real beach north of San Francisco. Sometimes a brave soul sampled the freezing water before they made the return hike. On the beach, Alice got to throw a baseball with her brothers.

Dan knew a man from the club where he played handball nearly every night after work who lived in Mill Valley and often treated the hikers to a feast. Alice, who had a hearty appetite, never forgot the menu: "Home-raised chickens with brown gravy, and huge pieces of apple pie, with thick cream— all we could eat. Dan let me sleep on his shoulder all the way home, and the conductors on the train and tramcars always had to awaken us at the end of the run. Mother waited up for us and tucked us all in bed."[25]

Hazel compensated for her lack of athletic ability by earning high grades at school. Teachers sometimes scolded Alice for her less stellar performance, not that she cared. She claimed to love school for two reasons, morning recess and afternoon recess, both affording the chance to play baseball. A kind teacher named Miss Coyne noticed that Alice had a lisp that made her shy and fearful of reciting or reading aloud in front of her classmates. She encouraged Alice to stay after school and practice reading aloud to her, as the audience. Miss Coyne also suggested dancing lessons to correct Alice's tendency to walk with her toes pointed inward. Jessie eked out an extra ten cents from the family budget so Alice could study Irish step with a neighbor, and the problem vanished. Miss Coyne even pointed the teen to the tennis court, but Alice resisted "that sissy sport,"[26] though she did surface again in the new year to play in a girls' handicap doubles tournament for the Golden Gate Park tennis club, starting January 9, 1927.[27] In April 1927, the *Examiner* reported, "H. Lynch defeated A. Marble, 6–0, 7–5," in the San Francisco Girls' Tennis Championship at Golden Gate Park.[28]

When Marble graduated from the eighth grade, Miss Coyne announced the names of three children destined for great success, Alice among them. While she was entertaining her dream of becoming a teacher of physical education, the family experienced another derailment. At the age of sixteen, quiet Hazel, who always seemed to hide behind her spectacles and recede into her domestic chores, eloped with a bounder, who soon left her with a little boy, back under her mother's roof.

Alice and Tim continued to team up and slip away as often as possible, joining hundreds of other children who thronged Rec Park. Alice stood out, especially in competitions about who could throw a baseball the farthest before a Seals game started.[29] She was so superior at catching and throwing, day in and day out, that it came as no surprise when one day a player beckoned her onto the field: "Say, boy, how'd you like to climb down and play with me?"[30]

At first she demurred; the gender gaffe left her feeling indignant. Couldn't he see? She was a girl and proud of it. The player didn't care. He kept motioning to her to come out on the field. All those practice sessions with Uncle Woodie had paid off. The manager of the team invited her back to warm up with the players, "every Saturday and Sunday, and in holidays too."[31]

The attention from the Seals was no mere sentimental gesture. A passion for baseball had followed newcomers to California from all over the country. The Seals represented a respected franchise, a rung below the majors. Many of the team's players had to take pay cuts to join the majors. They were considered the big time.

In their day, the Seals were larger than life, well known to legions of fans, who loved to invoke their names and cite their statistics: Buck Weaver in the infield, Jimmy Johnston stealing 124 bases in one season, pitcher Spider Baum winning 260 games, and Ping Bodie slugging "a record thirty home runs in 1910—an incredible number for the Dead-ball Era."[32] Named for the balls used in the game—inferior by design and disintegrating during use so that low scores and lack of home runs were normal—the dead-ball era lasted roughly from 1900 until Babe Ruth hit twenty-nine home runs in 1919, a major-league record, forever raising the bar.

"Ping" is one of those great ballpark nicknames, inspired by the sound made by Bodie's weighty, four-pound bat when it slammed into a ball. Best of all, he was a local boy, who had built his strength as a kid by rolling rocks up Telegraph Hill. "Ping was very confident about his hitting and bragged that he could 'hemstitch the spheroid.' Nobody knew what that meant, but it sounded good," wrote Bodie's biographer. "Bugs Baer, a sportswriter for the Hearst Publications, once said of his attempt to steal a base: 'There was larceny in his heart, but his feet were honest.'"[33]

Alice Marble's growing prowess on the field caught the attention of the *Examiner*. In the summer after eighth grade, before Alice entered high school, a reporter called her mother and asked her to bring her daughter to the paper the next day for a photo shoot. Alice wore her best outfit, which happened to be her only outfit, a middy blouse and skirt and a homemade beanie. She toured the offices of the *Examiner*, and then went up to the roof for the photo session, where she reenacted the skills she showed on the field.

On July 12, 1927, the *Examiner* article ran with the headline ATTA BOY, ALICE, and with Alice's photo,[34] marking the moment in her life when she crossed the threshold from spectator to actor, from anonymity to recognition. The energy in the image is remarkable, earning her the nickname, "The Little Queen of Swat," employing a term with special resonance in baseball, denoting a powerful hit. With her wide stance and her arms unfurled in opposite directions, the mitted one held high in a kind of salute, she resembles the figurehead on a ship, with the usual messages of female empowerment and full speed ahead. The lengthy caption under the photo read:

> *Presenting Alice Marble, 13-year-old diamond star, who works out at Recreation Park with the Coast League baseballers. She makes her appearance on Kids' Day, chases flies during the practice and then retires to the bleachers to cheer her favorites and to denounce the umpires. This action photo shows her reaching for a wide one, just like any old-time diamond performer. Pitching is her favorite baseball pastime and the youngsters who have faced her at "Big Rec" at Golden Gate Park, will tell you that she throws a wicked curve.*

The reporter indicated that the "gallery gods" in left field all knew Alice and admired how she could be counted on during practice to catch the ball, perhaps to return it to a local legend, Frank O'Doul or Brick Eldred or Joe Bratcher. She moved with grace, her back to the ball, and when she reached a few feet from the fence, she wheeled about. Her judgment was excellent as she dead-aimed the ball toward home.

The article noted, "Miss Alice wears a 'Frank O'Doul Club' button on her sweater." Of all the players who attracted Marble's admiration, perhaps none was more popular than O'Doul, known as Lefty. After early success as a pitcher with the Seals and then the New York Yankees and the Boston Red Sox, he hurt his arm in 1923 and returned to the Seals, converting to a power-hitting outfielder. As the 1927 season wore on, O'Doul's status only grew as he hit thirty home runs and stole thirty bases. Kids like Alice and Tim, dashing to the left-field bleachers, screamed O'Doul's name, "as he stood on the field in front of them and screamed even louder when he sneaked away baseballs between innings and tossed them into the stands," his biographer notes. "What O'Doul had, they wanted. And he was going to give it to them. The kids organized a rooting section and wore buttons bearing his image."[35]

Even though the *Examiner* article didn't say whether he was on hand when she shagged balls, just being mentioned in the same breath as Lefty raised Alice's status and further cemented her loyalty to the Seals. Whenever the team was in town, she tried not to miss a game.

AT THE TIME, Alice considered Dan an already "old man, burdened by eight years of responsibility."[36] He put in long hours at work six days a week, but occasionally enjoyed Saturday-night poker games in the second upstairs bedroom he had built, on his own in his precious spare time. His sister would serve him and his friends sandwiches and beer, a rare example of spirits in the Marble household. Alice would sometimes steal a sip. She distributed the refreshments slowly, spying on the game so she could learn how to play.

Dan still played handball and eventually could claim to be the best player in Northern California. Though he earned trophies, he lost games from time to time, and when he did, his temper often got the better of him. When in a rage, he found "great release in banging his head against the wall or pushing his fist through the side wall," Alice recalled.[37] She knew it hurt him to have had only six months of high school, and she tried to keep an even keel in his presence. However, one time, she admits, she teased him with "a very naughty word, one he frequently used. As I said it, I started running down the sixty stairs, Dan following me. When he caught up, he gave me such a sound wallop on the jaw that the bruise lasted for weeks. We didn't speak for days, until Dan, who would not apologize to God, said, 'Is my little sister still mad?' That was his way of apologizing, so I accepted it, because I loved him so much and because I knew so well that he must have felt cheated in life."[38]

It did not take long for the diminutive creature in the newspaper photo, the tiny dynamo, to disappear or, more precisely, fill out. During her freshman year in high school, Alice reported, she gained forty-five pounds and shot up seven inches, to five feet seven inches tall and a weight of 150 pounds.[39] If accurate, these figures represent an extraordinary growth over the course of a single year. In *The Road to Wimbledon*, Alice confessed to a certain awkwardness and to a desire to be like other girls in her school, to wear dresses and primp her hair, but something held her back—the mockery she imagined from the kids at Rec Park who might belittle her efforts at frills and finery. During that first year in high school, while still a mascot for the Seals, she was pleased to find other girls who also loved baseball, and she added track and basketball to her repertoire. Basketball held special appeal because she got to play games at night and then socialize at the sweet shop. It helped that two girls on the team were willing to tutor Alice in history and geometry in exchange for her tips on how to improve their game.[40]

Dan, forever strategizing to keep the family afloat, formulated what he considered a solid plan to steer his sister in the right direction. Dan did not want Alice to have Hazel's romantic fate. He also wanted her to pursue more frankly feminine athletic goals. As a reporter summed it up years later, Dan was afraid "she might be chewing tobacco next."[41]

"Allie," he said, "You've got to stop being a tomboy."

Dan offered her a gift, a brand-new Bancroft racket, costing about five dollars, purchased with his own earnings.

Alice always said this occurred when she was fifteen, already a sophomore in high school, but the written record of her tournament play in newspapers indicates it might have been earlier. Whatever the exact date, Dan told her she had to stop playing rough games, "like basketball and even baseball. I want you always to play and enjoy sports, but you must play a ladylike game."[42]

CHAPTER 3

WHERE IT IS ALWAYS JUNE

THE SPORT THAT Dan Marble pressed upon his sister started in France or the Netherlands with a game called "*jeu de paume*, game of the palm." Players used their hands to hit the ball, eventually wore gloves, and then adopted rackets. The early game was popular with monks, as it was "suited to the confines of the cloister." Royalty, too, embraced *jeu de paume* despite its likely roots as a street game. Whatever its beginnings, it became "something of a craze during the Renaissance, when the first professional players—women as well as men—appeared."[1]

The game continued to attract followers, and its fortunes changed dramatically in 1874. On March 7, London's *Court Journal* tipped off readers to a "a new and interesting game," with appeal to people who were tired of croquet and in need of novelty. It was granted a patent by Queen Victoria, under the Greek-derived name "Sphairistike," which went nowhere. The alternative name "lawn tennis" did.[2] Created by Major Walter Clopton Wingfield, the Major's Game of Lawn Tennis was sold in a painted box containing the props needed for play: poles, pegs, netting, four tennis bats, and balls.[3] The rigging was not cheap, at five guineas, about $800 today.[4] Wingfield's version of the game moved it outdoors, where it could be played on any flat lawn with enough room—as opposed to the earlier version, called "real tennis" or "court tennis," played indoors.[5]

Two inventions helped propel the game: the lawn mower (patented in 1830) and vulcanized rubber (patented in 1844, a process that led to bouncing balls). After croquet fell out of favor, well-tended lawns became available for tennis courts.

Wingfield's game sets were illustrated with pictures of both male and female tennis players.[6] In contrast to other sports of the Victorian era, in tennis, "uniquely, men and women shared the pitch, playing in partnerships usually of two on each side of the net," a history of the game explains.[7] The suffrage movement, with its emphasis on the rights of women to vote, own property, and receive an education, also supported the notion that exercise, along with its health benefits, should be enjoyed by women as well as men.

When tennis first arrived in the United States in the late 1880s, wealthy easterners gave the game an aristocratic gloss, building courts on their own land and founding private clubs across the mid-Atlantic and Northeast.[8] A Wimbledon referee named Henry Jones gets credit for adjusting the net height and arriving at what is today's standard of three and a half feet at the posts and three feet at the center, with the service line twenty-one feet from the net.[9] The lower net meant that the serve could be overhand, and thus the seeds were planted to transform tennis into a power sport.

The United States National Lawn Tennis Association ("National" and then "Lawn" were later dropped) formed in the spring of 1881 and held the first men's national tournament that summer at the Newport Casino in Newport, Rhode Island. Richard D. Sears, who won the singles final, wrote that the nets were flimsy but were not a problem because "none of the services was particularly severe; in fact a few of the players served underhand, but I must confess without much success."[10]

Six years later, in 1887, the Philadelphia Cricket Club hosted the first national championships for women. Seventeen-year-old Ellen Hansell, the winner, was conscious of expenses, such as tennis shoes and a yearly club fee of ten dollars. She practiced a small economy by walking a mile and a half to play rather than spend a nickel for a horsecar.[11]

In the United States, from early on, tension existed between eastern and western tennis. The former was snobby and inbred, limiting rather than welcoming participants, while the latter was freewheeling and, even before Alice Marble's ascendance, produced an array of national champions. California built an abundance of hard courts, which cost less to construct and maintain than the grass courts favored by private clubs in the caste-driven East. Hard courts offered another advantage: they could be used year-round, especially in sunny Southern California. A New York sportswriter, observing the dominance of western players, declared, "Of course they play well out there, where it is always June."[12]

Not surprisingly, given weather advantages and the profusion of opportunities, the caliber of tennis played in California escalated rapidly. Tournament play started in Southern California in Santa Monica in 1887, followed by Ojai in 1896. In 1905, Californian May Sutton Bundy, from Pasadena, became the first American to win Wimbledon, the tournament established in 1877.

The East Coast establishment guarded its sense of superiority, and the word "lawn" remained in official descriptions of tennis for decades. Alice Marble would discover, like western champions before her, that only the eastern tournaments mattered because they were the ones on grass. As one tennis insider wrote: "The rain-soaked turf courts of the Eastern circuit stretched the length and breadth of the 'in' resorts from Boston to Philadelphia, and before being 'acceptable' to the various national selection committees, all California players had to prove themselves in these areas."[13]

Writer Larry Engelmann describes a fan base in the early days of California tennis that demonstrated its enthusiasm by color-coordinating outfits and organizing cheers, displaying none of the prim quiet-enough-to-hear-a-needle-drop decorum that characterized tennis audiences in the East. In Engelmann's view, the raucousness helped the athletes from the West develop a useful immunity to distractions. He called western tennis "more emancipated" than eastern, citing how women worked as scorers and line judges from the get-go.[14] Women were encouraged to play against men, thus returning more powerful strokes than they might if playing only other women, emulating a masculine style of play.[15]

Northern California, even with a less ideal climate, embraced tennis with a fervor equal to that of its southern counterpart. Two Bay Area private institutions, the California Tennis Club, founded in 1884, and the Berkeley Tennis Club, founded in 1906, took tennis excellence seriously and alternated as hosts of the California State Tennis Championships. Coaches from both venues combed the public courts for new talent to recruit. As William C. "Pop" Fuller, junior coach at the club in Berkeley and tennis coach for the Golden Bears at the university, put it, using a cliché with at least the modest merit of local roots, given California's reputation as a prospector's paradise, "Like gold, tennis players are where you find them."[16]

The Bay Area thus produced some of America's earliest tennis stars. Maurice McLoughlin, known as the "California Comet," was born in Nevada and moved to California as a teen. He trained on the public courts in San Francisco, and in 1909 he played in the US National Championships in Newport. His game was so spirited, so unlike the significantly more polite game the spectators were used to, that by the end of a match, fans had climbed onto chairs to get a better view of his performance. In 1913, the year of Marble's birth, McLoughlin became the first American male finalist at Wimbledon. Many years later, she would write about him, "Tennis has not belonged to that select group since the days of Maurice McLoughlin, who, by 1910, had blasted his way into prominence by brute force, a big serve, red hair, a winning smile and a lot of courage. The public, long used to referring to tennis as a 'pantywaist game' began to prick up its ears and open its eyes."[17]

Among the luminaries of early Bay Area tennis was a compact, elegant man named Billy Johnston, a patron of the Berkeley Tennis Club, especially after his own amateur career had ended. Johnston won the men's singles at the 1915 US National Championships, the first to be held at the West Side Tennis Club in Forest Hills, after it changed locale from Newport owing to the greater concentration of players in the New York area. Known as "Little Bill," he grew up in San Francisco and learned the game at Golden Gate Park, pursuing the sport nearly full-time starting at age eleven, during the period of upheaval after the earthquake, when there was no formal school to attend. After volunteering for service during World War I, Johnston regained his number-one world ranking in 1919 with Gerald Paterson, and again in 1922, with Bill Tilden, and won the Wimbledon singles title in 1923. He was known for possessing one of the fiercest forehands in tennis, a marvel in and of itself but especially given his small frame. Spectators loved his rivalry with East Coaster "Big Bill" Tilden, who at six feet two towered over Little Bill, and who ranked as the number-one amateur in the world from 1920 to 1925. Tilden was known for possessing the world's fiercest serve, allegedly clocked at 163.6 mph in 1931, a figure now held in doubt because Tilden was using a wooden racket and the measuring tools were less sophisticated than current technology. Johnston's return to the game after he served in the war hit a chord with Americans, who appreciated his sacrifice and welcomed his return to the courts as a sign of normalcy and a reason for renewed hope.

A decade after Johnston's run, two young women from Northern California named Helen came to dominate women's tennis and would become early rivals for Alice Marble. In addition to their first name, they shared an alma mater, the University of California at Berkeley, and a coach, Pop Fuller. When Helen Jacobs's parents purchased a house once owned by Helen Wills's family, Jacobs took over her rival's old bedroom, which had been decorated with images of movie stars, and chose to decorate with images of her idol, Helen Wills. They both dominated the headlines during the early golden years of tennis.

Helen Wills, later Helen Wills Moody and then Helen Wills Roark, was born in 1905 in Centerville (now Fremont), near San Francisco. She enjoyed a long reign as a force in women's tennis, starting in 1921. A prodigy, Wills entered her first tournament in 1919, at age thirteen. Three years later, she played in the US National Championships and lost, and the next year she won the first of seven national titles.

The only child of a doctor father and a mother so omnipresent she was sometimes confused for her best friend, Wills took up swimming and horseback riding as a child and often went duck hunting with her father.[18] He gave her a tennis racket at age eight and practiced with her incessantly on the courts at Alameda County Hospital where he served as head surgeon. In time she would come to practice regularly against men. She kept her emotions under control, and the lack of animation was sometimes seen as a liability, earning her the nickname "Little Miss Poker Face." Her defense against the adjective "imperial" was simple: "I had one thought and that was to put the ball across the net. I was simply myself, too deeply concentrated on my game for any extraneous thought."[19]

Born in 1908 in Globe, Arizona, Helen Hull Jacobs moved with her family to California in 1914 and eventually to Berkeley. Her father's poor health motivated her start in the game. He needed exercise, and Jacobs became his tennis partner, forsaking her favorite sport, swimming. A prodigy, like Wills, she won the National Junior Championships in Philadelphia at sixteen. Dependable and sturdy, Jacobs could beat back almost everyone except Wills, losing to her continually until finally defeating her for the US women's title in 1933, the year Alice Marble made her first mark at the national level.

Despite their frequent pairing in the press and their many court meetups, the women possessed opposite personalities. Wills played up her femininity, dressing in understated but flattering outfits and using makeup. Jacobs managed her hair by throwing a net over it when she played and eschewed makeup. She preferred women, a proclivity reported by *Time* magazine in 1936 with the phrase, "has thus far shown no romantic interest in men." While Wills had developed a reputation for being cold and imperious, Jacobs was known to be warm and kindly. Their first matchup went poorly for fifteen-year-old Jacobs, a harbinger of the future. Pop Fuller had arranged for her to play against Wills, who had ascended to the national title at age eighteen. Wills was relentless: "She didn't care to rally. She just scored," as Larry Engelmann put it.[20] In twenty minutes Jacobs lost twelve games in a row.

In the aftermath, she was left wondering whether the "unchanging expression on my opponent's face and her silence . . . were owing entirely to deep concentration; or whether they weren't perhaps a psychological weapon."[21] As the years went on, Jacobs concluded the latter.

One further Bay Area contemporary of Marble's would eventually end up in a fruitful partnership with her. From a working-class background, Don Budge grew up in Oakland, the youngest of three children. His distinctive face verged on the comic: big ears, weak chin, a mouth that drooped open. Any concerns about irregularities in his appearance dissolved when he played tennis, which he took up after excelling at baseball and basketball. He was so flexible that a magazine once did a photo shoot of him in motion next to an image of Fred Astaire dancing. The motions were entirely the same, one man wielding a racket and the other a cane and top hat. Budge would win Wimbledon and the US National Championships in 1937, and he became and remains the only American male player to win all four Grand Slam tournaments in one year (Australian Open, French Open, Wimbledon, US Open), which he did in 1938.

For Marble, with her eventual goal of becoming a champion, there was no better place of origin than California. She had much in her favor, from the generally good weather in the Bay Area to free hard courts to a glittering roster of established and upcoming coaches and players who would help define the golden age of tennis, all on tap, all hers for the asking.

CHAPTER 4

HIGH HAT

"HERE'S A RACQUET I bought you. Go out and play tennis. It's a game you can enjoy for the rest of your life."[1]

Years later, Alice Marble recalled the anxiety she felt at her brother's insistence that she give up other sports. "My heart was broken, and even Dan's kind pat on the shoulder and offer to take me to the movies didn't help my spirits. I went to bed and cried all night, dreading the next day, knowing I would no longer have the fun of shagging flies at Recreation Park, nor all the hot dogs, peanuts and candy bars; that I would lose the interest of all the people in the stands, my public. But more than anything else, I would lose the proud title I had won from the men players, 'Little Queen of Swat.'"[2]

She thought about running away, but in the end, she obeyed his edict. "Heaven knows what would have happened to us if Dan had not taken on those burdens," she conceded in her memoir.[3]

At school the next day, having seen her new racket, some boys teased her about taking up a sissy sport. Nonetheless, that afternoon, she headed to the free courts at Golden Gate Park, which soon became her daily destination. The park itself was the visionary creation of horticulturist John McLaren. The great landscape architect Frederick Law Olmsted, co-creator of New York City's Central Park, passed on the chance to build a similar refuge in San Francisco, on 1,013 acres of windswept sand dunes: "There is not a full-grown tree of beautiful proportions near San Francisco, nor have I seen any young trees that promised fairly," he wrote in a report after the city of San Francisco asked him after the Civil War had ended to create a "pleasure-ground" in their environs, widely quoted to this day. McLaren thought otherwise. Born in 1846 in Scotland, he came to the United States as a young man after studying horticulture at the Edinburgh Royal Botanic Garden.

When he assumed the job of superintendent of Golden Gate Park in 1887, McLaren anticipated, accurately, that a park would inspire visitors to want to live nearby. He believed public land was to be enjoyed, not just admired. He deplored "keep off the grass" signs, and he disdained statues because they demanded undue attention, interrupting the natural beauty with their narcissistic bulk. When pressed to accept monuments of war heroes or literary giants or deceased politicians, he acquiesced and then obscured them with dense shrubbery. He believed, above all, that every child should live within walking distance of a park.

McLaren used bent-grass seed from France to cover the ground and planted Monterey pine, Monterey cypress, and eucalyptus trees, the roots of which stabilized the dunes. His green vision became Alice's windfall—a luxuriant auxiliary backyard. Alice practiced at the park's courts on weekdays, but Saturdays were special. Arising at six, she put on a white pleated tennis dress, freshly laundered and pressed the night before, a task she remembered taking hours. As a further badge of honor, she kept her tennis shoes the whitest white, preserving their purity by dodging puddles during her nearly two-mile journey to the park.[4] Often, the four courts at the top level were damp with dew, so she and the other girls who arrived for both pickup tennis and organized matches began the day's workout by dragging blankets across the asphalt to absorb the moisture, a ritual she grew to enjoy.

Marble's early training came not only late in her development as an athlete but also, at the beginning, seemed almost casual, which makes her eventual ascent so astonishing. She claimed she attained a ranking of number seven in the nation without ever having the benefit of a formal lesson.[5] Her initial achievements were almost certainly the result of her innate athleticism, encouraged by a kindly woman Alice remembered as Mrs. Kress, who organized junior tennis at the park and invited Alice to participate in the tournaments she ran each Saturday. Tennis offered Alice a future that baseball could not, and soon her Saturdays were devoted to the game. Uncle Woodie would suggest they catch a ballgame at Rec Park, but she had lost heart for the enterprise, claiming she could never enjoy baseball as long as she could not play. Her newfound dedication to tennis was such that even on Sundays, on a stroll through the park with her mother, Alice would gravitate toward the courts and watch older, stronger players hit the ball.

To afford the expenses of a tennis skirt, shoes, racket, and balls costing thirty-five cents each, Alice took on typical teenage jobs, recalling them later as a kind of negative résumé. They included babysitting (which bored her) and working at a soda fountain for a short time (fired for the crime of ice cream embezzlement when it became clear she was far too generous to her friends). She had a job in the high school cafeteria as part of a cooking class in which students had to show a profit to get a good grade. (She flunked that portion of the class but did win a prize for concocting the best candy, which she looked back on as her first real championship.)

In the spring of 1929, Alice became junior champion of the girls' tennis club in Golden Gate Park. This caught Pop Fuller's attention, and he encouraged her to train at the private Berkeley Tennis Club. "I had never played anywhere but on public courts," Alice later recalled. "And it was pretty exciting to carry my suitcase and racket all the way across the bay and to play at a real club."[6] In those days, the clubhouse consisted of a large room with wood paneling, maple flooring, and exposed trusses. Nearby, a train constantly belched smoke and created clatter. If anything, the club's lack of ostentation was its own form of snobbery, as the institution avoided glitz and placed the spotlight on the serious training of its players. As usual, Dan found a way to help with expenses. He was "papa," as Alice said, and his word ruled.

The *Examiner* zeroed in on Alice at the Pacific Coast championships, held at the Berkeley Tennis Club in mid-June. Only two out of 325 players had double wins—one of them fifteen-year-old Alice: "Alice Marble, Polytechnic High School girl and product of the Golden Gate Park courts, romped off with the Junior girls' under 16 title defeating Betty Wheatly, 7–5, 6–1 in the final round, and displayed a well-rounded game and plenty of future promise in her convincing victory."[7]

The euphoria carried over to the next win: "The junior girls' doubles title went to Ida Cross and Alice Marble on a surprise victory over Patsy McCoy and Evelyn Parsons, at 8–6, 5–7, 6–1. The two younger stars played with a reckless abandon that strangely enough defeated their heavily favored opponents, as they successfully handled seemingly impossible shots."[8]

It would be hard to overestimate Alice's astonishing rise. Within what appear to be mere months of formal training, she received her first trophy, which she remembered as all of two and a half inches in height. It was so poorly made it fell apart on the way home, but even in its discombobulated state, she displayed it with pride.

Alice continued to practice at the Berkeley Tennis Club, but no matter how much she longed to feel at home there, she felt like an interloper. In

September, her lack of confidence came to a head in the finals of the state tournament. Top seed in the under-sixteen category and third seed in the under-eighteen category, she could sense herself faltering. Going up against May Doeg in the sixteen-year-old age group, Alice was nervous. Junior champ May hailed from tennis royalty—she was a niece of May Sutton Bundy. The first set was an easy win for Marble, but she got rattled when Doeg hit a shot impossible to return. Alice impulsively went to retrieve a ball by climbing a fence, cutting her wrist on the metal. Her opponent's aunt kindly taped the bloody wound. "It really didn't hurt very much," Alice recalled, "but I felt very sorry for myself, and the disability took on greater proportions, and May won out quite easily. . . . Self-pity was stronger than the will to overcome it."[9]

Subsequently, she often lost to opponents she felt she should have beaten. Her mind wandered during play, and she found herself at times preparing to lose rather than concentrating on trying to win: "I would tell myself that I had had only eleven hours' sleep instead of twelve, that I had broken my best racket, twisted my foot or got something in my eye. My friends unfortunately did not say 'Lose like a lady,' but made still more excuses for me, offered more alibis."[10]

Dan showed no sympathy about a match he said she should have won: "You should be ashamed of yourself for letting such a bad player beat you."[11]

She told him she wanted to quit. At the table at the time, he just kept eating his dinner. To get his attention, she raided the closet that contained her tennis gear and proceeded to dump on the table her "racket, press, rubber case, balls and shoes," shouting that if tennis could not be fun, she wanted no part of it: "Take your old racket. I'll never play again, if you make this winning business a matter of life and death."[12]

Unusual for him, Dan did not show anger at her outburst. Instead, he smiled. Once again, he had a plan: if she didn't like playing tennis at one intimidating private club, she should play at more than one and thereby stop taking them personally. He purchased her a junior membership at the California Tennis Club in San Francisco, at the steep fee of forty-five dollars. Mary Therese Austin had founded the California Tennis Club in 1884 as a one-room clubhouse with a covered porch and the first three courts in San Francisco. Her goal was to encourage "an exuberant exchange across the net." It was a hit from the start. The courts, on the corner of Sutter Street and Van Ness Avenue, were paved—a novelty. "The macadamizing process of the courts is something which has never been done before on this Coast," the *Daily Alta California* reported, "and it will enable the members to pursue their favorite pastime in the wet season, as well as the dry period."[13]

The day after her demoralizing defeat against May Doeg, Alice won the state junior doubles by default. She and Ida Cross were to compete against May and Violet Doeg, but Violet had to leave the tournament early to tend to an injured foot.[14] In late September, at the Girls' Park Tennis Club tournament, Alice was handed another easy victory when the only competitor in her division did not show up.[15]

Throughout the fall, Alice appeared in sports pages of the *San Francisco Examiner* on a regular basis, her name making it into headlines, an open record of her early efforts. She most often shone on her home court, in Golden Gate Park, but entered competitions at other venues. She was one of "forty-five young lady stars" competing for the Bay Counties junior girls' championship starting in late October. Alice was singled out as worth watching; she was "less experienced [but] has just as bright a future."[16] In early November, on a Saturday morning, she returned to the park for the semifinals but lost to Marian Hunt, 9–7, 6–2.[17] The next day, Alice and Ida Cross won the city championship semifinal doubles at the California Tennis Club. A week later, the partners were defeated by players with more "court craft and experience," the *San Francisco Examiner* said.[18]

Alice's persistence paid off. The California Lawn Tennis Association (with Pop Fuller heading the committee) released rankings of top players in December, and Marble was ranked in four categories: she was number one for girls under-sixteen singles, number six for girls under-eighteen singles, number one for girls under-eighteen doubles (with Ida Cross), and number six for women's doubles (with Ida Cross).[19] Marble was elected president of the Girls' Park Tennis Club, evidence of her popularity and competitive savvy.[20]

Alice, with partner Joe Storss, started 1930 by winning the first round in the midwinter mixed doubles tournament but lost in the second round. In Golden Gate Park, the new season opened with a handicap singles competition. Alice was defeated, her "handicap too substantial to overcome."[21] By March, she won the first-class singles title for girls under sixteen at Golden Gate Park, "the third successive time she has won the event."[22]

Starting in late April and winding up in early May, Alice played in the handicap singles competition at the park, adding "another Girls' Park Club title to her extensive collection," the *Examiner* noted.[23] In mid-June Alice lost the state championship for girls under eighteen,[24] but with Marian Hunt she won the junior girls' doubles, defeating Dorothy Workman and Marion Wood, 6–4, 6–2.[25]

The last weekend in June, at Golden Gate Park, was a triumph. A half-dozen players competed "to name an undisputed champion" of the Women's Park Tennis Club.[26] Alice won the title in three rounds (one by default) "against wiser but less able foes." The *Examiner* noted that "Misses Marble and Postlethwaite and Mrs. Perow leave here on July 8 for an invasion of northwestern courts."[27] (Contemporary accounts give a different spelling of Postlethwaite's name and refer to her as Miss, not Mrs. as opposed to Marble's version of her name and marital status in *The Road to Wimbledon*.)

Alice alternated between club tennis and playing at the public park. The situation was not ideal. At the clubs, she thought she wasn't worthy of her opponents, and some players ostracized her. It did not help that she was some-times shabbily attired. "I wasn't very popular there with the snobs," she told Larry Engelmann. "I often had to run out to Golden Gate Park to find a game because my brother would have killed me if I came home without playing."[28]

At Golden Gate Park, her old friends snubbed her because they felt she had abandoned them and gone "high hat." Somehow, she made peace with the various settings, just as Dan had hoped. Even with the expanded orbit, she held the courts at Golden Gate close to her heart all her life, despite a terrible incident when her sanctuary, her "favorite place," as she called it, harbored danger. "I never dreamed I could come to harm there."[29]

ONE EVENING, as Alice headed home from the park, the feeble light from a streetlamp caused shadows to stretch across the Stanyan Street entrance. Someone grabbed her from behind, dragging her into the bushes, a hand heavy across her mouth. For a split second, she entertained the hope that it might be a joke. Pushing her to the ground, he pressed a rag across her mouth, preventing any screams or cries for help. With his other hand, he tore off her underwear. After fumbling with his own belt and zipper, he raped her: "Pain shot through me, and screams rose in my throat, only to be blocked by his savage hold on my windpipe and the filthy cloth in my mouth. I thought I was going to die, and almost wished it, to stop the pain. Mercifully, I fainted."[30]

She regained consciousness to the sound of her own weeping. The pain caused her to vomit from a sitting position. Blood running down her legs, she staggered in the darkness to the nearby house of her aunt Josephine, who took her in, cleaned her up, and called a doctor, who came to the house and confirmed the rape. Her aunt also called Alice's mother and, sparing her the truth, said that the teen had come down with the flu and would be staying with her for a few days. Alice later explained the cuts on her face and bruises as the result of a fall.

"Aunt Jo encouraged me to forget the incident, to put this terrible thing behind me," she later wrote.[31]

Alice kept the story under wraps for almost her entire life, acknowledging it only with the publication of her second memoir, *Courting Danger*. She never gave a precise year or month to indicate when the incident occurred but said she was living at home, during her high school years. She regretted that she had not been more public about the violation, reflecting: "Perhaps if I had talked about my feelings, like rape victims today who seek counseling, my life would have been very different. I never hated men in general, just the bastard who raped me, but it was ten years before I could bring myself to have a physical relationship."[32]

Despite the one horrific memory, the courts at Golden Gate were among the great loves of her life. She idealized everything about them, from the fleshy odor of grilled meat to the stinky musk of a bison that children could ride for a nickel, two at time, to the headache-causing music of a nearby merry-go-round. She loved the baseball diamonds, bowling greens, handball courts, bridge paths, and concerts. She was so adept at the games in the amusement center, smashing milk bottles with bricks or driving a long nail in just three strokes, that she reaped cheap prizes by the armful. One concessionaire put out a closed-for-business sign when he saw her coming.

Even the defects of the courts were endearing. They were way too close together, and much playing time was spent avoiding balls from other courts. The balls lost their luster soon after being put in play as they absorbed the gray surface of the courts. She and her pals baked dead balls in the oven to restore their bounce.[33] It was hard to concentrate. People gabbed on the sidelines, a constant distraction. It could take forever to get a court, up to three hours on a Saturday afternoon or a Sunday. Yet, the negatives were outweighed by one overwhelming positive: "There were always matches to watch and tennis enthusiasts everywhere." There was something, as she always put it, "so real" about those people playing on the courts. "I look back on those carefree days in the park and think how very little we appreciated the small but wonderful pleasures—the freedom, the advantages and the beauties of the park itself, the magnificent trees and flowers, the bandstand and the tea gardens, Stow Lake, the greenhouse, bowling greens, playgrounds. I can appreciate them now. And I will always be grateful for my public-park beginnings in tennis. One learned many bad habits in tennis, but one learned to play against all kinds of players and all kinds of odds."[34]

Tennis and athletic stardom may not have been the most pressing concerns in the aftermath of Harry Marble's death, but Alice had stumbled into a subculture conducive to the pursuit of both, offering her a way up and a way out.

CHAPTER 5

THREE CRISP
TWENTY-DOLLAR BILLS

E ARLY ONE EVENING in the summer of 1930, a slim man knocked on the Marbles' door. Alice was elated to meet Billy Johnston in person for the first time. When he retired from the tennis circuit, he refused to turn professional, instead moving home and supporting himself with work in a brokerage. He devoted his off hours to scouting and promoting new tennis talent, whether from the private clubs or from humble roots that more closely resembled his own. As a representative of the Northern California Tennis Association, he offered to put the official stamp on Alice's prospects as a tennis player, seeking the family's permission for the sixteen-year-old to play in the Canadian and Northwest championships. She would be bankrolled by a stipend of seventy-five dollars to cover expenses for the two and half months she would be on the road. A chaperone would see to her safety, Johnston promised, and the experience and attention she would gain as a competitor would be of immeasurable value.

Alice may have been thrilled, but her mother did not think it wise for her to be gone so long. Her brother Dan objected to the expense; a reasonable position given the arithmetic of their cash-strapped household. He did not see how seventy-five dollars would be enough, and there was no way the family could pick up the slack. The next day he contacted Johnston and said it wouldn't work. To his sister, he counseled patience. She could try again the following year.

"I pleaded and begged, but Dan was firm," she later wrote.[1] In Alice's telling, she responded by taking babysitting jobs and helping at a grocery store. She raised cash by selling her baseball mitt and ball—a symbol of her resolve—coming up with twenty dollars. And then, in one of those manifestations of good luck that blossomed in her path from time to time—one that she spoke about for the rest of her life—"a plain envelope addressed to me" with three "crisp twenty-dollar bills" arrived in the mail. The source of the money was never identified, although the most obvious benefactor was Johnston himself. Dan and Jessie withdrew their objections and gave Alice permission to go.

Alice allocated thirty of those dollars to a shopping spree with her mother, purchasing "shoes, a dress, underthings, and a tennis sweater. And I had two brand new Kro Bat rackets given to me by Spalding's as part of their advertising program. Uncle Woodie had surprised me by adding ten dollars." What made the mother-daughter excursion even more exhilarating was that passersby recognized the up-and-coming tennis star as she walked up Market Street and called her by name. "Mother just couldn't make it out. How did strangers know me? She never read the sports pages, and although she knew when I had my picture in the paper, she could never understand why people made such a fuss over tennis. She had never, up to that time, seen me play in competition."[2]

On the day she left, Alice's entire family including Uncle Woodie poured out of the house to wave goodbye. In *The Road to Wimbledon*, she wrote about boarding a "powerful-looking Buick sedan," joining Mrs. Postlewaite, the owner of the car; her chaperone Dorothea Perow, a ranked player and Alice's partner in doubles; and a young man of twenty-five named Roger. Alice observed how Mrs. Postlewaite urged an abrupt departure, as if there were something gaudy about her family's enthusiasm, unseemly and peasant-like.

The Canadian press kept track of the American tennis players as they headed north. "It appears that there will be a regular influx of southern stars," the *Vancouver Sun* reported. "Tennis circles are buzzing with anticipation." The Buick navigated the recently built Redwood Highway, a winding road where nature unspooled, offering visions of elk, firs, and redwoods that stretched hundreds of feet into the sky. The travelers stopped in Seattle, a city of 350,000 citizens, proud of its streetlights, an amenity of only two years standing, launched by Thomas Edison himself.

The group left Seattle by boat, heading to what Alice quaintly called "a foreign land," Canada. Vancouver offered a near even trade with San Francisco in terms of climate and topography, with the old familiars of fog, steep hills, and an ocean in the distance, but with a bonus, the North Shore Mountains, visible from almost every direction. The city rejoiced in its displays of neon, known as "letters of fire." Installation ceremonies were commonplace, with crowds applauding whenever a new set of lights blazed into being, a vibrancy of color never seen before.

Not everything about Vancouver burst with natural beauty and bright display. The Marble family had been in its own financial struggle for years, but it was early in the Depression, and so far, much of her hometown had been spared economic collapse. New construction in the 1920s inoculated San Francisco, for a time.[3] Vancouver, however, was suffering, as young men from all over Canada fled there in the hope of finding work, creating "hobo jungles." In a contemporary barb, a person could "starve to death before freezing to death."

Alice and her twenty-one-year-old chaperone and doubles partner, Dorothea Perow, economized on a bare-bones hotel room for seventy-five cents a night. Alice kept track of every penny. Nothing about this trip would be indulgent. She spent ten cents on breakfast, usually coffee and donuts, and otherwise tried to limit her spending to a dollar a day.

The newspapers gave thorough accounts of the various matches. A few days into the Canadian championships, the *Vancouver Sun* expressed high hopes for Marble: "With experience and careful coaching, this young lady should go far in the future."[4] At the first tournament in Vancouver, Marble lost in the women's singles semifinals, but her "play was one of the features of the day" because of the way she "competed against her more experienced opponent." Right after—with barely a break—Marble won the junior girls' title, although she was "badly tired, [and] just managed to pull out on top, 5–7, 6–1, 8–6."[5]

Recounting that tournament years later, Marble shared memories from both on and off the court. Early in the matches, she went to her first dance. She was enjoying the company of an older member of the club as he introduced her around, when he collapsed suddenly and died of a heart attack. The matches were postponed for several days, and then the players still in the tournament had to compete in two or three matches in one day. "This was my first experience on clay courts," Alice recalled, "and, as I slid around, one blister after another developed. My new brown-and-white shoes had rubbed my heels. A blister was all in the day's work, but after several days I couldn't sleep, and the doctor told me I had bad infections in both heels, and that it wouldn't be safe to continue playing my matches. But I couldn't quit. I was representing California. Next day in the final round I played with the backs cut out of my tennis shoes, wearing rubber bands to hold them on, and I won my first championship in a foreign country."[6]

Blisters may sound like a mere annoyance, but they had the potential to be deadly. While playing tennis without socks on the White House courts in 1924, Calvin Coolidge's sixteen-year-old son formed a blister on one of his toes that became infected. He died eight days later of sepsis. Discovery of the penicillin that might have saved him was four years away, and the drug was not popularly available until the 1940s. It was a well-known cautionary tale in the era before antibiotics, and those running the tournament were surely aware of the potential danger.

At the Western Canada tournament at the Vancouver Lawn Tennis Club, the tour's second stop, the *Province* tagged her as, "Alice Marble, brilliant San Francisco youngster."[7] Marble won the girls' title, 6–1, 6–3.[8]

In the women's finals, Alice faced fellow Californian Charlotte Miller, who played "sterling tennis," according to the *Vancouver Sun*. Miller hit "beautiful drives" both forehand and backhand. Marble, at the ready, "cut off many of these with neat short drop shots on which she put lots of stop, leaving her opponent flatfooted in trying to return them. She also showed to better advantage in her overheads." Marble won: 6–3, 6–3.[9]

Alice was pronounced a "young California marvel"[10] on opening day of her third Canadian tournament, the British Columbia tennis championships at the Victoria Lawn Tennis Club. However, the spotlight was short-lived—she lost in mixed doubles, women's doubles, and singles. She was able to regain her form in the final competition, the Washington State tennis tournament in Seattle, sweeping the event with wins in women's singles, junior girls' singles, women's doubles, and mixed doubles.

After the tournament, with chaperone Dorothea off the clock, Alice claimed in *The Road to Wimbledon* that she managed some personal frolic: an evening on the town with a "dashing young tennis official." She drew a veil over the particulars, except to indicate that she broke curfew (no one noticed), and the next day she received an orchid and a note from the beau, who immediately had to leave town on other business and was never heard from again. On the way home, the tall, strong, redheaded Roger stole a kiss. Alice recalled that he anticipated an upbraiding from Mrs. Postlethwaite. A scolding did ensue, but at Alice, in which the older woman said that a girl of her type, "born on the wrong side of the tracks," had no business consorting with a young man from his superior background.[11]

Despite the tirade, Alice regarded the trip as a triumph. Pleased to return with $6.37 in her pocket, she heeded her mother and Dan when they instructed her to get a money order made out to the Northern California Tennis Association immediately. There would be no embezzlement, no matter how petty, on their watch.

The bubble deflated when the Pacific Coast championships commenced in late September, after her return, the same tournament where she had won the junior singles and doubles the year before. Alice made it to the women's quarterfinals. She won handily in the early rounds of the juniors, but spotting Dan at the entrance to the club before the finals, she lost her ability to concentrate, finding his eagerness to see her succeed disabling. She blamed him for her loss.[12]

BACK HOME, Alice had her senior year of high school to look forward to. If all went well, the fourth-born of the Marble children would distinguish herself as the first to attain a high school diploma. Over the years she would tell reporters that her devotion to tennis had interfered with classwork, but back at San Francisco Polytechnic High School, with her eye on Berkeley, alma mater of the two Helens, she applied herself to her studies more than in the past.

During her senior year she met someone who appears to have been her first serious romantic interest. John Murio, known as "the king of the public courts," introduced her to Harold Dickenson, and the pair began playing doubles every day. He often treated her to lunch. Dickenson was thirty years old, and she was barely seventeen. The Marbles had reason to disapprove of the relationship based on the age gap alone, but after Hazel's debacle, the family worried that Alice might show no better judgment about suitors. "They didn't forbid beaux," Alice wrote in *The Road to Wimbledon*, "but it was uncomfortable to bring them home, so I didn't."[13] She added that she hid his presence from her family.

Dickenson went so far as to propose matrimony. During a meal at the always crammed Solari's Grill, he made his bid. The timing was awkward, just as a voracious Alice tore into a steak. She felt "furious and very frightened," as well as miffed that he chose such a frenetic setting. Yet, later, she wrote that while walking home alone, "I cried and cried because I realized that I wanted very much to marry him. We spoke no more of marriage for the time being, because my family felt I was too young."[14]

Marble was vague about what Dickenson did for a living—he was, as she wrote in the 1946 memoir, "involved somehow in the promotion of tennis." She understood he was from Los Angeles, and he conveyed an impression of knowing everyone who was anyone in the tennis scene in California. In fact, he was well connected in part because of his work at Wilson Sporting Goods, and he was prepared to use that association to her benefit.

One day during her senior year at Polytechnic, while she was working out at Golden Gate Park, Dickenson dropped by to urge Alice to leave practice to go meet an old friend of his. "He was very secretive and I was curious," she recalled, so she found herself with him, on a March day in 1931, headed to O'Connor, Moffat, and Company, a dry-goods store known for quality merchandise, where she would meet "the person who was to change my whole life."[15]

CHAPTER 6

"TEACH"

H AROLD TELLS ME you are a fine player,"[1] said the muscular, compact woman to Alice by way of introduction. At thirty-five years old, Eleanor Tennant had short, prematurely gray hair and a no-nonsense attitude embodied in a jutting chin. A sinewy powerhouse who moved with quick, narrow precision, she would indeed change Alice's life.

Born in 1895, Eleanor, like Alice, grew up in San Francisco. Like Alice, she learned tennis in the egalitarian embrace of the public courts. And like her yet again, her childhood had a spotty sense of security.

The seventh child and the baby of the family, she grew up in a large house on Broderick Street where every child in the family had a household chore. Eleanor was assigned, from the age of eight on, to the woodpile, which she attended to with handsaws, a hacksaw, three hatchets, and an ax that she sharpened herself. The house had to be in perfect order before the children left for school. Saturdays were devoted to a major cleanup, and if everyone did their job, they might get a treat—a six- to eight-mile walk, the chance to pick wildflowers, or a sweet, like gingerbread.[2]

Tennant's parents had stayed married, but they were estranged. Her mother did not speak directly to her father for years, using the children as a conversational conduit. "Please tell your father I want . . . ," she would request. Eleanor's biographer believed her parents' refusal to utter a direct word to each other may have contributed to her own speech difficulties as a child. She stammered and could not pronounce the letter *r*, impediments that showed up in adulthood when Tennant was under extreme stress.

Her father spent his days at home philosophizing, drinking coffee, and delivering lectures—to the cat. He left the family in a state of near poverty. Like Alice's grandfather, Eleanor's father was a gold rush dreamer. Originally from England, he never lost his accent, and his daughter displayed its traces from time to time. John Tennant died when she was fifteen.

From an early age, Eleanor Tennant appreciated money and found ways to make it. She retrieved men's hats when they blew off streetcars (earning a dime for each returned). "Indeed," her biographer wrote, "Eleanor considered it a bad day when she didn't pull down at least a dollar."[3]

She acquired her first tennis racket by stealing it from a houseguest and hiding it in her private domain, the woodpile. She was not sure what to do with it, but one day, spotting a woman carrying the same device as she boarded a horse-drawn bus, Eleanor gave chase on foot all the way to Golden Gate Park, where the woman alighted, and there the child watched her first tennis match in wonderment. She later told a reporter for the *Los Angeles Times* that she would watch other players, including "Helen Wills, Helen Jacobs, Maurice McLoughlin," and then "go home and practice the strokes in the bathroom."[4]

Eleanor skipped school to play tennis, and when her bossy older brother Lytton (who influenced her as Dan later did Alice) found out, he insisted she find a real job. Her inability to spell doomed a stenography prospect. Selling newspaper subscriptions door-to-door evaporated as an option when she was discovered to be double-dealing, representing both major papers at the same time, urging disgruntled *Examiner* readers to change to the *Chronicle* and vice versa, while she reaped financial gain either way.

In 1917, twenty-two-year-old Eleanor Tennant laid claim to being the first and only "woman traveler" (traveling salesperson) for Standard Oil, a job she took partly because she loved to drive. On her first vacation, she headed to Los Angeles, where she looked up her old tennis inspiration from San Francisco, Maurice McLoughlin. She had a genius for making connections and collecting the right people at the right time. Her early appreciation for McLoughlin, when she watched him play tennis and later played with him, paid dividends now. They reunited at the Beverly Hills Hotel, with its two mottoes: "A Country Club in the Heart of the City" and "Eleven acres of sunshine for twelve months of playtime." McLoughlin asked Tennant to join him in doubles. She partnered with Willy DeMille, brother of Cecil, the movie producer, and a man known as Admiral Winslow, from Newport, Rhode Island, vacationing at the hotel with his family. The quartet played every day of her two-week holiday.

Tennant couldn't have landed in a sweeter place. The Beverly Hills Hotel was new, with a knack for luring guests into falling in love with Beverly Hills and buying into the "high-class subdivision."[5] Margaret Anderson owned and ran the hotel with her son Stanley. The establishment attracted movie stars such as the reigning queen and king of Hollywood, Mary Pickford and Douglas Fairbanks, who bought a hunting lodge nearby for their rendezvous.[6] Stanley Anderson got Tennant to quit Standard Oil when he hired her to teach tennis to the guests. In that way, she earned the distinction of being, as she was described in the *Los Angeles Times*, the "first woman tennis player to turn professional in this country."[7] She was thrilled but somewhat troubled. Her biographer writes: "She had never taught anything in her life before—let alone tennis. She didn't know if she could do it."[8] McLoughlin suggested she grab a bucket of balls and analyze her own strokes, breaking them down into their component parts, the better to be able to build skills in future students. Tennant followed his advice, liked the results, and pronounced herself a natural: "Teaching was duck soup."[9] When the comic actress Marion Davies, the paramour of newspaper mogul William Randolph Hearst, sought her out for private lessons, her fate as instructor to the stars was sealed.

Tennant made excellent money, between $350 and $400 a month. In addition to tennis instructor, she served as an all-purpose activity participant. She bowled with the guests. She rode on horseback to picnic destinations with them, creating photo spreads of their good times to be placed in their hometown papers, in the hope of prompting jealous neighbors to sign up for the same vacation. For the older, less active tourists, she organized bridge games. She lived with friends six miles away and walked to and from work every day, sending as much money as she could home to her mother.

Hoping to expand her reach, Tennant left the hotel in 1918 for a summer at a tennis club with two clay courts in Cleveland. Her boss turned out to be an embezzler—as she put it, "He just went a little bit overboard with other people's money." After some travels, she returned to the hotel, where Stanley's mother was now in charge. She found Tennant less charming than her son did and promptly demoted her to the kitchen, perhaps as a punishment for leaving. She quit.

She missed her amateur standing and sought to win it back in 1919, making her pitch to George Wightman, husband of Hazel Hotchkiss Wightman, who sponsored an international competition for women called, indeed, the Wightman Cup. George Wightman bought Tennant's argument that her income as a professional had been devoted to the care of her widowed mother and should not be held against her. Amazingly, it was not, and Tennant reentered competitive tennis as an amateur. In a tournament at the Field Club in Greenwich, Connecticut, she beat Edith Sigourney, the national indoor runner-up, losing only five games. It was her first time playing on a grass court.[10] She achieved the rank of number three in the United States in 1920, the year she and partner Helen Baker got to the women's doubles final at the US National Championships.

At age twenty-six, Tennant married Lyman J. Potter, a stockbroker in San Francisco. They moved to Burlingame, in San Mateo County, for the duration of their union of three years. When her husband demanded that she give up tennis, Eleanor took up golf in its stead. When he had an affair with a woman, she retaliated with her own affair, with a woman. The divorce was ugly. As Tennant put it, "All of that tish-tush came out," by which she meant accusations of mental cruelty and infidelity. The stress of divorce court drained her mentally and physically. She feared she might have a nervous breakdown, contract tuberculosis, or perhaps both.[11] She often trumpeted her convictions with the phrase "the sum and substance of it is . . ." In this case, the sum and substance of divorce was that it threw her, as she put it, for a loop. The divorce rate at the time was 15 percent, and the female party carried the brunt of the stigma, perceived of as a "moral fire alarm."[12]

Eleanor ended up as a nighttime receptionist at another, less tony hotel, calling her salary an "Irishman's promotion in comparison to what I had,"[13] a commonplace slur for a demotion in pay or prestige or both. She worked to regain her health by walking everywhere and playing golf, badminton, and tennis. She had plenty of time to read, finding consolation in the wisdom of the philosophers Plato, Socrates, and Epictetus. Eventually, she moved to La Jolla, San Diego County, and gave tennis lessons on the courts at the Bishop's School without permission. Here, out of desperation, she came up with the concept of "tennis clinics," inventing the phrase while out on a walk and immediately cottoning to its ring. It sounded modern and rigorous, much better than "group lessons." Soon, pupils enrolled, up to one hundred at a time, and she instructed them en masse, on the theory that if she corrected one child's wobbly backhand, the other ninety-nine would benefit just as much. She geared the large sessions to children but also taught adults from time to time. The headmistress of the Bishop's School took note of Tennant's success and, instead of running her off, formalized the relationship with the offer of a full-time job running the school's tennis department, providing Tennant with a base of operations in La Jolla for the next eleven years. So, in 1924, she gave up her amateur standing again. "I dreaded that job," she told a reporter years later, "because I thought women were petty and small and hated the idea of a girls' school. I've had to eat that. I doubt whether anything proved so beneficial to me as those girls."[14]

To her students she spewed zingers. When one of her protégées would freeze after missing a shot, she goaded: "Don't just stand there with egg on your face—move when you're on the court"; or when someone worried about what to do with her right elbow, "Why don't you mail it home to your grandmother?"[15] Tennant also liked to say that five sets of singles in practice equaled three in a match.

Ever eager to create extra income, she sold her students equipment from Wilson Sporting Goods as a sideline. She was so successful, Wilson marketed a racket with her name on it, and she became adept at on-the-spot consultations as to which size of her name-emblazoned racket would most suit a student.

Hollywood was 118 miles away, close enough that Tennant cultivated a clientele there, including "Carole Lombard, Joan Crawford, Clifton Webb, Jean Harlow and the great Charlie Chaplin himself."[16] Tennant thought that her Hollywood students, whom she called Show People, had something in common with tennis stars: "Their footlights were our tournaments."[17] It was at that time that the infinitely glamorous Lombard gave Tennant the nickname that became her calling card. "Yes, Teacher, dear," Lombard often said, with exaggerated gratitude, when responding to a corrective, finally shortening the term of address to a one-syllable punch. From then on, no other name would do. The stars showered Teach with expressions of their gratitude, including, in a letter from famous film villain Peter Lorre: "My love for you is as great as my respect (that's enough, ain't it?)."[18]

During those years in La Jolla, Teach displayed her scouting instincts. One of the pupils who caught her eye was fourteen-year-old Bobby Riggs, who like her had come from the "municipal bracket." As she recounted in *"Teach": The Story of Eleanor "Teach" Tennant*, she got him on the "free list," meaning that one of the sporting concerns supplied him with equipment, and she even helped him out financially in getting the proper outfits to play in. She knew the world of tennis was bigger than just Southern California and dreamed of taking a star player to the highest reaches. Lest anyone doubt the scale of her ambition, she made it clear she had England in mind: "Wimbledon is tennis heaven, that's all. Don't sell that little number short."

A clinic brought Tennant to San Francisco that day in March 1931 when she met Alice Marble, encouraged by Harold Dickenson, an associate at Wilson. Teach always thought he had his eye on Alice: "As a matter of fact I think he was very much in love."[19] Teach invited Alice and Dickenson to accompany her to Dominican College (now Dominican University of California), where she would conduct one of her clinics. It was less than Alice had hoped for: "Harold promised to invite her the next day to the park to watch me play, but Miss Tennant went back to Los Angeles and my hopes were dashed at least temporarily."[20]

Alice had begun to perceive that the scattershot approach to her coaching, a combination of Dan's scolding voice and the sporadic attention of various local tennis legends, would take her only so far. After meeting Teach, she had one wish: "If only I had a teacher like that!"[21]

It turns out that Teach had identified someone as a bright new talent, news that she conveyed in a chatty letter to *American Lawn Tennis* published on July 5, 1931: "You may be pleased to learn that I am giving my services to a youngster," she wrote. "It is my belief that she has championship material, and maybe, in my small way, I can contribute a worthwhile player to the amateur world." The description may have fit Alice, but the player Teach had in mind was someone else entirely, a young woman named Mary Greason, who faded into obscurity as Alice's own fortunes began to rise.

ALICE FINISHED HER SENIOR YEAR of high school, graduating in a class of 177 students. She earned seven varsity letters in track, softball, soccer, and basketball. The school offered tennis to female students only as a beginner sport in the younger grades, and she was not welcome on the boys' team.

A couple of years before, she had subbed in a tournament and played against a male high school classmate, Rudy Wagner, who happened to be a football star and president of her class. He was not thrilled when she trounced him, in front of his friends no less, and Alice said he never spoke to her again. Perhaps she had a crush on him. The experience caused her to conclude that she would be better off looking for beaus outside the world of tennis. "It was a very grim victory and taught me that romance and tennis do not mix, and that men hate to be beaten by women at anything."[22]

In a letter to his fellow graduates published in their high school yearbook, Wagner pointed out some of the pursuits his female classmates had settled on. He noted that fourteen young women would be training for office work: "What a lot of good secretaries San Francisco will have pretty soon!" He also mentioned that "many of our girls are planning to take up nursing" and others wanted to learn how to "marcel," create the popular hairdo, which entailed using a hot iron rod to create rows of curls, taking hours to perfect. His enthusiastic recitation outlined predictable choices. World-class athlete was not among them.

Dan kept pushing college to Alice, who went so far as to write what she called a thesis as part of the admissions process. She chose to focus on playwright George Bernard Shaw, the most famous literary figure of the day, the subject of newsreel after newsreel at Alice's beloved movies, a scampish figure with a long beard and an elfin expression at odds with how acerbic he could be. She made herself an expert on all his plays, including *Pygmalion*.[23] Based on a tale from Ovid, the plot involves a wager between Henry Higgins and a male friend about whether Higgins could mold a lower-class flower girl, Eliza Doolittle, into a figure of well-spoken rectitude by chipping away at her deficits, including her heavy cockney accent. He claimed he could create someone so graceful that no one would ever guess her true lineage.

Alice earned a grade of B on the entrance exams for admission into the California university system and, the evening after winning on the first day of the California state tournaments in early June, celebrated with dinner and, naturally, a movie, inviting her mother along. The drumbeat of publicity continued in her favor, with a notice in the *San Francisco Examiner* quoting Howard Kinsey, a coach at the Berkeley Tennis Club, who labeled her already one of the state's "best young net stars," praising "her speed of foot" and her coordination. "Alice is only seventeen, but she's strong."

The *Examiner* predicted that the title of state champion would go to Helen Wills Moody, an understandable forecast, as Moody was the world's dominant woman player, with many titles in her past and many more to come. Marble was the third contender, after Dorothy Weisel.[24] The next day, the *Examiner* retracted its prediction. Moody would not be competing after all, a "distinct surprise," the newspaper reported. "The State tourney was to have been Helen's first taste of competition of the season."[25] Alice

Marble, identified as a "Golden Gate Park girl," ended up stealing "all the thunder" of the competitions, winning the women's singles and the girls' under-eighteen singles, one after the other.[26]

Once again, Billy Johnston served as the bearer of good news. Marble had been selected to represent Northern California in East Coast championships that summer. This time she would not have to rely on a haughty patroness and her big Buick. The United States Lawn Tennis Association had decreed that a chaperone had to accompany sixteen-year-olds when traveling to tournaments, as had been the case for Alice the previous summer. However, by the time a player had reached the exalted age of seventeen, such protection was no longer considered necessary, so Alice undertook the journey to New York City on her own by transcontinental train. Her family showed up in force to see her depart from the Oakland Mole, a wharf and transportation hub across the bay: her mother, three brothers, Hazel, Hazel's four-year-old, and even Uncle Woodie. The well-wishers arrived an hour ahead of time, the better to inspect Alice's accommodations as they bestowed the standard bouquet of advice—hide your money, don't speak to strangers—with a specific reminder to the young athlete to drink plenty of milk.

Dan was the last to hug her goodbye, telling her: "Bring back the cup."[27]

The train was a rolling hotel, with haircuts and manicures available, fresh flowers, and daily papers taken on at appropriate points. During the journey, Alice listened as an older woman interpreted the shifting landscape, especially eloquent about the mountains and the desert and Mormonism as the train crossed Utah. She later became a friend, whom Alice would sometimes visit when she was in the Boston area. The speeding train took only four days from coast to coast—*Sunset* magazine hailed it as "Aladdin's carpet."[28] It followed the usual route of Sacramento, Ogden, Green River, Cheyenne, Julesburg, Omaha, Council Bluffs, and Chicago. After that was a long stretch of 715 miles before it pulled into New York City.

CHAPTER 7

PRECARIOUS

UPON ARRIVING AT New York's Grand Central Station, Alice exited the shadows of the platform area and entered a soaring space with a vaulted ceiling, twelve stories high, decorated with twenty-five hundred stars, including zodiac constellations. A four-faced opal-glass and brass clock at the information center informed travelers heading in any direction of the precise time. Grand Central was itself young, having opened to the public in 1913, the year of Alice's birth. Conductors bellowed the names of cities and towns (Larchmont, Mamaroneck, New Rochelle, Bridgeport, Stamford, New Haven), adding even more echoes to a space that was already an echo chamber.

Billy Johnston had arranged for Alice to be met by Stephen Wallis Merrihew, the editor of *American Lawn Tennis*, so she was on the lookout for a man in his late sixties carrying a copy of his publication. She scanned the crowds, hoping to spot his white hair amid the younger men in business attire, wearing hats, lighting cigarettes, newspapers wedged under their arms. They gave an impression they were on their way to work or some other place with equal gravity, but the country was two years into the Great Depression, and at least a portion of the men at the station merely posed as wage earners, using the bustle of the crowd as a cover for their lack of purpose, their clothing a costume meant to imply respectability. The poet Langston Hughes, who made the inequities, racial and economic, of that era the centerpiece of his work, pointed out the indisputable truth in his poem "Advertisement for the Waldorf-Astoria." These men were fooling no one: "Your pawnshop overcoat's a ragged banner on your hungry frame."

Signs of hardship proliferated throughout the city: men, and sometimes women, selling apples for a nickel apiece—or shoestrings or pencils—a public admission of hard luck. The *New York Times* sent a reporter around the city to observe small acts of mercy toward peddlers one day during the cold of winter. A bus driver tossed a pair of gloves to a vendor; a woman bought an overcoat for an "apple man, young, slight."[1] Street vendors expanded their inventory, selling oranges, tangerines, flowers, even chocolate. They were so abundant that the police commissioner ordered peddlers off certain streets for blocking sidewalks and access to businesses.[2]

Money problems could erupt anywhere, anytime. One weekday afternoon that summer, "before the wondering eyes of guests," nearly all the furniture in the lobby, lounge, and dining room of the Hotel Victoria on Seventh Avenue and Fifty-First Street was hauled away for nonpayment.[3] New York was a magnet for people desperate for work, meals, and shelter, an increasing problem for the city. It was not uncommon for a patrolman to find nearly unconscious men collapsed on the sidewalk, "suffering from starvation."[4] Some of the newly homeless camped outdoors: twenty-two jobless men—"not ordinary bums"—were charged with sleeping in Central Park. The magistrate was so disposed toward these "mostly neatly dressed men" that he freed them and handed each two dollars.[5] Breadlines formed at places like the Salvation Army food depot, the Bowery Mission, the Municipal Lodging House. The Salvation Army reported that the majority of patrons appeared to have "spent their nights in the open."[6] Women were reluctant to join a breadline unless it was for the sake of their children. "Women still carry in their minds psychological remnants of the Age of Protection; to admit publicly that they are totally unprotected is often too bitter to endure," said Ollie Randall of the Emergency Work Bureau.[7] As a young woman on her own in the city, Alice did not fit a welcome demographic. The Welfare Council let it be known that "idle girls" should stay away from New York unless they had a job.[8]

Standing in the station, Alice had to acknowledge that somehow signals had crossed. All this humanity swirling around her, and the one person she hoped to spot, Merrihew, was nowhere to be seen. Finally, she overcame her shyness, asked for directions, and proceeded from the terminal into a tunnel[9] that spanned several city blocks and guided her to an entrance to the well-lit lobby of the Roosevelt Hotel, where accommodations had been arranged beforehand. A bellman carried her luggage to her room. She conscientiously offered the dime that her mother had counseled her to give as a tip. Ten cents could buy a ticket to the movies, two shoeshines, or a hot lunch. He refused to accept it.

She had been assigned to a suite where she would be joined by another player, Bonnie Miller, a junior champion from Los Angeles, and her mother. The two young women would often team up as doubles partners at prestigious venues in the upcoming competitions. While awaiting her companions, Alice attended to her dress, covered with soot during the trip. She could have paid a dollar for valet service on the train, but she elected to wait until she got to the city to freshen the garment on her own, placing it on a hanger and then turning on the bath water to the highest heat to create enough steam to smooth out the wrinkles and dislodge the grime. She closed the door of the bathroom to facilitate the process.

A half hour later, she was shocked by the results: "The entire side wall was covered with a combination of black dye and a four-day collection of dirt."

Scrubbing the walls only made matters worse, creating even more streaks. Adding to the confusion, an electric iron overheated, breaking the glass top of a table where she had placed it.

"I was perfectly safe," Alice recounted years later, "but mother was right—it was a little precarious."[10]

Although she did not know Bonnie Miller well, Alice felt relieved to meet up with her and her mother. They celebrated in the Roosevelt Grill with a bite to eat while listening to Guy Lombardo's orchestra. As members of the house band—before becoming world famous—Lombardo and his three brothers teamed up to play what they billed as "the sweetest music this side of heaven." Their nightly specialty, loud and nostalgic, was an orchestral rendition of the Scottish ballad "Auld Lang Syne."

As soon as they could on the following day, the trio left for the Forest Hills Inn, near the grass courts at the West Side Tennis Club, where Marble and Miller could practice on the challenging, unfamiliar grass and clay surfaces before commencing their seven-week tour. The first stop was at Seabright Lawn Tennis and Cricket Club in Rumson, New Jersey, from July 27 to August 1, 1931. It was vintage East Coast at its clenched-teeth finest: a high-toned institution where the ocean breezes consorted with the understated scent of old money. Founded in 1876, Seabright's sense of getting it right extended to its grass turf, imported from England. The clubhouse, built in the popular Shingle style of architecture, conveyed a forceful horizontality. The revelry of previous competitions was preserved for all to admire in the main room, a near riot of plaques and trophies and framed photos, amid dark wicker furniture.

Seabright drew the "greatest galaxy of tennis notables to assemble for any tournament of the current season," tennis writer Allison Danzig observed in the *New York Times*. So grand, said Danzig, even losers were winners—players "could be culled from the beaten group to regiment the seeded list of several tournaments." The "casualty list" included "Miss Alice Marble of California, who has been heralded as a second Helen Wills."[11]

The defeats for Alice at Seabright piled up, and they rankled. Alice's approach was rough and untutored. She quickly learned that her reckless-abandon style of play didn't go over so well on grass and against a different level of experience. Seabright had "little to offer me, and I to it. . . . My first and only opponent, a Mrs. Lamme, to me an utter stranger in tennis, beat me in the first round [7–9, 6–3, 8–6]. After the match I wanted to die quietly by myself, but it was too hot even for that."[12]

Alice and her partner Dorothy Weisel lost in the women's doubles, and she and Jack Tidball also fell in mixed doubles. The balls bounced much lower than Alice was used to. She flailed at them when she should have been using finesse. "The change from cement to grass was almost impossible if you had the wrong grips, which I did."[13]

The next stop was the Maidstone Club in East Hampton, New York, where she lost easily in the women's singles and the women's doubles. Marble also came away empty-handed from the Eastern Turf Court Championships at the Westchester Country Club in Rye, New York.

When Alice prepared to go to Forest Hills for the US National Championships, she discovered, to her dismay, that she was not even in the draw. She had hoped for a good position, to avoid early play against either of the two Helens, but she had been overlooked entirely. She turned to her contact at the Berkeley Tennis Club, Billy Johnston, to provide proof that he had submitted the paperwork so a new draw could be ordered. Having Johnston intervene on her behalf was no small influence, and he came to her rescue, providing all the necessary documentation. When the new draw was announced, players who had faced easy opponents in the first draw reviled Marble if they now faced tough ones, and players who lucked into easier prospects pretended to be her "best friends," as she put it.

By the time Marble got onto the court, she was feeling frazzled: "From the moment I walked down the four steps of the marquee onto the grass court I was frozen with fright. I felt every eye peering at me. A dozen photographers snapped pictures of us. The bevy of stalwart linesmen and the umpire took their places as we warmed up."[14] The outcome of her first match against Mary Greef Harris, whom she thought of as only "moderately good," reflected her state of mind. It ended quickly, in less than half an hour, Marble losing, 6–2, 6–2. She and Bonnie Miller also lost in the opening round of the women's doubles. The news coverage was harsh.

"The little matter of a letter which became lost between California and New York," the Associated Press reported, "caused more trouble for the United States Lawn Tennis association than all of the 64 entries for the women's national tennis championships that arrived and were duly accepted."[15]

East Coasters expressed prejudice against California, with its history of touting players who often fizzled: too much "wolf, wolf" and not enough real results. Reporter J. P. Allen sounded a sour note, calling Marble the "victim of too much trumpeting. There is undeniably a certain rugged attacking game at which Marble displays more than the usual amount of ability." The article pointed out that "like the majority of the players from the Pacific coast" her overhead shots were "spectacular" but she had "no defensive game to speak of" and her ground strokes reflected "uncertainty."[16]

The biggest blow wasn't that she lost, rather that she found herself siding with her detractors: "To be champion of Northern California meant nothing. Everybody could beat me."[17]

The girls' national championships were held at the Philadelphia Cricket Club, among the oldest country clubs in the United States, a founding member of the USNLTA in 1881 and host of the women's singles national championships from 1887 until 1921, when the tournament moved to Forest Hills. Gauging herself against her competitors, who were almost all accompanied by their mothers or their aunts, while she traveled on her own, she felt "rather lonely because most of the girls were chaperoned."[18]

The Germantown Cricket Club, also in Philadelphia, provided a base for Bill Tilden, the dominant men's player in the 1920s, who won his last major title at Wimbledon in 1930, before turning professional the next year. So great had been Tilden's appeal in the 1920s that it is said the Roland-Garros Stadium in Paris and the horseshoe-shaped stadium in Forest Hills were both built to accommodate the crowds who could not get enough of him.

Marble's debut on Tilden's home ground was a rousing success, as reported in an Associated Press story: Alice "made good her top seeding; as she drove with plenty of pace and mixed her shots for a second round victory. . . . [She] displayed poise, self-confidence and a game far above that of her competitors."[19] Marble beat Marjorie LeBoutillier (6–0, 6–0), Marion Wood (6–1, 6–2), Elizabeth Keating (6–3, 5–7, 6–2), and Hilda Boehm (6–0, 2–6, 6–2) to reach the finals.

Her jubilation faded after she lost in the finals (6–1, 6–4) to fellow Californian Ruby Bishop. Humiliated, because she felt she was clearly superior, Marble managed to win only five games. The same age as Marble, Bishop was from Pasadena and headed to college in the fall. The *Philadelphia Inquirer* reported: "Miss Marble, a husky athletic blonde . . . who is reputed for her burning drives and volcanic service, found herself completely outsmarted by the clever brunette, Miss Bishop."[20]

In a story about the Philadelphia tournament in *American Lawn Tennis*, a writer observed that the "only difference in the game between these youngsters and the grown-ups is that the youngsters can't handle themselves psychologically as well as the more experienced players do."[21] The writer then focused on Marble:

> *The girl with the most rounded game for her age is Alice Marble. She seems to have a natural tendency towards a chop, a drive, a lob, and a volley. At least it looks natural. I never saw a girl play her shots with more confidence. There is almost a scornful confidence in the way she conducts herself on the court and this characteristic I would say, should be tempered before she will reach her heights. For when she makes errors, she is outraged, and it is only with extreme self-control that she can manage to be careful, subtle and restrained. She was a good sport, however, after Ruby Bishop beat her in two sets in the finals. . . . Alice said afterward in the dressing room, "She was too good for me." All things considered; she was.*[22]

When the woman who chaired the tournament committee handed Alice the runner-up trophy, her good manners deserted her, and she threw it across the room and almost refused to play in the upcoming doubles finals. Persuaded back on the court, Alice once again showed no self-control and played recklessly. While she was toweling off during the break after losing the first set, the chairwoman approached her, reminding her that her partner, Bonnie Miller, had nothing to do with Alice's previous defeat. This time the words penetrated, and she and Bonnie won the match. Ruby Bishop was among the well-wishers.

Histrionics aside, the experience was far from a total loss. Alice could now speak a rudimentary version of a new language, East Coast Tennis, and she had had a crash course in meeting some of the players who would weave in and out of her life in the coming years. Two people took the time to give her unsolicited pep talks: the first, the woman at the Germantown Cricket Club, and the second, Mary K. Browne, who would become a lifelong friend. Nicknamed Brownie, she had been a national tennis champion in 1912, 1913, and 1914, and later, in the mid-1920s, distinguished herself in golf. Brownie had played Suzanne Lenglen in the exhibition match in San Francisco at which Marble had fallen asleep. Marble paid attention when Brownie said she too was from California and had had difficulty during her first three seasons playing in the East, losing in the first round three years in a row. Brownie assured the younger player that she had "great possibilities, but you want to play like a champion before you learn to be a beginner. You have worlds of natural ability, but you know nothing about strokes and strategy." Brownie urged Alice to develop a system whereby she could learn what was necessary when she got home. Among her advice was to watch all the tennis she could—players like Helen Wills and some of the English girls. "They do not rely on trick shots," Brownie observed. "They have learned three major shots by years of hard work, patience and practice. You must do the same."[23]

After Alice returned home, Dan asked her to reconsider the notion of college, but she decided against it and instead found a job in a bookstore. It had begun to dawn on her that if she wanted to excel at tennis, she was look-ing at an arduous apprenticeship. The overriding impression among fans and the press was of a talented player who lacked discipline. Yes, she possessed immense strength, but she showed poor command, and emotional control also eluded her. Alice had to face the simple fact that Ruby Bishop possessed actual ground strokes as opposed to a grab bag of power shots with a trajectory of their own, not to mention Alice's equally haphazard grips. To succeed, Alice needed to be taken apart and built back up, and as far as she was concerned, one person was meant to do the job: Ruby Bishop's brilliant instructor, the no-nonsense, fast-walking, fast-talking Eleanor "Teach" Tennant.

PART TWO

1932–1934

CHAPTER 8

CANNONBALL

I F ONLY IT WERE THAT EASY: pick the perfect mentor, and presto, she's yours. But that scenario would have required Teach Tennant to share the same high opinion of Alice that Alice did of her. Alice would have been humiliated if she had known that Teach's assessment of her abilities lined up with those of her detractors and was, if anything, harsher. Responding to pressure from Harold Dickenson, Teach found the time to watch Alice play at Golden Gate during a visit to San Francisco. Teach did not specify exactly when, but logic dictates it would have been after Alice's trip east in 1931.

On the plus side, Teach observed that Alice had coordination and ball sense, but otherwise her play was appalling. Alice struck Teach as "fat and heavy. Her stroke-production was eccentric, worst of all she had no control over her temper." Teach watched, in horror, as Alice batted a tennis ball far afield in anger. Marble would "sock the ball—and I'm not kidding: it would go almost to the Chicken Coop, a block from where we were playing."[1] The Chicken Coop was the most remote court in the park, a raggedy outpost filled with shadows and bad spots where the novices gathered to "scratch" (thus the name) in impromptu teams.

Yet Teach had an instinct: "Something happened in my solar plexus. This thing came to me which said she can be a world's champion."[2] As a result, she did not abandon the young athlete altogether. Teach declined to work with Alice, but she did arrange for her to train with Howard Kinsey.

The referral was no small matter, as Kinsey was considered the leading tennis teacher in the Bay Area. Kinsey boasted his own impressive credentials as a player. He and his brother, Robert, won the national men's doubles championship in 1924 at Forest Hills. Kinsey achieved top ranking among American men's singles players from 1922 through 1925. His reputation as a back-court player was legendary.[3] One time, he and Helen Wills Moody volleyed a tennis ball back and forth 2,001 times without missing over the course of one hour and eighteen minutes. The only reason they stopped was that Kinsey had to go teach a previously scheduled tennis lesson.

Kinsey set out to train Marble in strategy and in how to put spin on the ball as well as in patience and decorum. Alice repaid Kinsey for his tutelage by playing tennis with his other students, a not uncommon barter system in those days. The fruits of their collaboration became apparent when she beat top-ranked Edith Cross in June 1932 and won the California women's singles championship.[4]

Alice was considered deserving of "Eastern experience," and the Northern California Tennis Association went all out to support her. (Two other novices, Sam Lee and Charlie Hunt, were also deemed worthy.)[5] In a can-do spirit, young and seasoned players put on exhibition matches in July to "transport three Californians to the national championships in the east." One of the stars who showed up to play was Hazel Hotchkiss Wightman, founder of the Wightman Cup.[6]

Alice, now aged out of the juniors, headed for matches in Rye, New York, where her previous experience came back to haunt her. First, the *Brooklyn Daily Eagle* reminded sports page readers of the trouble Alice had stirred at the US National Championships, saying, she "will be remembered as the young lady who caused the national tournament officials to revise their draw because her entry blank had been overlooked." Second, Mrs. Lamme, the "utter stranger" who beat Alice in her first match of her 1931 East Coast tour, did the exact same thing in 1932 at the Rye championships. Alice lost in the third round.[7] But her confidence was better. The previous year she wanted to "die quietly" after Mrs. Lamme defeated her. Now, she went straight for Forest Hills. Alice had submitted five applications to be on the safe side, "thus proving that the girl has a sense of humor," one reporter commented.[8]

In an early round she went up against Sarah Palfrey, seeded number five, who had seven seasons in major tournaments under her belt to Marble's one. A year older than Alice, Palfrey came from Massachusetts and had a pedigree that contrasted with Marble's more rationed circumstances. Palfrey's parents owned a farm outside of Boston, where their five children summered on 250 acres that included a tennis court.

Every sport loves a new champion, and starting around 4:15 in the afternoon on August 16, 1932, at Forest Hills, tennis found one. The press was on top of the story. Marble's first set was "replete with brilliant rallies," an account in the *New York Times* reported. "Miss Palfrey had the service and won it after deuce, following it by breaking through at thirty. Miss Marble immediately retaliated, and the long struggle was on." Calling it a "splendidly round game," the paper said that Marble "gradually wore down the New Englander." The final tally was 6–8, 6–4, 6–2.

The crowd erupted. Alice's hometown paper, the *San Francisco Examiner*, reported the next day that the spectators "stood up and cheered in the Forest Hills Stadium until their throats were hoarse, and that's something of a record. And for whom would they cheer, but another Californian, a newcomer to the ranks of the mighty, a smashing, dashing, fighting blonde-headed San Francisco girl, Alice Marble." The *Brooklyn Daily Eagle* called Marble the "answer to the fervent prayers of the committee in charge of the national women's singles championship for a sensation and great was the rejoicing in the marquee at Forest Hills." The newspaper noted that an "enthusiastic gallery . . . means a contented box office, something devoutly to be desired, what with times being what they are." The *Brooklyn Times Union* echoed the praise: "The tennis public, ever on the alert for a possible successor to Mrs. Helen Wills Moody, found a new candidate at Forest Hills yesterday afternoon in the person of Miss Alice Marble, of San Francisco."

Alice's inconsistency was on display the next afternoon, August 17, as she lost in three sets to Joan Ridley of England, 3–6, 6–4, 6–3. The *New York Times* reported: "Miss Marble handed the match to her opponent after having won the first set. Miss Ridley . . . allowed the California girl to defeat herself on errors."[9] Alice's serve won widespread admiration for its power, but her play lacked discipline, as evinced by twenty-four unforced errors in the second set. It was as if she felt compelled to spell out all her weaknesses in capital letters before a crowd that had been primed to embrace her.

Marble roared back two days later, August 19, playing doubles with Marjorie Morrill Painter against Elsie Pittman and Joan Ridley. Alice was "smashing overhead and straight through the court with masculine power." The game went to three sets, with Marble and Painter winning, 6–3, 3–6, 8–6.[10]

The press dubbed her "Cannonball Alice." The *New York Herald Tribune* cited the "sheer speed and crushing power of the blonde and stalwart California girl."

Marble and her partner eventually lost to Helen Jacobs (who won the singles title and earlier had won the Wimbledon ladies' doubles) and Sarah

Palfrey, 8–6, 6–1, in the final, but at least she had the satisfaction of carrying a runner-up trophy home to California.

Pleased with the results and with the outpouring of goodwill from the press, Alice returned by train to San Francisco and then headed, in late September, to the Pacific Southwest Championships at the Los Angeles Tennis Club, where movie stars engaged in their two favorite sports, watching tennis and watching each other. The club was the brainchild of 1905 Wimbledon champion May Sutton Bundy and her husband, Thomas Bundy. She liked to say she married him because he was the rare person, male or female, who could beat her in tennis. In 1920, she led a venture that eventually converted the site of an old cow path into the club, where competitors entertained fans sitting in booths with red leather seats. The club's handy location around the corner from Paramount Studios guaranteed a steady flow of stars. Clark Gable and Carole Lombard maintained their own courtside box. The club combined a commanding design with old-world charm. Years later, Billie Jean King said it looked like a "colonial Spanish palace with its white stucco walls, pillared entryway and red tile roof."[11] She too enjoyed the scent of celebrity: "On any given day Errol Flynn and Bette Davis might be around . . . playing a friendly match."

Alice loved seeing the stars, the "breed apart," as she called them, gatekeepers to a world she considered nothing less than miraculous.

At the tournament that year, she lost to a reputable opponent, Anna Harper, who had been a finalist at Forest Hills two years before. Marble managed to beat her the following week on her home turf for the Pacific Coast title, thus finishing first in Northern California and seventh in the nation, numbers that won Teach Tennant's favor.

Encouraged by Alice's obvious improvement, Teach suggested an arrangement: Marble would live with her and her invalid sister Gwen in La Jolla for intervals, earning her keep by coaching younger players and doing secretarial work before rotating back home, where she would clerk for Wilson Sporting Goods. Teach had an ongoing relationship with Wilson, which routinely employed amateur tennis players as typists and in other clerical jobs to subsidize their careers and promote tennis without violating any rules about pay for play. Alice would earn forty dollars a month, and she would have the afternoons off to play tennis.

The money mattered, at least to Alice. Tennis, as portrayed in the pages of *American Lawn Tennis* magazine, enjoyed an upper-crust immunity from the Depression. An article in the summer of 1932, headlined "Young Girls Have Their Day," made light of money woes: "In these days of the Great Depression it is a fine sight to see forty-five girls, all but half a dozen in white, prancing about the two rows of green tennis courts at the Philadelphia C.C. [Cricket Club]. Notwithstanding Daddy's financial troubles he can dig into his pocket for an entrance fee."[12] A few months later, an ad appearing with the slogan "There's no Depression on the Courts," claimed: "Tennis puts low spirits to rout. Competition starts blood to boiling, a few smashing drives raise the spirits amazingly. Maybe that's the reason the courts are crowded this year."[13]

Once again, the approval of the two-person tribunal consisting of Dan and Jessie Marble would be necessary to put Teach's plan in action. This time, Dan signed up right away, but Jessie was more reluctant, especially when Teach took Alice to Berkeley for a musical evening that lasted two hours beyond the agreed-upon curfew of ten. Dan eventually won out, and both he and his mother gave their blessing.

Upon arriving at Teach's house in La Jolla, Alice failed the first test. Teach was aghast when Alice created the equivalent of a bread-crumb trail throughout the house by dropping "her coat on a chair and her hat in someplace else and her bag someplace else."[14]

Alice's version of that same initial meeting confirms Teach's impression: "I was a very undisciplined person and Teach was the one who was going to discipline me. I put my coat on the chair and she said, 'Hang it up. It'll have to go there eventually.' Very English background."[15]

Teach was just as frustrated with her new charge's sloppiness on the court. Tennis, Teach told her, "is a game of control and discipline. Tennis is built on dimensions, and you have a limited area in which to work. That requires, to my way of thinking, conformity and a very orderly way of mind."[16] After observing the scattershot nature of Alice's shots and grips, Teach said, "Get in the car. We're going somewhere."

That vague "somewhere" turned out to be the Santa Barbara home of yet another of Teach's many contacts in the world of tennis, Harwood White, known as "Beese." Teach believed that no one understood the dynamics of the game better than he did. Tall and courtly, he was, in Teach's view, a philosopher of the game, confirmed by the ten books he eventually wrote about tennis. A graduate of Princeton University, the father of five sons, and the tennis pro at the Montecito Country Club, in Santa Barbara, Beese observed Alice practicing and immediately announced, "It'll never do. Your shots won't do, and that's all there is to it."[17]

Alice resisted at first, dismissing Beese's approach as "no fun, no exercise." She loved flailing after the ball and could not see the joy in Beese's smoother stroke even if it resulted in a powerful shot. Beese stood his ground. He urged Alice to throw out everything she thought she knew. Over and over, he counseled, "Step into the ball. Full swing, full follow-through. Don't *hit* the ball; *meet* it. This is not a game of strength."[18]

Beese set out to school Alice in the physics of how to use the racket to return the ball with icy efficiency. He taught her the fine points of technique: "Hold the racket loosely around the end with two fingers and thumb," he said, and suddenly, she realized, "with one-tenth the strength I used to use I got one hundred times the result."[19]

Alice could see that Beese wanted the racket head to do the work. "I could see what he was getting after, but I didn't want to admit it."[20]

Beese and Teach enacted the classic good cop–bad cop approach. Whereas Teach demanded "unreasoning obedience," Beese's less dictatorial style encouraged his students to think of themselves as allies in the learning process. After Beese managed to convince Alice to stop attacking the ball, she finally understood that a flat, strong stroke was a better response than a slice. With Beese guiding her, Alice got the instruction she needed to abandon her underhand, Western-style grip, in favor of the handshake approach, in which the hand ideally feels fused with the racket.[21] Beese taught her how to change grips depending on whether her shot was backhand, forehand, or serve. Teach accompanied Alice to her lessons with Beese and was a patient observer, playing the role of a human ball machine, feeding shots to her over and over.

Beese instilled one lesson above all: "The minute you get the idea that you don't attack the ball, that you let the racket do the work, you've made real progress."

Alice saw the wisdom in Beese's coaching and in Teach's as well. Years later, she expressed amazement that Teach and Beese ever thought she would amount to anything:

> *I did have one wonderful ability, what is called "natural ball sense." This means coordination of eye and hand and muscle, plus accurate timing and a*

sense of distance. I could toss a paper wad into a distant wastebasket because I could gauge the distance accurately with my eye. In the same way a person can catch a baseball in the outfield by knowing just the spot at which it will fall down into his glove with a thunk. *Or his eye sees maybe just a foot wide opening in which to hit the ball past his opponent at the tennis net. White recognized this ability. I had got a long way with the foulest stroke equipment—I don't know now how they had the courage to take on someone so wrong.*[22]

Alice was not Teach's only exceptional pupil. Bobby Riggs showed up for occasional lessons, already enjoying a reputation as the "bad boy of tennis." From an early age, Riggs clowned around on the court, substituting antics for rigor. Teach disapproved, as she did his increasingly well-known gambling habit. He did not drink nor smoke, but he loved to wager bets for and against himself and often stayed up all night playing cards. Teach would pit her two charges against each other, telling Riggs how great Alice had played and telling Alice how well he had done, fostering tension. "It always stimulated their adrenalin gland," she would say by way of justification.[23] Alice not only resented the attention Riggs was getting; she was incensed when Teach recruited her to help Riggs pick out clothes: "He's nothing but a selfish little guy and I don't see why I should waste my time buying his clothes and you your money."

Teach's instruction extended beyond the tennis court to diet, decorum, appearance, and schedule. In Teach, Alice had her own Henry Higgins, and Teach was aware of the dynamic, telling interviewers that her charge had "until the age of eighteen known nothing but irregularity." That would have to change, and Teach led the charge. She picked out Alice's wardrobe. She prevailed upon Alice to use her fork in her left hand, "in the English manner, as she did." Marble wasn't "allowed to cook or drive or make decisions. She convinced me I was good at nothing *but* tennis, and I focused entirely on my sport, just as she intended."[24] The day began with a healthy breakfast of lemon juice, half a grapefruit, egg, one piece of toast, and a cup of coffee. Teach was petite and did not have much interest in food. Alice thought of Teach as a "real scrawny woman," with no idea how anyone got fat in the first place. Alice knew only too well: "I thought life wasn't decent unless you had five ice cream sodas every day."[25]

Teach saw to it that Alice "looked like a bandbox" on the court, referring to a lightweight cylindrical box used to house delicate items of apparel,
such as a hat or a collar. Alice was not allowed to sit down before a match
lest her outfit wrinkle. She was to always keep her tennis shoes spotless and
be in bed by 10 p.m.[26]

On Sundays, Teach and Alice would go to the home of a different
movie star and play tennis the entire day, followed by a buffet dinner.[27]
Teach introduced Alice to the stars as if they were all peers: "It all seemed so
unreal. When I talked, famous directors actually listened, nodding, laughing, sipping their drinks, their eyes on *me*. It made me feel so sophisticated,
so worldly. . . . The stars I had idolized she made a part of my everyday life,
as they were of hers."[28] Teach often hosted the stars at catered dinners, and
she intended to pass her social network along to her protégée as a kind of
inheritance. Her efforts may have appeared high-minded on one level, an
unusual devotion of one human being to the betterment of another, but they
had their roots in pragmatism. Teach and Alice became each other's meal
ticket, financially and figuratively.

"Ours was a strange relationship," Alice said years later. "I've heard
it said that Teach was a 'second mother' to me, but that was far from the
truth. She treated me like a child, but without the warmth of a mother. It
was difficult for her to show affection, and I understood why when Gwen
told me of their childhood. Their parents had a disagreement, about what
no one ever knew, and although they continued to live together, they did not
speak to each other for *fifteen years*. They communicated, when they had to,
through the children."[29]

When Alice first joined forces with Teach, she was told that the coach
was a lesbian, a new word for Marble and a puzzling one. After consulting a
dictionary and learning that the word originally described women who came
from the island of Lesbos, she was even more confused. "I knew Teach's
parents were English. She had to be English or American. Lesbian? Finally,
an old friend enlightened me. . . . [Teach] never asked me to be her bedmate,
though some of the other players no doubt thought I was."[30]

Alice admired Teach for her energy and her competence, including
in the treatment of a "bad blister or a cut," and she forgave her for being
authoritarian: "Eleanor Tennant was a good driving coach. The best psy-
chologist I think I have ever known. I always say that without Teach I never
would have made it. She was the push. I had so much God-given ability that

I had to be champion. It was all there. I just had to work on it and believe that I could and she was probably the one person who instilled it in me."[31]

In subsequent years, long after their union dissolved, Teach tried again and again to train other players as she had Marble, including Pauline Betz and Maureen Connolly (to whom, at age seventeen, she gave this unappreciated advice before the Wimbledon final in 1952: "You have to be mean to be a champion. How can you lick someone if you feel friendly toward them?"). Yet, in terms of having a tight grip on someone who gave her no ifs, ands, or buts, Marble was the prize. Under Teach, Marble would get top-notch training, financial security, access to the upper levels of society, and world renown.

CHAPTER 9

A LITTLE HIDEAWAY

J ESSIE MARBLE ALMOST SAID NO. She did not approve when Alice received an invitation to be a guest at the Hearst Castle in San Simeon, California, in the spring of 1933, leery of the company that her nineteen-year-old daughter would be keeping, given the range of movie stars and other celebrities the newspaper magnate William Randolph Hearst constantly invited. Teach countered her objections by outlining a version of life at the castle that sounded so clean-cut, so convent-like, Alice thought she had surely overdone it.[1] Teach won her point, as usual, so at sunset on a March day,[2] with the nervous, newly licensed Alice at the wheel, the two women arrived at San Simeon from Los Angeles, 230 miles south. La Cuesta Encantada, as Hearst called the estate, arose seemingly from the mist. The sight was so impressive that even the usually cocky Teach had been overcome at her first visit: "I couldn't talk. And when I can't talk, that's something."[3] The Hearst Castle embodied its owner's eccentric vision of luxury and fantasy combined with engineering, whimsy, and ostentation, a cousin of the mansions of Newport and the Gold Coast of Long Island. The travelers had picked the best time to arrive, the evening, when the floodlights were turned on so that arriving guests would view the turreted castle from miles away.[4]

Teach was already a frequent guest at the castle, staying up to a month at a time, owing to an arrangement with Marion Davies. At times Davies paid Teach up to $1,000 a month to teach tennis to her and her friends.[5] Teach, and now her protégée, were the equivalent of tennis pets, available to play with other guests as another source of pleasure in what amounted to an amusement park for adults. In return, they got to consort as equals with the Hollywood stars, writers, newspaper columnists, and captains of industry.

Teach's spiel had worked with Jessie Marble, but Alice entertained her own misgivings. Along with her tennis racket and powerful serve, she carried the whispered version of the *Oneida* scandal to the castle—a Hollywood whodunit, not resolved to this day. Alice adored Hollywood gossip, and she feared meeting Hearst in person, cowed not so much by his vast holdings, his influence, or his seniority as by a troubling rumor about his involvement in a suspicious death years before. Was it true that Hearst had arranged for Thomas Ince, a famous director of silent films and a guest on his yacht, the *Oneida*, to be killed? Had he himself committed the murder? Hearst's order to his inner circle to withhold information from reporters further obscured what really happened on the night of November 16, 1924.

Upon arrival, the first challenge for Alice was a "bridge-like thing that they kept up in the V or tent position, and then when you came up it was lowered so that it was level." Someone helped her drive the car across her first moat.[6]

A single-lane dirt road led to the estate, about which its owner once wrote, "Now, I am going to board a train and go down to my ranch and find my little hideaway on my little hilltop at San Simeon, and look down on the blue sea and up at the blue sky, and bask in the glorious sunshine of the greatest State of the greatest nation in the whole world." In response, one observer noted that it was a stretch to consider "four Mediterranean-style buildings containing 165 rooms surrounded by two classically inspired swimming pools and acres of gardens . . . set on a hill sixteen hundred feet above sea level with three-hundred-sixty degree views of the ocean and mountains, as a 'little hideaway.'"[7]

The *New Yorker* writer Brendan Gill decades later caught the essence of how big houses strike a newcomer unaccustomed to opulence: "Speaking for myself, when it comes to a big house, I am instantly credulous; I will believe anything about its owner as long as it is outrageous. . . . Little by little, I learned not to gape."[8] In time, Alice too learned not to gape, and the Hearst Castle provided her initial training.

Almost seventy years old when Alice met him, Hearst had spent a rootless childhood that entailed multiple trips to Europe with frequent exposure to the grandest of castles. Inheriting a fortune from his father, George, who made his money in gold and copper mining, the younger Hearst's deepest desire as an adult was to copy those domains and claim one as his own. When his father left him the property at San Simeon in 1919, he hired the architect Julia Morgan, and over three decades they created a structure sufficiently grand that it echoed his gilded memories. He would use the estate to highlight art he collected from all over the world and to offer nearly nonstop hospitality to guests including President Woodrow Wilson, New York City mayor Jimmy Walker, Amelia Earhart, and Charles Lindbergh.

One of the most prominent powerbrokers of his day, with a newspaper empire at his command, Hearst stopped at practically nothing if it meant he could increase circulation. His newspapers specialized in so-called yellow journalism, which embraced shoddy practices, the most obvious being to make up stories to boost sales. In 1898, eager to sell papers, he sent an illustrator to document the growing unrest between Cuba and Spain. When his man in Havana reported relative quiet, Hearst allegedly issued the dictum: "You furnish the pictures. I'll furnish the war."[9]

Admirers of the castle knew its numbers by heart: "a total of 165 rooms, including 56 bedrooms and 61 bathrooms, 41 fireplaces, a 5,200-volume library, and over 90,000 square feet (8361 sq m) of floor space. The primary structures on the grounds are a main house ('Casa Grande') that resembles a Spanish cathedral and three smaller guest houses, plus a huge Greco-Roman outdoor pool as well as an indoor pool lined with gold and Venetian glass." A private airport welcomed guests and accepted delivery of daily copies of almost thirty newspapers Hearst published. Alice observed that construction never seemed finished, telling her mother that she thought Hearst would die if he could not keep on building.

Hearst and his wife, Millicent, had been estranged for years but never divorced. She lived in New York and knew that her husband kept company with Davies. During the early days of the affair, Hearst had arranged for Davies to live far away from San Simeon out of respect for his children and other members of the family who desired to visit the castle. He did not want Davies to suffer in reduced or second-class circumstances, so he purchased a stuccoed home in Beverly Hills for her, arranging for the ownership papers to be in her mother's name, a way of keeping reporters and gawkers at bay.[10] To make up for abandoning Davies (thirty-five years his junior) during times when he had to be away, Hearst threw parties whenever they were together at her house and also arranged for trips on the *Oneida*, among them the fateful voyage resulting in Thomas Ince's death.

Alice braced herself the first time she met her host.

"Thank you for having me," she said. Had Hearst in fact killed a man? It seemed unlikely. She scanned his face and found it to be kind. "Your house is . . . it looks like something from the movies," she added.[11] The first time they were alone together—in an elevator—she was especially nervous. "We had read so many tales in the paper that he got Thomas Ince killed and all this sort of stuff, that I was a little nervous. He had such a high squeaky voice and put his hand on my head and he said, 'Sleep well, child.' And sort of patted me on the head. From that time on, I was at ease."[12]

Hearst loved animals, maintaining a free-ranging menagerie comprising yaks, gnus, giraffes, zebras, ostriches, water buffaloes, wildebeests, and kangaroos, five hundred or so animals in all, representing seventy species. His fondness for creatures extended to the mice caught in traps inside the castle, where staff had orders to remove them with care from the devices before releasing them outdoors.

With humans, Hearst enforced a strict code of conduct. Guests could eat only in the grand hall, never in their rooms. They were limited to one cocktail at six o'clock, three hours before dinner. Anyone discovered to have imported his or her own liquor was asked to leave immediately. Guests who violated the rules often found their bags packed for them, ready for pickup.[13] The alcohol policy was aimed, ineffectually, at Davies in particular. With a joie de vivre that caused her to declare "dull" a four-letter word, Davies was often lubricated by spirits.

And yet Hearst could be playful, and he delighted in planning surprises. On one occasion he instructed his gardeners to plant lilies in the night by flashlight as an Easter morning present for his visitors.

The ranks of guests would swell on the weekends, sometimes to as many as fifty. A pecking order existed, revealed by where you sat at dinner, as recounted by the humorist P. G. Wodehouse: "The longer you're there, the further you get from the middle. I sat on Marion's right the first night, then found myself getting edged further and further away, till I got to the extreme end, when I thought it time to leave. Another day and I should be feeding on the floor."[14]

Alice called the dining room "the biggest room I had ever seen." Hearst, "a very big man—tall, heavy and kindly-looking,"[15] would summon guests by ringing a big cowbell, a clangorous responsibility he clearly enjoyed.

Men wore suits and women cocktail dresses. Charlie Chaplin remembered fine fare, "game of the season: pheasant, wild duck, partridge and venison."[16] What struck Alice was that, despite the formality, including large chairs trimmed with red velvet, the table was set with paper napkins, and the condiments were not decanted but served in their original commercial form:

ketchup in its bottle, mustard in its jar. The dining room easily accommodated sixty diners ("Just a few friends, dropped round for dinner," as Teach once put it), with "carefully labeled little gold-and-white place cards"[17] marking each person's position at the table. The seating pattern often flattered Alice: "Mr. Hearst and Marion sat right in the middle, right across from one another. And for some reason he was fond of me, because I played tennis with him, and so I very often got to sit by his side."[18]

As for Hearst and his tennis game, Alice had only praise. "He loved to play, and he had a lot of stamina," especially for someone his age. He appeared "ancient but played nicely for a big man."[19]

"Actually," Alice recalled years later, sounding a bit like the castle-praising Teach must have sounded to Jessie Marble, "it was a very healthy life. You could go riding if you chose to ride, and Marion had a riding costume for you." Tennis. Golf. Many guests enjoyed a dip in the Neptune Pool, lined with Vermont granite, though Teach forbade Alice to swim, claiming it made "the muscles too loose for tennis."[20] Her job was to play tennis with the guests. "Forgive me," Alice said to an interviewer many years later, hoping she didn't sound swell-headed, "they were just as impressed with knowing me as I was with knowing them, because they all wanted . . . to play good tennis."[21]

Dinner extended until ten thirty or so in the evening, usually followed by a movie, enjoyed by Alice, even if they were mostly Davies's movies and mostly "awful." The guests often stayed up until past three in the morning, lounging on one of Hearst's many fancy carpets, solving jigsaw puzzles, playing bridge, and staging costume parties with trunks of clothes from the studios. The hilarity associated with this latter activity appears in a posed photograph: Bette Davis in a beard, figure skater Sonja Henie and actor Tyrone Powers as clowns, David Niven as a pickpocket, and Jean Harlow in lederhosen.[22] One game—dubbed "Who are they?"—consisted of citing the initials of silent movie stars and guessing their identity. One time Alice tossed out the letters "H. B." After an hour-plus, when no one could answer, she informed the guests: "Holbrook Blinn, the villain who tied girls to the railroad tracks."[23] Marble was proud to be a ringer. She claimed to have studied the silent movie stars as if she were studying to be a doctor: "I was the final authority."[24]

When the movies were over and dressing up in costumes grew old, guests might enjoy a talent show with Chaplin playing his left-handed violin or Hearst yodeling. Hearst's fondness for Alice took the form of encouraging her to sing. She had inherited her mother's contralto voice, which had once filled the farmhouse in the mountains on Christmas evenings.

"He was always bringing me out," Alice recalled. "I was shy, but I loved to sing, so he would always get me to sing a song. He was very complimentary. Here were all these pros, but I was just young enough and dumb enough not to be scared. My mother had taught me to sing quite well. So they would 'hush-hush, hush-hush.'"[25]

Alice enjoyed the company of Davies. "She was a very real person and someone I was enormously fond of."[26] Alice learned to refrain from admiring Davies's baubles such as a pretty ring, because Davies was likely to remove it from her hand and thrust it at Marble, claiming she had a dozen more.[27] Alice would be included in conversations with the other female guests, many of whom were Davies's friends from show business, various chorus lines or the Ziegfeld Follies. They gathered in Davies's dressing room, nicknamed the "loo." The conversations Alice overheard propelled her into a world about as far away as a person could get from Plumas County and the homespun amusements of stringing popcorn and dried fruit and singing hymns at holidays. She remembered:

> *They would talk about their abortions and to me this was sinful. But I listened and I certainly got an education. They told about how they went on diets, and they would eat and then throw up, so they would not get fat. They never told naughty stories or anything like that. They just had these things when they were going up the ladder, joining chorus lines, and some in the Ziegfeld Follies. They told them with great glee when they were starving to death. They loved this life they had in New York. There was a special kind of camaraderie with all the chorus girls.*[28]

Hearst asked Alice about college plans. She said she had hoped to go, but tennis "got in the way." He showed particular interest when he found out that Alice, as part of the application process for Berkeley, had written about "a very famous author,"[29] soon to be a guest of honor at the castle.

For years Hearst had been trying to get George Bernard Shaw, a long-time contributor to his papers, to pay a visit: "Of all the illustrious names that crowded Hearst's pages, none appeared more often than that of George Bernard Shaw—in large measure because his opinions on so many subjects were close to Hearst's. In 1906 and 1907, Hearst reprinted Shaw's articles on women's suffrage, which they both supported, on religion, which they distrusted, and on Fabian socialism, whose basic tenets they both championed—at least at the time."[30]

Hearst had extended to Shaw what he called a "formal and fervent invitation to be my guest and ride the range in California with me." Shaw said he would love to visit, but what he required most in his travels is a "nice desert island," to which Hearst responded that the castle had all the isolation of a desert island and could easily substitute for one.[31] Shaw finally agreed to a visit from March 24 to 27, 1933.

The man the newsreels billed as "The World's Most Outstanding Literary Genius" traveled to the United States aboard the *Empress of Britain*, arriving in San Francisco on March 23, 1933. The next morning, he gave a press conference that captured some of his contradictions. He could be good-humored yet condescending, completely off the mark or dead-on, sometimes in the same breath. He ridiculed the reporters for running out of questions, requested their gratitude for having supplied them with three weeks' worth of great material, predicted there would not be a new world war (because people remembered the last one and that would give them pause), and sounded no special alarm about Hitler: "The whole of Germany is in suspense and chaos just like the United States. They've decided to try Hitler just like the United States has decided to try Franklin Roosevelt."[32]

The next day Shaw flew two hundred miles south to San Simeon, where nervous guests were already auditioning their outfits and their repartee. Such an eminence required more than even the usual attentiveness to couture and grooming, and Marion Davies insisted that Alice choose a new outfit and have a makeover. Fortunately, Marble's hostess had "rooms and rooms and rooms" devoted to clothing and shoes and accessories, and Alice had her pick. Davies did her hair, Jean Harlow did her makeup, and Dorothy Mackaill ("a very interesting English movie star") was in charge of her nails.[33]

When the guests gathered in the dining room, Marble noticed an old man with a beard. "He came over and said, "Young lady, I admire the moles on your back."[34]

Alice, not recognizing him, took in in his long white beard, and concluded: "That dirty old man."[35] Before she could berate him, Davies interceded, explaining to Marble that she had just met her dinner partner, George Bernard Shaw, Nobel Prize laureate.

At dinner that night, Shaw avoided the pheasant, wild duck, partridge, and venison. A vegetarian since the age of twenty-four, he used to joke that when he died, instead of a parade of people following his casket, he hoped to be trailed by all the animals who were grateful that he had not eaten them.

During the meal, Marble summoned the research she had done on Shaw, chatting him up and sticking to a subject dear to his heart: him. "I knew the names and characters of every one of his plays, so I talked about his work, and he talked about himself. He was a delightful old coot, but so egotistical."[36]

Another guest, the gossip columnist Louella Parsons, profiled Shaw for the Hearst syndicate. Shaw demanded the right to edit her prose beforehand, which may account for its effulgence:

> HEARST RANCH, SAN SIMEON. *Seventy-seven years old, as straight as an arrow, as slim as a stripling of nineteen, the pink cheeks of a girl, the great Bernard Shaw had all the guests at the William Randolph Hearst ranch sitting at his feet. Shaw, with more appeal than a Maurice Chevalier, more charm than Charlie Chaplin, held court every afternoon while he drank his tea. . . . Seldom do we meet a man who measures up to every expectation as completely as does this cherubic faced youngster of seventy-seven. True, his publicized wit is even sharper than we were led to expect, but sharp as his matchless wit is, it lacks the venom so often attributed to him. With equal equanimity he discusses world disarmament, the gold standard, what's wrong with the movies, sex appeal and stage celebrities of the last 60 years, always with the same disarming twinkle in his clear blue eyes.*

Shaw took his leave of the castle. Before heading back to England, he stopped in New York City to deliver a speech to the Academy of Political Science on April 11 at the Metropolitan Opera House before a full-capacity crowd of thirty-five hundred. Broadcast on radio, the talk addressed American democracy. Among the highlights, he referred to the American Constitution as a "charter of anarchism." He said it was "not really a constitution at all. It was not an instrument of government; it was a guarantee to a whole nation that it could never be governed at all. And that is exactly what they wanted." The next day, the *New York Times* printed the text, annotating laughter and applause in a painstaking effort at calibrating the reaction to Shaw.[37]

* * *

OVER THE NEXT FEW YEARS, Marble would return on many occasions to San Simeon, sometimes staying for as long as a month. However, her main focus was on qualifying for and winning the tournaments that would determine whether she would be invited to head east for the third year in a row. The eyes of the tennis elite were on her, recording every move, thanks in part to remarks by the great Bill Tilden. As reported in the *San Francisco Examiner*, Tilden had happened upon a training session of Alice's with Howard Kinsey at the California Tennis Club. Tilden threw his hat in the air to signal his enthusiasm and began to "talk, then to gesticulate, and finally to rave over the talents of the young lady across the net. His manner was fervent, his praise profuse." The *Examiner* quoted Tilden at length:

> *"Never have I seen such speed with ease of motion in a woman player, not only as she strokes the ball but as she covers the court. It's a tremendous factor, and something that neither Mrs. Moody nor Miss Jacobs has at least in this degree.*
>
> *"Mme. Lenglen, Miss Aussem and Miss Alvarez have this speed and ease of motion, but none of them has the 'mechanics' of the game upon which Mrs. Moody and Miss Jacobs almost solely depend. . . . But here is someone who seems to have the speed and freedom of motion of a Lenglen, an Aussem or an Alvarez and it's all backed up by great mechanics as well. No players in the world have all these qualities, but as I live and breathe, this girl certainly has. When she meets any of the others in a little while, the results will be inevitable."*[38]

Tilden's words indicate that perhaps Teach's formula had paid off at long last. The efforts of Kinsey and Beese combined with Teach's exacting standards had changed Marble's game. No longer an unruly force of nature, she more closely resembled a sleek machine.

Uneasy can be the head that wears the crown: within weeks of Bill Tilden's high praise, Alice won the title at the Ojai Valley tournament handily but did not fare as well in the Southern California championships in May. Her match in the semifinals against Helen Marlowe Dimitrijevic lasted three hours and fifteen minutes. The contest was well fought, and Marble, at match point, hit a pitch-perfect return that should have demolished her opponent. Instead, Dimitrijevic's riposte arced inches above Marble as she stretched in vain to swat it before the ball landed squarely on the baseline. After that,

Marble lost five games in a row. The final score, of 8–6, 10–12, 7–5, reflected the closeness of the match.

Alice's confidence was shaken, and when she arrived back home for the state championships at Berkeley, she felt diminished. It did not help when the local press pursued a theme of "Who does she think she is?" prompted by peevish anger at Marble's decision to train in the southern part of the state.[39] Nonetheless, Alice won another state title, against Anna Harper (6–2, 10–8), also scoring her third transcontinental train ride in as many years.

On board, she ignored the passing landscape and instead pored over Beese's written notes of advice. She astonished her fellow passengers by constantly practicing her forehand drive in the aisle of the train. "People thought I was crazy."[40]

She headed straight to Massachusetts, where she won the Longwood Cricket Club (Chestnut Hill) and Essex County Club (Manchester-by-the-Sea) tournaments handily, beating top-seeded Carolin Babcock in both venues. The press took note of Marble's increasing prowess on grass, as for the first time she claimed two eastern titles.

At Seabright, however, she lost badly to Sarah Palfrey in the semifinals. It lifted her spirits somewhat when, partnered with Josephine Cruickshank, she later won the women's doubles. The next stop was in East Hampton on Long Island, at the Maidstone Club (which took its name from a town in Kent, England), where her performance would determine whether she would have a spot on the six-member annual Wightman Cup team, inaugurated a decade earlier by Hazel Hotchkiss Wightman, who had played at the Berkeley Tennis Club as a youngster.

Sickly as a child, Wightman grew up in California at the turn of the century and took up tennis to conquer asthma and build stamina, winning forty-five US tournaments in her lifetime, including sixteen national titles, four in singles and the others in women's and mixed doubles. She credited an uneven backyard for her skills, because it forced her to hustle as she swung at erratic balls. Her marriage into a Boston family that owed its wealth to steel caused her to move east, where she eventually gave birth to five children. Her father encouraged her to be the first female titled player in the United States to return to a major competition after having a baby, which she did, in 1915. In Chestnut Hill, Massachusetts, where she mentored players at the Longwood Cricket Club, Wightman became known as the "Queen Mother of American Tennis." She had a regal air, captured when she appeared in the press, for instance, on a luxury liner en route to the overseas competition bearing her name, smartly dressed in a cloche hat and a suit bearing a corsage—just the kind of tableau that underscored tennis's status as international, elite, and glamorous.

When she originated the Wightman Cup, donating a silver vase for a trophy to the United States Lawn Tennis Association, Wightman envisioned the competition as a way of offering women an international opportunity akin to the Davis Cup for men. Originally, she hoped to involve many countries, especially France, where Suzanne Lenglen held such sway. But partly on the advice of Julian Myrick, who was running the Maidstone Club's eighth annual (1933) invitational tennis tournament, she settled for an American–British rivalry, with each country hosting in alternate years, even in Britain and odd in the United States.

Wealthy summer residents relished opening their homes to visiting tennis players at Maidstone, and they equally relished opening their newspapers to get the lowdown on who was hosting whom—a kind of social chess. By now Alice knew it was her job to act as if it were a routine matter to see her name in the Society News section of the *East Hampton Star*. This year, she and Carolin Babcock got the nod as the guests of Mr. and Mrs. Auguste Cordier. The athletes and their hosts were not the only recipients of publicity that weekend. In another gala event, Mrs. James T. Lee entertained a group of children Friday afternoon, at a party to celebrate the fourth birthday of her granddaughter Jacqueline Bouvier.

Maidstone had originated in 1894, as a seven-hole golf course for a newly imported game that some called "cow pasture pool," when East Hampton was a backwater. After the first and second clubhouses were destroyed by fire in 1901 and 1922, architect Roger Bullard created the third version, with ivied walls and dormers and peaked roofs, on a bluff overlooking the Atlantic, in the neighborhood where, in the 1930s, socialites Gerald and Sara Murphy, said to be the inspiration for the protagonists of F. Scott Fitzgerald's *Tender Is the Night*, held court. Even today, Maidstone bullies with its grandeur. For Alice, the experience of playing at Maidstone should have been, like the setting, bathed in glory. Instead, it was anything but.

CHAPTER 10

HEAT WAVE

THE HEAT WAS ALREADY MERCILESS when Marble took to the courts at 10:20 a.m. on July 31, 1933, the final day of the Maidstone invitational tournament as well as the deciding matches for American players hoping to make the Wightman Cup team. Days earlier, Alice had planned to play in the singles competition only, but Julian Myrick, the chairman of the event, informed her that she had to play doubles as well, partnered with Helen Wills Moody. Marble disliked Myrick "at first sight," deploring his manner and his voice, "an irritating staccato," in which he issued commands "like a dictator whose decisions were above question."[1] He made it clear that her preferences carried no weight. His sway in tennis circles and his social prominence far outstripped the power of a teenager from California with a promising but uneven record. She had no right to interfere with his judgment as to who played in what contests and with whom. She should be thrilled to be associated with Helen Wills Moody in any capacity. From 1927 to 1933, Moody won 180 straight matches and for nine years was the top female player in the world. She entered twenty-four Grand Slam tournaments, winning nineteen, and she won eight Wimbledon singles titles, a record that was not broken until 1990, when Martina Navratilova won her ninth.

"Mrs. Moody has afforded you the honor of playing with her in the doubles," Myrick said, causing Marble to recoil, "God, the little man was pompous!"[2]

An insurance executive, Myrick founded the first training college for insurance agents and later helped set up the American College of Life Underwriters. His allegiance to the sport of tennis was well known. On June 9, 1918, the *New York Times* published a letter he wrote to college presidents, making a familiar pitch:

The United States Lawn Tennis Association is exceedingly desirous that your institution consider the advisability of making tennis a major sport. The two outstanding reasons are, first, that it is one of the few games of use to a man after he is 25 years old, and, second, that the sooner the game is taught, the more pleasure the individual gets out of it as he grows older.

By making tennis a major sport in your institution many more boys will begin to learn it in the schools, with the idea of continuing it through college and later life.

With regard to this first point: We recognize that sports such as football, baseball and rowing are great body-builders. It very often happens, however, that the men who participate in these sports in college do not continue their exercise after graduating and the reaction, therefore, is distinctly harmful to their physical condition. The second point is so obvious as to require no elaboration.

Your institution develops a man's mind and gives him information upon which he may continue to develop mentally so long as he retains his faculties. Is it not worth while also to emphasize the necessity for physical exercise to keep one's body fit after leaving college, as a most important adjunct to proper mental functions? Our association has undertaken to develop tennis among boys and girls; if the colleges for which they are preparing would recognize its benefit upon their lives by making it a major sport, the effect upon future generations would be remarkable.

Myrick made the first nationwide address on tennis to a radio audience in 1922, echoing the themes in his letter to the *Times*, in his capacity as president of the United States Lawn Tennis Association. His general comments extolling the sport were accompanied by specific remarks about the Davis Cup matches. Myrick served as president of the West Side Tennis Club, in Forest Hills, from 1915 to 1917; president of the USLTA from 1920 to 1922; chairman of the Davis Cup committee from 1920 to 1927; and chairman of the Wightman Cup committee in 1929 and again in 1933 and 1934. He sat on the executive committee of the USLTA for decades and was president of Maidstone from 1930 to 1937.

The player with whom Myrick had paired Alice for doubles, Helen Wills Moody, was far from her favorite person. Alice respected Moody's brilliant record, but early impressions of her from the Berkeley Tennis Club gave her pause. Moody's hauteur was not lost on Alice. She overheard another player wonder why Moody, by then a multiple Grand Slam player, had her own dressing room, while twenty-five other players shared a common area, to which someone replied, "Would Garbo bathe with chorus girls?"[3] When Dan Marble had purchased the membership at the California Tennis Club for Alice in 1929, Moody was one of the established players who wanted nothing to do with her. They never played together but would see each other several times within the space of hours, and exchange greetings, as Alice recounted: "She would say hello three or four times in the same day, and each time look through me and not recall saying anything earlier. That was, I thought, because she hadn't seen me. Now you are awfully impressionable at the age of eighteen. And that made an indelible mark on me."[4]

One day Pop Fuller asked Helen outright if she might be willing to "help a young hopeful like Alice here to get her start so she can do what you've done?"

Helen gave Alice a cold look, and said, "No, I wouldn't."[5]

Then, she walked away.

Bill Tilden considered Moody "the coldest, most self-centered, most ruthless champion ever known to tennis."[6]

As Alice argued to play in either singles or doubles but not both, Myrick's bespectacled face showed no sympathy. He told her she could give up the singles competition but not doubles. "I'll be the judge of who's to play, not you." he added.[7]

Myrick was so influential, it was said that "one word from [him] was enough to keep a lesser player off the circuit."[8] Alice could have declined the doubles slot and taken her chances on getting to play singles, but being, as she put it in *The Road to Wimbledon*, "nineteen, ambitious and stubborn," she agreed to both. Rain had forced tournament organizers to compress the matches, and the organizers were determined to announce the Wightman slate by evening. And thus, Alice was, in the genteel phrasing of *American Lawn Tennis*, "obliged to engage in two semifinals and two finals" on the same day, a challenge made even more punishing by the hideous heat.

For days the mercury had been climbing, and people had begun to resort to desperate measures. In Clyde, New York, almost a thousand worshippers had gathered at St. John's Catholic Church to pray for relief. Animals suffered, and New York City authorities documented sixty-four cases of overworked horses, many of which had to be euthanized. At the Bronx Zoo's aquarium, even the tropical fish appeared listless, despite fresh water supplied by attendants. Coney Island boasted record-breaking crowds, more than a half million people passing through the bathhouses. On Brook Avenue and 144th Street in the Bronx, children turned on a fire hydrant to create Coney Island on their own block. Tenement dwellers in the city bedded down in the parks, with approval of the police department, which added patrols to guard against thefts and assaults. Not only the police were lenient; judges imposed lighter sentences on criminals, such as two days in jail instead of ten for Prohibition violators.

John J. A. O'Neill, the science editor of the *Brooklyn Daily Eagle*, explained the heat wave in human terms: "The weather is exactly the same as you and I and that is the cause of all the trouble. A high-pressure area is stagnating to the south of us without energy enough to move. The longer it stagnates the hotter it gets and the hotter it gets the less energy it has to move. It acts in very human fashion. No relief in sight today. . . . The most aggravating phase of the situation is that there is a plentiful supply of nice low temperatures extending over the boundary from Canada."[9]

As might be expected, upper-class spectators were not going to let a little excess mercury nor the news of a few petulant dairymen on strike upstate interfere with their fun. A report in the New York *Daily News* ran under the headline "Shebas of Tennis Swelter, but 400 Sticks to Seats." The word *sheba* would be known to audiences at the time as slang for a woman with sex appeal, also known as a "tomato," "dish," or "looker." The article extended sympathy to the fans for tolerating the weather, praising one clever spectator's pith helmet and another's "enormous linen hat." A young woman came dressed in "a pair of checked blue and white gingham rompers of such brevity as to wring admiration from a Vanities chorus girl," flaunting the no-shorts rule—but she had an acceptable excuse, having arrived at the courts from a rehearsal for an amateur revue.

The *News* opined, "Well, it's better than taking in washing. But that's about all that can be said in favor of amateur tennis play when both the players and the gallery rapidly melt away before one's eyes. Broiled to a crisp—that's what the sun did today to the fashionables in the unprotected grandstands and the pretty gals playing in the Maidstone Club's swank annual invitation tournament."[10]

Spectators might be able to get away with skimpy outfits, but signs in the clubhouse reminded tennis players the no-shorts rule applied to them. The heat was no excuse to lower standards.[11] Alice preferred shorts—"the only sensible costume for modern play"—but didn't want to be the first woman to break the rules. "When you're in tournament play you have to watch what the others do . . . but with any encouragement I'll go into shorts in a minute," she told a reporter earlier in the summer.[12]

The day before, July 30, Alice had triumphed in two matches. She and Moody had defeated Virginia Rice and Marjorie Sachs, 6–3, 6–0; and in singles, she had defeated Josephine Cruickshank, 6–4, 6–2. Allison Danzig, writing for the *New York Times*, was complimentary: "Miss Marble took her place in the semi-finals by virtue of a well-earned victory over Miss Josephine Cruickshank of Santa Ana, Cal. Finding the form again that swept all before her at Essex and Longwood, the San Francisco girl stood off the sturdy drives of Miss Cruickshank and prevailed with her drastic volleying and overhead smashing."[13]

On the final day of the tournament, Alice won the early singles match against Marjorie Gladman Van Ryn, 6–3, 6–8, 6–1. Alice knew how close it was, telling her opponent she almost won. She had already started to feel ill. "My cockiness had long since evaporated, baked out of me by a relentless sun that was nearing its zenith and growing hotter by the minute," she remembered. "How did New Yorkers stand this humidity? The pounding in my temples reverberated through my body, echoing painfully in my joints and turning my stomach into a queasy knot."[14]

As the day wore on, the temperature rose to 104 degrees.[15]

The minute Alice finished her first singles match, the edict came down from on high: "Mrs. Moody is ready to play doubles," to which Alice responded, in the privacy of her own mind, "Mustn't keep royalty waiting."[16] During the doubles semifinal, Moody indicated that her back hurt and instructed Marble to take all the overhead shots through three challenging sets. They won, but Alice was feeling the strain. By one in the afternoon, she was exhausted. She had the singles final against England's Betty Nuthall an hour later, and the doubles final after that. She had already lost five pounds that morning and during her break could not eat anything more than "a piece of toast and some hot tea with lots of sugar."[17] When Nuthall saw her opponent looking weak and pale, she asked if she was all right.

Alice at first held her own against Nuthall, winning the first set, 7–5. The second set featured weak play from both players, and neither won their serve through the first seven games. But Nuthall found her footing and took the second set, 6–3. Beset with muscle cramps during the ten-minute interval before the third set, Alice could scarcely walk and lost at love in ten minutes, offering no resistance to Nuthall. She then had only a few minutes to put on a fresh outfit for the doubles final, which she and Moody lost in straight sets, with Moody wordlessly exiting the court upon their defeat.

The initial reports treated Alice kindly:

> *Playing in the warmest weather East Hampton has seen in several years . . . the defeat of Mrs. Moody and Miss Marble, prospective number 1 Wightman Cup team, came as a surprise to the gallery, and despite the heavy task allotted to Miss Marble, it was she who did the major share of the work for her team. Mrs. Moody displayed championship form only at rare intervals. . . . Mrs. Moody served six games, losing and winning three each, and dropped the first game of each set on her own service. Miss Marble's backhand was lamentably weak, but her sizzling forehand drives accounted for many points.*[18]

Four matches, eleven sets, 108 games: by the end of the day, Marble had lost twelve pounds.

The press latched onto the grotesquerie of the scene at Maidstone, picturing Marble as David up against Myrick's Goliath. The *New York Times* blamed the setback in the doubles match on "the exhaustion of Miss Marble." The editors of the tennis bible, *American Lawn Tennis*, also did not hold back: "The principal victim of the tournament was Alice Marble. She had the extreme misfortune of being successful enough to gain the final rounds in both events, with the result that on Monday, the hottest day of the year and one of the most torrid on record—100 degrees Fahr, she was obliged to engage in two semi-final and two final matches, three of them extra set affairs and the other unusually long and hard."[19]

Teach long argued that the worst could have been avoided if only Alice had been quickly restored with a salt injection instead of having water thrown on her: "The sum and substance of it was she was talked into it [the doubles match in addition to the singles] against her wishes."[20]

Her views enjoyed support in many quarters. Ted Tinling,[21] who served as the master of ceremonies at Wimbledon for years, put it plainly: "Myrick said no play, no Wightman Cup Team. It was desperately unfair because Alice honestly only wanted to scratch in one event."[22]

Davis J. Walsh, the International News Service sports editor, heaped scorn on the tennis officials who forced Marble through such inhumane paces. Describing the play at Maidstone in a column that ran in the *St. Louis Star-Times*, he had one question, "Is it sport?" Known among his peers as the newsman who had covered more Olympics competition than anyone else and admired as an accomplished athlete in track and golf, Walsh believed the officials rushed the schedule to reach an arbitrary deadline for naming the team, and the victim of their poor planning was Marble.

The night of the competition, at the home of her host, Marble fainted. The stories vary. Teach's was the more dramatic, claiming that Alice fell down a flight of stairs. Alice's version was less precipitous: she had toppled onto a couch. Either way, she was exhausted physically and rattled mentally. When interviewed later, she cast her anger in artfully chosen words, "Tennis training doesn't prepare one for a marathon."[23]

Alice's use of the word "marathon" bore a specific subtext in that era, evoking an image of someone at a dance marathon, a popular entertainment that began in the 1920s and crested in the 1930s, consisting of endurance contests of the most extreme sort. Many never forgave Myrick for the spectacle of Alice shrinking, one agonizing step at a time, as if she were a desperate girl at a dance pavilion, hoping to strike it rich for what was almost always just a slender purse.

CHAPTER 11

HELLO, VENUS

DESPITE THE DEBACLE AT MAIDSTONE, Marble was chosen as part of the American team for the Wightman Cup at Forest Hills. One observer called it her "'consolation' for gutsing it out."[1] The team doctor forbade her to play singles. She played doubles on the final day, paired with Marjorie Gladman Van Ryn, quickly losing to Betty Nuthall and Freda James, 7–5, 6–2. The United States retained the title by a score of 4–3. A photograph of the competitors in *American Lawn Tennis* makes no secret of the ongoing dynamic between Julian Myrick and Marble. Myrick is turned entirely in the direction of Nuthall, beside him, ignoring Alice, who is off the side, staring straight ahead, hands shoved in her pockets, a visor shading her face, not so much against the sun as to conceal her glum expression.

Before the US National Championships, soon to follow Maidstone, Helen Jacobs announced her intention to wear shorts, and no one stopped her. As Bud Collins observed years later, "Her daring as a superb volleying attacker seemed matched in 1933 by her nerve in introducing what was considered an outrageous article of clothing for a woman on the court: shorts."[2]

On August 19, 1933, following Jacobs's lead, Nuthall and Marble wore white shorts with a blue stripe on the side to play in the quarterfinals. Alice won the first set, 8–6, coming to the net to "zowie the balls with a kill." Marble lost the second, at love, when Nuthall "kept her returns so deep that Miss Marble had to stand back of the base-line to get them."[3] In the third set, Marble was back on track, winning five of the first six games. Marble "ran the count to 40–15, one point from victory; two chances to get it. And that was when Betty decided to put on her own private show," coming back from the brink to win the final set, 7–5.[4] Marble was sufficiently frustrated that she threw her racket in the air.

A different moment still resonates among hard-core tennis buffs, an appalling display of bad sportsmanship at the singles final between the two Helens, Moody and Jacobs. The contest began evenhandedly, with each winning a set. Jacobs easily won the first three games of the third set, and at that, Moody walked off court. Her back was giving her trouble, and after retrieving her sweater, she moved at a steady pace, with her head high, the two blocks to the clubhouse, thus forfeiting the match. Many fans thought that if Moody had the energy to walk, she could just as easily have summoned the graciousness to see the match through. Later that day, Moody, scheduled for doubles, indicated her willingness to compete, but officials nixed the idea, partly to protect Moody. What would the spectators think if she waltzed back into the competition after vacating the premises with such cold composure hours earlier? Skepticism abounded as to the seriousness of Moody's ailment. Her doctors called it "sub-acute unstable fifth lumbar vertebrae symptoms," which then sportswriter Westbrook Pegler interpreted as "a crick in her back."[5]

Betty Nuthall and Freda James thus won the doubles title in a walk-over, and then they played an exhibition match against Elizabeth Ryan and Marble, who took what would have been Moody's place. As luck would have it, that match was never completed either: Marble took a bad hit in the eye from Nuthall and had to be carried off the court.

By the end of the 1933 season, Alice had risen to number three in the national ranking, behind Moody and Jacobs, up from number seven in 1932. She now enjoyed the same milestone that Teach had achieved at the height of her career. Alice compared her apprenticeship with Teach to the kind of total commitment an opera singer might have to a superior. Her public profile continued to expand, such that anything about her was good copy. When brother Tim, now sixteen, got bit by the family dog, the incident was considered noteworthy enough to earn a headline in the *San Francisco Examiner* on November 26, 1933.

A week later, at another visit to the Hearst Castle, Alice found herself being hailed by her fellow guests with an unfamiliar salutation: "Hello, Venus." The reason was a December 3, 1933, column by Arthur Brisbane, a close friend of Hearst's and frequent guest at the castle. He was a powerful figure in journalism with a readership said to reach twenty million or more. His column, titled Today, appeared in all the Hearst papers and was syndicated in over fifteen hundred weekly newspapers, often featured on page one.

The salutation was inspired by Brisbane's effusive assessment: "What a girl Alice Marble is, with everything the Venus of [*sic*] Milo has, plus two muscular bare, sunburned arms marvelously efficient. Her legs are like two columns of polished mahogany, bare to the knees, her figure perfect. Frederick MacMonnies [a highly regarded contemporary sculptor who worked in the Beaux Arts tradition of idealized forms] should do a statue of her. And she should marry the most intelligent young man in America, and be the perfect mother, with twelve children, not merely the world's best tennis player, which she probably will be." As a rule, the Marble family enjoyed each other's shining moments, but this newsman's intended praise seemed ambiguous at best. He had crossed a line, at least in the view of Alice's mother. Jessie Marble did not focus on Brisbane's impressive credentials or his life story or on his strong ties to Hearst. From her point of view, a stranger—it hardly mattered how prominent he was—had the temerity to draw unseemly attention to her daughter's body, to her arms and legs, in a semi-leering manner, and to imply she should have a future as a font of fertility.

Jessie Marble called the column "suggestive," not a word one applied lightly to a woman in that era.[6] As far as she was concerned, her daughter should stop gallivanting and come home. For generations, the Marbles had been "nose-to-the-grindstone folk,"[7] with plain tastes and a strong work ethic. Maybe the matriarch even envisioned her daughter settling into the kind of low-key, respectable life she led, pickling beets and salting down cabbage and mending worn-out garments—anything but this circus. For her part, Alice did not appear to be unhappy to be summoned home. As she later put it in *The Road to Wimbledon*, life had improved for her brother Dan. He was now a member of the police force, with a uniform to prove it, but she could see the strain in her mother. Alice got back her old job at the Wilson Sporting Goods Company. She played in local tournaments, palling around briefly with a male admirer, portrayed in vague terms, cited mostly as sharing his love of music with her and her mother for hours on end.

Despite her annoyance at Brisbane, Jessie soon forgave him. "I think she was secretly proud that the columnist had thought so highly of me," Alice later reflected. "When he came to our house and asked my mother if I could spend Christmas in Miami with his family, she agreed."[8] Brisbane covered her expenses, and he paid her missed wages, the forty dollars a month that she would have earned as a stenographer at Wilson Sporting Goods had she stayed home. Alice reported that she had a "wild romance with [Brisbane's] eighteen-year-old son who was about six feet three inches." She added, "I had a marvelous two weeks."[9]

When Teach and Beese beckoned Alice back to Los Angeles after the turn of the new year, she did as she was bade, once again following the routines set forth by her two coaches. In January 1934, Bill Tilden praised Marble, this time to the estimable Curley Grieve of the *San Francisco Examiner*: "She has the physique and the strokes. The rest is up to her. She must learn that ability to hit the ball is not ALL there is to tennis. Only time and experience can tell whether she will develop the patience. And patience is exactly what she needs—patience to overcome that impulsive habit of youth to smash and thunder on every return. Come to think about it, patience is one of the great assets of tennis. Mrs. Helen Wills Moody and Helen Jacobs had it. If Miss Marble develops it, she should succeed to the throne."[10]

In February, Grieve picked up on Tilden's endorsement and described Alice as "bubbling with enthusiasm" and "filled with a healthy confidence" as he outlined her prospects for the upcoming season: "A shiny new car awaits Miss Alice Marble, San Francisco's newest tennis sensation, if she can un-crown Miss Helen Jacobs, also of this city, in the national singles this fall. . . . Miss Marble already has been named on the Wightman Cup team that will oppose the British queens of the court at [Wimbledon] this summer, and she is now practicing her strokes for her first tournaments abroad."[11]

Later that spring, Marble was thrilled to win the Northern California Championships. She was also elated to make the Wightman Cup team without having to qualify, and, with Moody not part of the team this year, she would play number two in singles after team captain Helen Jacobs. As a bonus, she would sail to France on May 1 to play an exhibition match before going to London. Undercutting the excitement, however, was a vague sense of unease about Marble's health. For a while now, she had been plagued with sudden fatigue and unexplained aches in her joints and muscles. She was disappointed to learn that Teach could not afford to take time off to accompany her on the journey. Beese was too and went so far as to tell Teach, "I'm afraid something will happen to Alice if you're not there."[12] Beese, Teach, and Teach's famous student Carole Lombard all believed in astrology and hunches and extrasensory signs. For the most part Alice dismissed their predictions as hocus-pocus: "My mother had taught me that God was the only one who knew our destinies." But this time all the talk of bad premonitions made an impression, cemented when she sought the services of a psychic, whose disturbing prediction struck a note of doom she could not shake: "You will rise like a skyrocket and then fall to the ground." Another bad omen intruded when she got to New York to gather with the team: she apparently misplaced in her hotel room a diamond and ruby pin in the shape of tennis racket that Teach had given her, experiencing the disproportionate anguish that often follows the loss of a prized object. In a further blow to her equilibrium, among those who came to see off the team in New York was Julian Myrick, who said, in his unctuous way, "I trust your health has improved?" Alice loathed everything about him, but in deference to his tremendous power in tennis circles, she managed a civil response: "I feel great. I'm a California girl. I just needed to get back to the sun and my mother's cooking!"[13]

Alice was feeling sufficiently spunky that she had packed a half dozen pairs of shorts and, for backup, some skirts, not knowing which she might wear. "I will see how the land lies over there," she told a reporter.[14]

American Lawn Tennis described the team's practice play before the journey as "very good," adding: "Girls' doubles can be dull and tiresome, but this match was marked throughout by fast, offensive play and the mixture of all the good shots known to the game, combined with headwork and fine judgment in the choice of shots. Miss Marble was the hardest hitter of the four, and some of her smashes were veritable thunderbolts."[15] The night before departure, the team attended a dance with the kind of music Marble loved: "Blue Moon," "The Continental," "Stars Fell on Alabama," and her favorite, Cole Porter's dreamy "All Through the Night."[16]

The next day, Alice boarded the German ocean liner *Bremen*, joining teammates Sarah Palfrey, Carolin Babcock, and Josephine Cruickshank on their way to Paris. Team captain Jacobs had gone ahead earlier. *American Lawn Tennis* featured a photograph of the four young women, all wearing corsages or carrying flowers, on board the ship. Nothing about their relaxed appearance would suggest that they were aware of their luxury liner's sad history, as the first vessel to sail through the debris field left by the *Titanic* in 1912, where passengers observed hundreds of bodies, many strapped to deck chairs and tied together, including women clutching children. The *Bremen* did not stop to retrieve the dead because another boat deputized to perform that task was on the way, but nonetheless a kind of unresolved grief attached to the ship.

Marble walked the decks incessantly and hit balls against the walls of the ship's gym, but she sensed her energy was low, especially in contrast to her cabinmate, who stayed up late into the night to partake of the party atmosphere.

When Helen Jacobs, reliable as ever, met her players at the train station in Paris, she was struck by how pale and sickly Alice looked. Jacobs assumed the passage had been rough, but Alice said it had been fine. Jacobs wondered whether Alice might simply be homesick. A tour of the city seemed to give her a lift, but Alice acknowledged later that as she took in the rooftops and the Seine, her thoughts traveled west six thousand miles to her mother and of how much she would have enjoyed such a trip: "I blinked back the sudden tears."[17]

The French and American teams would be playing at the walled-in Roland-Garros Stadium, named after a French aviator who had been killed during World War I, located in the outskirts of Paris. This was home base for Suzanne Lenglen,[18] by then retired from tennis but running a school on the stadium grounds.

Roland-Garros may have been rich in history, but it was short on oxygen. Famous for its trapped air in the best of times, the stadium pioneered a surface that looks like red clay but is far more water-resistant, consisting of white limestone and crushed brick. The two elements combined to create a fine dust, to the dismay of the players and the detriment of their lungs, worse on hot days. Instead of experiencing euphoria in the face of a new venue and a fresh challenge, Alice felt woozy and irritable. Everything annoyed her, especially the scoring, eccentric enough in one's native language, indecipherable in French. The numbers sounded gargled and guttural, confusing her to the point of madness. "I had always assumed that wherever I went, *someone* would speak English. Aside from my roommates, everyone—even the visiting Europeans—spoke French. A day of deciphering the score—*quarante-quinze* instead of forty-fifteen—left me so morose that I skipped dinner and stayed in my rooms, writing letters home."[19]

As evening fell, she recalled, "I wanted only to be alone. My muscles ached and I couldn't sleep."[20] Jacobs called the team doctor, who said Alice's hemoglobin count was low but did not forbid play.

The warm-ups for the mixed doubles exhibition match on the suffocating courts made Alice swelter. The heat kicked up memories of the panicked hours at Maidstone. Her hands were so damp that her racket kept slipping, and "no amount of sawdust from the box at the courtside would help."[21] The French players knew how to work with the slower pace of clay courts.

Marble did not. She lost in mixed doubles, teamed with Marcel Bernard, against Sarah Palfrey and Harry Hopman. She thought she would fare better in singles, but her opponent, Sylvia Henrotin, number two on the French team, destabilized her with a variety of unpredictable shots, causing Alice to careen hither and yon across the court. As Alice recalled years later, "Sylvia was clever—and she knew her turf. . . . The woman was playing *my* game and beating me at it!"[22]

Helen Jacobs later wrote about the match in her book *Gallery of Champions*: "Alice lost the first game, won the second on service. Then the score soon went 4–1 against her as Mme. Henrotin ran her all over the court with an adroit mixture of angled drives, chops and volleys. Starting the sixth game with a double fault, Alice suddenly crumpled in a faint."[23]

Alice's vision began to fail before she blacked out. She had one final image before collapsing and eventually regaining consciousness at the American hospital in Neuilly. She could see herself reaching to return a ball that had suddenly, in her mind, shape-shifted into a balloon, floating away, untethered, nearly weightless, beyond all reach. The photo of Alice Marble in a heap on the red courts at Roland-Garros—slack-muscled, enervated to the point of immobility, watched over by two men in suits while her opponent attempted to deliver aid to her prone body—went around the world. That image was soon replaced by another one: the same two men, acting as human crutches, carrying her limp body off the courts.

Alice feared something worse than sunstroke was responsible for the pain in her back and chest: "I felt as if I'd been speared."[24] Jacobs consulted with Dr. Robert Dax, who issued orders for Marble to return home as soon as she was physically able to travel. "Alice was a very unhappy and discouraged girl when I told her the only wise decision was to send her back to the United States," Jacobs later recalled.

> We sat and talked for a long time in her hospital room, and I knew how she felt. I had been alone on the Riviera when I developed pleurisy and quinsy which resulted in a heart strain that had kept me out of the 1930 American season. I had thought my tennis days were over. It is a terribly depressing and hopeless possibility to face. But Alice had her future before her, which, it seemed to me, would be needlessly impaired by any effort to play until she was fully recovered. Even had I not felt so strongly about it, Dr. Dax's opinion left no alternative.[25]

Nothing consoled the invalid. It did not help that Dr. Dax's diagnosis kept escalating in seriousness from sunstroke to anemia to gall bladder problems to pleurisy to, most dire of all, tuberculosis, which likely spelled the end of not just her tennis career but perhaps even her life. When a nurse sliced her some peaches, a gift from the ever-thoughtful Jacobs, and served them with sour cream, Alice threw the fruit and the plate, utensils included, into a wastebasket.

After six weeks in France, she was bundled into a wheelchair to board the *Aquitania*, headed for New York, on a voyage that lasted a week, from June 16 to 23. A man on his way home to bury his son, who had died in an accident, made certain that she got out on deck for fresh air and that she ate, she recalled, "marrow bones one day, snails the next, frog's legs another, and always finished off with delectable desserts like baked Alaska and cherries jubilee."[26] Teach met her in New York and arranged for a room at the Roosevelt Hotel so Alice could gather her strength for the train trip home.

One day, confined to her hotel bed, Alice overheard Teach locked in a heated exchange with two men. One male voice sorted itself out from the other—that of Julian Myrick, demanding repayment of the money the United States Lawn Tennis Association had invested in Alice's trip to France, which included "her fares, her hospital expenses, doctor's bills." They complained, Teach recounted, that "Alice hadn't even played in the Wightman Cup Matches. And the doctors said she would never play again—so why should they help her any further?"[27]

Teach questioned just whose money Myrick was protecting, causing one interpreter of the scene to later comment that she had a "strong point, because before sponsorships, national associations' funds derived almost entirely from tournament receipts, which in turn derived essentially from the box-office appeal of the players."[28]

Myrick's demand gave Teach the opportunity to remind him that if he hadn't forced Marble to play under grueling conditions the year before, the nightmare in France might not have ever happened. But he had selfishly sent her down the slippery slope to ill health.

Then Teach raised the ante: Not only was Alice not returning any money, but the USLTA should cover the cost of her current and upcoming medical bills in addition to her expenses while she was abroad. Myrick should take the blame for Alice's health, and it was cruel of him to doom her to an inactive insular life when she had the makings of a great athlete. Teach sometimes talked out the side of her mouth like a gangster's moll in an old-time movie. She loved slang, and she now employed one of her favorite phrases to denote easy street, telling Myrick that he was "a very rich man and lived in the well-known pot of jelly." Getting personal, she reminded him that he had "lovely daughters and he would not have wanted *them* treated in that fashion."[29]

Myrick had not heard the last of her nor of her pupil, Teach told him. Alice Marble would be back, Teach insisted, and she would take "her rightful place as Tennis Champion of the World," information that Myrick greeted with "a very cynical smile,"[30] a smile Teach put in her tool kit of future motivators.

On July 5, 1934, *American Lawn Tennis* published a report on Alice's health and prognosis: "Miss Marble will stay with Miss Tennant at La Jolla for some time, in the endeavor to regain health and strength. Physicians have prescribed rest and residence in a warm, sunny climate, such as Southern California has."[31] Commenting on her collapse in Paris, the article stated that the hospital had diagnosed her as suffering from pleurisy, often associated with tuberculosis.

As soon as Teach felt it was safe for her charge to travel, they headed back to San Francisco, so Alice could recuperate in a familiar setting. Alice gave an upbeat interview to Curley Grieve of the *Examiner*, saying she was sorry to have missed the Wightman Cup, which the American team managed to win despite her absence, but "I'm not the kind to cry over spilt milk. I'm looking forward to the future, I still have hopes of Wimbledon."

She told him she felt well after what he called "the long trip over the Atlantic and across the continent." She said she was looking forward to a "long loafing spell. Nothing but rest. Maybe I'll practice up on my singing. I still have hopes in that direction, you know."[32]

She took her family's temperature while they took hers. Dan's face could not disguise his pain at seeing his sister suffering. George stayed upbeat. Tim, now a teen, remained aloof. He never understood why she gave up baseball for tennis, anyway, abandoning him for all practical purposes. After leaving her bad marriage and moving home, Hazel now worked for the phone company. Most troubling, Alice's mother possessed barely enough strength to climb all those stairs, inside and out, let alone while carrying trays laden with food, drink, and medicine as she tended to a bedridden daughter.[33]

Alice told Grieve that she felt weak, and pains shot through her right side whenever she picked up a racket. "Because of her age," he wrote, "which is 20, she has been advised that a rest of six months to one year, depending upon the speed of convalescence, will enable her to start anew on her campaign for tennis laurels."[34]

Soon Teach, who came from a background where patience for infirmity was nonexistent, was supervising Alice's medical decisions. Teach's mother did not believe sick children should be coddled, interpreting most maladies as a form of malingering. Her policy was to place bedridden children in rooms with windows so they would be forced to eavesdrop on happier children at play. Young patients were spoon-fed castor oil and given water but not food. Teach grew up sharing the opinion that most of the time illness was "treated too softly."[35]

Even with her deeply embedded skepticism, it was clear to Teach that Alice's condition required something beyond mere home care. Teach prided herself on knowing the best places and the right people, from restaurants and hotels to dressmakers and doctors. Teach had in mind what she considered an excellent prospect.

CHAPTER 12

"YOU DON'T KNOW ME, BUT . . ."

TEACH'S IDEA OF AN EXCELLENT prospect was Alice's idea of hell: "From the moment I walked into the square-shaped bungalow, screened on three sides, I knew I would hate it."[1]

Teach had arranged for the twenty-year-old to go to the Pottenger Sanatorium for Diseases of the Lungs and Throat in Monrovia, about twenty miles northeast of Los Angeles,[2] and eight miles east of Pasadena, with the promise that she would be there for only six weeks.

A large white administration building dominating the grounds also served as home to the sickest patients. The majority were assigned to cottages or bungalows—structures open to the elements save for a small dressing area and bathroom. Canvas curtains in the bedroom could be lowered for privacy or extended outward like awnings to divert rain. Despite Marble's negative reaction to Pottenger's, Teach appears to have done her best to find a reputable facility, lauded by its founder in an article in the *British Journal of Tuberculosis* that made it sound like a superior tourist destination: "The sanatorium is situated on the southern slope of the Sierra Madre Mountains, 1,000 feet above sea level, at the mouth of one of the most beautiful canyons in Southern California . . . thirty miles from the ocean . . . far enough inland to escape most of the sea fog and dampness, and yet not so distant but that it receives the stimulating and cooling marine breezes."[3]

Whether Alice had tuberculosis or a lesser but serious diagnosis was unclear, but Teach was taking no chances. For centuries, TB had been among the most feared diseases to rack humankind. In the late 1890s, a futile but well-intended crusade by American public health officials to control the disease took aim at spitting: "The expectoration of persons suspected to have consumption should be caught in earthen or glass dishes containing the following solution: Corrosive sublimate, seven grains; water, one pint, and finally thrown into the sewer or burned."[4] The National Tuberculosis Association released a poster with the image of a llama expectorating:

> *When a Llama Gets Sore*
> **He Spits!**
> *He's the world's best spitter*
> *But*
> Who *Wants to be a Llama?*[5]

The campaign ignored the reality that tuberculosis is spread almost exclusively by dried tubercle bacilli coughed into the air.[6]

The Pottenger Sanatorium embraced the best practices of the time. Dr. Pottenger expressed his theories about treating the disease in *The Diagnosis and Treatment of Pulmonary Tuberculosis*, published in 1908, including instructions intended to calm and comfort the patient. He suggested linen undergarments, less likely to cause the patient to chill after perspiring. Wool was the worst, "not only unscientific, but harmful and barbarous." Light dress was better than heavy, and the feet required constant changing of stockings and shoes. Bed covers should be spare.[7]

Of all his recommendations, the most outlandish in today's terms was his advocacy of bacon—the more the better: "Patients who will eat plenty of bacon, butter and milk do not need cod liver oil. In fact, I never find it necessary to prescribe it. I have found bacon an easy form of fat for most people to digest and use it in liberal quantities."[8]

Pottenger endorsed a well-ventilated room as if it were its own drug. He even gave instructions for creating fresh-air sanctuaries at home. He included a sketch of a floor plan and photo of a bungalow, like the one where Marble stayed, with a front porch, bedroom, and dressing room–bath. Such a bungalow could be "constructed in a yard adjacent to the house at a small cost." Failing that, a screened-in porch or bed placed correctly to catch a crosscurrent would suffice.[9] In Pottenger's view, the peaceful atmosphere of his facility calmed the soul and nudged the body along in its healing mission amid the tumble of flowers and what the writer Joan Didion would later call the talismanic fruit of Southern California, especially the orange groves.

None of this came at a cheap price. Choice rooms such as Alice's, paid for by Teach, went for thirty-five dollars a week and up. Alice could hardly be described as grateful. While a setting so lacking in stimulation might work for some patients, the extreme serenity was one of the reasons Marble loathed it. The beauty and the calm made her even more impatient, especially when she reached the first six-week deadline, only to be told by Pottenger that she needed to stay at least six more weeks. Marble had heard conversations among other discouraged patients, some having finished their second full year, about how they also had been falsely promised a prompt exit at six-week intervals, time and time again. For Alice, the cure was its own agony: "I tried to read, but I couldn't retain the meaning of the previous sentence. All my life I loved to sing, but I couldn't remember the words of any song. I longed to walk in the gardens, but I was not allowed to get out of bed. All day long I listened to the radio, to the mystery plays and the soap operas, which were sometimes very sad, though not as sad as I was. I cried for hours every day."[10]

Like someone in prison, where the chief activity is the forced march of minutes, Alice welcomed interruptions, although they were rarely as satisfying as she hoped. Letters from her mother arrived but only once a week. Teach visited daily but made no promise of release. Teach's sister, Gwen, supplied tea towels to embroider, but Alice had always despised sewing. Worst of all, listening to the tennis matches at Forest Hills on the radio made her feel all but forgotten, a has-been at the age of twenty. Fred Perry defeated Wilmer Allison in a five-set men's singles. Helen Jacobs defeated Sarah Palfrey in women's singles. The two women then teamed up to defeat Carolin Babcock and Dorothy Andrews in women's doubles.

Alice had by now cultivated a public face and a private one. In an interview with the *San Francisco News* on September 11, 1934, she called her time in the sanatorium "simply swell." It was as if by acting cheerful, she could fool people into thinking she was:

> I am allowed to sit up in a chair one hour a day. I have a radio, listen to all the broadcast matches and dream of the time when the doctors will let me pick up my rackets again. Tennis is still my one big ambition in life. . . .
>
> I have gone domestic in a big way, making pillows, bridge sets, etc. . . .
>
> I am discovering many things I missed in my almost 21 years—I have a big birthday this month, you know. . . .

I write letters by the dozens to my family, tennis players, etc. Friends have been marvelous about coming to see me, bringing me books and magazines. . . .

I am very glad Helen Jacobs won at the women's nationals—I heard the broadcast. She is a real person and deserves her success. . . .

In case you are interested, I have vocal ambitions. I hope to learn to play some musical instruments while I'm laid up and surprise everybody. . . .

As for marriage, skip it.[11]

Five months passed. Finally, Alice was allowed to walk to a nearby pond. This was followed by permission to sit outdoors for fifteen minutes. She took up smoking cigarettes, then marketed as a beauty-enhancing prop with no mention of any injurious side effects.

The rich diet (bacon, liver, butter, cream, and eggs) and the sedentary lifestyle pumped Alice's weight up as high as 185 pounds. "My body had become an obscene thing, bloated and slack, and all my cockiness was gone," she lamented.[12] After about eight and a half months, Teach said the doctor thought Alice could leave—in a month. Marble had heard the same promise four times previously, and she told Teach she no longer trusted either her or the doctor.

In Alice's telling, the turning point occurred when she received a letter from the movie star Carole Lombard. In *The Road to Wimbledon*, she quoted it as "something like this":

Dear Alice,

You don't know me, but your tennis teacher is also my teacher, and she has told me all about you. It really makes very little difference who I am, but once I thought I had a great career in front of me, just like you thought you did. Then one day I was in a terrible accident. For six months I lay on a hospital bed, just like you are today. Doctors told me I was through, but then I began to fight. Well—I proved the doctors wrong. I made my career come true, just as you can—if you'll fight.[13]

The terrible accident happened when Lombard was a teenager, a passenger in a Bugatti roadster driven by a teenage boy. Some accounts say another car rolled backward and smashed into theirs, and other reports say their car was rear-ended. Either Lombard went through the windshield, or the windshield shattered on impact and glass sliced her face, creating a cut from her nose to her cheekbone. A plastic surgeon stitched Lombard without anesthesia, believing that would ensure the facial muscles stayed taut.[14] She sued the driver and his parents for $35,000, but the judge was "spared the necessity of determining how much it is worth for a motion-picture actress to carry a scar on her cheek," wrote the *Los Angeles Times*, because the suit was settled out of court.[15] In time, the scar faded, and makeup and lighting picked up the slack.

Lombard's words to Alice had the desired effect, sinking in as a call to action: "I was tired of people telling me what I *couldn't* do. My six-week stay had turned into eight months, at great expense to Teach. The doctor had finally given me permission to spend fifteen minutes a day outside, and to walk to the pond seventy-five feet away. This wasn't living! It wasn't me! When Teach came to visit, my bags were packed."[16]

As Teach told the story,[17] the stay at Pottenger's did not appear to be doing much good, and she finally took action. Convinced that Alice did not have TB, Teach told her pupil that if she had the strength to leave at that minute, they would both make a run for it. Teach was disgusted by the way Alice had gorged on milk and starch: "Here's this nice athletic body disintegrating into a lump of fat, which I loathe and despise."[18] Teach compared the extra thirty pounds to a sack of flour.

Teach grabbed what few items Alice had brought with her while the disgruntled patient struggled to squirm into a dress now way too small. Humiliated, Alice threw a coat over her pajamas and inched her way to freedom across the fruit-laden terrain. At one point Teach carried her, firefighter style. When Teach started the engine of her car, Marble heard her say: "I'm not breaking any laws. So why do I feel like I'm making a getaway?"[19] They both smoked cigarettes by way of celebration.

Teach's sister, Gwen, who suffered with a heart condition, supervised Alice's routine while Teach was away coaching. She took a daily walk, slow at first, just a block, but eventually she hit the three-mile mark. Teach prescribed jumping rope to improve footwork, a training technique favored by prizefighters, because "some of the exercises necessary to become a good tennis player are almost identical."[20] Alice sang an hour a day to strengthen her diaphragm. She read inspirational messages. She helped with Teach's paperwork.

Teach found a chiropractor to assess Alice, telling him she could not pay his steep fees but would make it up to him in referrals. She instructed him to forgo the usual medical markers such as X-rays, which had unsettled Alice in the past. Instead, he should appear to check her lungs and say, "Hocus-pocus, meeny-mocus," and tell her she was now able to jump over the moon. Teach abandoned him when he made the mistake of forbidding meat. At the end of her fourth month away from Pottenger's, Alice had a checkup with Dr. Ernest Commons. After taking her history and an examination with a fluoroscope, he shared his opinion. "I can't tell definitely without the X-rays, but I don't believe you have tuberculosis or that you *ever* had it."[21]

While less of a threat than TB, a diagnosis of pleurisy with effusion seemed probable, which could explain her shortness of breath and chest pain when breathing deeply—nightmarish symptoms for anyone but especially frightening for an athlete. Dr. Commons asked what she wished to do most in the world, and when she said she wanted to play tennis again, he said he saw no reason she couldn't. The doctor struck a deal. As soon as her bloodwork improved and she lost fifteen pounds, Alice could pick up a racket.

After leaving the sanatorium, an invitation to dinner with Lombard and her family proved to be the tonic Alice needed most. Lombard was nearing the height of her fame. As *Life* magazine reported, Lombard had launched the genre of screwball comedies that took off during the Great Depression, with their fail-safe class-warfare plotlines, in 1934—the same year she met Alice—with a picture called *Twentieth Century*.[22]

In person, Alice found Lombard, five years her senior, even more wonderful than she had come across in her letter. It pleased her that "our backgrounds were similar. Neither of us had a father, and both of us had older brothers we competed with like crazy. The only thing that troubled me about her was that she had such a good-sized entourage of people I didn't like. But she was such a kindly person."[23] Lombard's mother, Mrs. Peters (known as Petie), was just as upbeat as her daughter, and her two brothers reminded Alice of her own. Lombard had moved from her hometown of Fort Wayne, Indiana, to Los Angeles in grade school. Like Alice, she got her athletic start playing baseball. "When the neighborhood kids organized a ball team, Carole was the star first baseman. A tomboy, and a good one, she defended her position until her battle-scarred teammates became resigned to it," the *Los Angeles Times* reported. Lombard continued to excel athletically, winning prizes in junior high school for running and broad-jumping and in high school taking on swimming, horseback riding, golf, and tennis.[24]

At five feet three inches and 110 pounds, Lombard was agile on movie sets. Her stride was known to be quicker than anyone else's, male or female.[25] Lombard's figure was made for the divine clothes of Hollywood's golden age. One Hollywood costume designer said of her: "You could throw a bolt of material at Carole and whichever way it landed, she looked smart."[26]

Lombard made Alice promise to come to Marion Davies's house to observe her tennis lesson, and from that moment on, Alice's health began to improve. She took up tennis again, tentatively at first, merely as an observer of Lombard and others as they took lessons, then assumed a more active role of playing doubles and of running tournaments for Teach for women connected to Hollywood. The first time out, Lombard and Teach challenged Alice and Louise Macy,[27] and each day she continued to play for longer intervals. After the husbands arrived on the scene and joined the group for supper and awards ceremonies, some of the women pressed Alice to sing: "When I did, there was never a sound in the room, and often I saw tears in their eyes."[28]

In the Marble household, alcohol was regarded as sinful, except for the beer at Dan's poker parties. It flowed freely in Hollywood. One evening, a bartender supervised an array of offerings. Upon his recommendation, Alice settled on a Bacardi cocktail, and then had eight more. The next day she made a vow to give up drinking from that day forward.

Lombard was paid well for her pictures and insisted on helping out Alice financially. "After I got out of the TB Sanatorium, I was sad, I had acne, I didn't know much about clothes. She helped me with all these things," Alice wrote. "I was so ashamed of myself. And she sent me to a dermatologist— never charged—never let me pay her back. And if I mentioned it, she'd use some pretty strong language."[29] Lombard also paid for Alice to take a course in clothing design. Lombard took note of Alice's singing voice and subsidized voice, drama, acting, and fencing lessons at Paramount.

Alice lacked intimate female company. Her sister had her own problems, her mother was exhausted, and Teach and the ailing Gwen did not offer much diversion. Lombard was fun and easy with advice. She flirted with the occult and had a fondness for psychics and astrologers and fortune tellers, often looping Marble into these extrasensory explorations, including sessions with people who had messages from other worlds. Lombard was also candid. When Alice asked why she had divorced the debonair William

Powell, her costar in several movies, she said, "I couldn't stand the fact that he acted even when he was taking off his pajamas."[30]

Alice bore a resemblance to the actress Virginia Bruce, and Lombard would sometimes introduce her friend as the lookalike star and wait to see whether anyone noticed the ruse. In Lombard's company, Alice finally had someone to gossip with, someone with whom she could be giddy and could discuss clothes and makeup. Years later Alice recalled, "I lost forty-five pounds and then we began to talk about clothes. And she said, 'Honey, you're going to be going East or going to Europe.' So, she sent me to the University of Southern California, and I took a course in costume design."[31]

Alice gained the impression Teach was not thrilled with the friendship, confiding to an interviewer years later: "Teach was a funny person. She loved Carole very much indeed, but she didn't like anything that sort of took me away from her."[32]

Teach's disapproval aside, together Alice and Lombard created a force field all their own. In their photos together, it is hard to tell which is the world-famous actress and which the merely world-famous tennis star. The caption writers agreed, as in a cutline accompanying an image of the two women some years later: "Miss Marble looks as glamorous as Carole Lombard as they watch a game together."[33]

PART THREE

1935–1939

CHAPTER 13

STARRY NIGHTS

WHEN TEACH RECEIVED AN OFFER to manage and coach at the Racquet Club in Palm Springs in 1935, a year after it opened, she jumped at the chance and took Alice along as an assistant. Palm Springs in the 1930s represented life in the relatively slow lane, as Alice recounts: "We didn't party. One street, one movie theater. Teach and I had an apartment over the drugstore. Teach might stay up and play bridge. I was in bed by nine o'clock. It was a very quiet life. Occasional movie. That was a big deal."[1]

A hundred miles east of Los Angeles, the Coachella Valley is defined, in a horseshoe shape, by the Santa Rosa, San Jacinto, and Little San Bernardino Mountains, and bordered in the southeast by the Salton Sea. It lays claim to being the sunniest place in America, sees regular temperatures in the hundreds in July, and is one of the driest, with less than six inches of rainfall a year, generally spread over some ten days total, guaranteeing outdoor sports year-round. The land is brown and tan and dry, filled with cacti, date palms, and bougainvillea.

During the cold months, the tallest peaks are crowned by snow. High up, desert bighorn sheep roam free alongside bobcats, burrowing owls, cactus mice, fringe-toed lizards, and Gambel's quails. Close up, the mountains look like steep shaggy piles of stones and dirt, their aspect otherworldly. Locals urge vigilance in the event of rockslides, coyotes, and rattlesnakes. The desert is a strong taste, not for everyone, but perfect for those who are sustained by it. Alice felt sustained.

Charles Farrell and Ralph Bellamy,[2] the two actors who founded the Racquet Club, had purchased the two hundred acres of open land in 1932 at the appealing price of thirty dollars an acre. They hired an expert court constructor and had tamarisk trees planted as a shield against the wind and the sand.[3] At first they charged players a dollar a day, with no time limit on how long a person could play. They decided to sell memberships at the end of the 1933–34 season. Initially, it cost fifty dollars to join. There were four takers. Showmen at heart, Farrell and Bellamy announced more openings for members, now seventy-five dollars a shot. As the *Desert Sun* reported, "Every 15 days they sent another set of announcements, and each time they raised the price. By the time the fee was $650, there was a waiting list."[4]

As their revenue increased, Farrell and Bellamy added buildings. The stylish Bamboo Lounge claimed the distinction—sometimes disputed in the world of mixology—as the birthplace of the Bloody Mary. Clark Gable, William Powell, and Spencer Tracy had their own assigned perches there, off-limits to mere mortals. Marble recalled movie stars could not get enough of Palm Springs and Palm Desert: "They would fly their planes down here just for the weekend to get away from the mad world of Hollywood. . . . I was the maddest movie fan in the world, and they were all tennis fans so it was just natural that I should know these people."[5]

Alice ran the pro shop at the club, tolerating the locker-room banter of the men who frequented it. She had three brothers after all, and she usually stayed one step ahead, but when the actor Errol Flynn requested a jockstrap, she fell into an easy trap.

"What size?"

"The largest you have, of course!"[6]

Alice's job playing tennis with guests at the club in friendly, low-stakes games gave her the chance to stress skills over scores. She was finally having fun again, laughing as she hit the ball. In *The Road to Wimbledon*, Alice recalled that Teach's roster of pupils featured the big stars of the day, including George Brent, Marlene Dietrich, and Robert Taylor. Teach was nowhere near the movie expert Alice was. When Teach had trouble placing an actress such as Jeanette MacDonald, Alice would subtly bring her up to speed.

Alice and Teach enjoyed standing dinner dates with the Arkells, Claire and Jimmy. American success stories are filled with entrepreneurs who stumble on a single magical concept or ingredient and take it to dizzying capitalistic heights. In the case of the Arkells, a family member traveling in South America noticed a substance called *chicle*—a sap obtained by tapping into sapodilla trees—which, after it is processed and flavored, provides the basis of chewing gum. By adding baby food in 1931, and eventually chewing gum and Life Savers to a business that began as a seller of smoked hams in

New York State in the late 1800s, the family prospered, and by the 1930s the Arkells could easily afford a retreat in the desert, to which they gave a Spanish name, La Finca de Esperanza.

Amid the calm of those days and evenings, Alice considered whether to resume her career or torpedo it forever. Dr. Commons urged caution and suggested she concentrate on local events before heading east. She went home to play in a tournament, noticing that "Dan was fatter; George's forehead twice as high; and the house smaller."[7] When she went to hug her once plump mother, she could feel "her bones through the cotton dress." Jessie, Alice continued, "had sworn the others to silence about her cancer, saying I had my own health to worry about. I should have suspected something, but I was too thrilled at being home."[8]

Her family embraced her, even Hazel. Alice assumed it was because they were "both grown women now."[9] The two sisters had never been close, circumstances exacerbated when Hazel become a single teenaged mother and Alice set forth, however she faltered, to find her fortune in the larger world. Marble did not feel so welcome at the Berkeley Tennis Club and found herself arranging her old tennis connections into a hierarchy: who was friendly (Pop Fuller and Billy Johnston), who was fake friendly (players who had shown no inclination to be in touch when she was ill but now embraced her celebrity status thanks to her connections to movie stars), and who was hostile and thought she was a traitor for moving to Los Angeles. She brushed them off: "How silly. Wherever Teach Tennant was, that's where I would be."[10]

Her face-off in the finals of the 1935 California State Tennis Championships in June against up-and-coming Margaret Osborne, age seventeen, at the Berkeley Tennis Club gave Marble the jitters. She could sense that, even though both combatants were from Northern California, Margaret attracted the hometown applause, thanking the crowds with a tip of her racket, making Alice feel forgotten.

Alice won, 6–4, 6–3. The *San Francisco Examiner* described a match that was sloppy on both sides, but it must have been satisfying to receive the trophy in singles from Carole Lombard, who was on hand to present all the awards, and to win another title in doubles with Frances Umphred. Visions of Forest Hills could once again dance in Alice's head.

Before she got too far ahead of herself, the East Coast tennis establishment, in the form of Julian Myrick, intervened. He decreed that before she could play tennis in the East, she would have to be evaluated by a doctor in

New York. The evaluation in New York would have to be within the time frame he demanded, which would mean missing the qualifying tournaments at home that would have led to the chance to play in tournaments in the East.

Teach greeted this news with her usual vim and vinegar, sharing her opinion that the tennis authorities had treated Alice shamefully.

> *No less than 12 physical examinations have been demanded. Not once did the committee contact the girl direct or show any sign that they were cognizant of her existence. Forced two years ago to play and practice for eight hours with the thermometer at 108, it is small wonder that Alice collapsed at East Hampton. Last year she had a spell while playing in Paris. She was over-worked, overplayed and over-practiced to suit the exactions of committees.*
>
> *The committee has put every possible hurdle in the girl's path, and yet she is perhaps a better player than any of the girls named. . . . I would like to see the girl get a square deal, and then America would have one more GREAT woman player of whom California, in particular, could well be proud.*
>
> *But please dissipate the idea that the girl is not rugged and healthy. She is five feet seven and weighs 135 pounds today. Her game never was sounder nor her stroking more accurate and powerful. It is simply that, the "persecution" of the committee has her mentally down and quite upset.*[11]

The press acted as puzzled as Teach, with one outlet calling it "the strange case of Alice Marble." Alice announced she would not be playing competitively for the time being. She would miss the US National Championships for the second year in a row. Marble headed back to Los Angeles and redoubled her efforts at training. She would do paperwork for Teach in the morning, then head to the courts for a lesson with her, in which they would pick up on mistakes from the previous day and keep practicing until they had been rectified, and then she would play all afternoon with male opponents. No parties, no movies. She "lived, breathed and dreamed tennis until bedtime at ten o'clock."[12]

Marble's first test in 1936 came in early March at the Hotel Huntington invitational tournament in Pasadena, California. In mixed doubles, Marble and Ray Casey defeated Carolin Babcock and Gerald Bartosh, 3–6, 6–4, 7–5.[13] The Palm Springs Racquet Club celebrated and took some credit because Marble and Teach had practiced there beforehand.[14] "Those who saw Alice in action were surprised at the excellence of her form," said one reporter.[15]

In other matches, Don Budge beat Jack Tidball, 6–2, 6–1, in the singles. Budge won again, partnering with Gene Mako to defeat Bobby Riggs and Lawrence Nelson, 6–3, 1–6, 6–3, in doubles.[16]

At the end of March, Marble proved her mettle in two matches. At an exhibition at UCLA, she had no trouble defeating Gracyn Wheeler, ranked number six nationally, 6–1, 6–0.[17]

Best of all was the second annual Palm Springs invitational tournament. Carole Lombard pushed for it, proposing an idea widely hailed as inspired. She acknowledged that Marble would have stiff competition, playing against Carolin Babcock, but because the contest was local, it posed no financial burden. Alice, and more to the point, Teach, agreed.

"With some trepidation," Alice later recounted, "I added my name to the list of entrants that included Southern California's best women players—Dorothy Bundy, Carolin Babcock, Dorothy Workman, and Gracyn Wheeler."[18]

Marble defeated Bundy in the quarterfinals and Workman in the semifinals. In the finals, fierce winds threw her competitor off, and Alice made good use of the home-court advantage. She defeated Babcock, now number four in national rankings, 6–3, 6–4, in the women's finals. No matter how fiercely Babcock played, she couldn't "pass the cool San Francisco girl."[19]

At least one bartender, Alice remembered, "had done a land-office business before that match, fortifying members against the possibility of my losing; now he fueled a thirsty celebration."[20] In the revelry that followed, Teach was treated to a generous round of martinis while everyone toasted Alice Marble, her resilient acolyte.

Despite beating two of the nation's top ten women players and winning the Palm Springs tournament, Marble was handed another setback. On March 31, 1936, newspapers reported that the Wightman Cup committee sent a letter saying she would not be part of the team headed to England in the spring: "Committeemen said they felt they would like to see how she could stand up under a season's play before sending her across the sea. Close friends of the girl here said she was keenly disappointed in being refused the trip and added that her health was fully restored."[21]

Teach protested to the press: "She eats like a team of farm horses and sleeps nine or 10 hours a night. Her footwork on the court is like Tilden's. She has attained great speed through rhythm. Her top spin on the second serve is dangerous for any opponent."

Alice did not give her detractors the satisfaction of hearing her voice her disappointment over not being chosen for the Wightman Cup team. All she allowed was, "I'm happy because I've got my health back. The doctors say I'm ready for any kind of competitive tennis now."[22]

In early May, Alice won the Southern California championship (formal name: Southern California Golden Jubilee Tennis Championship) against Dorothy Bundy, 6–2, 6–4, which was "not unexpected as she has sailed through a long series of exhibition matches and tournaments this year," the *Los Angeles Times* reported.[23]

Alice maintained her training regimen and refused to accept that a small group of influential higher-ups in the tennis establishment seemed to want her career to be over.

On May 23, 1936, Marble and Tennant began their road trip to the East for tournaments, making news wherever they went.[24] They crossed the country in Teach's new Buick convertible, a marvel of geometry and engineering known to car enthusiasts as Art Deco on wheels, planning to be on the road until September, for the US National Championships. Teach would use her earnings from clinics to support them both. As Marble wrote, "No normal girl in town or country has to own ten pairs of tennis shorts and ten blouses. She doesn't need three evening dresses either. But the girl who plays in amateur tennis championships has to have them and the tennis association does not pay for them. This is a considerable and necessary expense borne by her family, in addition to laundry, meals and pocket money. The association pays her way on the fastest trains and provides living quarters at the most elegant hotels, but the player is really on a shoestring."[25]

Their first stop was Salt Lake City, Utah. Teach was "emphatic" when scheduling Alice's matches: Male players only.[26] Marble "played a 'man's game,' throughout the afternoon," a local paper reported, winning one of the two singles sets and the doubles.[27]

In Omaha, Nebraska, Marble again played against a man: "Reason for this appears to be that Miss Marble is merely seeking conditioning matches for a big comeback in the net game this year," the *Omaha Bee-News* reported.[28] The reporter covering the match, in which Alice won one of two sets, was enthralled: "The 1936 national women's tennis champion played at the Omaha Tennis club Wednesday. How could there be a women's champion in 1936 when the meet isn't held until September? Well, it's just one tennis enthusiast's way of getting out on a limb for one thing. Alice Marble is the kind of girl a person would get out on a twig for, with said twig protruding out over the Grand Canyon." The reporter loved most of all Marble's polite reply— "Why yes, I'd be glad to if I have the time"—to a girl who asked Alice to play a match with her and her friends.[29]

The May 29, 1936, edition of the *Daily Times* of Davenport, Iowa, carried a three-deck headline announcing:

Miss Alice Marble,
Tennis Star, Stops
Here for Luncheon

For weeks it was smooth sailing. In the evenings, Teach would dictate articles to Alice to type up for publication in the Hearst papers. By day, they stopped at prearranged destinations for exhibition matches, and there Teach could conduct her clinics and sell rackets bearing her name for Wilson Sporting Goods. Marble said Teach was "wonderful to watch" as she gave clinics in a variety of settings from department stores to schools to public parks. She would choose a few students to help her in demonstrations, and the others would follow suit on their own. Marble said Teach worked miracles, getting the most sluggish student to run and the least gifted to hit the ball back with precision.[30]

Teach shared stock advice. First rule: "Enjoy the game!" Then:

Take it easy always. Let the head of the racket do the work. Don't clench your fist in clutching your racket. Make your grip a handshake. Associate hitting the ball with slapping someone in the face. Always keep moving on the tennis court. Return to the middle base line after every stroke. Running on the court is just dancing. Start your backswing to hit an oncoming ball when the ball has hit the ground. When you are told that you are hitting the ball late, it means that you are taking the backswing late. If you are hitting the ball into the net, let your racket head clear the net. In that way you will hit up on the ball and clear the net by a safe margin. If your shots are short, aim at the backstop. If your shots are out, hit for the service line. If you are serving into the net, toss the ball higher, hit sooner. If your serve is out, move the toss forward.[31]

The same words of wisdom, the same rackets sold, over and over, in Salt Lake City, Omaha, Chicago, St. Louis, Pittsburgh, and eventually, at the last stop before New York, in Willoughby, Ohio, a suburb of Cleveland, to visit Mary K. Browne. Brownie had been Suzanne Lenglen's opponent when Alice as a girl had dozed off at their exhibition match. Brownie and Alice had first met in person at Forest Hills in 1931. Then, Brownie had advised more discipline, praising Alice's "natural ability" but cautioning, "you know nothing about strokes and strategy." Brownie supported herself as a part-time tennis coach at Lake Erie College for women, originally modeled as a seminary for female students in the same mold as Mount Holyoke College in the East, with an emphasis on intellectual accomplishment, gracious living, and piety. She had a side vocation painting animals' portraits from photographs in watercolor. When Alice and Teach arrived, in late June, Brownie was at the easel, capturing an Irish setter with all its stubborn, redheaded energy.

Brownie greeted Alice warmly: "I knew we would meet again."[32]

Alice told the *Pittsburgh Press*, "These two great teachers will work on me and thus give a last-minute bit of schooling before I enter the series of eastern events."[33] The trio practiced tennis in the morning on Brownie's home court, with Teach and Brownie patiently coaching Alice while she hit ball after ball. In the afternoons, Teach taught clinics while Alice played with men in matches arranged by Brownie. At night after dinner, they gossiped and talked tennis. Brownie shared insights about her pro tour with Lenglen, good-naturedly dishing about an interlude that must have been challenging to her morale (Brownie lost thirty-eight straight matches and won sets only twice): "Suzanne was always angry. She was so good that I used to earn bonuses on the tour whenever I won three games from her. I remember her taking a swing at a photographer who chased her. The rest of us on the tour steered clear of her. She dined alone with her mother and complained incessantly that she wanted to go home. She was one hell of a player, though."[34]

The three women planned to travel to New York together. Teach and Brownie would provide a cheering section while Alice pursued glory that would redound to all three. The eastward and upward momentum came to a halt, thanks to a telegram sent from California informing Alice that the United States Lawn Tennis Association remained unconvinced of her health. In light of those misgivings, she would not be allowed in any of the eastern tournaments prior to the US National Championships. A committee of five men, including Julian Myrick, had reached this disappointing verdict. Alice called it unthinkable. Teach was apoplectic, telling Alice, "They think you're not well enough. That you'll collapse again. They don't want to be responsible. Myrick did this."[35] Teach felt that Marble's recent wins over Carolin Babcock and Gracyn Wheeler should have been enough to establish her mettle.

Brownie sensed that Teach was too angry to be trusted to act in either her own or Alice's best interests. Consumed with her financial investment in her pupil, estimated at $5,000, Teach had a high stake in appealing this decision. While Teach could be a firebrand, Brownie was known for her even disposition and was well liked in the tennis establishment. When Teach threatened to give a piece of her mind to "that little weasel," Brownie decided to act on Alice's behalf instead.

Brownie's plan, inspired by a suggestion from Alice, was far more effective than a mere tirade. She proposed that Alice prove her mettle by playing men and men only, in a series of qualifying matches at Forest Hills. Several members of the committee who had objected to Alice's inclusion agreed to watch and offer their judgment. Myrick was not one of them.

On the appointed day, Alice proved unstoppable. What made her performance especially sweet was her indifference to the weather, "so hot the birds stopped flying."[36] If Marble could play this well in the conditions most likely to demoralize her and derail her game, then the committee would have to admit she had the stamina to compete. One by one her competitors gave up. Her final opponent "quit when he was down 5–2 in the first set. 'If she's sick, I'm at death's door,'" Alice later recalled him saying. "'It's too hot for me, and Alice is hardly sweating.'"[37] She had achieved Teach's highest accolade: she had learned to be a "fighter at last."[38]

Tennis enthusiasts were appalled that Myrick had gone so far in his animus against Alice. Ted Tinling, who for two years, starting when he was thirteen, had served as helper and consultant to Suzanne Lenglen, calling himself her personal umpire, and who later enjoyed a long career designing tennis dresses for leading players, called the qualifying matches a charade, believing that Myrick knew he had to capitulate or face the true wrath of Teach, a show of force no one would lightly invite.[39]

Alice got the go-ahead to play in the tournaments leading up to the US National Championships at Forest Hills. She followed a strong start, with a victory at the Longwood Cricket Club in Massachusetts over Carolyn Roberts for the singles title (6–1, 8–6). Together Alice and Gracyn Wheeler won at doubles (7–5, 3–6, 6–3). Then she beat Carolin Babcock at Seabright

Lawn Tennis and Cricket Club in New Jersey. Her momentum faltered at the Westchester Country Club, in Rye, New York, where she lost to Sylvia Henrotin, against whom she had been playing when she collapsed in France. Teach guessed, correctly, that Marble was back at Roland-Garros Stadium in her mind's eye and exhorted her: "You'll have to get rid of your ghosts. Play today's match today. Yesterday's matches are history."[40]

At the Essex County Club in Manchester-by-the-Sea, Massachusetts, Alice lost a matchup against Helen Jacobs. Afterward, she reviewed the play with an eye toward what she might do differently in the future: "Unlike most players who favor their forehands, my opponent had a deadly backhand. She pounced on my returns to her strong side, made me eat them, and won 6–3, to take the match. . . . I didn't like losing, but I felt that I was playing better than ever before and that I had learned a lesson. If I wanted to take the champion's crown from her, I couldn't ease into the game. I would have to play one hundred percent from the first service, and never let up. *And* avoid that backhand."[41]

During the crush of tournament play, Marble learned that her Uncle Woodie had died on June 26 at the age of sixty-four, harbinger of an even greater loss at the end of the year.

Soon she and Teach would be heading to Forest Hills, New York, for the US National Championship. By now the rags to riches to rags routine of life as an amateur tennis player was familiar. Teach and Alice economized on their cross-country travel by staying at cheap accommodations, but sometimes they landed in what Teach liked to call a pot of jelly—a storybook setting—an estate so grand that it gave even the Hearst Castle a run for its money.

CHAPTER 14

AND THEN . . . SHE KISSED IT

ALICE HAD NOT QUITE mastered the art of not gaping, as her reaction to Gilbert Kahn's family spread on the Gold Coast of Long Island indicates. She took in its grandeur: pitched rooftops, a formal sunken garden, greenhouses, stables, a nine-hole golf course, five hundred acres, and a sixty-two-thousand-square-foot house with seventy-two rooms and twenty-five baths.[1] The impressive proportions of the drawing room caused Alice to blurt out to Teach, "You could move the furniture back and play tennis in here," prompting Teach to hush her charge.[2]

The edifice was the dream vision of Kahn's father, Otto, known by the press as the "King of New York." Otto Kahn made a fortune, much of which he delighted in spending to support the arts. His largesse benefited the Metropolitan Opera Company. He helped restore the Parthenon in Athens. He gave prize money to Black artists in New York and paid for art classes.[3]

The estate was known for its elaborate parties: the grand dining hall could seat two hundred, presided over by Kahn at one end, never without his dachshunds. The eclectic guest list included "penniless bohemians, members of the clergy, kings, socialites, actors, boisterous musicians, and Ziegfeld girls."[4] This time it would include two competing tennis players at the Nationals: Alice and fellow guest Kay Stammers,[5] Britain's left-handed player, who in 1935 had reached the semifinals at the US National Championships and won the doubles titles at both the French championships and Wimbledon. Alice joined the long line of those who were entranced by her, finding her to be "beautiful, honest and scatterbrained, and could tell a dirty story with the dignity of a queen. Men competed shamelessly for her attention, and she adroitly kept them all at bay without hurt feelings."[6] Alice turned to her new friend for advice on cosmetics. People kept saying she looked peaked when she did not feel it. She needed something that would put some pink on her mahogany-colored cheeks and something else to hide the circles under her eyes and the fine lines around them. Stammers and she spent an entire evening perfecting Alice's makeup routine, and after that, strangers finally stopped expressing concern for how wan Alice looked.

A "will she or won't she?" rumble attached to reports about Helen Wills Moody and whether or not, as the previous year's Wimbledon champion, she would enter the competition at Forest Hills in 1936. She herself was back and forth, in one day, out the next. She said she was willing to play smaller tournaments but wanted to concentrate on her writing and painting. Tennis would be a hobby evermore.

"I believe that different ages should adjust themselves gracefully, if possible, to pursuits suited to them," she said. She perceived that she had been "too sober and serious" as a young player, and only in her later years did she truly enjoy the game. She wanted to time her retirement so that she left while retaining a love of the sport. Without that, she felt any future victories would be hollow.[7]

In the quarterfinals, Alice beat Gracyn Wheeler, and the day before the semifinals, Teach and Alice took a busman's holiday and traveled to a nearby country club to play singles, something they never did, just the two of them. The court was empty, and no wonder: its grass was in deep need of a trimming. As they volleyed, both stumbled comically. The laughter, not the score, was the point.

Kay Stammers had lost to Helen Jacobs in the semifinals, after Jacobs hurt her thumb slipping on the grass. The Kahn household, courteous and evenhanded in its support of both Stammers and Marble, could now rally around "Allie" with single-minded enthusiasm. In the semifinals, Alice beat Helen Pedersen, 6–1, 6–1.

Alice believed two gestures from members of Kahn's staff affected her attitude during the finals. A butler delivered several artfully arranged leaves of cabbage—on a silver tray—to wear, under her hat. Dr. Commons, who helped her back to health after her time at Pottenger's, had been told that workers in hot climates line their caps with cabbage leaves to promote cool-ness, and suggested Alice do the same.[8] She had added this element to her tennis couture, and it had become something of a signature. Then, a maid from Scotland ran from the house just as Alice was leaving for the finals, waving a sprig of heather. "I saved this for a long time. Take it. It will bring you luck."[9] Scots attribute superpowers to the plant, saying it grows on the graves of fairies and in gentle places where no blood has ever been shed. Alice slipped the offering into the pocket of her tennis shorts.

On September 12, third-seeded Alice squared off against top-seeded Jacobs, who wore a bandage on her right hand and thumb. Alice respected her opponent's resolute nature. Jacobs looked, in Alice's reckoning, as Teach might say, bandbox: "The champion exuded confidence, moving easily in her tailored flannel shorts and English-made knit blouse. She looked strong."[10]

The announcer seemed to suggest Marble had overreached, contrasting Jacobs's stellar track record with a mere geographical description for Marble: "This match will be between Miss Helen Jacobs, four times national champion and winner of the Wimbledon championship, and Miss Alice Marble of San Francisco."[11]

Alice took a quick 3–1 lead in the first set, but Jacobs fought back to win it, 6–4. In a frantic and crowd-pleasing second set, Alice pulled even, at 6–3.

Between the second and third set, players were allowed a quick break in the locker room, a swallow of tea, and a pep talk. Alice and Teach arrived simultaneously, at a sense of peace about the proceedings. Getting this far had been unimaginable not all that long ago, when Alice's body was bloated on cream and bacon and the world felt bleak and profitless. As the underdog, Alice had felt lifted by the enthusiasm of the fans, but that was not all. There was something about the moment of equipoise, with one mere set of tennis standing between her and national glory. Alice soothed her wrists with cold water from a faucet. Teach stayed practical, reprising her often proffered earlier advice about how to how to beat Jacobs: "Hit to her forehand. Work the net. Mix it up. Make her hurry her shots." Alice told Teach that no matter, even if she did not win, she had not lost.

Teach agreed. And then she gave what was probably the best, the simplest, and the most pure advice she had ever offered: "Have fun."[12]

And with that, Alice put on a fresh top, reattached her lucky pin, and reentered the arena.

In the final set, Alice stormed ahead, 4–0, keeping Jacobs on the run, and she served the match at 6–2.

Teach sealed the victory with two comments when she rushed over to give her protégée an embrace. "I'm so proud of you," she said, adding a delicious aside: "Was Myrick's face red!"[13]

Among the commentators who hailed Alice was fellow Californian Ellsworth Vines, a power player known for a swift corner-to-corner game. Like Alice, he had faltered early in his career, stating after one defeat, "I guess I am just a false alarm," though he was ranked or co-ranked number one in the world in 1932 and 1934–37. He appreciated Alice's style of play, reporting: "The defending champion tried everything in her varied bag of tricks, but Miss Marble had the answer every time. If Miss Jacobs elected to play from the backcourt she was run unmercifully from side to side; if she elected to chop, Miss Marble was at the net to cut off these slower and higher returns with beautifully placed stop volleys which time and again caught Miss Jacobs flat-footed behind the baseline."[14]

An example of good sportsmanship also made the paper. Eula Jacobs, Helen's mother, called Jessie Marble to offer her congratulations. "I'm so glad such a lovely girl as your Alice was the one to win," said Mrs. Jacobs. "Naturally I wanted Helen to win, but if she had to lose, it is nice to know she lost to a fellow townswoman."[15] The gesture so touched Alice's mother that she asked a local newspaper, the *San Francisco Chronicle*, to mention the call.

Dan Marble took advantage of the swirl of goodwill surrounding his sister to sound a different note in the *San Francisco Examiner*, finally free to express anger at the way she had been treated after the collapse at Forest Hills: "The association, which was responsible for the collapse of Alice's health when they forced her to play four matches, or 108 games in eleven sets in a blazing heat, washed its hands of her completely in 1934. It declined to give her financial aid. Then in 1935, it even refused her entry to the nationals, and this year declined to name her on the Wightman Cup team. The association did everything they could to discourage her—but she succeeded in spite of it. It can be said now—for it won't do Alice any harm."[16]

Upon being presented with a silver bowl as her trophy for being the national champion, Alice played the press perfectly. First, she thrust it above her head. Lowering it, she closed her eyes as if in prayer, and then, to the delight of the photographers and to the click of their cameras, she kissed it.

That night, at a buffet dinner, the music in the ballroom was provided by the orchestra leader Emil Coleman. Never one to downplay his high opinion of himself—in his marketing material, he claimed that if a debutante had a coming-out party and he was not playing at it, "the debutante simply hasn't come out"—he invented the medley style of playing one song after another, the better to keep dancers on the dance floor for as long as possible. Five hundred guests swayed to his nonstop sounds, though Coleman did pause long enough to invite Alice to sing in front of the adoring audience. She chose "Pennies from Heaven," impressing him with her abilities, as would become evident when they met again. Teach made certain the revels ended, at least for Alice, at midnight, but she did allow her charge to sleep in until ten the next morning. Alice enjoyed breakfast in bed, served on a tray along with flowers and telegrams—from family members as well as Beese, Marion Davies, Hearst, and Lombard.

In what appears to be a rare recognition of dissociation between her public persona and her private self, Alice said that in the days to come, "I told my story of illness, despair, and comeback so many times, I began to feel as if I were talking about someone else, some fictional character."[17] On Tuesday, September 15, a few days after her victory, Alice returned to Southern California for more glad-handing and displays of tennis expertise. Not until mid-October did she finally make it back to San Francisco, a visit trumpeted in the *Examiner*: "Alice Due Tomorrow." The use of just her first name indicated the degree of celebrity she had achieved. She arrived by train at nine a.m. on September 17. Mayor Angelo Joseph Rossi presented the tennis queen with a bouquet. At a city hall reception, the press peppered her with questions, and she handled their curiosity like a pro, immediately identifying certain topics as off-limits. She "had nothing to say about (1) the European political situation, (2) the American political situation, (3) the new book she is writing, (4) the designing of feminine undergarments, (5) the romance between the King and Mrs. Simpson."[18]

Teach fended off any discussion of Alice's love life as reported in the *Examiner*: "Alice just plays the field. She gets lots of presents from lots of people, but they don't mean anything."

Teach was far more interested in praising her charge's skills in the world of commerce: "I believe Alice's business acumen has had a great deal to do with her becoming champion. Through her handling of my affairs, Alice has learned a great deal about human nature. She has learned how to grab every opportunity presented to her. She has learned to take every advantage that appears, no matter how briefly. I know—because I have to go to Alice for every cent I get."

Alice had not been in her hometown in a year, and the press wanted to her to choose between Los Angeles and San Francisco. She gave a diplomatic response: "I never said San Francisco was not my home, but I travel around quite a bit and it appears that my home is where I hang my hat."[19]

When no one in the Marble family showed up to greet her, the press sniffed a rift. Teach covered for Alice, saying she was very close to her family and suggested it might have been a hardship to be on hand so early in the day. Alice then set the record straight. Her mother had been ill. It would have been too much for her physically to make a public appearance. The rest of the Marbles were at home, taking care of her.

When Alice finally made it to Twelfth Avenue, waiting for her in addition to the family, was gift from Marion Davies and Hearst, a new green Buick, with a note, "To the winner go the spoils." She was not the only one being celebrated in the family. Dan had recently been runner-up in the national handball championships, Tim had signed on as a shortstop for the San Francisco Missions, and George had earned a reputation as a swimmer.

However, in the year since Alice's last visit, her mother had lost more ground. She now weighed less than one hundred pounds. When pressed, Jessie Marble revealed that the cause was cancer. Yet she refused her daughter's offer to stay home and help, as Alice later recalled: "No, you won't. You will go live your own life—a wonderful life, too, now that you're well."[20]

More hoopla ensued, including the opening of new tennis courts at the Olympic as well as a dinner dance at the San Francisco Press Club, where she was a guest of honor along with tennis buddies Budge and Edward "Bud" Chandler.

Alice paid a sentimental visit on her own to Golden Gate Park and watched some young people at play, hopeful that like her, even if they lacked a middle-class background to pave the way, they too might achieve great heights. She relished her status as a hero in her hometown. She was proud that, like movie stars, athletes took everyone's mind off the "real world that was pretty dismal and getting worse all the time."[21] But the lack of money for amateurs nettled her. Here she was, "at home in the glamorous environs of the country's upper class," but she lacked the money to open a checking account.[22] Teach's fulsome praise of Alice's business skills didn't match up with Alice's sense of never-ending debt. Any money she made outside of tennis fed the always growing debt that Teach accrued while caring for her. Without a major cash infusion, the cycle appeared doomed to continue.

During an outing to the movies with her mother, Alice made an embarrassing discovery. She and her mother watched a newsreel as it transitioned from crime news with fresh developments in the Lindbergh baby kidnapping case to sports, beginning with a story about Olympic sprinter Jesse Owens, who had won four gold medals at the 1936 Olympics, followed by footage of Alice winning the US National Championships. Seeing herself on the big screen, larger than life, shaking hands with Jacobs, Alice could not keep from shouting, "That's me!" in the theater, jumping up and pointing to the image. "I was satisfied with my strokes; they looked much as I expected." But then her mood changed: she liked seeing how she played, but she didn't like how she looked, especially after the match. When she observed herself "striding to the net to shake hands with Helen," she wrote later, "I groaned and slid deeper into my seat. The girl on the screen walked like a stevedore, or a farm girl following a plow. Why hadn't Teach told me?"[23]

When Marble did ask Teach, she replied, "I didn't think much about it. I was worried about your game."

Before she left San Francisco for Palm Springs, Alice gave one last interview, to Harry B. Smith, the sports editor of the *Chronicle*: "I don't believe I have half reached the top. I still have much to work for and with that in mind I am returning south with Miss Tennant where I intend to practice three or four times a week to improve my game."[24]

In Palm Springs, Alice started training again as well as basking in "thousands of letters—from fans, from people wanting to know how I managed to come back from tuberculosis, and from players seeking advice."[25] Carole Lombard rented a house for the holidays, the press reported, and "one of her guests will be Alice Marble, the tennis champion."[26]

Alice confided in her friend about how awkward she looked in the newsreel. Once again, Lombard offered a solution. She counseled her to enroll in the John Robert Powers "charm school"—a popular resource at the time for women who felt they needed refinement as they sought to find a mate or success in public.

Powers welcomed women of all ages and stations in life into his suite of offices on New York's Park Avenue[27] and at his many satellite offices across the country. Clients would get "magic advice," which, if heeded, translated, "open sesame," to "fame, fortune and happiness." Powers's system of betterment, as enshrined in his book *Secrets of Charm*, bombarded readers with the minutiae of self-improvement, a delicate trellis that could be climbed forever. Marble, eager to improve her bearing, had expressed her concerns none too soon. Without an intercession, Powers intimated that she and others like her, who suffered from a clumsy carriage, risked a cornucopia of figure flaws, from "spare tire, the 'bustle' in the back, dropped bosom lines, bony shoulders, Dowager's hump, puffball knees, stick legs, ballooning calves" and other defects "too gloomy to dwell upon."[28] It is easy to ridicule his scare-tactic verbiage and to imagine how little it had to do with the intrinsic grace of a gifted athlete like Marble, but Powers could cite many women of note among his clients, including Norma Shearer, Ava Gardner, Barbara Stanwyck, and Lucille Ball. It is not clear which of his many offices Marble visited, though in later years she credited his methods for raising her sense of confidence, especially before an audience on the lecture circuit.

Lombard was experiencing both professional prosperity and romance. She and Clark Gable had made a movie together in 1932, *No Man of Her Own*, but it was all business then. At the beginning of 1936, they met again at the Mayfair Ball in Hollywood, which Lombard planned. Guests, men and women, were to dress in white only. (The actress Norma Shearer infuriated Lombard by wearing red, an act of defiance that later inspired a similar scene in the Bette Davis movie *Jezebel*.) Gable was married to his second wife at the time, but that did not stop him from making his interest in Lombard clear. She had one of the all-time great responses to his overtures: "Who do you think you are, Clark Gable?"[29]

Later that year, when Lombard turned twenty-eight, on October 6, Louella Parsons, the gossip doyenne of Hollywood, wrote, "Carole Lombard's family and about eighteen close friends celebrated her birthday Sunday night; Clark Gable's gift a sports bracelet in gold and a pedigreed cocker spaniel; tennis at midnight with Alice Marble wielding a mean racket, and a bridge game with Carole's mother as the star player, kept the party going until the wee sma' hours."[30] Gable was Hollywood's king, an Oscar winner for *It Happened One Night*. Lombard was about to become the highest-paid movie actress, the queen of screwball comedy. Alice had entered the center of Hollywood celebrity.

THEN, JUST BEFORE NEW YEAR'S DAY 1937, the news Alice feared above all arrived, an awful way to punctuate what had been her comeback year. Her mother had died, at the age of fifty-nine, in San Francisco on December 31, 1936.

"I'm praying for you," wrote her mother in her final letter. She signed off with a phrase that Alice loved so much she also used it to sign off letters to close friends: "God bless, angels keep."

Alice's father had died on New Year's Day 1920, so now the holiday season would always have two sad anniversaries attached to it. A funeral for Jessie was held a few days later, but Alice chose not to mark the death with a trip home. "You will go live your own life," her mother had urged, and Marble took the words at face value. She kept busy, eschewing formal mourning for the spotlight. *Physical Culture: The Personal Problem Magazine* published a four-page feature story in January 1937, titled "How the Girl Weakling Became Champion." The writer praised Alice for combining "more power and speed afoot than any player ever seen on the feminine side of the Forest Hills program. . . . In fact, the ultimate in women's tennis finally had been realized—the speed and finesse of Lenglen, the power of Wills and the tenacity and competitive urge of Jacobs."[31]

The USLTA agreed, naming Marble as number one in women's tennis in the United States, knocking Helen Jacobs from the perch she had held for the previous four years, with the press predicting that Alice's new spot at the top would likely elicit howls of protest. The debate revolved around Jacobs winning Wimbledon and defeating Alice at the Essex County Club in Manchester-by-the-Sea, Massachusetts, the previous summer. In England, Jacobs was called the world's best female player, an opinion that carried weight in the United States, even as Marble defeated Jacobs at the US National Championships.

Stepping up as the voice of reason, Stephen Wallis Merrihew, *American Lawn Tennis* editor and member of the USLTA committee, said: "After all there must be some reward for winning the national championship."[32]

Alice was unfazed. "I would have been surprised if it had been otherwise," she told the *San Francisco Examiner.*[33]

CHAPTER 15

THE HEART OF THEIR UNIVERSE

I N THE SPRING OF 1937, Marble observed from afar a world fraying at the seams. Japan was gearing up to invade China, and Amelia Earhart was putting the finishing touches on her soon-to-be doomed plan to circumnavigate the world. The German airship *Hindenburg* blew up in flames in New Jersey as it attempted to dock, killing thirty-six. The stock market crashed, again, and the Dust Bowl, with its "black blizzards" composed of thick dust formed from loose topsoil, dislocated farmers and their families on the Great Plains, relentlessly pushing them west. In Germany, the Nazis were putting the finishing touches on their first concentration camp, Buchenwald, including electrified barbed-wire fences, watchtowers, and sentries equipped with machine guns. The first occupants, male political prisoners, would arrive in the summer.

By contrast, Alice spent much of her time in training with Beese but found a window in February to take a screen test under Carole Lombard's guidance. Star Dust, a syndicated movie column, observed: "Carole Lombard was right there on the sidelines making suggestions and cheering. Some people might think that Alice Marble won enough glory in tennis tournaments for one young girl but Carole thinks it would be nicer for her to get in the big earnings that come with glory in pictures."[1]

Dreams of Hollywood have not gone to her head, one interviewer said, explaining that Marble is from "a family of moderate circumstances, [and] has battled for most of the things she has." Alice approaches everything with "calm seriousness," including the English championships, several months away:

"I'm looking forward now, most of all, to playing at Wimbledon," said the determined young woman, stretching one of the shapely Marble legs covered by slacks instead of the familiar non-covering of the famous Marble tennis shorts over a coffee table in front of the divan. Flicking a cigaret ash into a tray, she continued: "And don't think I have the idea that I am going to win in England. I don't. It's easy for someone to say, 'Yes, Alice, after you win at Wimbledon, and so on,' but I know it's not that easy. My, I wish it were."[2]

Alice returned to competition in early March. At the UCLA gym, she split two sets with Jack Kramer, the national boys' champion.[3] In the annual invitational tournament in Palm Springs, California, in early April, Marble defeated Dorothy Workman in singles, won mixed doubles with partner Owen Anderson, but then lost when she paired with Workman in a women-versus-men match.[4]

Alice's social life picked up. Teach and Alice were given a buffet supper in their honor at the Palm Springs Racquet Club in late March. Gossip columnist Louella Parsons let it be known that Alice had lunched with Marion Davies, her screen test had gone well, and she was getting ready for Wimbledon.[5] Years later, Marble would admit that Parsons's positive assessment had not precisely reflected her experience, but for now, she luxuriated in giving the impression that acting talent oozed from her pores, and she would put "Hollywood actress" on her résumé as soon as it was convenient. Alice and Teach left in mid-April by train, heading east. Teach made plans to accompany Alice to Wimbledon, though she groused about how she would be sacrificing the money she could have made teaching tennis. Alice felt guilty but relieved. She did not want to break the spell of their partnership, and she gladly handed off all the decision-making for the two of them to Teach, the better to concentrate on tennis exclusively.[6]

At a stop in Missouri, a man was recruited to play against Marble, because "St. Louis has no woman player who could cope with the California star," the *St. Louis Post-Dispatch* reported.[7] Robert Weinstock, the district's indoor tennis champion, won the first set, but Alice rebounded to take the second.[8]

On April 24, newspapers reported, Tennant and Marble reached New York and soon set sail for England, amid an exodus that took place May 4–5, 1937, as 5,290 passengers left New York for Europe in twenty-four hours.

Travelers who wanted to get to England before the coronation of George VI packed the ships. The new king would take over now that his elder brother, Edward VIII, had abdicated the throne for his love, the twice-divorced Wallis Simpson.[9] Five ships sailed in those twenty-four hours, including the Cunard White Star liner *Berengaria*, with Alice and Teach on board. Alice wore a jacket trimmed with piping over a dress with a piped neckline. She looked "the picture of health," according to the Associated Press.[10] A newsreel interviewer asked what was drawing her to England, the coronation or Wimbledon. She set the record straight: tennis and only tennis, explaining that this was her first attempt at Wimbledon and she hoped to bring "something back for America."

The interviewer wondered whether she expected Helen Wills to show up, to which Alice replied, "I'm afraid I don't know. I hope she does. I think it will be a great thing for tennis."[11]

Alice's voice sounded polite but direct. Her smile was effortless. She did not dwell on the gloomy fact that only four women in fifty-three years had won Wimbledon on their first try. Nor did she mimic Teach's mouthy overreach, when the coach declared to the press that nothing could stand in Alice's way.

To ease the financial pressures of travel, Teach managed to convince a small group of patrons to pick up some of the tab, including Gil Kahn, whose estate had hosted Teach and Alice the previous year during the US National Championships and would again in 1937, and Freddy Warburg, of the banking Warburgs, known for attracting foreign capital for US investments. Teach and Alice had played tennis at Warburg's lavish estate in Westchester County, New York. Recognized for their philanthropy, especially toward struggling artists, the family apparently had no qualms about reaching a struggling athlete and her coach with their largesse as well.

En route to England, Alice could not help but remember how terrible she had felt on her previous ocean crossing, to France, and notice how much more festive this one seemed now that she was in good health. Even so, Teach forbade her from socializing. Alice wondered whether romance would ever come her way. If Teach could control it, the answer was never or at least not for a long time. She used to say, "Love is just a tennis score." Nonetheless, as she later revealed, Alice wished Teach could be a bit less vigilant. "I was twenty-three, my hormones were in full tilt, and there were several attractive young men whose attention I found very pleasing. I could have been coaxed into a shipboard romance."[12]

Men made overtures, but Alice had yet to take a lover. She thought her reluctance was attributable to a combination of the lingering emotional aftermath of the rape and to the tight rein of Teach, who shut her charge off from the world of couples just as she forbade desserts. On the boat, Teach enforced a ten p.m. curfew, warning Alice that all eyes were on her and not just to appraise whether or not she held her purse correctly or whether she stood up straight—her status as national champion made her vulnerable. People were gunning for a misstep: "I don't want you to get cocky. You think it was hard to reach the top? Wait till you see how hard it is to stay there. As the challenger, you have nothing to lose; as the champion, you have *everything* to lose, *every* time you step on a court."[13]

Even as Teach worked to keep Alice's ego in check, she readily touted her pupil's prospects to reporters, predicting that she would make a clean sweep of the pre-Wimbledon tournaments in Britain. Such would not be the case.

At the Surrey Championships in Surbiton, Marble's fate could be read in the rain-soaked field, so soggy that for one match Marble followed the lead of her competitors and put socks on over her shoes. Her play that day told an old story: her volleying was spirited, even if slower than usual thanks to the mud, but her ground strokes were weak. At Chiswick, the Middlesex County championship tournament of "impressive antiquity," she lost to Anita Lizana. At St. George's Hill Club at Weybridge in Surrey, she lost in singles again, beaten by the Polish player Jadwiga Jedrzejowska, known to all as Ja-Ja. At her fourth tournament, at Beckenham, Alice lost to Ja-Ja again. Observers noted an overall hesitancy in her game. These disappointing results challenged her confidence.[14]

When she finally made her way to the All England Lawn Tennis and Croquet Club at Wimbledon, in the suburbs of London, a journey universally regarded by tennis players as a sacred pilgrimage to a holy land, she was overcome by the weight of the occasion. The first time Alice saw Centre Court, she felt she had entered another dimension.

I was escorted, along with six other visiting players, to view for the first time the historic center court. Our guide was a member of the old guard at Wimbledon; a charming elderly man, Commander Hillyard. It was

two weeks before the championship and a very rainy day. The eight of us
stood there under the roof, viewing the beautiful green surface, as smooth
as a billiard table. There were no lines on the court, no net posts, no one in
the stands but us. Yet we heard clearly the sound of a racket hitting a ball.
Knowing that there could be no one playing for miles around in the heavy
downpour, I felt the hair rise on the back of my neck. The other spectators
looked as I felt, that we'd heard a ghost. Commander Hillyard smiled and
said, "No, you are not suffering from hallucinations. Everyone hears
what you have heard. There are many explanations, but this is the one I
like best. I like to think that the sound you heard comes from the spirits of
the great English players, the Gores, Doherties and Roper-Barretts who
come back to uphold England's tradition in tennis." And then he added
prophetically (it was two whole years before the start of World War II),
"Just as I'm sure that if we have another world conflict the spirits of the
great English leaders, Drake and Wellington, will come back to uphold
England's traditions of the battlefield."[15]

Many players refer to Wimbledon as "church."[16] Billie Jean King said
it was "love at first sight." The writer David Foster Wallace used the term
"cathedral." The altar is Centre Court, where the words of Rudyard Kipling
are inscribed, "If you can meet with Triumph and Disaster, and treat those
two imposters just the same . . ."[17] Suzanne Lenglen called Centre Court the
"most frightening place I know."[18] Don Budge liked to tell the story of his first
visit to Wimbledon, two years before Alice's. Having arrived in London at
six in the evening before the competition, he could not bear to wait until the
next day to see the facility firsthand. Hailing a cab, he arrived at dusk to an
empty stadium. After wandering a bit, he finally found Centre Court: "I was
not two steps onto the grass when suddenly from somewhere above, there
rang an authoritative and literal, 'Halt.' I froze." A kindly older man explained
that no one was allowed on the court in anything other than tennis shoes.[19]

Founded in 1877, Wimbledon sits in a small village that seems not just
miles but decades away from modern London. The colors of Wimbledon are
green, purple, and white—and, in a rare lapse of record keeping, no one is
precisely sure why. The general theory is white for the tennis attire, green
for the grass, and purple for the game's royal origins.

"Just being there regardless of who plays and comes crashing through
those gates seems enough," wrote America's best tennis journalist, Bud Col-

lins. "They could set up TV screens on each court and show reruns of old matches, and it wouldn't make much difference. . . . Dusky green and high, the walls at either end of the amphitheater provide the best background in the business. Champion after champion will tell you . . . that it is the heart of their universe."[20]

The year that Alice experienced her first Wimbledon, the institution also celebrated a milestone, its first television broadcast. Early viewers were told that if they showed patience, sifting through the grainy waves of black and white, they might, with luck, be able to see the ball, aloft and discernible, on the screen, and that, with enough refinements, television might even replace radio someday.

New Yorker writer and humorist James Thurber watched Don Budge play Frank Parker on a screen twelve miles from the action. His reaction was mixed. "Budge, the size of your index finger, against Parker, the size of your little finger; wielding match-stem racquets hitting a speck of white. You could hear the impact of the racquets, the judge's droning count, and the barking of the linesmen. You could see the tiny, tense faces in the stands, the tiny heads moving in unison, following the infinitesimal ball. . . . It was like watching a photograph in an album come to life. Extremely interesting, but not entirely satisfactory, because you can't get a grasp or feeling of the match as a whole."[21]

Alice's showing in singles was more than respectable. She defeated Mary Hardwick in an early matchup. With her curls and her local provenance, Hardwick was the crowd favorite. After the spirited first set, which lasted forty-five minutes, it seemed Hardwick might prevail, but Alice asserted her superiority, taking the match (9–11, 6–4, 6–3). Alice won the next two rounds easily, with scores of 6–1, 6–0, and 6–0, 6–2. She then faced a much greater foe in Hilde Sperling, who, at six feet, was the tallest woman playing tennis at the time and had a repertoire of unpredictable strokes. Bruce Harris, writing in the *Evening Standard*, had praise for Marble, but he also had reservations: "Miss Marble is as brilliant a player as anyone, man or women, at this Wimbledon. Yet in this country she has not yet shown sufficient constancy of form, nor enough stamina, to last a long match against a rival like the implacable Miss Sperling."[22] Nonetheless, Marble won a competitive first set, 7–5; Sperling walked away with the second set, 6–2, and leaped ahead in the third, 3–0. At that point Marble changed her tactics, repeatedly getting to the net, forcing awkward returns, to take six straight games and the match, 6–3.

Alice then met an even more formidable opponent in the semifinals. Ja-Ja Jedrzejowska had beaten Marble in the warm-up tournaments and did so again, 8–6, 6–2. Ahead 5–3 in the first set, Marble lost the ninth game when her service betrayed her, and Ja-Ja capitalized on Alice's difficulty. The second set was less rigorously fought.

Under a subhead "Alice in Blunderland," a British reporter said of her disappointing performance, "A match of exactly an hour's length was taken by Warsaw at the expense of the Pacific West."[23]

Alice vividly recalled the match years later: "[Ja-Ja] had a hit like a mule's kick and it was working for her that day. She blasted drives deep in the corners, spinning chalk from the line time after time with her deadly placement. She pounced on my returns with unnerving enthusiasm, sturdy legs churning and all the force of her blocky muscular body addressing the ball. I turned to putty, like papier-mâché in the rain."[24]

Ja-Ja then lost the finals to the British player Dorothy Round, who took her second singles title.

Alice lost again in the women's doubles second round but in the mixed doubles finally had a good ending. She and her teammate, fellow Californian Don Budge, made their wins seem effortless, defeating Raymond Tuckey and Peggy Scriven, 6–2, 6–2 in the quarterfinals; Gene Mako and Ja-Ja Jedrzejowska in the semifinals, 6–3, 6–2; and Yvon Petra and Simonne Mathieu, 6–4, 6–1, for the crown. Budge was thrilled to team up with Marble: "If you are lucky enough to have a partner with the abilities of someone like Alice Marble, just consider yourself blessed and don't worry about a thing." He called her "any man's favorite doubles partner."[25]

Budge owned Wimbledon that year, becoming the first man to take all three events, singles, men's doubles, and mixed doubles, as he would again in 1938. (The first woman was Suzanne Lenglen, in 1920.) Marble owned the fashion front, with the Associated Press reporting: "The American champion scored something of a personal triumph . . . with her trim shorts and white jockey's cap. Wimbledon had seen nothing like them before."[26]

Under the headline "Ocean Travelers," the *New York Times* announced Alice would arrive in New York on July 13, 1937, on the Cunard White Star's *Aquitania*, the same liner she took home after collapsing in France three years earlier. When she did disembark, the *Daily News* informed its readers: "Our top-notch gal tennis star is back . . . prettier and more sun-kissed than ever."

Newspapers carried a consistent message: yes, Alice would try again at Wimbledon next year. Marble said: "Naturally I wanted to win on my first attempt . . . but after all, I did no worse than the many others who have attempted this feat."[27] Marble planned to go to Forest Hills to practice before competing at Seabright, where she made it to the singles finals to meet none other than the Polish star Ja-Ja Jedrzejowska, who had just defeated her three times. Ja-Ja was telling reporters two things: she loved American idioms ("O.K., Toots, so what, swell"), and she would beat Alice.[28]

The crowd—and the reporting—were over the top for the Alice-versus-Ja-Ja match. "In all the history of this grass court fixture," the *New York Times* wrote, "it is doubtful whether a gallery has witnessed more exciting drama than was unfolded in this fluctuating, cruelly punishing battle of champions." Alice eked out the win, 6–3, 5–7, 8–6, as she "averted disaster by the thin margin of a stroke."[29]

At the Rye, New York, tournament, Alice and Ja-Ja met in the finals, setting off a frenzy for fans hoping for a Seabright repeat. The *Daily News* frothed over the prospect: "Our Alice Is Out for Revenge!"[30] Spectators "stormed" the Westchester Country Club, and every seat was taken, while hundreds more sat on the ground, and some perched in trees or on the "scaffolding erected for moving-picture cameras," the *New York Times* reported.[31] Fireworks never happened. Alice put up a fight, but she was defeated in straight sets, 7–5, 6–4.[32] In doubles, however, she and Sarah Palfrey prevailed against Carolin Babcock and Marjorie Gladman Van Ryn, 9–7, 6–1.

In the middle of the tournaments, newspapers dropped the news that Alice would head the Wightman Cup team. The announcement was so casual, as if Alice's struggles to belong had evaporated. Alice did her bit to help the United States successfully capture the Wightman Cup, winning two matches of the four on opening day, one against Mary Hardwick in singles, 4–6, 6–2, 6–4; and the other, teamed with Sarah Palfrey, in doubles, 6–3, 6–2.[33]

At the end of August, at the Longwood Cricket Club national doubles championship in Chestnut Hill, Massachusetts, partners Alice and Sarah Palfrey once again triumphed against Carolin Babcock and Marjorie Gladman Van Ryn, 7–5, 6–4.[34]

By the time Alice got to the US National Championships in Forest Hills, she could sense that the spark of the previous year was missing. She felt melancholy, perhaps in reaction to the death of her mother.

Shockingly, she stumbled in the quarterfinals, losing to Dorothy Bundy, the daughter of May Sutton Bundy, even after winning an easy first set and holding match point in the second. When she lost that set, Marble could not control her frustration, screaming and throwing her racket. Bundy dominated the third set, hitting one strong driving shot after another, to which Marble responded feebly, and Bundy won it, 1–6, 7–5, 6–1. Three years younger than Alice, Bundy seemed almost embarrassed to dethrone the champ, the *New York Times* observed: "Miss Bundy, in her moment of greatest triumph on the courts, stood quietly at her baseline with a look of regret on her face."[35] Marble ran from the court to the clubhouse, weeping. Later, she recovered her poise enough to acknowledge that Dodo, as Bundy was called, had won fair and square: "What can you say when one plays better than you."[36] In the semifinals, Ja-Ja Jedrzejowska beat Helen Jacobs, and Anita Lizana of Chile beat Bundy. The South American star went on to take the prize against Ja-Ja, 6–4, 6–2. For Alice, winning the doubles title with Sarah Palfrey hardly compensated for the early loss against Bundy, which the papers covered in excruciating detail.

A party at the Kahn estate in honor of Marble and Kay Stammers was low-key compared to the one the previous year, when five hundred guests swayed to the music of Emil Coleman. When Alice walked into the ballroom for the dinner dance, her first impulse was to flee, and she would have, if not for a stern look from Teach.[37] Alice found a chair on the sidelines, where she hoped to remain unnoticed. Even so, her patron Freddy Warburg managed to seek her out. Harvard educated, with an amiable personality and the ability to write doggerel, deliberately inferior poetry crafted for comic effect, at a moment's notice, Freddy enjoyed performing the odd kindness. On that evening his generosity took the form of delivering a beautifully wrapped gift to Alice, a silver cigarette box engraved with Kipling's inscription from Wimbledon. The gesture worked wonders on Alice's doldrums. She joined the party and led the assembly in a toast to her successor, Anita Lizana. After that, she went to the microphone and belted out a couple of tunes.

As the merriment wound down, Alice sank into a sofa next to Freddy's father, Felix Moritz Warburg, and chatted with him until Teach enforced her curfew. To her sorrow, she recounted years later, the next morning Felix Warburg was found dead in his bed of a heart attack. Marble remembered feeling honored to be called upon by the family to fill them in on their casual conversation, as it had been his last social interaction. "His family was heartbroken and begged me to recall everything their patriarch had said during the last hours of his life. I did, and I was grateful that I could use my memory to comfort people who were so dear to me."[38]

BY THE TIME Alice entered the Pacific Southwest tournament, which she dismissed as a trivial tournament, she was ready to give up, telling Teach, "I don't want to play today. Tell them I'm sick. I don't want to play today. All our movie friends will be there, and I can't bear to lose in front of them."[39] Teach would hear none of it: "You can't quit now, not like this. The tournament sponsors are your friends, too. You're the attraction, and they're counting on you."[40]

"Carole and Clark were in the first box," Alice recounted. I was all dressed with my racket and about to go in and I heard Clark say, 'Honey, look, Carole, we all love Alice,' Allie he called me, A-l-l-i-e, 'but she just doesn't have it.' Now, this was what I said about myself but damn it, no one's going to say it about me. I went on that court and I annihilated that girl."[41] Gracyn Wheeler was swiftly defeated, 6–1, 6–0.

Alice continued: "I came back and I was still burning when I walked into the box and Clark looked at me with that cute sideways grin and said, 'Hi champ.' And naturally I melted like all of his other fans."[42]

Gable's dismissal of her talent gave her the impetus "to go out and practice and beat everybody as badly as I could whether it was my best friend or not. So, I told Clark the story and he was so mortified and he sent me three dozen American beauties, and he still apologized and apologized, and I told him 'maybe these are the little pushes we need and then you gave me that push.'"[43]

The nudge, along with the specter of being a one-trick pony, made a difference as Alice devoted the fall of 1937 to working on her game, though she remained intrigued by the notion of launching a secondary career as well and was soon selling her own fashions. In December 1937, at Bullock's in Los Angeles, one could buy, for $39.75, a Marble-designed three-piece tweed suit in toast beige, fog blue, court green, or sunset blue. The caption for a newspaper ad announced, "Alice Marble enters a new field."[44]

A few weeks later, a United Press photo, widely published in the beginning of 1938, showed Alice reaching "skyward for a high lob at the Beverly

Hills Tennis Club, where she is preparing for the coming major tournaments in America and in Europe this spring and summer."[45]

Marble told the sportswriter Curley Grieve that she had spent the winter perfecting her "strategy against all leading players." One new technique was "a slightly different forehand with a new topspin," she said. "I can bang the daylights out of the ball now."[46]

April's tournament at La Cienega courts in Beverly Hills was billed as the "climax event of the spring season." The *Los Angeles Times* assured readers that "leading stars—Don Budge, Alice Marble, Gene Mako, Dot Bundy—and others of international reputation are using it as their springboard into the whirl of 1938 competition."[47] In mixed doubles, Budge and Marble won against Jack Tidball and Bundy, 8–6, 6–3.[48] Alice won the singles, 6–3, 6–4, against Barbara Winslow, a "sound and dangerous challenger."[49]

On April 25, 1938, Alice and Teach headed east by train[50] before sailing to England.[51] The *Chicago Tribune* kept close track of their goings-on when they arrived in the city two days later. On their first evening, they appeared on radio station WGN radio's *Sports Celebrity Parade*, promoted as "two famous tennis personalities."[52]

The committee of the Junior Wightman Cup gave a tea at the Drake Hotel in honor of Alice and Teach. The United States Lawn Tennis Association had organized the Junior Wightman that year in six cities to develop new talent. For two days, Teach and Alice worked with the young players, first at the University of Chicago and then at the country club in Evanston, Illinois.[53]

A gossip columnist spotted Alice and Teach, mentioning them along with author Thomas Mann, by then in exile from Hitler and Germany, who was "alighting from a cab" at the Drake Hotel, while Dale Carnegie, author of *How to Win Friends and Influence People*, was "dining in the Boston Oyster house, winning a friend in Mario, handsome maître d'hotel from the Island of Capri." As for Alice and Eleanor, they were "sticking to a nonalcoholic regimen at a fashionable dining bar."[54]

During a two-day stop in St. Louis, on the final weekend in April, the local Junior Wightman Cup group threw a luncheon for Alice and Teach at the Coronado Hotel. Their friend Mary K. Browne, in town for tennis lectures, joined them. Both Brownie and Teach predicted a Wimbledon win for Marble. With her trademark manner of expression, Tennant said of Alice's health: "Her nerves . . . are 'padded' now."[55]

Arrived in New York, Marble practiced against Francis Hunter, whose opinion was gold. He won the Wimbledon men's doubles title in 1924 and 1927 and the mixed doubles in 1927 and 1929. Alice was Wimbledon-worthy, he said. Her lobbing, her deep court drive, her timing, her speed, and her strength made "her almost unbeatable," said Hunter to the New York *Daily News*. "Alice is the strongest woman player I have ever seen."[56] United Press echoed the praise in a report transmitted to newspapers nationwide.

Not everyone agreed; readers of the *Brooklyn Daily Eagle* learned an entirely different story. Alice's "new forehand has a lot of wrist snap in it, but it is a shot that Miss Marble cannot always keep in the court. . . . She was missing the setups, giving up too easily, and playing much as the erratic Marble of old did. Only her backhand looked really fine."[57]

On May 11, 1938, twenty-four-year-old Marble sailed from New York to England on the Cunard White Star liner *Queen Mary*, heading toward an ever-more menacing Europe. Since her last visit, Germany's propaganda ministry had opened an anti-Semitic exhibition at the Deutsches Museum in Munich called *Der Ewige Jude* (The Eternal Jew). It traveled to other cities, reaching as many as four hundred thousand viewers. In March, Hitler had successfully annexed Austria, and forced Polish Jews there to relocate to Poland, which consigned most to the border between both countries.

In the world of international tennis, the news centered on one of its own. Baron Gottfried von Cramm had been accused of homosexuality by the Nazis. For three straight years, from 1935 to 1937, he had been the men's singles runner-up at Wimbledon. Don Budge rallied twenty-five American sports figures, including Alice and Joe DiMaggio, to send a letter testifying to Cramm's character. The signatories praised him as the "ideal sportsman, a perfect gentleman and decency personified. . . . No country could have wished for a finer representative—no sport for a more creditable exponent."[58]

On the ship, Teach met Roz Schiffer Bloomingdale Cowen, a divorced woman traveling with her four children. The well-connected Roz took a liking to Alice and insisted that she have her portrait painted by the celebrated artist Dorothy Vicaji when they arrived in London. The London-born Vicaji demanded total cooperation from her subjects. She specialized in painting American women used to being admired for their wealth or connections, such as debutante sensation Brenda Frazier and Mina Miller Edison (wife of Thomas Edison). The artist said she had to be firm with her subjects from the United States in order to get them to slow down and pose, as "they lead a life of such perpetual activity." Alice had no interest in having her portrait done, but Teach insisted, and she acquiesced. Vicaji demanded compliance from Alice, five sittings in all. Bold colors distinguish the artist's work: "I love luminous color. Color is sunlight, and sunlight, you know, is happiness."[59] Vicaji made Alice look like a sunburst framed by a sunburst. In the portrait, Alice's face, surrounded by blond curls, bore a self-assured, even regal expression, her posture ramrod straight, her future golden.

When Teach finally glimpsed the finished product, she zoomed in on the one element that disappointed her. Always proud of the signature racket Wilson Sporting Goods had named after her, and often claiming to be the first person ever to have had such a tribute, she was dismayed when she did not see her name clearly spelled out on the racket in the painting, amazed that an artist of any magnitude would ignore such a salient detail.[60]

Alice joked with Teach and the artist, "If I lose in the early rounds, my portrait will probably end up in some smoky bar," to which Teach replied, "Then see that you don't!"[61]

Five hundred dollars for the finished project far exceeded Alice's budget, but it pleased her to know that among the artist's other subjects had been Queen Alexandra of the United Kingdom. Marble always appreciated good company.

The theme of beauty continued when Britain's *Daily Mirror* sponsored a contest to name the fairest of all the female tennis players. On June 14, 1938, the paper ran the results of a reader-driven poll as part of the buildup to the upcoming Wimbledon competition. The *Mirror* had given readers a list of fifteen players and seven categories—vivacity, poise, style, confidence, sociability, figure, and sportsmanship. Readers could give up to ten points for each attribute. Naturally, Kay Stammers, the favored local daughter, won, though the newspaper made it sound close: "Competition was keen, for Kay Stammers was only a few points ahead of Helen Wills Moody. Followed in order Anita Lizana, Helen Jacobs, Betty Nuthall and Alice Marble—the glamour six of big lawn tennis."

Alice drew in fans of her own. The *Daily Mirror* said one reader "went all lyrical" with a poem:

Alice Marble, glamour girl,
Looks like Venus, but she's real.

I love to see her on the courts,
Cute and smart in week-end shorts.
Every time she hits a ball
Men feel small, she's so tall.
Alice plays a sporting game,
Really she deserves her fame.
But I hope when she has won
Lots of prizes, she'll have fun,
Ere she leaves our Wimbledon.

And a nineteen-year-old fan "waxes eloquent": "I choose Alice Marble because I admire her for her plucky fight back after her serious illness. She has beauty both of face and form, and an inner beauty which we call charm or personality."

Helen Wills Moody, back on the scene from a three-year retirement, was favored to win at Wimbledon, with Alice as second seed. Jacobs was unseeded. Yet no one thought Moody was a shoo-in. One tournament official noted that "time was catching up with her."[62]

News that Suzanne Lenglen was ill haunted the matches. In 1933, she had launched a career in coaching, and in May 1938 she was appointed inaugural director of the French National Tennis School in Paris. She had grown mysteriously and precipitously weak in the middle of June. Diagnosed with anemia, she did not improve despite several blood transfusions. The word from Lenglen's sickbed was that she was following the tournament, eager for scores and gossip.

Cruising through the early rounds, Alice faced Simonne Mathieu of France in the quarterfinals, winning the first set and falling behind in the second before settling on a strategy of lobs and drop shots that carried her to victory. She then squared off once again against Helen Jacobs in the semifinals. As the Associated Press reported, "One heart-breaking shot, followed by a flash of anger, led to the downfall of Alice Marble of San Francisco in her celebrated match with Helen Jacobs of Berkeley here today."[63]

The single shot that led to ultimate defeat occurred in the tenth game of the first set. Ahead 5–4, Jacobs had launched a weak lob just above the net. It was, according to onlookers, a perfect setup, and Marble belted it, but it landed on top of the net and rolled back to her feet. Her immediate loss of decorum spelled doom.

"Furious, she took a wicked kick at it and sent it aloft," the AP report continued. "Miss Jacobs, calm in the face of this storm, battered back the San Francisco girl's next three services and won game and set."

Hazel Wightman observed the play and knew in the moment that Alice had lost the match.

Jacobs won the second set by the same score, and Alice later acknowledged, "Helen made fewer than twelve errors in two sets. She was on; I was not."[64]

Hazel Wightman was far more impassioned when she laced into Alice. As she bungled the shot, she should have immediately adopted a fighter's stance. Instead, Alice had played shamelessly to the crowd. Wightman continued: "While you were amusing everyone you netted two more simple shots and tossed Helen the set. Your mind wasn't on your tennis. It took you two full games before you were back in business, and after that you never caught up. Even a girl with your natural equipment can't win if she allows *anything* to break her concentration."[65]

The final singles match began on a mournful note: an announcement over the loudspeaker informed the crowd that Suzanne Lenglen was near death.

Helen Jacobs was given a good shot against Helen Wills Moody, but she had hurt her right Achilles tendon, and it soon became clear to spectators that Jacobs not only could not run, she could barely walk. Yet she made every effort to return any shot that she could. The vision of Jacobs dragging herself across the court and continuing to play despite the obvious pain cemented her reputation for sportsmanship and stood in stark contrast to the inglorious moment, five years earlier, when Moody forsook Jacobs mid-match because of a bad back at Forest Hills. Moody won (6–4, 6–0)—her nineteenth and last Grand Slam title. Later, *Life* magazine reported that Jacobs had limped off the court in tears. Jacobs urged the publication to examine its own photos, in which there was no evidence of tears, demanding, and getting, a retraction.

Alice took top honors in both women's doubles and mixed doubles. She and Sarah Palfrey beat Simonne Mathieu and Adeline "Billie" Yorke (6–2, 6–3), and she and Don Budge defended their title, beating Palfrey and Henner Henkel in mixed doubles (6–1, 6–4).[66] Alice felt entitled to hold her head high at the Wimbledon Ball, though she was not pleased when Samuel Hoare, chairman of Wimbledon, described her as "the girl who's so very nice, but never wins" or when Ambassador Kennedy told her she had better hurry up and "do it soon" if she wanted to win the Wimbledon crown, because "there's going to be a war that will make all of us forget about tennis."[67] Disappointed as she was not to take the singles prize, she managed some light humor, telling a London paper, "Well, apparently I did come over here for the boat ride."[68]

Alice accepted an invitation to Lady Domini Crosfield's annual fund-raising party, one of those posh events with an underlying charitable purpose that at least partially obviates the excess. Guests roamed the eleven acres of the Crosfield mansion, with its rose garden and tennis courts. They paid to watch more tennis. At one earlier such event, the Duke of York (before he became King George VI) and Winston Churchill's wife, Clementine, had played in the matches. The party benefited the North Islington Infant Welfare Centre, of which Lady Crosfield was chairwoman. The center focused on malnutrition, a dire threat for the poor.

A pictorial in the *Sketch* showed Alice outdoors at the party, seated in a lawn chair, wearing mid-thigh shorts, ankle socks, cap, legs crossed, her feet resting on a rug. She was chatting with Princess Helena Victoria, granddaughter of Queen Victoria, by then well into her sixties, who was cloaked in dark garments. They appear to be engaged and friendly.

But Alice's skimpy tennis shorts caused their own stir, according to the column Miss Sketch's Diary, which offered a solution: "Lawn tennis stars were presented to the royal spectators and had some conversations with them. Mrs. Wills Moody's abbreviated but pleated attire allowed her to curtsy very gracefully, but the short shorts, worn by Miss Marble and some of the other well-known players were not so well adapted for sweeping a deep reverence. Wondered if it wouldn't be better for official ruling to be made instructing ladies wearing sports attire to make deep bows instead of giving the customary curtsy."[69]

ON JULY 4, two days after Wimbledon ended, Suzanne Lenglen died, of what was finally diagnosed as leukemia. The obituary in the *New York Times* emphasized both her dramatic personality and her skills as an athlete: "A genius of the court, Mlle. Lenglen had all the temperament of a great artiste. Her public life was a tale of foot-stampings, defiance and tears—a veritable comic opera in a tennis setting."[70] An editorial summarized her impact: "Whether or not she was the greatest in her field, Suzanne Lenglen was by easy odds the most colorful. . . . She never had a rival in accuracy and scientific placement. . . . She played so furiously that few could face her. Perhaps she wrote her own epitaph when she said, 'I just throw dignity to the winds and think of nothing but the game.'"[71]

In the aftermath of Wimbledon, *American Lawn Tennis* offered a verdict on Marble's game:

> *It seems certain that the women's game of the future will be of the masculine, all round style whose leading exponent today is Alice Marble. Sir Samuel Hoare hit the nail on the head when he said, during her match with Helen Jacobs, "Miss Marble is beating herself." He did not mean by that to lessen the merit of Miss Jacob's win but he was deploring the frightful errors Miss Marble made at 3-all in the first set. When Eleanor Tennant's pupil learns how to wait for the proper moment for a net advance, in other words when she is less impatient, she will be the best in the world. This grand volleyer has already made remarkable progress in her ground strokes.*[72]

AFTER WIMBLEDON, Alice and Teach took a quick consolation trip to the Continent, where fun-loving Roz Bloomingdale Cowen had a bead on a casino in Le Touquet, in the north of France on the English Channel. Once a wasteland of wild dunes (not unlike the Sunset District of San Francisco), the little town had turned into a popular seaside resort in the 1920s and a favorite spot of, among others, playwright Noel Coward. Cowen treated everyone in her party to luxurious hotel rooms.

Teach and Roz hit the gaming tables while Marble remained with Cowen's son Alfred Bloomingdale,[73] three years younger than she was, hobbled by self-consciousness about not being taller. They found themselves covering for each other's nascent love lives. Alfred had his eyes on a young woman, but he did not want his mother to know. In the hotel lobby, Marble ran into a man from Switzerland who had attended Wimbledon and recognized her in this new setting. Much later, in her autobiography, *Courting Danger*, she called him Hans Steinmetz, a pseudonym, and said that she accepted his invitation for drinks at a quiet bar and later to stroll by the water, where the surefire formula of sand, bare feet, music, and moonlight kicked in. After a long kiss, he spread his jacket on the beach and pulled her gently down beside him. "I moved into the circle of his arms as naturally as if we had been lovers for years. And we were to be lovers, I knew. I wanted him, with an urgency that had been building for years. I opened myself to him, welcoming the strange, ultimate bliss that came with our union, our moving together as one. At that moment, we were the only life on the planet, perhaps in the whole universe, and the stars were singing."[74]

Maybe the stars really did sing. Teach evidently thought so and, furious, ordered Alice to break it off. Secret meetups followed, with young Alfred serving as the alibi and lookout while the two lovers tooled around the countryside in a convertible, stopping along riverbanks for picnics. When Teach caught on, she delivered an ultimatum: "You've had your fun. Now end it. Or find another coach."[75]

The breakup, ordered by Teach, has a breathless quality in Alice's recounting from across the vale of years:

> He kissed the top of my head. "Was it bad?"
>
> "The worst. I have to stop seeing you."
>
> ". . . She's afraid I'll hurt you. I can talk to her, tell her we love each other. Then she'll understand."
>
> ". . . She won't ever understand. We can't see each other . . . at all."
>
> For a moment there was silence, except for the sound of his heart beneath my ear.
>
> "Teach and tennis mean more to you than I do?"
>
> "No!" I hit his chest with my fist. "Don't you ever think that! I love you! I've never loved anyone ever. But I've told you all Teach has done for me. She saved my life, Hans, and she made me a champion. I can't do this to her."[76]

DURING A DESPONDENT CROSSING BACK to the United States, Alice recognized that even if she wished to see Hans again, she had no idea of how to get in touch with him.

Good fortune came Alice's way at the Seabright tournament when she won the singles for the third year in a row, earning the trophy, a silver bowl, "one of the most-prized pieces of tennis silver."[77] Adding to the joy of her new possession, her victory was over Dorothy Bundy. (She also won the women's doubles with Sarah Palfrey and the mixed doubles with Hal Surface.)

Alice skipped the Maidstone tournament because, according to one reporter, the club "marks the spot where a sunstroke put a dramatic interval, and almost a full stop, to her tennis career" five years earlier.[78] Whatever the reason, Alice was battle-ready for the next contests.

At the Rye, New York, championships, Marble delivered the "best tennis of the tournament" in fourth-round play. Her opponent was "not playing badly," observed *American Lawn Tennis*. "It was, rather, she never had the opportunity to hit the ball." Alice "hit everything as hard as possible, and nearly every shot was a winner." She won the singles, and she and Sarah Palfrey again won the women's doubles.[79]

Alice then sailed through the Essex County Club tournament, winning the singles and the doubles again with Sarah Palfrey,[80] and at the Longwood Cricket Club, she won the women's title with Sarah Palfrey and the mixed doubles with Don Budge.

Finally, at the US Nationals at Forest Hills, Alice blew through the first three matches to reach the quarterfinals, against Kay Stammers, losing the first set but winning the deciding third set in a rout, 6–8, 6–3, 6–0.

At this point the massive hurricane of 1938 interrupted play for an entire week. After the storm, the details of the full damage came to light: over seven hundred people were killed, forty-five hundred houses and farms were destroyed, and an untold number of trees toppled over when the combination of flooding and high winds disrupted the contact of their roots with the soil.

When the tournament resumed, after the turf had recovered from wind and rain damage, the semifinal between Sarah Palfrey and Marble was "a see-saw contest." Marble jumped to a 5–1 lead in the first set, then Palfrey won the next nine games in a row. Marble responded with, as Allison Danzig wrote in the *New York Times*, "tennis that was simply invincible in its power and control." Facing tennis match points at 2–5 in the second set, she reeled off five straight games and won the third set and match, 7–5.

Danzig observed that Palfrey lost "under heartbreaking circumstances. But at least she had the satisfaction of knowing that she had failed not because of any deficiencies on her part but owing to the magnificent shot-making of her opponent."[81]

The finals were an easy win for Marble against the Australian player Nancye Wynne.[82] The twenty-two-year-old Wynne was a long shot to begin with. A bit of a party girl who hand-rolled her cigarettes, she was, by her own admission, loud and tall and smoked a lot. Her attitude of not taking things seriously netted her the nickname "Nonchalant Nancye."[83]

"It was actually more one-sided than the 6–0, 6–3 score indicates," *American Lawn Tennis* reported. "Miss Wynne could do no right and showed no signs of working out of it. Miss Marble rightfully kept up the pace, a very fast one by which she won the first set with the loss of only eight points. She made five placements and only four errors, leaving the latter to her opponent. It is possible that never has a woman displayed such controlled average speed of shot as Miss Marble."[84] At least thirteen thousand fans had witnessed the shellacking, with tickets selling for up to twenty-five dollars. The first set lasted seven minutes, the second twenty-two, the final over in record time.

Alice Marble was big sports news as someone who had fallen and risen again, but the title of number-one newsmaker in the country belonged not to a person but to Seabiscuit, the horse that beat War Admiral at Baltimore's Pimlico Race Course on November 1, 1938, in the "race of the century." Forty million people tuned into that race by radio, including President Franklin D. Roosevelt, who paused the government for one minute and fifty-six seconds to listen to the commentators. The stoic "people's horse" beat his more refined competition by an amazing four lengths. In the elite levels of horse racing, the relatively small Seabiscuit was cast as a mongrel, an upstart, even a juvenile delinquent. When he won, it was as if he had carried every person in the United States of humble origin or conditions to a new and better finish line or at least provided the hope of one.

Alice was also big fashion news. Marble enjoyed the limelight as a taste-maker, engaged in designing a "line of sports clothes under her own name," reported the Associated Press. "And one of her best-known patrons is one of the well-dressed women of the screen, Carole Lombard."[85] Sportswriter Curley Grieve called her a "full-fledged stylist in women's sports clothes."[86]

"As far as I am concerned," wrote Babette, the *San Francisco Examiner*'s fashion columnist, Marble's designs "have all the details you want sport clothes to have. Nothing tricky. Nothing flashy. But with lots of character."[87]

"It's getting to be the 'road they travel'—first championships in tennis, or some other sport, and then on to designing and our costume world!" wrote a fashion columnist in the *Santa Cruz Sentinel*, mentioning that Marble was out and about promoting her clothes. "But what woman—in her soul—hasn't wanted to be both actress and designer at some happy day-dreaming moment of her life?"[88]

At no point did Marble make clear how much money came from the use of her name on these various garments or how much work she did, if any, but the field of fashion never translated into a post-tennis career. If nothing else, Marble's involvement fed Teach's instinctive attraction to publicity and her perceived need to keep Marble before the public whenever possible.

In any event, Alice was feeling good about herself. Now restored to tennis stardom on the home front, she hatched a plan. She had achieved renown in one field, tennis, and was gaining attention in another. Perhaps she could do so in a third.

CHAPTER 16

DEBUT TONIGHT!

As Cole Porter wrote, "It was just one of those things, Just one of those crazy flings."

The Waldorf-Astoria hotel on New York's Park Avenue had a job opening for a soloist. Alice had often confided her love of singing to interviewers, and a talent agency had called Alice out of the blue in November 1938, asking whether she could she come in for a tryout right away. She would be auditioning in front of orchestra leader Emil Coleman, familiar from the party when she got to sing "Pennies from Heaven," and Lucius Boomer, the president of the Waldorf-Astoria—two busy men used to acting decisively. The audition was over in a matter of minutes.

Marble sang about four bars. She thought they could at least pay her the courtesy of sitting through an entire song, but Coleman quickly said, "I think she'll do fine."[1]

Boomer informed her she would open in eleven days.

The moment Alice was offered a contract to sing at the hotel's famous Sert Room—and to stay at the hotel—she encountered an array of amenities. Each additional luxury revealed the gap between her backwoods origins and the world stage that now beckoned. The hotel was the first to offer room service (breakfast in bed) and the first in America to have a men's barbershop and a women's beauty salon.[2] Indulgence was everywhere: rooms imported from English manor houses and reassembled at the hotel, Art Deco designs, the two-tiered Grand Ballroom.[3] Boomer had written a 519-page manifesto, *Hotel Management*, on running the ideal hotel. "The perfect host," he wrote, "whether in his own home or in his hotel, seems to know instinctively what little services will please. He knows which should be rendered automatically and which only upon request. A too persistent effort to serve is sometimes as annoying as lack of service." Boomer quoted the creed of another hotelier: "to afflict them with no unwarranted assistance."[4]

Services at the Waldorf met every wish: hat cleaning, trunk packing and unpacking, ladies' dress repairing, tailoring, a newsstand with about forty newspapers from cities outside New York City, a haberdashery, a brokerage, and theater ticket offices. Cigar clerks were told: "Personal taste is not a matter of argument."[5] At tearooms and candy shops, workers had to maintain a "constant and unfailing atmosphere of courtesy and hospitality. No patron or visitor should ever come through the door of the shop without receiving *immediately* a smiling, friendly greeting." Alice, as was the Waldorf custom, would be addressed as "madam."[6] The saleswomen delivering greetings would be clad in black shoes, stockings, and dresses "of a conservative style," with no jewelry, costume or otherwise. In the summer months, they were permitted to wear white instead of black as long as everyone coordinated ahead of time.[7]

The hotel offered state-of-the-art communications: not just telephones in the rooms but also radios, with a choice of six programs, and "in the not distant future," management envisioned a similar supply of televisions.[8]

The hotel was like a palace for rent—for overnight, for the week, even for life. Lyricist Cole Porter made his home within its walls for thirty years, in a ten-room suite in the Waldorf Towers. Porter wrote the musical *Anything Goes* in which the song "You're the Top" gave a nod to the hotel: *You're the top, you're a Waldorf salad / You're the top, you're a Berlin ballad.*[9]

The hotel opened in 1931, at the very time when, as the poet Langston Hughes pointed out, "people were sleeping on newspapers in doorways, because they had no place to go." Seven years later the repercussions of the Depression continued to affect the country, and Hughes latched onto the Waldorf-Astoria as a place that embodied the magnitude of the gap between rich and poor: "Suites in the Waldorf ran into thousands a year, and dinner in the Sert Room was ten dollars! (Negroes, even if they had the money, couldn't eat there. So naturally, I didn't care much for the Waldorf-Astoria.)."[10] His poem "Advertisement for the Waldorf-Astoria" made his dislike clear, mimicking an ad in *Vanity Fair* magazine promoting the hotel's opening. In six parts ("Listen Hungry Ones!," "Roomers," "Evicted Families," "Negroes," "Everybody," "Christmas Card"), he satirized the hotel's splendor and invited all the poor to enjoy the new hotel's sweet frills, to swap sleeping in subways for suites, to sample the delights of "peach melba" and "small onions in cream." Homeless families should live at the hotel because, after all, "$10,000 and $1.00 are about the same to you, aren't they?"

The Waldorf told a different tale. Intent on billing itself as a symbol of prosperity even in hard times, the hotel carried on as if everything was just fine. During periods of low occupancy, chambermaids had orders to turn on the lights in empty rooms so the building would look less spectral.[11]

On Thanksgiving Day, a week before Alice's opening night, a blizzard hit New York and other parts of the eastern United States.[12] The next day, November 25, Marble gave interviews in the Waldorf-Astoria's Jansen Suite, one of three suites on the fourth floor set aside for gatherings, with its own vestibule, reception area, and dining room. Outside, workers were clearing snowy roads and sidewalks. Inside, Marble was "shivering delicately," as the International News Service reported under the headline, "Tennis Champion Goes Glamouring":

> *Equipped with a diaphanous gown of scarlet tulle and a full complement of woolen undergarments, Alice Marble, 25, National Women's tennis champion, is prepared to make her debut as a café singer in the Sert room at the Waldorf-Astoria next Thursday night.*
>
> *The gown was chosen by the fair-haired, green-eyed queen of American tennis herself, one lady athlete who is a sight for sore eyes. But the woollies are the contribution of her tennis coach and business manager, Eleanor Tennant.*
>
> *"I've never been in the East before in the winter," said sunny California's Miss Marble today, shivering delicately in the Waldorf's Janssen [sic] suite as New York tried to shovel its way out of the season's first blizzard. "The snow looks beautiful but I wouldn't touch it for anything."*
>
> *"We don't know what to do in cold weather," added Miss Tennant, who thought up the woolen underwear as one solution.*
>
> *When Miss Marble dons the scarlet gown next Thursday night, she will be further proof that lady athletes can be glamour girls and not, of necessity, muscle molls. She will also be taking the first note in what she fondly hopes will be a radio career.*
>
> *"If I were a good singer, I'd be called a contralto," she said with becoming modesty. "I love to sing and it's really fun."*

This was not the first time Alice had flirted with a career as a performer, although the screen test she took in late winter 1937 under Carole Lombard's guidance was not as successful as she liked to imply: "The director had me wear a brightly colored spangled dress and a black wig. He sat me on a piano and had me sing the song, 'My Bill,' from the movie, 'Showboat.' Imagine an outdoor girl dressed like that, seated on that dammn [sic] piano and singing the words, 'along came Bill?'" She was so wooden that her performance was good for only laughs. Clark Gable had secured a copy of her acting audition tape and evidently agreed. Alice took what might have seemed like an insult in stride: "Clark Gable bought it and made it into a comedy film and would show it at parties. It was hilarious. We all took it as a joke."[13]

Nonetheless, the desire for the more realistic possibility of a singing career still simmered. Carole Lombard had paid for voice lessons in 1935 when Alice was recovering from her collapse, with the full approval of Teach, who believed singing opened the lungs and led to increased stamina. Thanks to Lombard, Alice trained with some of the most prominent vocalists of her day, including opera singer Nina Koshetz.[14] Marble also studied with Ted Straeter, who worked on "God Bless America" singer Kate Smith's show.[15]

Alice made it into *Life* magazine on December 5, 1938, joining a trend that season of young women looking to croon in front of an audience. "All over Manhattan," the magazine reported, "society girls are now singing and crooning and moaning into microphones. More than half the current singers in the expensive East Side cafes are socialites singing for champagne suppers. A few of them need money, work hard. But most want publicity and glamour and do little work." Alice was singled out as an exception: "A new kind of society singer is Alice Marble, U.S. tennis champion, who sang in a choir when she was a girl." The choir credential created a sanctimonious glow, handy under the circumstances.

On Thursday, December 1, 1938, a Shirley Temple movie was about to open at the Roxy on 153 West Fiftieth Street. The title, *Just Around the Corner*, took on unintended menace given the historic upheaval on the horizon. A front-page story in the *New York Times* indicated the growing turmoil in Europe: JEWS' MOVEMENTS LIMITED BY NAZIS.

The *Times* quoted a German newspaper, which had called the United States a "land of lynch justice, kidnapping, false prophets and strip dancers. . . . While America mixes in the most violent manner in the inner affairs of Germany and laments over the Jews without helping them, it forgets completely to attend to its own affairs. They are dirty enough and we all have reason enough to remind them."

The economic prospects of New Yorkers could be seen in the Help Wanted section of the paper. The few lucrative opportunities, as accountants, dentists, architects, and veterinarians, were for men only. Women had the chance to be stenographers, but only if they met specific physical or ethnic or religious requirements from prospective employees, as in the ad seeking an "attractive Jewess Bklyn." One job required not just "knowledge of the plugboard" (an old-fashioned electrical switchboard); the successful candidate also had to evince "personality."

The *Queen Mary* was set to dock at West Fiftieth Street at six p.m. Corn led the grain market, and cotton sales were on the rise. If money were no object, a Persian lamb coat could be purchased for $295 or a Cadillac for $795. The rink at Rockefeller Center was available to skaters for ninety-nine cents, a bargain by comparison. And for anyone seeking an escape from the sense of dread over the history unfolding abroad or the economic travails at home, a small ad in the back pages of the *New York Times* offered relief in its promise of frivolity.

The Sert Room
Paul Draper
Emil Coleman
and His Orchestra
Debut tonight!
Alice Marble
Songs
Two performances Nightly
Dinner and Supper Dancing
The Waldorf Astoria

Earlier, some concern had been raised that Alice's new career might be against USLTA regulations, but after consideration, the organization ruled there was no conflict, as the singing bore no relationship to her status as an amateur tennis player. Alice was paid considerably more than a plugboard operator, even one with a good personality. On opening night, she wore a red dress, one of two gowns she bought for $600 together at an elegant couturier store. "They cost a week's salary,"[16] she later revealed. Alice would wear the red dress at future events, but the manager at the hotel did not like the color and preferred she stick to the other, more sedate selection, with its bolero jacket, cummerbund, and gathered skirt.

Alice performed in the Sert Room, named for Josep María Sert, the Catalan artist who created fifteen murals in the room celebrating Don Quixote, painted in black and silver with a "sufficient infusion of rose to heighten the brilliance of the ensemble."[17]

She liked to launch each performance with a song by Arthur Schwartz and Howard Dietz, a recent hit tune in the Broadway musical *Between the Devil*.

The evening roared with success as the room filled up with air kisses and heartbreak songs. Her admirers called her "a peach" and "a honey" and said she was "wonderfully marvelous." She returned the phrases in kind, calling her fans "darlings."

She said she sang sad songs because her voice was low and husky, and she could not reach the high notes. She said she liked the light-hearted songs, but the low register of her voice made them impossible to sing, claiming that as a teen, her voice became a baritone. She joked that the only way she would ever be able to hit high C was with a tennis racket.

One member of the audience, the actress Gloria Swanson, gave tips to Alice on how to improve. Swanson had been the highest-paid silent movie star, so she knew a thing or two about gesture language. She said she liked Marble's voice, but her delivery was without emotion, "like the English actor who when he says, 'I love you' might just as well be asking for a cup of weak tea."[18]

Swanson told her, Alice recalled, that "I seemed afraid to make any gesture for fear I would overdo it. My voice showed feeling, but my face never changed, no matter how gay or how sad the song." Marble attributed the lack of emotion to the game face she had cultivated over the years. Tennis "required concentration, and concentration has a way of making one look serious. I had learned to control my temper, my joy or disappointment and my facial expression rarely changed no matter how keenly I felt anything. Therefore, in my singing, although I am incurably romantic and sentimental, I found it difficult to register on my face the things I felt inside."[19] In a longer review of entertainment at the Sert Room published more than a month later on January 28, 1939, Sol Zatt of *Billboard* gave Marble two sentences: "Also on the bill is tennis champion Alice Marble, who has turned singer. Why?"

Others were more effusive. *American Lawn Tennis* reported that "one feminine scribe asserted that the audience could not have been more enthusiastic if Miss Marble had been Flagstad,"[20] referring to the Norwegian star soprano Kirsten Flagstad.

Alice Hughes, in her newspaper column A Woman's New York, expressed delight.

> *Everyone who can sing a lick wants to unloose her best notes in New York, believing from this dot on the map stretch those radio contracts, those Hollywood careers, those pictures in the papers. Bless their trusting little tonsils! . . . The deboo I really hung back for was that of Alice Marble, the tennis champ in the Sert Room of the Waldorf. I wanted to see if anyone who looked so lovely on the court in short shorts could sing pretty in a café. The answer is yes, she could. . . . Nice work, Alice old kid—and you can get it!*[21]

A *New Yorker* ad suggested making New Year's Eve reservations. Of all the expressions of goodwill that came her way, none rivaled the irony in the nod from Julian Myrick, who sent Alice a telegram, wishing her "every success" and expressing the hope that she might one day end up at the Metropolitan Opera.[22] Not everyone approved of Marble's new career. She was besieged with letters from fans who "seemed to think I was deserting the clean sports world for one of smoky night clubs filled with drunken people."[23] She said that was not the case, but the negative reaction made her realize tennis in fact came first.

A few days into the new year, George Tucker, author of a column called Man about Manhattan, shared a cup of tea with Alice in her suite at the Waldorf where she told him how much she enjoyed singing in the Sert Room. She downplayed rumors that she might abandon tennis for a full-time singing career, confirming she played every day, indoors at this time of year. Eleanor Tennant sat in on the interview, predicting that one day her "masterpiece" would rival, if not outstrip, Lenglen and Tilden as a great tennis legend.

In mid-February 1939, Alice gave up her Sert Room gig. If her point had been to establish her star quality, that mission was accomplished. Even a staid personage such as Hazel Wightman noticed that quality. When asked years later which woman player she admired the most, she responded: "That's a difficult question to answer. I would say that up through the first era, the era I knew best, it was Suzanne Lenglen. She was so homely . . . but she was graceful, a wonderful player. And Helen Wills, of course. . . . And Alice Marble. Alice was the first girl who became sensational."[24]

CHAPTER 17

JULY 8, 1939

B ACK IN CALIFORNIA, Marble received some happy news from Hollywood about her two favorite movie stars. Clark Gable's divorce from Houston socialite Maria Langham was final, and he was free to marry Carole Lombard. During a break in his shooting schedule of *Gone with the Wind*, he and Lombard eloped in Kingman, Arizona, on March 29, 1939.

By the end of May, the press was back to reporting on Marble the athlete. The headline in a Maryland paper proclaimed:[1]

ONLY MARBLE CAN BEAT MARBLE IN ENGLISH TOURNEY

The subhead drew a powerful comparison:

U.S. CHAMPION SAILS FOR ENGLAND WITH GAME COMPARABLE TO LENGLEN'S

"We are here," Teach announced on their arrival, "to commit tennis murder."[2] The striking phrase matched her striking appearance, the skull-clinging snow-white hair contrasting with what one observer called an "olive, almost waxed complexion that resembled that of a Tibetan monk."[3] She obviously had not learned any lessons about bragging in advance.

The 1939 season could only be called subdued, despite Teach's bloodthirsty sloganeering. Intermittent rains throughout the tournament dampened everyone's spirits. The threat of Hitler made the national mood both jumpy and dispirited. The German dictator had been pressuring Bulgaria lately, attempting to secure its loyalty in a squeeze play against Romania and Greece. Jews in Germany faced a "crushing task" according to the *New York Times*.[4] A new decree required that one-fourth of the Jewish population, in addition to paying "the highest taxes possible under German law," was now responsible to "feed, clothe and educate the overwhelming majority of Jews in Germany who have no income." The threat of war loomed such that defense workers in France were told they could not take their usual summer vacations until October, so as not to jeopardize output.

Alice and Teach stayed at the Hyde Park Hotel, the epitome of London at its most elegant. Assigned to room 803, Teach asked for a change. The numbers added up to eleven, which she believed was an unlucky number. Alice came up with a quick fix. She asked the hoteliers to change the number to 802-A for the length of their stay.

Royal-watchers wondered whether Queen Mary, the queen mother, would be able to attend Wimbledon. An avid motorist, like most members of the royal family, she had experienced a fright earlier in the spring. On Wednesday, May 24, 1939, the day before her seventy-second birthday, her car had collided with a truck at a dangerous intersection in southwest London. Despite her advanced years, she had climbed out of the vehicle and walked to a nearby house, where she waited for another car to take her home. Doctors indicated there were no serious injuries, just shock and bruising. Her presence in the royal box in Centre Court always brightened the mood of the games, as had the presence of her husband, King George V. When he died in 1936, their eldest son took the throne as King Edward VIII, and Mary became queen mother, though she preferred the title Her Majesty Queen Mary. Edward soon abdicated the throne to marry the American Wallis Simpson, to be replaced by another son, affectionately known as Bertie, who became King George VI. The government had recently promulgated the slogan, "Keep calm and carry on," which fit Mary perfectly.

As always, the state of the grass was scrutinized: "Wimbledon's turf is dieted and fed to make it durable and velvety. Such a common thing as rain is not allowed on the main courts. . . . A week or so before the games start, up to ten men comb the grass on their hands and knees. . . . Not a daisy or a blade of coarse grass was allowed to show its vulgar head."[5]

Eddie Fuller, a man of serious mien, himself almost as lean as a grass blade, was serving his twenty-third year as head groundskeeper. Among his assistants, starlings hunted "ceaselessly for the leatherjackets which, unmolested, would ruin the turf."[6] He could be seen all year, roaming the premises, inspecting his kingdom of chlorophyll and cellulose, ensuring that each blade was or eventually would be the prescribed height and density.

Just prior to the tournament's start, the *Daily Mail* assessed Alice, the women's favorite. The paper identified three chief rivals: Helen Jacobs, "quiet and undemonstrative, also practices strenuously"; Ja-Ja Jedrzejowska, "hardest forehand drive of any woman playing"; and "our own glamorous Kay Stammers," of whom the paper said, "People will be surprised to see how thin she has got lately. Indeed, Kay has been trying to put on weight by drinking quarts of milk daily."[7]

Stammers went so far as to predict she would make it to at least the semifinals in women's singles, having corrected her grip on her forehand, saying, "I suppose it is immodest to tip myself, but I do think I have as good a chance as others."[8]

Alice had sounded even more confident during an earlier interview with the *San Francisco Examiner*: "The first time I went to Wimbledon I said I would never quit until I win that championship. This, I believe, is my year. I have won all the other championships I hoped to win when I started playing. Now if I can get this one, I will be satisfied."

She added, "No, I may not quit tennis if I win, but at least I will be able to if I care to. I will have reached the goal I set for myself when I started."[9]

IN THE QUARTERFINALS, Kay Stammers beat Helen Jacobs, 6–2, 6–2; and Marble dispatched the challenging Ja-Ja Jedrzejowska, also in two sets, 6–1, 6–4. Sarah Palfrey Fabyan beat Simonne Mathieu, 6–4, 6–0; and the German-Danish player Hilde Sperling beat Mary Hardwick, 6–4, 6–0. Stammers then dispatched Palfrey Fabyan, 7–5, 2–6, 6–3, in the first semifinal. Despite an ill-advised indulgence in sweets beforehand (the match began earlier than Marble had expected, and she feared the sugar might make her sluggish) and the challenges of a wet surface and bad weather, Marble overwhelmed Hilde Sperling in the other semifinal in less than twenty minutes, 6–0, 6–0, in a brilliantly efficient display, setting up the final against Britain's favorite. Alice had equal success in women's and mixed doubles; playing with Palfrey Fabyan and Bobby Riggs, respectively, she reached her second and third finals, all three to be contested on July 8.

The day before, the men's singles final was played between two Americans and was regarded as hugely disappointing. Bobby Riggs and his opponent, Elwood Cooke, played so lackadaisically, spectators and commentators alike agreed, they could have easily been mistaken for two pals at a country club engaged in a seemingly endless afternoon of friendly volleys. Fans fled, and the press scolded the players for their subpar performance.

Clifford Webb's column As I See Wimbledon in the *Daily Herald* captured the disappointment: "Robert L. Riggs, 21-year-old Californian, won the men's singles championship at Wimbledon, beating another American,

Elwood T. Cooke, 2–6, 8–6, 3–6, 6–3, 6–2, in a 130-minute final that was almost incredibly lacking in thrills. . . . There were Robot rallies containing so many perfect strokes that it seemed impossible for either player to make a mistake. . . . After two sets, there was a centre-court exodus the like of which has not been seen on a Wimbledon finals day for many a year."

Columnist Godfrey Winn was equally disappointed: "For has there ever been a drearier match between two young men of supposed world class who played throughout their encounter as though they were taking part in a practice knock-up on a private court, politely returning the ball well within each other's reach."

Riggs had a playing style that both intrigued and infuriated fellow players. Don Budge gave a piercing analysis of how Riggs liked to toy with his opponents, with the ability to raise and lower his game at will: "Riggs was like a race horse that stays head and head, whatever the pace, and then takes off on his own whim and wins by ten lengths down the stretch. That was Bobby. Against someone whom he could obviously whip, his whole game was suddenly cat-and-mouse. He'd drop shot, lob, lose interest (and a few games), slice and spin—but always make it very obvious to all that he could win when he really wanted to. And then he would."[10]

It thus fell to the women to save the day and play quality tennis in the singles championship, a challenge made greater for Marble because during one of the two victorious doubles semifinals, she had stretched to hit a smash and felt a slight twitch in her abdomen. She thought it was nothing more than a passing spasm, but the next morning, the day of the finals, she woke up unable to move. Teach immediately summoned the hotel doctor, who diagnosed a torn stomach muscle. He asked Teach's assistance in helping Alice sit up so he could tape the injured area. Alice begged to know whether she could play: "I'm in three finals today. I can't default." The doctor did not forbid her to play but said it would be painful and she should not expect to excel. Marble steeled herself for the worst: "I just prayed, please dear God, don't let me make a fool of myself."[11]

Just before the opening, groundkeeper Eddie Fuller knelt to appraise the grass, observed by a reporter from the *Daily Mail*. Bespectacled, dressed in a dark suit with a vest and a hat, he tested the sod with his long fingers, taking pleasure in the hardiness of his handiwork at Centre Court. "He peered through glasses, shot a hand through already rumpled sandy hair, and said: 'Reckon she don't look so bad. Rain done her a lot of good.'"[12]

Marble strode onto the court, her countenance as impassive as possible to mask the pain from her pulled stomach muscle. She wore the tennis pin given to her by Teach that she had mistakenly thought she had lost before the trip to France in 1934—her good-luck charm. The press made note of her fashion choices for all three of the finals: all in white for ladies' doubles, with a pink cardigan and blue cap for mixed doubles, and for the singles final, a blue cardigan and white cap and abbreviated shorts with a hip pocket.

The stands were nearly full, enthusiasm having remained high despite the dismal Riggs–Cooke match the day before, many hoping the homegrown Stammers could somehow overcome Marble's power. Some spectators had lined up overnight,[13] camping out as they sought admission, a ritual that impressed Marble with the length to which British fans were willing to go.

For her part, the queen mother had not let the car accident keep her away and was ensconced in the royal box along with the American ambassador to the Court of St. James's, Joseph Kennedy, and his wife, Rose. Onlookers swore she looked no older than twenty-five, "as vivacious as a screen-star, as wise as a dowager,"[14] and no one could believe she was already the mother of nine.

Stammers won the spin and chose to have Alice serve first. After a bow from the waist to the queen and a nod of recognition to Teach in the stands, the twenty-five-year-old painfully launched her first serve, in a game that went to deuce four times before Alice finally prevailed. Sensing that Stammers had seen her wince as she stretched to hit the ball and would use the weakness against her, Marble, in an example of pure mind over frail matter, was somehow able to put the pain aside and invite the voice of her old coach Harwood "Beese" White into her head, obliterating all other thoughts and considerations, summoning the mantra he had instilled in her, over and over, "Step and swing. Step and swing. Find your rhythm."[15]

Observers were stunned by the quality of Marble's play, calling it cyclonic, astonishing, the ultimate. The strokes were so solid and self-assured, it was as if she had been playing this match in her dreams her entire life. The next day, the *Times* of London noted that Stammers was on the defensive most of the time, and even her vastly improved forehand could not prevail "in such a storm." The key, according to the paper, was Marble's "unflinching defense in the backhand corner as a parry to Miss Stammers' best stroke—the cross-drive of a left-hander. . . . Miss Marble covered the court so quickly that she could reach almost any shot in a stride or two."

Match point consisted of a backhand blasted down the line so powerfully
that Stammers had no hope of reaching it and simply started walking toward
a stunned Alice to congratulate her. Her pain had miraculously disappeared
(until the next day, when it returned with a vengeance): "After the second game,
I didn't remember I had anything wrong with me."[16] Marble won the first
set, 6–2, and then shut the door on Stammers, 6–0, in the second.

Afterward, *American Lawn Tennis* reported that Marble not only won but
proved herself "worthy of the Olympian Heights in company with Suzanne
Lenglen and Mrs. Moody. Her errors were astoundingly few and the forehand drive, which of old was spoilt by faulty footwork, rarely failed to race
to its allocated target. Her high geared stride frequently enabled her to reach
some of the most deadly of Kay's drives and turn the tables by an equally
deadly counter." The publication pronounced the match "short but sweet" and
"full of color."[17] Marble's expression and "deliberate, calm, businesslike tennis" remained so steady that afterward she earned the accolade "poker-faced
successor to poker-faced Helen Wills."[18]

The London *Times* called Alice's triumph a "London fairy tale": "It
was delightful at all events, to have Miss K. E. Stammers surviving to the
last match of the ladies' championship, just as it was to have British players
in all the other finals, but Miss Marble left her never the ghost of a chance
in another unsurpassed display of feminine severity. One hardly thought she
would find again quite the ruthless touch that had dumbfounded Frau Sperling; but . . . Miss Marble was simply invincible. She played a masculine type
of attacking lawn tennis that has never been equaled in the ladies' game."[19]

One of Marble's first impulses was to seek Teach out in the crowd: "My
victory was her victory, the culmination of a lifetime of striving. I was the
best in the world, and so was she. I hugged my racquet to my chest, prouder
than I'd been ever in my life."[20] Marble danced her way into the main hall
of the All England Club and gave Teach a huge hug.

The Associated Press recounted: "Miss Marble said she felt 'this was the
climax of my comeback after my collapse in Paris a few years ago. When my
health broke down in Paris and I had to return home, three specialists told
me I never would play tennis again. Now that I have been lucky enough to
win at Wimbledon, I'd just like to give credit to Eleanor Tennant, who not
only convinced me I could play tennis again but taught me how to play.'"[21]

Still dazed, Marble rushed over to Stammers to apologize: "I'm sorry,"
she said. "I just hated beating you."[22]

Stammers was gracious in defeat: "Alice played amazing tennis. Actually, I was lucky to get two games from her. Quite honestly, I've never seen anything like that in tennis before."[23]

Ambassador Kennedy introduced Alice to the queen mother, who merely mouthed pleasantries—"Thank you for a fascinating match," and "I like your cap"—but such utterances from royal lips rang in Alice's ears for a lifetime.[24] Marble would retell the story of that brief meeting with fresh enthusiasm at endless interviews and luncheon speeches long into the future—overlooking the gaffe that followed. Instead of backing away from the royal eminence, as protocol dictates, she had turned her back and strode off. Teach's constant lessons in decorum and John Robert Powers's in charm proved to be of no help in the heat of the moment.

"How does it feel to be the world champion?" asked a reporter.

"Better than anything I've ever known."[25]

Alice returned to the locker room to prepare for the two upcoming matches. She was "simply wonderful," Teach told her. "If you never play another match in your life, I'll still be a happy woman."[26] Alice's muscles hurt, and if she could have, she would have sunk into a tub of hot water, but there was no rest in sight. She was soon summoned to play in the women's doubles, winning convincingly with Sarah Palfrey Fabyan over an aging Helen Jacobs and Billie Yorke, 6–1, 6–0. After a short break, the mixed doubles final was to begin, with Riggs as her partner against Frank Wilde and Nina Brown.

The day was dragging on. Alice was irritated with Riggs, who always seemed offhand and above it all. With his perpetual little boy persona, Riggs invited a sibling dynamic, the kind of friction that flares up between a brother and a sister all too familiar with each other's foibles. Alice told him to shape up: she had won doubles twice before with Don Budge, and if she lost on this day, he would be the cause of her failure. To her surprise, he vowed to be serious. Later, she figured out why. He had placed a bet on himself winning.

Nina Brown gave Riggs a run for his money. *American Lawn Tennis* reported that she "frequently out-maneuvered Riggs in a way that elicited from him a look of surprised admiration." The match was not going well, when "Miss Marble awakened with a start and swept the chess table to the ground."[27] The final score was 9–7, 6–1. Associated Press reporter James "Scotty" Reston's ecstatic account echoed that of the media at large, appearing under the headline:

ALICE MARBLE WINS WIMBLEDON TITLE, DOWNS KAY STAMMERS

"Think of all the attributes of a great tennis player and Miss Marble had them all today as she became the first woman in the history of international tennis to hold three American and three all-England titles at the same time," Reston wrote. "Tonight they were saying that Marble 'plays like Lenglen—only harder.'"[28]

Just as in years past, Carole Lombard and Clark Gable were among the first to congratulate Alice, but this time their goodwill was conveyed by an international phone call. Later that night, Marble prepared for the Wimbledon Ball at the Grosvenor House Hotel, known for its luxury. She wore the same red dress as when she made her debut at the Waldorf as a torch singer—form-fitting in the bodice but otherwise all swoosh and glitter, "featuring yards and yards of red tulle" and straps bedecked with sequins.

Pressed by the crowd into performing as a chanteuse, she chose Hoagy Carmichael's "Stardust," with lyrics by Mitchell Parish, a song about how the singer desires a reunion not with a person but with something more gossamer, with the memory of a melody and the feelings it inspired. It was precisely the kind of sad song Marble felt her mother might not have approved of, the lyrics suffused with a feeling deeper and potentially more disabling than mere melancholy.

When the crowd demanded more, Marble changed gears and treated them to "This Can't Be Love," a hit song from the previous year's Rodgers and Hart musical, *The Boys from Syracuse*, a staple of her repertoire at the Waldorf. The lyrics, coy and oppositional, upend the usual approach to songs about romance. Instead of being lovesick, the crooner is love-healthy, experiencing "no sobs, no sorrows, no sighs," no "dizzy spells," and she possesses a heart that is beating just fine: "This can't be love because I feel so well."

Marble and Riggs occupied places of honor to the right and left of Sir Samuel Hoare, the British Lawn Tennis Association president. Hoare toasted the health of the champions and they responded with warm speeches. He then remarked with stuffy gratitude on Queen Mary's loyal presence at the games.[29] Hoare also served as Britain's home secretary and was known as an appeaser, arguing that war with Hitler was shortsighted and not in the national interest. He even made a political crack during his speech: "I wish that politicians had the same anticipation in their sphere as these two champions."[30]

Always good for a joke, Riggs ridiculed his performance in the singles match on the previous day: "Teach told me that everybody got up and left and had tea and she was the only one who sat and watched me. And at that she woke herself up several times snoring."[31] He could be ridiculous; often, especially during the mixed doubles match, Alice would have willingly hit him in the head with the heaviest racket she could find.

But not tonight.

For her first dance, Alice placed her hands on Riggs's shoulders, her face glowing. As the couple swept across the room, he boasted about the money he had made that day—by betting on himself. His life's philosophy, often shared, boiled down to: "If I can't play for big money, I play for a little money. And if I can't play for a little money, I stay in bed that day."

Alice shrugged it off.

Nothing marred her good humor, certainly not Riggs's goofy grin and his gambler's heart. She did not even care that her high heels made her "two inches taller than Bobby, or that his broken tooth gave him a 'Dennis the Menace' look." At one point she detached the corsage of cypripedium orchids at her shoulder and tossed it high into the crowd—the gesture of a bride.

"I forgot everything but the joy."[32]

SWING HIGH, SWING LOW

AFTER DANCING UNTIL four in the morning, then returning to her hotel and collapsing, Marble had one day off before heading to Dublin to compete for the Irish title. She traveled with as many as twenty suitcases, including athletic gear and her ball gowns. The cost of this finery, along with transportation, pleasing hotels, and meals on the road, was subsidized by a variety of revenue streams, including the income from Alice's warbling at the Waldorf and Teach's incessant clinics. The United States Lawn Tennis Association covered the costliest items for players of Marble's caliber: hotel rooms and transportation. Occasionally, private citizens contributed money to Teach to use for other items, including clothing and incidentals, and a network of wealthy individuals enjoyed the status attached to hosting the more famous and accomplished players. The two women had a fifty–fifty partnership, and Teach was banking on the tables turning, looking forward to the day when Alice would bring in more than her mentor. The temptation to turn professional and compete for prize money was growing, encouraged in part by Don Budge's example. In 1938, he won the first Grand Slam ever, capturing the singles titles in Australia, France, Wimbledon, and the United States. By late 1938, he had renounced his amateur status.

Across the Irish Sea, more elegant housing greeted the new champion, the south Dublin home of Irish tenor John McCormack, with views beyond marshland to the sea and an ornate interior featuring formal appointments such as an oak-paneled dining room, stained glass, and an oratory.[1] McCormack had a fondness for tennis and frequented the Racquet Club in Palm Springs, where Teach had been manager and Marble had relaunched her career after her involuntary hiatus.

Alice played in the Irish Lawn Tennis Championships at Dublin's Fitz-william Club, and she cruised to another victory, defeating Susan Noel in the final, 6–2, 6–4.

After an exhibition match held following the tournament, one headline said it all: "Girl Beats Man at Lawn Tennis." Marble had beaten Cyril Kemp, a strong Irish player, 9–7, 8–6. Kemp enjoyed high regard among Irish players and was "on the very top of his form."[2] Teaming up, Marble and Susan Noel won the women's doubles, but Marble and her partner lost in mixed doubles.

For his part, John McCormack claimed to be so impressed with Alice's singing ("I believe that she will be a better singer than tennis player") that he arranged to give her lessons in London the next week.[3]

On July 12, during the Irish championships, the *New York Times* ran a wire story with the headline ALICE MARBLE TO ENTER MOVIES: "Alice Marble, who plays tennis well enough to win Wimbledon's historic cup, and who sings well enough to win praise from New York's night club patrons, soon will try a movie career. Frank Orsatti, Hollywood agent, said he had signed a contract for her, but that it forbids any role as a tennis player. Her acting will not interfere with her amateur status as a tennis player, he added."

Orsatti had a track history of signing up athletes, laying claim to having discovered Sonja Henie after she won Olympic gold in women's ice-skating in 1928, 1932, and 1936.[4] Perhaps Marble had amnesia about the audition, which she had always regarded as humiliating, that Carole Lombard had arranged a few years earlier.

Alice and Teach headed back to the United States on July 19, 1939, leaving from Southampton, known for its docks, its walls, and its double high tides, and famous as well as the launching site of the *Titanic*. She told the British press she had had a "marvelous time" (inspiring at least one headline to feature the inevitable pun "Marble-ous") and that she would be back again next summer: "Most certainly I will be coming back. I always enjoy my trips to England, and I am looking forward to next Wimbledon."[5]

Four tugs towed the *Champlain* out to sea under strong currents.[6] With a carrying capacity of a thousand passengers, the transatlantic French liner, built only seven years earlier, conveyed modernity with a high funnel on top that deflected smoke and soot away from the decks, so the passengers could enjoy the sun without distraction. The ship, considered "one of the most smartly decorated liners on the Atlantic in the thirties,"[7] arrived in New

York early in the afternoon of July 26. Dressed in a wide-brimmed hat and a dress with a round collar and long billowing sleeves, a clutch purse beneath her arm, Alice floated off the ship, to be greeted by an adoring press. Their curiosity extended beyond tennis to the silver screen.

"There is no definite deal on," she told the press in New York. "I understand my agent is negotiating with a couple of companies for a film test for me, but as far as I know that's as far as it has gone."

She refused to be tied down to any one possibility, whether tennis, singing, or playacting.

"I like them all," she said. "One at a time."[8]

In New York, more fancy lodgings greeted Marble, thanks again to Roz Bloomingdale Cowen, this time a free suite at the Sherry-Netherland Hotel on Fifth Avenue usually occupied by Cowen's parents, away on a summer holiday. Cowen hosted a tea in Alice's honor, comprising a small group of theater people and First Lady Eleanor Roosevelt.[9] Alice was to address the group with a practice run of what she came to call her "will to win" spiel, which she hoped would lead to a career in public speaking. The term came from a radio program in which Mary K. Browne, with whom Alice stayed in touch, "depicted the lives of famous people who overcame adversity, such as Dr. [Edward] Trudeau, Beethoven and many more."[10] Alice's story was an easy fit.

Alice said she had never felt so nervous in her life: "This wasn't like playing tennis or singing songs before a group. These were my thoughts, my opinions, and though I knew the words were firmly locked in my memory, I was unsure as to how they would be received. For the first time, I worried about boring an audience."[11] Pressed to share her opinion by one of the hosts, Eleanor Roosevelt said she was so impressed that she was going to straighten all the dresser drawers when she got back to the White House. Marble took it as a good sign that her speech had inspired the First Lady to take some action.

Acknowledging her historic Wimbledon, *Life* magazine, read in millions of American households each week, featured Marble on the cover of the August 28, 1939, issue, photographed by the illustrious Alfred Eisenstaedt. *Life* told its readers: "With Helen Wills Moody in retirement, the No. 1 U.S. woman tennis player is 26-year-old Alice Marble. She has won every tournament she has entered this year, is top-heavy favorite to win again the National Championships, Sept. 7, at Forest Hills. When not playing tennis, Miss Marble works as a night-club singer or a dress designer. In fact, she herself designed the famous shorts which she wears on the courts."

Life was known for employing the greatest photographers in the world, and Eisenstaedt may well have been the greatest.[12] His style remained consistent over his long career. He preferred existing light, and he tried, he said, "not to push people around. I have to be as much of a diplomat as a photographer. People often didn't take me seriously because I carry so little equipment and make so little fuss. When I married . . . my wife asked me, 'But where are your real cameras?' I never carried a lot of equipment. My motto has always been, 'Keep it simple.'"[13]

Seen through Eisenstaedt's lens, Marble is at the net, hunched slightly forward, racket in hand, wearing her visor. Her expression is both sunlit and appraising. A web of incipient wrinkles wreaths her eyes. The sun would do her no favors when the years began to add up, but in this image, Eisenstaedt captured a look of quiet assessment as well as a quality of being open to the world. An interior photo revealed a different aspect of her personality. Leaping over a tennis net, legs in midair, eyes wide, huge smile, a racket in one hand and a hat in the other, she radiates the same exuberance as in that now ancient "Little Queen of Swat" photo from childhood.

ON THE DAY of Marble's triple wins at Wimbledon, the first passenger flight from the United States taking a northern route to England, via Newfoundland and Ireland, left New York. Pan Am service was limited to about two dozen passengers, almost all members of the press. The journey would take twenty-four and a half hours. The travelers would spread out upon their arrival, and each speak with as many people as possible, the better to report back to their countrymen the state of upheaval throughout Europe and their conclusions about how it might affect the United States. They spent three hurried days in England and France and then flew back to the States, where they attempted to answer the question that was on everyone's mind: "Will there be war?" Diligent reporters, they weighed official utterances against the opinions of "the man in the street." *Life* reported their verdict: "England is calm but determined." Virtually unanimously, they predicted, "There will be no war this year."[14]

Some six weeks later, on September 1, 1939, Germany invaded Poland. Two days after that, England declared war against Germany. Following air-raid warnings, many families sent their children as far north as possible to get them away from London and environs. In France, a sacred tennis facility instantly became profane when hundreds of political prisoners were detained at Roland-Garros. Later during the German occupation, Roland-Garros would be a way station for Jews being shipped to their deaths. The United States remained neutral, with many Americans believing that its ocean borders and vast distance from Europe would and should protect it from the turmoil.

Against the dramatic backdrop of war in Europe, the US National Championships went forward as planned, starting on September 7 at Forest Hills. A few days in, given her celebrity, Alice was invited to appear as a guest on a radio program called *Information Please*, which announced itself with a crowing rooster followed by, "Wake Up, America! Time to Stump the Experts!" A panel of four experts answered obscure questions, and listeners could judge for themselves who was smart and who was not.

Clifton Fadiman, book editor of the *New Yorker*, was the show's host. His voice was so forceful that one newspaper called him "the inquisitor." The name of the show referenced the days when one could ask for information (please) from a telephone operator. At its peak, fifteen million people tuned in, including, as Fadiman's daughter Anne wrote in her memoir *The Wine Lover's Daughter*, "Justice Felix Frankfurter and a New York cab driver who tried to avoid fares between 8:30 and 9:00 every Tuesday night." Fadiman presided "over a panel of wits who, as *Time* put it, were 'baited, stung, encouraged, wounded' by a series of pointed questions. . . . Each week sixty thousand listeners sent in questions. If they stumped the experts, they were awarded prize money (to *the thrrring-thrrring* of a cash register) and, starting in the second year, a set of the *Encyclopedia Britannica*. The right answer wasn't important; what mattered was the pun, the ad lib, the deliciously acidulous riposte."[15]

Alice, referred to by Fadiman as "the youngest expert we've ever had," joined newspaper columnist Franklin D. Adams and book authors John Kieran and Bernard Jaffe—all certifiable eggheads. Questions jumped from chemistry to etymology to literature.

"Name the imaginary country created by L. Frank Baum."

"Oz."

"That country was greatly invaded by MGM," Fadiman commented.

"Which requires the most food in sustenance in proportion to his weight: fish, bird, baby, dog?"

"Bird."

In the category of tennis, Alice was set up for an easy victory.

"For what particular stroke or technique is each of the following tennis stars famed?"

"George Lott?"

"The lob."

"Vincent Richards?"

"The volley and the half volley."

"Wallace Johnson?"

"The chop."

"Billy Johnston?"

"Forehand drive."

In another category, she was asked to name a song that has a tennis term in the title.

"Swing High, Swing Low," she said.

A subsequent one-page spread in *Look* magazine criticized most female guests on the show for looking bored or frightened or for giggling. Included was a series of black-and-white headshots of women who ruined the merriment. The article noted two exceptions: Helen Wills Moody, "an ornament to the program," and Alice Marble, whose photo was not included. She was excused from the lineup of spoilsports thanks to her ability to win "the respect of the experts."[16]

Alice made another clean sweep at Forest Hills in 1939. The press generated little advance suspense:

> *Alice Marble's vast superiority over the best of the other tennis females has knocked all the interest out of the Ladies' League in the national championships. . . . The pretty San Francisco bomber is considered a mortal cinch to win here as easily as she won at Wimbledon. It's only a question, really, of whether Helen Jacobs or Kay Stammers will be offered up as the sacrifice in the finals. . . . Some of the critics who have been watching them all for upward of ten years think that Alice, in her present form, could have trimmed Suzanne Lenglen or Helen Wills Moody in their prime. Certainly, they say, she comes nearer having a man's game than either of them—the hard, kicking service, the deep smoking ground strokes and the deadly overhead "kill."[17]*

Marble and, as predicted, Helen Jacobs navigated their way to the women's finals, which held more suspense than expected. Allison Danzig wrote, "Here was one of the most dramatic battles that women's tennis has produced in years, fought out for an hour-and-a-half in gusty crosscurrents of wind that raised havoc with the strokes, while the gallery of 8,500 roared and screamed its encouragement at Miss Jacobs. The crescendo of the enthusiasm was reached in the final game, a furiously disputed 20-point session in which Miss Jacobs five times came within a stroke of 5-all and twice stood off match points, only to yield finally to Miss Marble's more powerful attacking weapons."[18]

Marble's hard-fought victory—6–0, 8–10, 6–4—gave her a third national title, sealing her reputation as a power player. She made a clean sweep. In women's doubles she and Sarah Palfrey beat Kay Stammers and Freda James Hammersley, 7–5, 8–6; and she paired with Australian Harry Hopman to take the mixed doubles title over Palfrey and Elwood Cooke, 9–7, 6–1.

"She is the first woman to play tennis like a man," intoned a regional California paper.

> *A natural athlete who played baseball well, she can be compared only to masculine players. With both feet off the ground as she hits the ball, this girl's smash is like that of Maurice E. McLoughlin. She has more speed than any woman who ever played. Her footwork is compared to that of Big Bill Tilden. She has masculine imperturbability when the going is tough. She is a fighter from way back. Yet people who think of topnotch women athletes as being athletic-appearing with short bobs and weather-beaten complexions have to alter their opinions when they get a close-up of lovely Alice Marble.*[19]

THE NEWS FROM ENGLAND was grim. By the third week in September 1939, photographs ran in British papers of women in nursing uniforms training for war: "Wimbledon fans will hardly recognize the sacred portals of the All-England Club, where international rivalry has given place to National Service. The Club now houses a first-aid, anti-gas and ambulance station and the familiar notices on the walls . . . are plastered with official instructions and warnings."[20]

San Francisco had long ceased to be home base for Marble. When good news arrived from the Bay Area, such as her brother Tim's selection to play third base for the Hollywood club of the Pacific Coast League,[21] she celebrated from afar. Alice returned to Palm Desert for the winter holidays, where she played an exhibition in the village tennis tournament.

Alice may have felt honored to be on *Information Please*, but the show hit a nerve, making her more conscious of gaps in her knowledge. She was hurt when Roz Cowen introduced her as "my friend Alice, whose knowledge is a mile wide and a half-inch deep."[22] She began taking courses, in everything "from upholstering to Latin American culture. I'd missed all that and I felt inadequate with my learned college friends."[23] She decided to study Spanish with Margarita "Tica" Madrigal, a popular language teacher. Like orchestra leader Emil Coleman before her, Madrigal did not refrain from praising her own skills: "I think I'm the best language teacher who ever existed. I have no pride, no sense of vanity. It's just a fact." Madrigal claimed a roster of clients including writers "Sherwood Anderson, Andre Maurois and, briefly, Ernest Hemingway, . . . FBI, the Rockefeller Institute and Time-Life International, . . . ambassadors, judges, generals and executives."[24]

Madrigal was as devoted to cognates as Teach to her clinics and John Powers to charm. She believed that once an English-speaking Spanish learner recognized the hordes of words that share the same roots and similar sounds, the acquisition of Spanish proficiency would follow. None could compare with Madrigal's "method for getting quick results." Plus, Madrigal was "thoroughly grounded in Spanish as spoken and written in South America." As one observer later said about Madrigal's exuberant approach, "Miss Madrigal believes that most conversation is past tense—I went, I did, I ate, I saw, I met, I slept, I traveled, I said. She therefore hacks out the cumbersome, complex rules of general grammar and gets to the nub of things. . . . 'DIVE IN,' she says, 'and mangle it, twist it, but keep going.'"[25]

Soon Alice fell in love with Madrigal, as she later acknowledged in *Courting Danger*, the only gay alliance she admitted to during her lifetime.

"One Thursday we were to have a lesson at my place," she recalled. "Tica came early, and found me sitting on the floor, intently fretting the strings of the guitar. She knelt behind me and reached around me to adjust my position. Something in me stirred at the touch of her hands on mine. I could feel her breath on my cheek, and the closeness of her body made my heart race."[26]

They started seeing each other outside of class, infuriating Teach, who felt sidelined. The affair was short-lived. Madrigal soon found another partner, but Alice remained loyal, even contributing to an ad in *Life* magazine touting Madrigal's unique teaching methods after they had broken up.

DECEMBER 1939 saw the release of *Gone with the Wind*, which Marble later described in a gush of adjectives and superlatives: *magical, gleaming, sheer grandeur, the best movie I have ever seen, the best movie ever made.*[27] Invited as a guest of Lombard and Gable to attend the premiere in Atlanta on December 15, she shared memories of the event having less to do with the huge celebration of the film than the more personal coup of securing a room that adjoined Lombard's at the Georgian Terrace Hotel. The movie star's room was within full view of another hotel.

One day Lombard knocked on Marble's door and whispered, "You have to see this." Word was out that Gable was taking a bath. Binoculars from many hotel windows across the way were trained on his in the Georgian Terrace. Lombard took ribald delight in pointing out the voyeurs would likely be disappointed, claiming that "his manly weapon" was just a "dinky little thing." Marble chastised her friend, calling her a "devilish woman." Lombard agreed.[28]

That off-color story became part of Marble's repertoire.

The year of miracles for Marble concluded with an outpouring of accolades. Journalist Dorothy Kilgallen named Marble one of the Outstanding Women of 1939, "because she was the country's foremost girl athlete and managed to look pretty in the newsreel shots."[29] Marble made a list of America's best-dressed women of 1939 selected by fashion designers. Sportswriter Bob Considine put Alice on his list of unforgettable sports moments: "The sweetly composed face of Alice Marble, so cleverly concealing the gal's good killer instinct on the tennis court. And the way she'd give a glittering smile to the bedraggled, sweaty girls she was beating—as they'd changed sides on the odd game. Then the sweet composure again—and boffo, another ace or placement."[30] The Associated Press voted Marble the Outstanding Woman Athlete of 1939, winning by the largest margin ever in the history of the poll.

PART FOUR

1940–1945

CHAPTER 19

$100,000 ON THE TABLE

A LICE MARBLE'S KNIGHT in shining armor was a scrawny man who often smelled of mud and manure, not that it mattered to him. He entered her life in the early months of 1940 and remained a significant presence until his death in 1965.

Will du Pont Jr.'s great-grandfather founded a gunpowder mill in 1802, which eventually became DuPont de Nemours, Inc. The DuPont company's fortunes rose during the Civil War when it supplied one-third of the gunpowder used by the Union Army. Tutored at home as a child, du Pont became president of the Delaware Trust Company in 1929, a position he inherited when his father died. As one of the richest men in America, Will du Pont didn't have to impress anyone, and he went out of his way not to. He aspired to shabbiness and valued thrift, known to repair his rubber boots with tire patches. The sportswriter Red Smith called him "thin-shanked," using equine terminology. A neighbor said du Pont's clothes were "rumpled and mildewy, and, to say the least, tended to announce his presence."[1] Du Pont's nickname was "Dirty Willie." If interpreted in a charitable light, the name could be said to have heralded his love of the outdoors. A Delaware newspaper wrote: "He was a man of basic simplicity of tastes whose keenest interests sprang in one way or another from the land. He always looked most comfortable in riding clothes that had survived plenty of horses' sweat and mud from horses' hoofs. At a Cecil County fair on his Fair Hill estate, smoking his pipe, he was as much a countryman as any other farmer with a keen eye for a good horse or a Guernsey bull."[2]

Du Pont's main love was horses—breeding them, entering them into races, and building racetracks. He was known for getting up extra early at Bellevue Hall, his six-hundred-acre estate, two miles from downtown Wilmington, Delaware, with grass tennis courts, a pool, an indoor racetrack, and a dressage training center. By four a.m. he was doing paperwork, and he would arrive at his office in the Delaware Trust Building at seven.[3]

Du Pont's second passion was tennis. A mutual friend had written to Alice in Beverly Hills, where she was sharing an apartment with Teach, and arranged an introduction. Du Pont was ostensibly seeking advice for construction of some new tennis courts at Bellevue. Up until then, he appears to have lived an orderly life, married to Jean Liseter du Pont since January 1, 1919, with whom he had four children. He was a born archivist, as evidenced by his proclivity for keeping meticulous records along with massive amounts of saved correspondence.[4] He even saved typed copies of requests for items of clothing from Brooks Brothers, including a regretful letter from the company informing him that his underwear order would arrive later than his shirts. The Depression made no dent as he planned expensive surprises for his wife. In December 1937, he initiated a special order from Warren D. Perry and Silversmiths on Fifth Avenue in New York as a Christmas gift. Du Pont reviewed designs for pins in the shape of rabbits, foxes, and ducks, and a horse's head in platinum embedded with diamonds.

Years later, Alice remembered her first impression of du Pont in California: "I watched him walk toward me in a rambling, farmer's gait, his long arms swinging loosely. He wasn't a big man, and his aquiline face and long nose gave him a sorrowful look. He was dressed in high-top black basketball shoes (he had weak ankles), rumpled khaki pants, a sweater fastened with a big safety pin, and a badly stained tennis cap."[5]

Seventeen years Marble's senior, du Pont told her he was a fan. She claimed to have no clue as to who he might be, relying on Teach, with better radar, to figure it out by asking whether he was related to the "munitions family." When he said yes, Teach perked up. Finally, Alice had a suitor to her mentor's liking.[6]

The inconvenient truth that du Pont was still married to Jean when he became infatuated with Alice did not lessen Teach's enthusiasm nor curb his. When he returned home to Wilmington, he sent an invitation to Marble and Tennant to visit him there. Du Pont began his letter in formal terms, addressing it to "Dear Miss Tennant," almost as if he were a suitor conducting an old-fashioned courtship seeking permission from his intended's parents. In this case, Teach filled the role of both father and mother. Du Pont used a soft sell to win the favor of both women, seeking their advice and offering low-key bribes.

March 8, 1940
I want to thank you for all the trouble you went to in my behalf to give me
a most wonderful time in playing tennis on all the different courts and to
track down Pop Davis and all the color schemes. . . .

I hope that you and Miss Marble will come to Wilmington and stay
with me and try out our grass courts. I am going to send you a set of plans
of them that you can hold. If the courts come up to all the expectations in
the Spring that I anticipate and if you are pleased with them, the plans
might be useful to you in the event that some one in Los Angeles could be
persuaded to put in a battery of grass courts.[7]

In the same letter, he sought Teach's opinion of nylon stockings, offering
them for free from his company, which was hardly necessary. Word was out
that nylons were less thick and cumbersome than wool or cotton stockings,
so more flattering. Any woman, at least in that era, would have been thrilled
to receive them as a gift. Better yet, if Teach expressed enthusiasm, he was
prepared to send her more pairs.

The same day, March 8, 1940, he wrote separately and directly to Alice,
thanking her, in his stilted way, for "granting me the privilege of playing tennis
with you and in offering the hospitality of your home." He said he had had
a wonderful time and hoped it did not appear as if he were about to move in
permanently. Still, he said he would love to come back again and play more
tennis. In the meantime, perhaps she and Teach would visit him in Wilmington
and give their opinion of his new grass courts and their lights. By April 4,
Teach and Alice had replied that they would visit. As etiquette required,
Mrs. du Pont wrote separately, confirming the arrangement. Du Pont offered
a convoluted description of his wife's athletic inclinations: "While she is not
a tennis player and is more on the order of Mrs. John Hay Whitney, whom
you know, being interested in horses and hounds, and rather thinks 'tennis nuts' is a certain form of insanity, she enjoys all sports even though she
doesn't participate in them to a reasonable degree."[8]

Early on in their relationship, du Pont took Marble's financial future to
heart and scouted opportunities that might appeal to her. On April 12, he
wrote saying that he was trying to arrange work for her during the Delaware
Oaks horse race.

As she prepared to travel to the US National Championships in the summer of 1940, Marble once again sought Carole Lombard's advice, this time

on how she would finance the trip east. The competition promised to be less spirited than in years past. Players from Germany had already canceled plans to attend, along with many others from overseas. The specter of war captured everyone's fretful attention, and the matter of how a tennis player, even one of Marble's appeal, would finance her sport hardly occupied the top tier of anyone else's list of worries, except her own.

Always good for a solution, Lombard suggested that Teach and Alice team up, as they had in the past, and do another combination of exhibition matches for Alice and clinics for Teach. Wilson Sporting Goods readily came on board, agreeing to set up a thirty-stop tour. Whenever possible, Teach and Alice would stay with friends or accept the hospitality of patrons, which pleased Teach because then they could bank the ten-dollar-a-day living allowance.[9] There was no talk about taking a train instead of driving. Teach loved the open road.

With Alice at the wheel of a Studebaker provided by Wilson, she and Teach and a friend named Lily Yeates sped toward Shreveport, Louisiana, on sunny roads, reaching one hundred miles per hour. A timely directive to slow down from Teach prevented total disaster, as Alice tried to avoid a truck in the center of the road. She steered the car to the shoulder, where a tire caught in gravel, spinning the vehicle around three times. Their passenger, in the back seat, was spared serious injury. Teach hit her head on the windshield, and Alice hurt her neck and feared it had been broken. An ambulance transported them to a hospital, where in apparent deference to Alice's fame, they were seen in a cordoned-off room.

By the end of the day the three women were pronounced fit for release and ensconced in a hotel room before heading out the next day in a new vehicle, provided by Wilson, to replace the one that had been damaged.

This accident set a pattern for several such incidents that subsequently befell Marble, which were not made public at the time they occurred. Alice never explained what influence she employed to ensure silence, but said she had good reason to do so. If her competitors found out about her injured neck, for example, they would lob every ball they could to her. She recuperated for an entire week in Shreveport, using the excuse of strep throat, which du Pont believed sufficiently to send her a get-well note. On May 3, he was in touch again with good news. She would be presenting an award at the Delaware Oaks horse race as well as broadcasting on the radio. On the same day that du Pont invited Alice to present a trophy and stay at his home, he continued to address the needs and comfort of his family. He confirmed that he would be renting the ballroom at the Bellevue-Stratford Hotel in Philadelphia for $400 for the coming-out party of his eldest daughter on New Year's Day in 1941 and he also signed a four-month lease for a summer rental of a cottage on Fishers Island in New York for a sum of $1,750. He did not act like a man about to end his marriage, as he arranged for a tea dance for eight hundred people to be held at his mansion on September 13, seeking the advice of a parking specialist and hiring Pinkerton guards.[10]

WIMBLEDON WAS CANCELED IN 1940 and would not reopen for tennis until 1946, but that spring and summer, Alice played on the domestic front, in hinterlands and cities. Teach was her constant companion, which didn't always suit the press, for a good reason. "When Alice Marble, the tennis star, lunches with newspaper men (and other guys) she is chaperoned by her coach, Eleanor Tennant," wrote AP sports columnist Eddie Brietz. "All very pleasant, but it runs up the check, boys."[11]

Alice's exhibition match on May 5 in Shreveport was typical of what unfolded in the coming weeks. She made a thousand fans happy—getting "many rounds of applause from a more than pleased audience"—and won singles and doubles.[12]

The afternoon of May 13, in Clinton, South Carolina, twenty-five hundred spectators from "scattered points" in the Carolinas and Georgia watched Alice easily win a singles match in straight sets, and, with Californian Virginia Wolfenden, doubles in an exhibition game. In the audience were four hundred high school and college female tennis players from the three states. Eleanor, meanwhile, gave a lecture to one hundred physical-education teachers in the morning.[13] At the Atlanta invitational championship, Alice defeated Gracyn Wheeler, 6–0, 6–2, in the semifinals, and the *Atlanta Constitution* lavished praise: "Even as the Empire State building imposingly overlooks New York does Alice Marble stand majestically above the rest of the feminine tennis world."[14] On May 19, Virginia Wolfenden offered some competition for the singles title but was "worn down by the superior power stoking, forcing game and court strategy of the beautiful blond bomber,"[15] and Alice was victorious, 6–3, 6–3. On May 26, in Minneapolis, Marble defeated two male players from the Northwest in exhibition matches. However, the next day, local tennis champion Norm MacDonald beat Marble, 6–3, and then paired with her to win doubles. During "one of the grandest exhibitions ever staged" in Akron, Ohio, on June 2, Alice "pounded the ball with amazing might," defeating English player Mary Hardwick, 6–3, 7–5. Her buddy Mary K. Browne was among the five hundred fans.[16]

Alice ruled tennis, but the landscape was changing. Southern California was having trouble coming up with cash to send players (at a cost of $500 each, plus other expenses) to the eastern tournaments. The problem was that the Pacific Southwest Championships, a big moneymaker, had not been profitable the year before, according to a United Press news story. The diminishment was related directly to the war: "It is no secret that tennis isn't in a position to absorb too much cuffing about. The war already has extracted the 'international flavor' of the Australian, English and French cup teams from the recognized American tournaments. And this hits where it hurts the most, smack in the box office. During 1940 American players must support American tennis all by themselves."[17]

Marble and Tennant headed to Delaware for a week with the du Ponts in the beginning of June. They spent a day inspecting the DuPont nylon plant in Seaford, Delaware, the world's first nylon factory.[18] As Will du Pont had hoped, he found radio work for Alice as the guest speaker on a broadcast of the Polly Drummond Stakes at Delaware Park.[19] At the Wilmington Country Club, Don Budge and Marble won an exhibition matchup.[20] In mid-June, Alice joined the horse-racing crowd again when she presented a silver trophy to the owner of the Delaware Oaks Stakes' winner at Delaware Park.[21] The visit to Wilmington showed Marble how estranged Will and Jean du Pont were from each other, a subject Will would later discuss candidly with Alice, and also allowed her to witness firsthand the extent of his holdings.

Alice attracted a "capacity crowd" at the Merion Cricket Club in Haverford, Pennsylvania. She lost twice to male players but won mixed doubles in exhibition games.[22]

Marble headed west in late June. She won the singles in the National Clay Court Championships, defeating Gracyn Wheeler, 7–5, 6–0, in Chicago,[23] and the doubles with Mary Arnold, also coached by Eleanor Tennant. Alice's victory march continued in Evanston, Illinois, where she won the North Shore tournament singles, defeating Virginia Wolfenden, 6–4, 6–3. At the Western Tennis Tournament in Indianapolis, she defeated Wolfenden again, 6–2, 8–6, to win the singles, and joined forces with Bobby Riggs to win the mixed doubles.

The moment Marble showed up at the Baltimore Country Club for the Maryland–Middle Atlantic championships, she was on fire, as reported in the *Evening Sun*: "Alice Marble, queen of the courts, already is the most photographed and the busiest autographer. When she arrived late in the day, accompanied by her coach, Eleanor Tennant, swarms of cameras clicked. She spent several minutes obliging the signature hunters."[24]

Alice was more popular than any other player, male or female, "on and off the court," said Paul Menton, the *Evening Sun*'s sports columnist. He was often asked that week: Could Alice Marble beat Miss Poker Face, Helen Wills? His answer was definitive: "I don't believe Helen Wills was as good a tennis player in her prime as Alice Marble. She couldn't do as many things as well. She had nothing like the speed afoot, the quickness of action, the ability to volley. Miss Marble comes closer to playing tennis like the great men players of the world than any woman. Her footwork, her timing, the ease of her stroking are marvelous."[25]

She and Mary Arnold, Teach's student, won the Maryland–Middle Atlantic doubles against Mary Hardwick and Valerie Scott, 7–5, 6–4.[26] But the day of the singles finals, July 21, Marble overslept, recovering from heat fatigue. Moving slowly, she lost the first set to Pauline Betz. Teach exhorted Marble with her usual brio: "Get out there and stir your stumps." Will du Pont and S. Wallis Merrihew, the *American Lawn Tennis* editor, were also watching, as Alice rallied, winning 4–6, 6–4, 6–0.[27]

Alice put a good spin on missing out on overseas competitions, telling an interviewer: "Really, . . . one doesn't realize how much fun there is playing in tournaments right here in America when one usually is busy going abroad and just to the bigger meets in the East or West."[28]

In the finals at Seabright, in New Jersey, Alice easily defeated Mary Hardwick, 6–2, 6–0, while Bobby Riggs spent three and a half hours finally defeating Frank Kovacs. Marble dominated the women's field in a way Riggs, "even at his best," did not in the men's. She and Sarah Palfrey teamed to win the doubles.[29]

On August 10, Alice won another singles against Helen Jacobs, 6–1, 6–0, in the Eastern Grass Court Championships in Rye, New York, taking the victory for a third year in a row. She was presented with a silver bowl, a candelabra, gladioli, and acclaim from the *New York Times* for "hitting with withering speed from her backhand."[30]

So expected were Alice's triumphs that a *Fort Worth Star-Telegram* headline read "Ho-Hum! Alice Takes Tennis Tourney," when she defeated Pauline Betz, 6–2, 6–2, for her fourth singles title (1933, '38, '39, '40) on the grass at the Essex County Club in Manchester-by-the-Sea, Massachusetts, on August 17.

"It won't be news until she is defeated," one sports columnist wrote.[31]

Alice and Sarah Palfrey[32] then won the doubles championship at Longwood for the fourth time, at the end of August, defeating Dorothy Bundy and Marjorie Gladman Van Ryn, 6–4, 6–3. In mixed doubles, Marble and Riggs triumphed over Bundy and Jack Kramer, 9–7, 6–1.[33]

Right before the US Nationals at Forest Hills, Marble stood alone, monarch of a sport itself in a "sad slump," as one headline expressed it. International players could not get to the tournament, except for the handful who hadn't returned to their homelands when the war began. Even though Alice was, one reporter wrote, "statuesque, and beautiful and a tremendous attraction," she needed competition "such as we used to have when La Lenglen and Miss Wills were around." And the number-one male player, Bobby Riggs, did not inspire:

> It will be recalled that when he was winning his Wimbledon crown the English spectators departed the stadium in mass for tea in the middle of the match. He was that bad. . . . The horrors of war are being felt in this country where it hurts the promoters worst—in the box office. Having caused cancellation of the Olympic Games, Davis cup and Ryder cup matches and numerous other events that normally would be held, the fireworks in Europe also are affecting gate receipts over here, with a new low in public apathy likely for the national tennis singles championships, scheduled at Forest Hills.[34]

Marble spent the US National Championships, held September 2–9, at yet another grand mansion, Arthur Loew's estate in Glen Cove, Long Island. The president of Metro-Goldwyn-Mayer movie studios, Loew had inherited the estate from his father, Marcus, who had purchased it for $1 million in the 1920s from the sea captain who built it. Pembroke, as it was called, featured its own horticultural museum an acre in size stocked with palm trees and tropical birds. The manor house had eighty rooms with especially spacious ones on the first floor set up to entertain hundreds of guests.[35]

Alice traveled to the tournament in style, by limo or on the Loew family yacht from the private boathouse, depending on the weather.[36] It too was an inevitably deflated event, with fewer players and a diminished audience.

One incident from the tournament lives on in tennis lore, a kerfuffle that occurred during the men's singles quarterfinals. The top-seeded Joe Hunt became incensed when his opponent, Frank Kovacs, played to the crowd with some silly antics. Hunt sat down in protest at the baseline and allowed several of Kovacs's serves to fly by him, prompting Kovacs to then deposit himself at his baseline. Five minutes went by before the umpire ordered both men to resume play.

By contrast, Alice had a more straightforward time of it, reaching the finals in all three events. She and Sarah Palfrey defeated Dorothy Bundy and Marjorie Gladman Van Ryn to win the women's doubles, 6–4, 6–3. She and Bobby Riggs defeated Bundy and Jack Kramer in mixed doubles, 9–7, 6–1. And she easily routed Helen Jacobs for the singles title, 6–2, 6–3.

In his 795-page book called *History of Tennis: An Authoritative Encyclopedia and Record Book*, preeminent tennis historian Bud Collins offers this summary of Marble's stunning career:

> *Alice Marble, about to turn 27 . . . was supreme-plus, charging to her fourth U.S. singles title while never endangered, winning 12 sets, losing only 27 games. This put the finishing touches on her amateur career that had purred uninterruptedly victorious since a Wimbledon semifinal loss to Helen Jacobs in 1938. As in 1939, Alice won nine tournaments, and 45 straight singles matches. Moreover, she was 27–0 in doubles, 11–0 in mixed for a stupendous 83–0 record. She left intact a 22-tournament, 111-match streak, third only to Suzanne Lenglen's 44–179 and Helen Wills Moody's 27–158.*[37]

HAVING CONQUERED FRANCE IN JUNE, Germany now turned its attention to attacking Great Britain from the air. The Blitz began on September 7, during the US National Championships. Germany aimed to destroy British air bases and harbors, to greatly damage London, and to attack other highly populated areas as well as. Scotty Reston left the AP in favor of the London bureau of the *New York Times* where he was stationed on the seventh floor of the Reuters Building on Fleet Street. He described London at night in his first book, *Prelude to Victory,*

> *Before we got better sense, we used to put the lights off in the* Times *office every night and watch this effort. . . . "With uncanny regularity, the German bombers would come over just about 10 minutes after blackout and start dropping incendiary bombs all over this section. About an hour before we could see the flames, we would begin to hear the steady throb of scores of engines along the banks of the Thames; these were the pumps, driving the muddy water from the river up through miles of new hose. . . .*
>
> *A little later the sky would begin to change in color from midnight blue to a reddish glow, and soon the great dome of the cathedral would stand out in silhouette against the flames of perhaps a dozen raging fires. Night after night we watched this incredible scene, and morning after morning we marveled at the fact that the fires were somehow put out.*[38]

Wimbledon was attacked from the air on October 11, 1940. Twelve hundred seats were destroyed. Soon, the stadium would be conscripted as a mortuary. Despite the widespread destruction, an attitude of optimism prevailed, at least in tennis circles. Allison Danzig asked, "Will the day come when Briton, Frenchman, German, Italian, Spaniard, Japanese, Chinese, American and the nationals of a dozen other countries will all gather in the camaraderie and good sportsmanship of a world tennis championship? The answer is empathetically yes, as long as the Union Jack flies above No. 10 Downing Street."[39]

The cold facts told a less upbeat story. The city of Coventry in England suffered from the most concentrated air strike during the entire war on November 14. The Germans were so proud of their handiwork they formulated a new word, *coventrieren*, meaning to raze a city to the ground. Countrywide, forty thousand British civilians were killed during raids that lasted from September 1940 to May 1941.

Alice acknowledged that her triumphs meant little in the face of global conflagration. "Whenever possible," she said in a 1942 interview, "I play an exhibition game for one of the war funds, but tennis is secondary now. Unless a sport is doing something for the war today, it has no excuse for existence."[40] The tennis star who had worked so hard to reach the pinnacle now found herself in the curious and hardly enviable position of being on top of the world when there was no world to be on top of.

ON OCTOBER 2, Marble celebrated the New York wedding, and second marriage, of Sarah Palfrey, this time to tennis champion Elwood T. Cooke. Along with Teach, she gave the couple a reception at the Sherry-Netherland Hotel after the ceremony, attended mainly by family members and tennis heavyweights.

Will du Pont made marital news in the opposite direction when he and his wife separated later that year. Alice understood that the union was unhappy. Du Pont told her that he and his wife showed horses together, but that was about it. He said he was sometimes so depressed he wished he would just go down in a crash during an airplane ride. Alice got him to admit it would be unfair to the pilot, who happened to be his cousin. She noted that he seemed looser and happier in her company.

At first it puzzled her that when she and du Pont walked together, he always took the inside instead of walking close to the curb. She would change sides, which in turn puzzled him. Marble said, chivalry dictated that men walk on the outside to "protect the lady from runaway horses and splattering mud—that sort of thing." He explained that he put her on the right because that was how he had learned to lead livestock. It apparently did not occur to him that an adult woman might not like the comparison to cows and horses.[41]

Marble increasingly fretted about her future. The facts were not in her favor. International tennis was suspended, and the United States would likely enter the war soon and suspend tennis as well. She had no family money and only a high school diploma. The movies were never a real option. Publicly, she blamed the predatory nature of the film business. She also castigated the industry for overlooking talent—she considered Clark Gable's failure to get an Academy Award for Gone with the Wind a sign of disrespect. Yes, Hattie McDaniel and Vivien Leigh certainly deserved their Oscars, but so did he. Privately, Marble was more realistic about her limited prospects than she let on. She had no misgivings about performing as an athlete or making speeches, but whatever it was that made someone a convincing actor eluded her, and no amount of goading by Teach or crowing by Orsatti could change that.

She tried her hand at radio, debuting as a sports commentator for New York's WNEW on October 11, 1940, a pioneering job for a woman. On Fridays, at 7:45 p.m., in a fifteen-minute segment, Marble predicted the outcome of forty-five college football games to be played over the weekend. On Saturday evenings, in the same time slot for the same fifteen minutes, she announced winners and losers. Her first weekend was a success—she chose thirty-one out of forty-five games correctly, and another three games had tied.[42] Her radio manner was pleasing; Marble "zips along in a breezy style," one reporter wrote.[43] *Variety* magazine had a different view, calling the show a publicity stunt and panning her performance:

"*Variety* does not ordinarily review sports programs, but here makes an exception to the startling idea of a girl guessing which football teams will win the next day. Program bespeaks a flair for the unusual at WNEW. Alice Marble, the tennis player, does the session, which is also attention-commanding as a novelty. It may be Alice Marble, but it sounds like somebody else wrote the script and did the picking, and she's just reading from the script. Pretty flat in delivery over fifteen minutes time. In fact, it's more of an idea than an accomplishment. But still might be fixed up to get WNEW some effective word-of-mouth."[44]

In an interview with the *Brooklyn Daily Eagle*, Marble said she figured out how football works from her three brothers. "I admit I'll be sticking my neck out, but I have to admit I know football. A girl couldn't grow up in a family with three husky brothers without getting shoved around on the local football field. They dragged me to all the games until I learned how the game is played in a college stadium. Now I can tell who's likely to make the touchdowns."[45]

While the radio show diversified her portfolio and spoke to her astute athletic intelligence, it did not add to Marble's coffers in any significant way, nor did it lead to more amplified employment. She experienced some success and increased renown for designing clothes—a "Tomboy" line for Best & Company and a practical oxford shoe for Sadler in Boston—but Marble did not see how the revenue from those efforts would ever be enough to defray her debt to Teach. Neither would the tennis clinics nor the "will to win" speech.

There was one way out if she ever hoped to make money, and that was to turn professional.

Teach was thrilled, du Pont less so. He had his own ideas about her future, and when he got wind of her intention, he summoned both women to an emergency meeting. To present his case in the best light possible, he chose an elegant setting, the 21 club, in midtown Manhattan. Marble noticed that the waiter had placed a generous martini at Teach's seat before she even arrived.[46]

Du Pont got down to business right away. He had heard the rumor that Alice was going professional, so he put $100,000[47] on the table to keep Alice from doing so.

As she recounted the story years later to Dale Leatherman, Alice's first reaction was to demur, asking him, "Why would you do such a thing?"

He told her, "You're turning pro to make money. Take my offer and you won't have to."

As a fifty–fifty shareholder in Marble's earnings, Teach thought the offer was irresistible. She expressed her enthusiasm by repeatedly kicking her protégée in the shins under the table, but Alice remained undeterred. Marble saw it as a veiled proposal of marriage. As much as she liked du Pont and enjoyed frequent meals and theatrical offerings in his company, formalizing their union as husband and wife was not something she could bring herself to do.

In Alice's telling, du Pont accepted her refusal with grace, changing gears almost immediately, summoning the waiter to inquire about dinner and then eagerly asking Alice for details about a proposed tour.

CHAPTER 20

SIXTY-ONE STOPS

WITH DU PONT'S OFFER OFF THE TABLE, Teach did not waste a second as she strategized the best way to maximize the drama of Marble's decision to go pro. The wording of a letter from Teach, which she sent to various outlets, including the editors of *American Lawn Tennis*, was teasing, promising a surprise: "It gives me great pleasure to invite you to the reception I am planning for Miss Alice Marble at The Sherry-Netherland Hotel at one o'clock on November 12th, at which time Miss Marble will have an important announcement to make to the press and her friends."

The press joined promoter Jack Harris in the suite shared by Teach and Alice. Harris had organized several pro tennis tours in the past. Having worked for Spalding and Wilson Sporting Goods, he had made many contacts with tennis players. With Harris was Al Ennis, an advance man who had worked with him in the past.

Thanks to Harris and his network of contacts, Marble announced, she would be joining two of the world's most famous male tennis players on the tour: Bill Tilden, who had sung her praises for years, and Don Budge, her Oakland neighbor and championship mixed doubles partner, whom, she liked to say, she had known since he was knee-high. The risk for players who turned pro was that what they would make in money they would lose in prestige. After going professional, the saying went, a player would never again get into a country club, at least not through the front door. Yet players who had taken the high road often regretted their lofty stance. As Billy Johnston urged Budge: "Take the money, Don. The pats on the back don't last long."[1]

At forty-eight years of age, Bill Tilden was the senior player on the tour by far. Born into a wealthy family, Tilden was also born into tragedy. His parents' first three children died very young. Coming after those losses, he became the object of protective pampering on a disabling scale.[2] Tennis was the only sport that compelled him, but he always said he would give it up for music if he had to. His mother took ill and died when he was a freshman at the University of Pennsylvania, and his father died before his senior year, and soon after his brother succumbed to pneumonia. Tennis became his lifeline. He turned to the sport, according to one of his biographers, "not only to master it—and herein truly lies his supremacy—but to contribute to it as well. Years later, he wrote with disdain about the tennis he knew as a child, 'they played with such an air of elegance—a peculiar courtly grace that seemed to rob the game of its thrills. . . . There was a sort of inhumanity about it [and] it annoyed me. . . . I believed the game served something more vital and fundamental.'"[3]

Tilden was a mix of complete snob and common man. For years he believed amateurism was sacred, but when he went to other side in 1930, he became, in effect, "the Pied Piper of professionalism."[4] Shaped by the knowledge that his family could not have been much more elite, he always acknowledged the ways in which tennis and sport in general struck him as unfair. He believed that tennis should abandon the expensive-to-maintain grass courts in favor of hard courts as the preferred venue globally. He thought, way ahead of today's debate, that college athletes should be able to participate in the profits they generated, arguing that if a man can get paid well to be a good waiter or a good musician, why not also be paid well to be a good athlete?

At six feet one inch and 160 pounds, Don Budge used his lankiness as a weapon, covering space more quickly than his opponents. *American Lawn Tennis* editor S. Wallis Merrihew described him as "cheery, spontaneous, full of the joy of life—and not caring who knows it."[5] Budge had known and liked Harris for years and the feeling was mutual. Harris had tried to convince Budge to go pro in 1937, but Budge wanted to give himself another year, privately hoping for, and achieving, a Grand Slam. Harris was patient, but he did warn Budge: "A year of tennis is a lot of matches and a lot of quick stops and a lot of falls." He asked Budge to consider what would happen if he turned a knee or ripped a muscle in a meaningless tournament: "You'll be through as a player with nothing to show for it except the silverware. You've thought of that?"[6]

Budge took his chances, signing up with Harris the following year. He later explained: "Pro tennis operated for decades on the premise that the man who controlled the champion, controlled the game. One reason the pros never established themselves as a viable force was that there was never any stable, coordinating professional organization to compete with the amateur organizations. Pro tennis was carried in the hat of the man who had the best player under contract, and sometimes, in the case of first Bobby Riggs and then Jack Kramer, the organization was simplified even more since promoter and champion wore the same fedora."[7]

Budge always said he turned pro because he had to: "I simply ran out of fields to conquer in the amateur ranks. Another factor that hurried us all to the pros was a common proclivity for eating and dressing well and putting some money in the bank. Believe me, as sure as nobody ever got rich running amateur tennis, nobody got rich playing it either." Once in a while, there might be a windfall, "a lucky bonus and not something to be regularly expected."[8] The highest he recalled was $125.

Budge believed it was as irrational to ask a "young man of twenty-three or twenty-five to use his special talents playing tennis for free as it is to ask him to play baseball for free or to sell insurance or to drive a bus for the sheer pleasure of it."[9] Budge was in much better shape and fifteen years younger than Tilden, who had deteriorated, especially in terms of his lungs and breathing capacity. In a cruel ellipsis, the press reported that his wind was "gone with the . . ." making a sardonic play on the title of the popular movie.

Harris was coy about naming the fourth member of the troupe. Harris allowed that he was far along with negotiations with a suitable candidate, at least 90 percent there, but until the remaining 10 percent fell into place, he would remain mum.

Marble's reasons for going pro did not differ all that much from those of the first woman to do so, Suzanne Lenglen. Billie Jean King quotes her directly to make the case in her book *We Have Come a Long Way*:

> *"In the twelve years I have been champion I have earned literally millions of francs for tennis," said Lenglen, announcing her decision in 1926, "and have paid thousands of francs in entrance fees to be allowed to do so. . . . I have worked as hard at my career as any man or woman has worked at any career. And in my whole lifetime I have not earned $5,000—not one cent of that by my specialty, my life study—tennis. . . . I am twenty-seven and not wealthy—should I embark on any other career and leave the one for which I have what people call genius? Or should I smile at the prospect of actual poverty and continue to earn a fortune—for whom?"[10]*

Lenglen decried the rules requiring tennis at the tournament level to be amateur as "antiquated" and "absurd": "Only a wealthy person can compete, and the fact of the matter is that only wealthy people *do* compete. Is that fair? Does it advance the sport? Does it make tennis more popular—or does it tend to suppress and hinder an enormous amount of tennis talent lying dormant in the bodies of young men and women whose names are not in the social register?"[11]

Lenglen's one and only professional tour featured forty stops.

The British star Bunny Austin, less dramatically, said he went pro because he did not want to be a "useless old man living in a one-room flat." His countryman, columnist Trevor Wignall, put it bluntly: "As things are today, the tennis star who turns professional kisses farewell to the very desirable trimmings of the game. Mongrels are not welcome in well-bred kennels. It is all monstrously unfair and unsportsmanlike, and contemptible. Amateur tennis is as much a professional occupation as working on a dock, balancing a ledger or writing a book."[12]

Marble may not have been a natural actress, but she was not above showmanship. A black-and-white news photograph captures Alice's ebullience at the time of her announcement. Hopping up on what looked like a desk or a bureau, and sitting side-legged, using lipstick as her pen, she wrote on a formally framed mirror, in an exuberant hand, "$25,000," the amount she had been guaranteed. Marble and Teach were hoping that sidelines from the tour would create even more revenue. She had already negotiated with Longines to promote the company as the official watchmaker for what it called the Alice Marble Professional Tour. There would be sixty-one stops in all, beginning in New York on January 6, 1941, and ending in Birmingham, Alabama, on May 10. She said she felt "practically like a millionaire." The new chapter inspired yet another commonly used pun-laden headline: "Alice in Moneyland."

The financial details were confirmed by Jack Harris. He placed Alice's guarantee for a four-and-a-half-month tour at $25,000, with an opportunity for her to better that figure if the receipts went above a certain amount.

American Lawn Tennis wrote: "As in the case of Budge's $75,000, Harris stated that he is personally the sole backer and underwriter. Miss Tennant—when Miss Marble was asked just how much she expected to gross on her playing, singing, sports clothes designing, endorsing, and possibly a name on a racket—vouchsafed the information that Alice would have to temper her expectations on the tour itself, since there were two other high-priced performers in the troupe—Budge and Tilden."[13]

The second piece of news that Marble related at her press conference was that when the tour was complete, she planned to invest in voice lessons with Dr. Mario Marafioti of Los Angeles, the former throat specialist for the Metropolitan Opera Company, who hoped to turn Alice away from the deeper registers into a mezzo-soprano.

"All my life I have wanted to sing," she told the crowd. "Mother wanted me to be a singer—she played the piano and father played the cornet—but they could not afford lessons for me. Last winter I took two months of fancy singing lessons—and that settled it. I just have to be a singer. I'm so excited about it I can't think of anything else. I'm excited too about making money—golly. I've been on the receiving end for so long that it will be a great thrill to do a lot of giving for a change."[14]

She hoped to donate some of her newfound wealth to young tennis players who, like her, might not have the money for the right equipment: "I've never had any money for extras," she said, recalling the shoes she wore to play in when she was sixteen, so small she lopped off the backs and turned them into slippers, securing them to her feet with elastic bands. (Years later, she would donate her time to young players, giving free or low-cost lessons to deserving pupils.) "You have to live high in the tennis world. From the middle of April to the middle of September each year, you have to be able to travel. You live in other people's houses—nice houses and nice people—but you've got to tip the servants and buy thank-you gifts and play the part of a winner."[15]

The 1941 professional tour would cover ample territory, over twenty-five thousand miles, but it would be somewhat less hectic than previous ones, in that Harris had worked out a new approach. In the past, such tours stopped in all forty-eight states, but he now favored a more streamlined version, with fewer stops and some of the sites closer together.[16] Harris planned to keep to his policy of transporting the players to the next engagement site as soon as the matches ended, on the theory that if they were excited from playing a match, they would have trouble sleeping and would be even more exhausted when they had to wake up early to leave the next day. The tour organizers urged the four players to observe certain protocols: get plenty of sleep, nine hours, if possible, and take a nap on days when they played. Watch the water: it could contain unfamiliar minerals that might upset their digestion. Avoid movies for two reasons: the strain on the eyes and the unhealthy sedentary nature of the activity. Cards, just not poker, were approved, along with shopping, in moderation.

In the weeks that followed Marble's announcement, the president of the United States Lawn Tennis Association, Holcombe Ward, in a statement that has grown even less appealing with time, quickly assured fans that her departure did not mean all glamour had fled the sport: "There are scores of beauteous gals just budding into bloom; gals who are restful and easy on the orbs, and who have that certain something which makes the male cash customers forget what the score is."[17]

The fourth member of the tour was finally announced: England's Mary Hardwick. Marble had beaten Hardwick every time they had played previously, but that did not prevent a hopeful press from hyping her prospects. Hardwick was sometimes referred to as the "English refugee," as she had been trapped in the United States in 1939 as a member of the Wightman Cup team by the outbreak of war in England. The *New York Times* called her "a diligent worker for British war relief," saying "her assets had thinned so precariously as a result of the foreign exchange situation that professional tennis beckoned to her as the solution to her problem." She had the consent of her family to join the tour and would be sending earnings home. The *Times* indicated that Hardwick, whose game was much less powerful than Marble's, was not likely to defeat Alice at her best, but if Marble faltered at all, Hardwick, who had previously beaten Sarah Palfrey Cooke and Pauline Betz in the US National Championships, might find an opening.[18]

In the *Times* article, Hardwick explained why the tour appealed to her: "I might have gone home to England and roll bandages or knit sweaters or do any of the thousand and one things which British women are doing today, but I honestly feel that I am accomplishing more by earning my own living here and sending the bulk of my income home to aid the suffering. There is no tennis in England now, and there may not be again in my lifetime, but some day the stands around center court at Wimbledon will be filled again, and I'd like to feel that I helped in some way, however small."

Mary K. Browne, ever the close friend, offered advice to Marble less than two weeks before the tour started, based on her own experience, having toured with Suzanne Lenglen two decades earlier. She reminded Alice that she would have matches every other day, but not to worry about weather-related delays and missed connections and other transportation snafus because she had no control over any of it. She said the indoor arenas would be crowded with cigarette smoke in the air and that she might experience trouble breathing. "The only thing to do is to school yourself to counteract it by going around outdoors during the day, collecting a stock of fresh air that will last through the evening."

She also counseled Alice to "avoid meeting too many people. There's nothing quite so tiring as people."[19]

While Brownie warned Alice about the challenges she would face on tour, the promoters were unabashedly enthusiastic, trumpeting Marble in a promotional brochure: "The Glamour Girl has arrived in tennis. Alice Marble brings to her new field of endeavor all the attributes of greatness: high purpose, skill, courage, modesty and vibrant health. Professional tennis salutes its newest luminary—the streamlined American girl, Alice Marble."

The logistics of cramming sixty-one venues into a four-and-a-half-month interval that began in the dead of winter would be daunting by any standards but were especially so in 1941, when air travel was barely past its infancy, cars were unreliable, and efficient interstates a figment of the future. Many of the arenas did not have tennis courts, so a property man and his assistant traveled by truck, transporting a makeshift court. Workers would lay the two halves of a sailcloth canvas, each weighing a half ton, out on the floor and secure them with ropes and pulleys. It took three hours to create a surface uniformly smooth enough that players would not trip over an unexpected crease in the fabric. Budge compared the tent truck to a circus wagon, festooned as it was with colorful lettering announcing the tour, which had a strain of vaudeville running through its veins. Amazingly, the troupe made it to every stop.

Marble entered the tour feeling depleted. She had spent the weeks since making her announcement racing around, honoring previous commitments to deliver her "will to win" speech. Christmas was quiet, spent with friends at her Sherry-Netherland Hotel suite.[20] The next day, she made her weeklong Broadway debut at Loew's State Theatre, part of a vaudeville show with acrobats, comedians, and tap dancers; she sang in four shows a day, from December 26 to January 2.

Alice and Jay C. Flippen, the emcee and an established actor, were equal headliners. Alice's ten-minute patter-and-song act included "Don't Rock the Boat"[21] and "It Was Just One of Those Things," with new lyrics about romance at the Westchester Country Club.[22] *Billboard* magazine's

tepid summation: her voice was "full but not too appealing."[23] *Variety* magazine dashed any hope: "Miss Marble's routine includes some specially written
verses in which there is included the query, 'You Might Be Wondering What
I'm Doing Here?' That in itself provides a wide opening."[24] Marble, recruited
for her name value, "incurs the admiration of the State's Wimbledon set more
for her courage in crashing a new medium than for her aptitude." She "got
away nicely with her expressionless service of several pop tunes," encouraged
by an indulgent audience in a holiday mood.[25] *Variety* praised Alice's "strong
contralto," finding more suited to clubs than the stage. "It's all too, too swanky
and dubiously entertaining. Okay for class niteries, however, in which field she
has already appeared."[26] Show people did not abandon Alice in the following
days. Mr. and Mrs. Arthur Loew—Arthur was an executive in the business his
father started—and emcee Flippen had box seats for her pro tennis debut.[27]

The lackluster critical reception would have been a wake-up to Marble;
if she thought a career in show biz was going to be a surefire exit plan when
she retired from tennis, it was time to think again.

The AP hailed her first tour stop, in Madison Square Garden, on January 6, 1941, with the headline "Alice Marble in Pro Debut Tonight" and
predicted sixteen thousand spectators would attend. Promoter Jack Harris
engaged a corps of linesmen from the Tennis Umpires Association, who
officiated dressed in dinner coats, and two women, attired in satin and velvet.
Mary Hardwick, wearing a red blazer over a sleeveless tennis white dress,
was introduced first. She walked to the center of the west baseline and stood
perfectly still while the British flag was raised to the tune of "God Save the
King." Marble, wearing a knitted middy sweater over a long-sleeved blouse
and shorts, advanced to the same spot, where an American flag was raised
to the tune of "The Star-Spangled Banner." For the first time in memory,
Alice forsook her jaunty little cap.[28]

Allison Danzig of the *New York Times* put the event in its historical
context:

> On the same brilliantly lit court whereon William Tilden hit the golden
> trail in 1931, to show the way to riches to Henri Cochet of France, Ellsworth
> Vines, Fred Perry of Great Britain, and J. Donald Budge, all world ama-
> teur champions, blonde, comely Alice Marble will have her premiere on a
> contracted tour across the country. . . . The appearance of Miss Marble and
> Miss Hardwick on the Garden court will make the first time that professional

tennis has presented women players of such rank since 1926. It was that year
Mlle. Suzanne Lenglen of France and Miss Mary K. Browne appeared
on a program under the auspices of C. C. Pyle, with Vincent Richards and
Howard O. Kinsey as the other headliners.[29]

Marble almost lost to Hardwick that first night (8–6, 8–6), before 12,371 fans, fewer than predicted. Danzig reported: "Miss Marble did not play as consistently as she can, her forehand being recalcitrant all through the match." He praised Hardwick for giving Marble a run for her money, pointing out her "tenacity of purpose and excellence off the ground." He thought Hardwick was so good that he predicted Marble could be in trouble and the tour might prove "more of an ordeal" than even her four national championships.

L. B. Icely, president of Wilson Sporting Goods and an organizer of the tour, misread Marble's missteps and congratulated her for throwing so many games to Hardwick. Marble was enraged: "Mr. Icely, I don't give anyone games," she retorted. Marble learned early on that such charity often backfired when a weaker opponent, likely buoyed by unexpected success, suddenly caught fire.

The Budge-Tilden matchup that night offered less in the way of suspense. One writer in *American Lawn Tennis* recalled that years earlier Tilden had hit shots that made spectators stand up on a chair, but those occasions were fewer and further between, and Tilden was now embracing the role of court jester. In the initial game against Budge, he broke his racket on the first stroke and then, after apologies to the audience, he managed to break a second racket. His "foolery brought down the house," but for his long-time admirers, seeing him replace brilliant stroke-making with antics was "not a pleasant augury for his future."[30]

The four players, Teach, and manager Jack Harris next traveled to Chicago by plane. As in the tour's opening ceremony, the American and British flags were raised before all the matches, and the American and British national anthems were sung or played. Soon a curious dynamic began to emerge among the players and organizers: Tilden behaved as if he, not Harris, were the manager. Whenever facilities struck him as inadequate, Tilden took charge, waging a special war against the scourge of poor lighting. Budge, amused by Tilden's ardor, did not share his concern. Bad lights could be a hindrance, but they were like the weather—something one just accepted in that both players were affected equally. Tilden, not appeased, ordered workers to move electrical devices on the ceiling back and forth, up and down, on and off, in a somewhat panicked fashion, causing onlookers to joke that despite the commotion, the lights probably all ended up exactly where they had been in the first place.

Tall, at six feet one and a half inches, Tilden had a long, narrow face, with wide shoulders atop a narrow frame. With his dramatic movements, and his sloping face accentuated by the deep Vs of the sweaters he favored, he seemed at times like a human cape, sweeping and swirling in several directions at once. Tilden was vivid in contrast to Budge, who with his fair coloring and accommodating manner, could recede off court, like an echo of himself. On court, his backhand was so formidable that one opponent said trying to return it was like volleying a piano.

A terrible businessman, Tilden interfered at the gate. He refunded promoters when there was no need to. It was such a common occurrence that one time when Harris spotted Tilden speaking to a functionary at a venue, he asked Budge what Tilden was up to.

"Oh," said Budge, "Bill's just telling them they can have their money back."[31]

Money quickly became a sticking point for Marble. After merely three stops on the tour, she began to resent that Don Budge was, at $75,000, making three times as much as she was. He was also getting a percentage of the gate, at least what remained after Tilden left his mark.[32] Tilden and Hardwick were getting paid more as well. She had agreed to the lower sum, at the urging of Teach, but it now seemed unfair. Marble was the darling of the press, who called her "queen." The red, white, and blue cover of the official program featured her image and not the others. The typography made it seem as if the tour bore her name, and it was in fact referred to in some quarters as the Alice Marble Professional Tour, such as in an ad from Longines, hailing Marble as the sponsor of the official watch of the United States Lawn Tennis Association.

Alice threatened to go on strike one hour before a match was to commence in Minneapolis, when the organizers caved, giving Marble the same deal as Budge. In addition to more than tripling her earnings, the incident gave her something else: the opportunity to see Teach in a new light. She had never doubted Teach's efficacy as her advocate, and now she did, a momentous shift in her thinking, giving Marble the ammunition that would lead to the eventual dissolution of their partnership.

Al Ennis, the publicity director, served as advance man, setting forth anywhere from one week to ten days ahead of the others, sowing enthusiasm at each stop. Newspapers didn't linger as often on Marble's fabled will-to-win story—swapping baseball for tennis, her illness, championships. There was fresh material. In St. Louis on January 17, a reporter met Tennant, Budge, and Marble for coffee, and recorded this exchange, asking what the tour was like:

> "It's fun," said Queen Alice with a semblance of royal dignity. Then she dropped a packet of paper matches in her coffee and as she fished it out with a spoon, the fun really began.
>
> "Anything to get attention," brooded Miss Tennant, the star's coach, who said Miss Marble was violently in love with Budge. . . .
>
> "Do you love me honey?" Queen Alice was asking him.
>
> In a jesting voice, Budge quavered: "I never felt like this about anyone before as I do about you, darling." . . .
>
> "Don thinks we ought to spend more time together before I propose," Miss Marble said, then hummed a few bars of "Only Forever" in her best singing voice as Budge leaned over to the reporter. "Psst," said he, "I don't know about her, but I'm only kidding."
>
> This madness has followed them since the start of the tour, Miss Marble declared. There's hardly a dull moment.[33]

Budge's wedding a few weeks after the tour ended smashed the Marble-Budge romance rumors once and for all.

That night, Tilden, having collided with a car the day before on an icy road and bruising his leg, shuffled onto the court with a cane. He announced it was the first time in twenty-five years that he missed a match, earning him the "biggest applause of the evening."[34]

January 23 in Boston at the old Garden would live in personal infamy for Marble. Playing before an audience of 5,121, the lackluster Marble at first seemed to be "merely toying" with Hardwick, "in the interests of showman-ship," reported the *Boston Globe*. But it soon became clear that Marble was off her game, and ultimately, she won only three points in the last three games, as Hardwick defeated her for the first time on the tour, 6–4, 4–6, 6–2. Marble had not lost a match since 1938, and she ungraciously "beat a hasty retreat from the court after her match, with the happy Miss Hardwick trailing after her. . . . Miss Marble, who has won every woman's title there is to win, didn't take her defeat too well, which is strange considering she is now one of a money-making troupe which depends on showmanship and good will."[35]

Some of the group was invited to President Franklin D. Roosevelt's birthday celebration, on January 30. For the eighth year in a row, Roosevelt turned his birthday into a nationwide fundraiser for polio, the disease that struck him in 1921, at age thirty-nine, leaving him paralyzed from the waist down. Birthday balls were orchestrated all over the country, with proceeds going to organizations providing local services and to Roosevelt's National Foundation for Infantile Paralysis, eventually named the March of Dimes. As Roosevelt said in a radio address, he couldn't think of a better birthday present. Dimes were arriving by mail at the White House, a fundraising campaign that sprang from the idea that if everyone in America sent in a dime, or extra change, the bank would grow exponentially.

Roosevelt's birthday festivities began with a private lunch at the White House. The guest list was heavy on entertainers, including swing bandleader Benny Goodman, actresses Maureen O'Hara and Lana Turner, actor Glenn Ford, comedian Red Skelton, *Information Please* TV host Clifton Fadiman, and, among others, Alice Marble, Mary Hardwick, and Eleanor Tennant.[36]

As was customary, Roosevelt was seated in the State Dining Room before the sixty guests arrived.[37] After lunch, Eleanor Roosevelt gave a tour of the White House, a task she performed with her usual warmth and friendliness. After the White House lunch, Marble and Hardwick had tea at the British embassy, invited by Lady Halifax, wife of Britain's new ambassador to the United States. Both had watched Marble and Hardwick at Wimbledon.[38]

For Marble and Hardwick, it was back to the normal routine the next day. Marble and Teach were to appear at Hecht's department store in Washington, followed by a tennis clinic. In the evening, the foursome played at Ritchie Coliseum at the University of Maryland at College Park.[39] The *Evening Star* gave fans a heads-up about the toll pregame partying might exact: "After their strenuous day and night yesterday, . . . the Misses Marble and Hardwick may be anxious to get it over with as fast as they can this evening. 'All' they did after arriving in Washington at 12:50, was to dash to a White House luncheon at 1 o'clock, take in a tea at the British Embassy at 5, attend the President's Birthday dinner last night and make the rounds of the balls."[40]

The 3,428 spectators got to watch a well-fought match, however fatigued Marble and Hardwick were, which Marble won, 7–5, 8–6.[41]

On February 6, in Charlotte, North Carolina, Mr. and Mrs. L. G. Osborne invited the tennis players to their home on Biltmore Drive for a dinner party that took tennis as its theme. Their table was set to resemble a miniature court, with a net across the middle and baselines marked with chalk. They served sandwiches shaped like miniature rackets, with olives rolled in cream cheese representing tennis balls.[42]

Later that month, after playing in Havana, Cuba, the troupe had to make a quick turnaround to Nassau, Bahamas, then a British colony, to play a charity match to benefit the Red Cross in front of the Duke and Duchess of Windsor. However, no direct flights connected the two cities. The Duke of Windsor, governor of Nassau, came to the rescue, sending his private plane to Cuba.[43] Only five people—the four players plus their manager—could fit aboard, and Teach was temporarily left behind.

On February 23, in Fort Worth, Texas, "old geezer" Tilden, forty-eight, defeated Budge (6–8, 6–1, 6–2) for the second time on the tour. In between games, he would say things like: "I won that game, Don, by the grace of a stinking bounce."[44] By then Tilden was in something of a free fall. His choice of clothing and his erratic behavior on court cemented an impression that he was an oddball. In the middle of matches, he would suddenly go barefoot or play in his stocking feet, thinking that gave him more traction. Rather than wear a simple warm-up, he dressed extravagantly, in a camel-hair jacket.[45] He was sometimes mocked with the girl's nickname "Tilly." Tilden's habitual cigarette smoking did nothing to lift his game, and his rumored sexual predilection for young boys threatened his reputation, a circumstance that the tennis hierarchy did its best to ignore.

One Fort Worth reporter, reviewing the looks of the players, called Marble pretty, Tilden "old and tall and wonderful," Hardwick a ballet dancer, and Budge "so homely he's handsome."[46]

In Los Angeles, on March 2, a fake court was stretched out over part of an indoor ice-skating rink at the Westwood Tropical Ice Company. Bob Hope emceed, quipping, "Big Bill appeared through the courtesy of the Westwood Adrenalin Co."[47]

The ball boys wore skates, and between matches skaters performed skits. At times the players bounded off their fake court and skidded onto the ice. Marble later recalled that Bing Crosby, whose baritone was once described by Louis Armstrong as "gold being poured out of a cup," helped introduce the players and that actress Barbara Stanwyck was in the audience. Best of all, from Marble's point of view, Lombard and Gable, beautiful and handsome as ever, cheered her on.

Alice left Los Angeles a day early, flying to San Francisco to catch up with her family. She had not been home in two years and had not played in her hometown in four. She looked, as was so often the case at this point in her life, like a starlet as she disembarked from the plane in a knee-length leopard-skin coat. During an interview, her sister Hazel and brother Tim were in another room, "spilling over with happiness at seeing their famed 'Sis.'" A reporter asked Marble to clarify where home was—San Francisco or Los Angeles?

"My home?? My home right now is in my suitcase. . . . But why bring that up? I suppose one's real home must always be the place where one's relatives are, where one was reared. But business and the world's demand sometimes require one to live elsewhere." Responding to a question about her future, she said possibilities, as usual, abounded, from designing clothes and singing, to movies, if they were Westerns. "Such pictures don't call for one being an actress, which I am not, so maybe I could get by with it. But I'd have to get acquainted with a horse."[48]

The triumphant visit included a parade down Market Street in an open car. The papers cared only for Alice. Tilden and Budge and Hardwick were merely "along for the ride." At city hall she was given a key to the city. Fans paid from fifty-five cents to $3.30 to watch their hometown heroine play at the Civic Auditorium, the same arena where Alice had fallen asleep during the Lenglen–Browne match in 1926.

It was a quick visit and only further emphasized the differences between Marble and the rest of her family. While they stayed put and toiled at workaday jobs, she enjoyed the limelight and constant attention from the press.

On April 3, Moline, Illinois, rolled out its idea of a red carpet for Alice Marble and friends. "Nothing has been spared to make the big exhibition here . . . the greatest in the history of quad-city tennis," said a local newspaper. "The big field house has been decked in flags around the balcony rails. The ushers and even the ball boys will appear in costumes featuring the Maroon and White of the Moline high school."[49]

A river town, filled with plants that manufactured pipe organs, furniture, cars, and above all John Deere farm equipment, Moline aspired to be another Pittsburgh. Known in neighboring towns as "Proud Moline," disparagingly, given the city's high self-regard, it prided itself on dullness and reliability. The many Swedes who immigrated there were welcomed as good workers, not inclined to go on strike.

"Moline tennis history," the *Daily Dispatch* predicted, "will be made."[50]

This was a chance to watch Big Bill Tilden in action one last time, at least in the Quad Cities region of Illinois and Iowa. Tilden had won his first national title in 1913, about two years before Budge was born, and "the services of a prophet" were not needed to predict Tilden's playing days were dwindling, according to the *Daily Dispatch*.[51]

The city's mood was "anxious"—not eager—as anticipation built for both Tilden and Marble. No "responsible tennis expert" on any continent in the world would say a woman could beat Marble. "It appears today," the newspaper reported, early in the week of the event, "that the largest crowd ever to see a tennis match in western Illinois or eastern Iowa will be on hand Thursday to see Queen Alice and her escort of tennis stars."[52]

All was well: twenty-six hundred fans attended, the biggest crowd "ever to witness tennis matches in the quad-cities." The city, with a population of 34,608, could be gratified that the "management of the professional troupe was amazed no little that in a city of the relatively small size of Moline, so large a crowd turned out despite miserable weather conditions."[53]

On April 14, in Indianapolis, Indiana, the focus was on the war effort. Throughout the tour, Hardwick had been raising money and supplies for England. She was active in Bundles for Britain, an organization that collected knitwear to send to her homeland. At the organization's Indianapolis chapter, Marble donated one hundred sweaters—short-sleeved pullovers—from her clothing line made at the Real Silk Hosiery Mills in town. The sweaters retailed for $4.95 (with three pairs of Realsilk brand stockings thrown in) and were versatile enough to wear at "home, office or outdoors" and "equally appropriate with skirts, slacks or shorts."[54] Hardwick accepted the sweaters and turned them over to a messenger to send to England. She invoked Churchill in her comment: "Anything I say will sound feeble, I know, when compared to the gratitude already brilliantly expressed to the people of the United States by our prime minister, Winston Churchill."[55]

On a tour with this many moving parts, one never knew when a remarkable moment would occur. On April 23, in Montreal, Tilden became more and more upset when a linesman called out three or four of Budge's clearly good shots. Tilden kept asking the linesman to change his calls, to no avail. Budge was flabbergasted. He had never seen anyone carry on so vociferously when the linesman was making mistakes that favored him and diminished his opponent.

Tilden's indignation grew to the point that he stopped play and asked the umpire to remove the linesman. Instead of admiring Tilden for being sportsmanlike, the crowd turned on him and began booing during points. Finally, Tilden, no stranger to drama, held up his hand to stop the match and commandeered the microphone. "Ladies and gentlemen," he said.

> *I believe you will observe the British way of letting a man defend himself before you condemn him. It is you, not I, who suffer the most from these bad calls. Mr. Budge is now the greatest player in the game, and you have paid good money to watch me try to put up a match against him. If I am to be disturbed by bad calls, I cannot play my best, and if you razz me or boo me during a point, you will only make it more difficult for me. Please boo me all you will between points. I have endured that all my life and am quite used to it, but if you wish to obtain the most for your money, hold off while I try to play the best player in the world. Thank you.*[56]

As Budge said later, he knew Tilden was persuasive, just not how persuasive. Play recommenced, to complete silence.[57]

On May 10, in Birmingham, Alabama, the tour breathed its last breath, with Tilden on his final tear about bad lighting and bad calls. This time, he stopped the match, demanding an electrician fix a light over the doors opening into the auditorium. As for Budge, when asked about whether the glare had bothered him, he wondered, "What glare?"[58]

And yet Marble always felt that Tilden enlivened the tour immeasurably, especially in the after-hours, when the players would socialize and decompress from the matches. Tilden took over, telling stories in dialect or reading a play he had written. He loved to act out each character and could be counted on to claim the spotlight for hours. His audience was grateful for the change of pace.

When the tour was over, the quartet could dwell on the comic side, how in Trenton they had played on a short basketball court and Hardwick's serve was caught by a boy in the balcony, or how in Los Angeles their tour had morphed into the Tennis-capades.

The final scores were woefully lopsided, with Marble beating her opponent 58–3, and Budge losing only seven matches to Tilden.

Jack Harris sent a letter to *American Lawn Tennis*, published on May
20, the event a rousing success.

> *In the 18 weeks of play our activities took us throughout the United States.
> We played a match in Havana, one in Nassau and three in Canada—
> Vancouver, Montreal and Toronto. Altogether 61 matches were played. . . .*
>
> *Despite the fact that Miss Hardwick won but three matches from Miss
> Marble, on several occasions in other matches Mary had excellent opportuni-
> ties to achieve victory, notably in Chicago, where on seven different occasions
> the English girl was at match point for a straight set victory. Tilden, too, in
> his matches with Budge, played magnificently throughout the entire tour, and
> though he won but seven times from Budge, demonstrated that he is still one of
> the world's greatest players and the most amazing athlete of this generation. . . .*
>
> *Attendance figures indicated that tennis interest is growing by leaps
> and bounds. In the neighborhood of 190,000 turned out to see our matches in
> the 4½ months we were on tour. Matches played at colleges and universities
> broke all previous records for attendance and financial returns. Without
> doubt, all in all, this was one of the most successful tours in history.*

At the finish line, Marble received a diagnosis of exhaustion and malnutrition and was given glucose for several days. Years later, she would share
an account of the tour that acknowledged just how grueling it had been, but
in the moment, the public was treated to a more sanguine version of events.

THE RUMORED MARRIAGE to Budge was all in good fun as far as Alice
was concerned, but a more serious prospect loomed. While Alice was on tour,
Will du Pont had gone to Reno to divorce Jean. Readers of the *Philadelphia
Inquirer* learned that Mrs. du Pont was now living separately, in Newtown
Square, Pennsylvania, "ever since rumors of a marital rift sped through Wilmington society circles. He has been interested in numerous sports and last
summer was principally occupied with tennis. It was reported that Miss Alice
Marble, pretty tennis star, was seen often in his company. She spent a week
in Wilmington last summer."[59]

The press practically announced nuptials for Marble and the equestrian from Delaware. Marble acknowledged that the rumor mill had her "smitten with a horseman who has four children." She admitted that he was "nice," but a spark was missing. She said about du Pont pretty much what she had said about Budge: "I love him in his way, but not that way."[60]

Du Pont was indeed eccentric. One friend and frequent visitor to his estate said, "You wouldn't think he had a quarter in his pocket. He probably didn't. He always carried a curved pipe and wore shirts that were always too big for him. He worked long hours. He was up with the colts at three thirty or four in the morning. He had the nicest horses. He loved tending his rose garden. When he had company, he would fix mint juleps for everyone and go to bed early, at seven thirty or so."[61]

Alice remembered someone warning her: "You can't marry him. Will's such an automaton, he would probably say, 'Alice, we'll have intercourse at eight thirty-one P.M.'"[62]

Alice always felt that the du Ponts's oldest child, Jean Ellen, who turned eighteen during the divorce proceedings, blamed the "pretty tennis star" (as the *Philadelphia Inquirer* called Marble) for her parents' divorce. True or not, years later, Marble would pay a heavy price for that perception.

Even if marriage to Alice was not in the cards, du Pont would have been hard put to evict her from his thoughts entirely. She maintained a sprightly presence in news columns and gossip items, her renown expanding beyond tennis. Her name surfaced frequently on the women's pages. She became an icon: almost anything she wore or said or did upheld her image as a trendsetter and tastemaker. Everywhere a reader looked, photographs of Alice appeared, offering fitness advice or beauty tips or sharing information on yet another new career. She told readers in Vineland, New Jersey, that like a pianist, she considered her hands among her most precious possessions, demonstrating a routine of finger, wrist, and arm exercises that she performed every morning and before matches in order to ensure her strong grip.[63] She told fans in Indianapolis that they should bleach the tips of their hair if they wanted to be more glamorous.[64]

Alice gained a reputation as a clothing designer and guru; her mother's rickety sewing machine had been a major influence after all. The *Detroit Free Press* wrote with admiration about Marble's rayon tennis dress. One unusual design element was "plaited inserts under the arm," the paper explained.

"They look like just a regular shirt sleeve when your arms are down but extend out like an accordion when you swing your arm in action."[65] In Ithaca, New York, readers learned that she required ten street-length dresses and four evening gowns a season to be pleased with her wardrobe.[66] The *Desert Sun*, in Palm Springs, California, ran a picture of a pensive Marble leaning against a ladder, praising shirtwaist dresses for day and night, dressed in a rayon-gabardine dress with metal buttons and bishop sleeves—a long, billowing sleeve gathered at the bottom with a cuff—described as her favorite.[67] A Boston readership was told of a more practical item of apparel that she had designed, a military oxford shoe "made of polished, supple calfskin with built-in arch support features plus a sturdy men's weight sole, as flexible as your own toes."[68] What remains murky is how much money, if any, these designs and endorsements generated. From her later protestations about poverty, the payoff appears to have consisted, in part, of the publicity itself and vague promises of more doors opening.

WITH THE UNITED STATES actively preparing to defend itself against Nazi Germany, Marble wanted to do her share. She tried to join the WAVES (the women's branch of the US Naval Reserve) but said she was turned down, as she was by other branches of the military, when she shared with them her history of tuberculosis, ignoring her actual medical history, in which doctors had eventually ruled it out.

Marble found what was at least temporarily a good placement, serving in the Office of Civilian Defense. New York City mayor Fiorello La Guardia headed the organization, spending half the week in Washington. He had been appointed to the post by FDR, who admired the mayor's brusque style, to the point of comparing him to Winston Churchill. La Guardia had a similarly direct way of speaking, warning his fellow citizens that they should toughen up. This was no clambake, he liked to say, nor was it a pinochle party. Eleanor Roosevelt served as assistant director, and on September 4, 1941, three months before the attack on Pearl Harbor and America's involvement in World War II, Marble was appointed to the office as cochair in charge of physical fitness for women. Her male counterpart in these efforts was John B. Kelly, a wealthy Olympic gold medalist in rowing from Philadelphia who promoted fitness through his writing. Their assignment was called Hale America.

Sheilah Graham, a Hollywood gossip columnist, wrote that Marble was joining forces with Mayor La Guardia to "put bone and muscle into the feminine 'form divine,' United States brand."

"The idea behind the organization," Marble told Graham, "is to make the women of this country better citizens by keeping them physically fit and thus prepared for any national emergency. . . . Walking is the cheapest and best way to keep well. I want women to walk to work, to walk to the movies, to walk to the stores. I want them to join our hiking clubs and walk on their weekends. I myself always walk two miles a day at least." Marble told Graham that there would be "no more singing in night clubs" and romance was out, including with du Pont.[69]

Marble would be paid a dollar a year for urging on the public with comments such as how there are too many watchers, not enough doers. She liked to cite the number of spectators at a football game, giving a figure of 90,000 people, on hand to watch 22 young men play. She lamented the softness of the American lifestyle, especially the reliance on cars as a means of transportation. Brownie volunteered to serve as her assistant, thus cementing a friendship that would be one of the most significant mainstays in Marble's life. Barely over five feet tall, Brownie's even temperament had been put to good use a few years back when her diplomacy with the tennis authorities got Marble reinstated at the highest levels.

Marble felt that American women lagged behind their British counterparts, based on observations she made in England during the summer of 1939, when she saw "thousands of women taking long hikes and bicycle trips" on the weekends. She also noticed Englishwomen playing tennis for recreation, some as old as sixty-five. She was not surprised that "they have been able to take over men's jobs in wartime. We should be able to do as much."[70] Marble said that in addition to walking, she jumped rope and played tennis with Teach five times a week: "If I can have an hour of tennis before dinner, I'm a new person."[71] She often played at the home of Arthur Loew, then vice president of Metro-Goldwyn-Mayer, whom she advised against double features as being too sedentary.[72]

This Week, a magazine of the *Los Angeles Times*, published Alice's message to "America's fifty million women" on October 26, 1941:

> *I have been given the job of getting 50 million American women in top-notch physical shape—to help our country meet the present emergency.*

> *Someone is going to ask: "What does physical fitness have to do with National Defense?"*
>
> *For an answer, look at Europe. More than ever before women are sharing the burdens and hardships of war. They are manning antiaircraft guns. They are driving ambulances and canteens through the rain of falling bombs. They are giving first aid by flashlight in demolished shelters. They are harvesting crops and manning the assembly lines in munitions factories.*

Alice unleashed a new slogan: "Bridge Clubs into Athletic Clubs." Acknowledging that exercise for exercise's sake was not her top choice for fun ("It's the game and competition that give you the lift"), she was determined to find a way to get women moving around in groups and enjoying it. To underscore her commitment to fitness, she sported a new low-maintenance "minute woman" hairdo, three inches long, requiring only a minute of brushing.[73] Alice's trips to Washington meant that she had occasion to converse with First Lady Eleanor Roosevelt, who worried she was not sufficiently active: "I walk from the White House to my office, about a mile. Then, when I get home at night, I go for a twenty-minute swim. Friday night, I go to Hyde Park and spend two days working in my garden. This is fair exercise, because I'm so tall I have to stoop a long way. Weekends I also get up early and go for a ride, but I don't get anywhere near enough exercise." Alice begged to differ.[74]

MARBLE WAS HARDLY the only celebrity putting herself forward to help in the war effort. Carole Lombard wanted to pitch in as well. After the attack on Pearl Harbor on December 7, people on the West Coast felt more vulnerable to attack than their East Coast counterparts and immediately scheduled "air raid drills, black-outs, brown-outs, and other civilian efforts at mobilization."[75] Lombard and Gable sent a letter to the president, asking how they could help.

Responding on December 16, 1941, Roosevelt thanked the couple and urged them to carry on: "For the present, at least, I think you can both render the very highest service to the nation by continuing your professional activities. In contributing your superb talents to the production of inspirational and patriotic pictures you will help maintain the spirit and morale of the nation. Such a contribution, always of incalculable value, is indispensable at this time."[76]

Unwilling to accept that their talents were the full extent of any contribution they could make, the couple figured out their own plan for pitching in. An isolationist before the war, Gable moderated his views and accepted a post as the head of the Hollywood Victory Committee. In that capacity, he was asked whether Lombard, a Hoosier, would consider heading home to Indiana to attend a statewide war-bond rally to raise money for World War II, held on January 15, 1942.[77] She would and did. Anyone buying a bond received a receipt with Lombard's picture and an autograph.

All told, Lombard raised about $2 million in a day. As a reporter wrote in the *Indianapolis Star*: "Those young gentlemen who wonder what Clark Gable has that they haven't got learned yesterday afternoon that it was Carole Lombard."[78]

After the rally, Lombard decided to fly home instead of taking the train, as planned. Lombard's mother and Otto Winkler (Gable's MGM publicist), who had accompanied Lombard, were against it. A coin toss in Lombard's favor sealed the decision, the Associated Press later reported.[79] They got tickets on a TWA flight that was scheduled to leave Indianapolis around four a.m. and arrive in California by evening.

Why Lombard wanted to get home so quickly invited gossip—was Gable romancing Lana Turner, his young costar in the movie *Somewhere I'll Find You*? Did Lombard need to get back to the premiere of her new movie, *To Be or Not to Be*? Was she hoping to become pregnant sooner rather than later? Maybe she was just plain tired. She told a photographer from *Life* magazine that she simply could not face three days on the "choo-choo train."[80]

The DC-3 plane that Lombard, her mother, and Winkler boarded made several departures and landings en route.[81] In the evening, the plane was cleared to depart Las Vegas for the last leg of the trip. Fifteen minutes later, at 7:20 PST, on January 16, 1942, the plane crashed into an "almost vertical rock cliff, near the top of Potosi Mountain in the Spring Mountain Range," according to the Civil Aeronautics Board report.[82] Everyone was killed, three crew and nineteen passengers.

Witnesses heard the crash and saw the fire on the mountain. Gable flew with a group to Las Vegas, hoping to join the search party, a task from which he was dissuaded. He gave moral support to the rescue mission that took three days to complete its grim task. An observer later said, "Clark put on the greatest act of his life, trying to keep everyone else from crumbling."[83]

Because she died in service to her country, Lombard was offered a military funeral, but her survivors honored a directive in her 1939 will, in which she requested a private event, to "be clothed in white," and entombed in a modestly priced crypt in Forest Lawn Memorial Park, Glendale, California. Afterward, friends noticed that Gable seemed kinder than he had ever been before but also deeply preoccupied, so much so that his doctor warned him against drink.

Upon hearing the news, both Teach and Alice broke down. It was the first time Alice had seen Teach grieve, and it felt awkward to hug her, but she did. Teach buried her face in Alice's neck. Alice's reaction to the loss of her friend was to follow in Lombard's footsteps and amplify her own war efforts. She visited wounded soldiers in hospitals in the New York area, singing, playing cards, and chatting with them.[84] A week earlier, the two friends had chatted on the phone for an hour. "Losing Carole was like losing a sister. We had such a wonderful kinship, an intuitive understanding of each other," Alice recalled years later.[85]

Lombard had been scheduled to start filming another comedy, *They All Kissed the Bride*, for Columbia Pictures. Joan Crawford stepped into the role in her place though not without difficulty. MGM chief Louis B. Mayer, who had Crawford under contract, did not want to release her. Crawford tried appealing to his emotions, but when that didn't work, she went straight to the bottom line: if he persisted in refusing to let her step in for Lombard, "one of the most beloved members of the film community, the whole town would hear about it, and fast."

Crawford assumed the role in her friend's place and turned over her salary—$128,000—to the American Red Cross, which had led the search through the Spring Mountain Range for Lombard and the other twenty-one victims of TWA Flight 3. When Crawford's agent refused to give up his 10 percent, she did what was honorable: She paid him the amount he demanded and then let him go.[86]

CHAPTER 21

WONDER WOMAN

N EW YORK CITY in the war years pulsed with common purpose. The city was awash with "soldier khaki and sailor blue"[1] as GIs marched in formation and sailors lounged in the parks and vice versa. The city served as the principal port of embarkation for the European theater, the Mediterranean, and North Africa as the war went on—almost three million men and even more supplies shipped out from New York.[2]

Weddings were hasty and commonplace. In 1942 alone, almost two million weddings took place across the nation, nearly double the number ten years earlier. Many of the grooms were new enlistees. A minister at an Episcopal church on Twenty-Ninth Street between Madison and Fifth Avenues performed three ceremonies in the morning and three in the afternoon, on what he called a slow day. Brides dressed modestly, sometimes in dresses fashioned from the silk parachutes that their husbands trained with. Cakes, nontraditional, like the lead cakes of Marble's childhood, sprang from rations.[3]

Kids collected tin cans for recycling, "to keep our munitions factories going," as Mayor La Guardia exhorted. Turning in scrap metal was a national effort, but in a "city of apartment dwellers, the humble tin can offers the best regular source of scrap metal," and Mayor La Guardia, the *Daily News* said, was determined to get back every last one.[4] One man snooped on uncooperative neighbors: "Believe it or not," said a letter writer to the *Brooklyn Daily Eagle*, "occupants of some big apartment houses are throwing tin cans in the incinerators or rubbish boxes instead of keeping them separate."[5]

In an era when the military—and America at large—was segregated, racism extended to Red Cross blood banks, which did not accept donations from Black people at the beginning of the war, and when they finally did, in

January 1942, the donations remained segregated. It made no difference that one of the world's leading authorities on blood banking was Dr. Charles Drew, an African American, or that the Nazis favored an Aryan-only blood policy.[6] (The Red Cross ended racial blood segregation in 1948.)

Volunteers signed up with the City Patrol Corps, a civilian defense organization cloaked in police authority.[7] Men, in uniforms provided by the city, patrolled from four p.m. to midnight, armed with nightsticks and revolvers, on the lookout for teenage gangs as well as foreign saboteurs. Women could also volunteer, working behind the scenes, arranging transportation, typing reports, and preparing food for the corps.[8]

By spring 1942, the city was under a military dimout order because of the fear of bombs, affecting Times Square, the Empire State Building, streetlamps, ships in the harbor, and trains along the shore route. The Brooklyn Navy Yard built battleships around the clock, employing seventy-five thousand,[9] including women, in jobs that were once off-limits to them.

As assistant director of civilian defense in charge of physical training for women, dressed in a drab green uniform, Marble fit into the mold, undertaking public displays of sacrifice and patriotism. Her job became even more demanding after Pearl Harbor, when she and Brownie were on the road or in Washington, giving speeches about the salubrious benefits of exercise, three days a week, every other week. It was hard to gauge what good they were doing. The women to whom they directed their pep talks were exhausted from working on assembly lines, and when they weren't at work or asleep, they were tending to their families. The lack of pay was more burdensome than Marble had envisioned. She and Teach continued to pool their earnings, a moot point now that Marble's amounted to a dollar a year. On January 24, 1942, du Pont sent a letter to "Dear Teach"—no more "Miss Tennant"—detailing how a joint account at the Delaware Trust Company he set up for Teach and Alice would work.

For the purpose of buying bonds and making any investments, you and Alice individually gave me a Power of Appointment that allows me to sign checks on the joint account, for which I am holding the check book, and also to make deposits in the account for you.

I think it would be very hazardous to play the stock market at this time, as it is so uncertain and there is the possibility that many of the companies, whose stocks and securities are listed on the board, may have to discontinue their regular business and do only war work. Consequently, I would rather have my money in cash or liquid form so that when the market crashes during the slump that is bound to occur after this world conflagration subsides, I would be in a position to buy at that time.

My advice would be at this time to use the cash balance of $1,125.00 and borrow the rest of what you need, which I could arrange for you, to pay your income taxes (you didn't tell me how much they were) and to cover your living expenses, as I could get you a loan for about 2 and ½% interest or half of what you are earning on your investment. . . . The security of the bonds would be perfectly good.[10]

The letter was all business until the end, when he wrote, somewhat ambiguously, "Perhaps sincere friendship has to have a few tests at times, but it always wins out." Then, he mentioned that he had a source for some hams, and if they turned out to be any good, he would leave one at the Sherry-Netherland, where Teach and Alice were staying. Du Pont had a touch of the quartermaster to him, and over the years he spent a good deal of energy provisioning his friends with treats, arranging deliveries of delicacies and luxuries, including out-of-season fruit, salmon from the finest streams, nylons, and now ham.

He signed the letter: "With love to Alice and yourself, I remain . . ."

A couple of weeks later, while at Union Station in Washington, DC, he was certain he heard Alice Marble being summoned by loudspeaker to the Western Union stand. He looked for her on the train to New York, thinking he might convince her to join him for supper, but to no avail. She was nowhere to be found.

In April, Marble announced her resignation from her civilian defense role as of May 1. The Associated Press reported: "When appointed to that post last September, she asserted she would continue in the dollar-a-year post 'until I go broke.' She indicated she was nearing that condition."[11]

She explained the stark financial truth to a reporter: "I am entirely self-supporting, having no independent means of my own." She said she wanted to serve in the defense effort, but "I haven't the least idea of what I'm going to do. There isn't any tennis to speak of. I'm going to try to organize some matches for the benefit of various war funds." She ended the exchange with a stab at levity. "Have you a good job for me?" she asked the reporter. "I like to eat steaks," she said, only half joking.[12]

Brownie left the Hale America job as well, heading to Australia to volunteer with the American Red Cross. Marble, never one to sit by idly, volunteered for the New York City branch of the Navy Relief Society. Eleanor Roosevelt, who published daily accounts of her own activities, mentioned Alice in her My Day column on May 29: "Then I went to the Navy Relief Society Headquarters and was photographed with Miss Alice Marble, who is helping to distribute the little banks throughout the city in which people can put small coins for the benefit of the Navy Relief Society."

Marble added exhibition tennis matches to help the war effort to her other out-of-town commitments. On May 9, 1942, she played in Northampton, Massachusetts, for the Navy Relief program.[13] On June 14, 1942, Marble was back in New York for an Army and Navy Relief sports fundraiser that "boasted more stars than the big and little dippers combined."[14] Among the sports were tennis, lacrosse, pole-vaulting, baseball, boxing, and track. Marble and Budge got top billing in tennis. World heavyweight champion Joe Louis, a recent army recruit, went four rounds, winning against sparring partner George Nicholson.[15]

In the city, Marble resumed her friendship with Will du Pont. The degree to which he continued to court Alice and later to simply keep her best interests in mind indicates, at least on his part, a depth of affection that never flagged. He usually visited New York once a week, always folding Alice into his dinner plans if she happened to be in town. He and Alice often played tennis with Bishop Fulton Sheen, a showman who took to the radio and later television to propagate his Catholic faith.

Alice could be a bit of a locker-room coquette, aware that certain off-color remarks were good for a laugh. One of her stock stories involved hitting a powerful forehand accidentally into the prelate's groin. Bishop Sheen fled the court in pain. When he returned, Alice was in a state of mirth. She could not help but remember her mother's advice: "When we got hit, she always told us to rub it."[16]

Du Pont marshaled his contacts, suggesting Alice meet up with someone he knew at the firm that published Wonder Woman and Superman comics. She had been a tennis champion, a torch singer, a spokesperson for the government, a clothing designer, a radio commentator, a giver of advice and beauty tips, and a fashion guru. Why not a writer, especially when the job came with an office on Lexington Avenue? At a cocktail party that spring, du Pont introduced her to Max Gaines. His publishing company was thinking of launching a new series based on the lives of real women. The person who came up with the idea, William Moulton Marston (who also developed the prototype for the modern lie detector), offered this rationale: "Not even girls want to be girls so long as our feminine archetype lacks force, strength, and power. Not wanting to be girls, they don't want to be tender, submissive, peace-loving as good women are. Women's strong qualities have become despised because of their weakness. The obvious remedy is to create a feminine character with all the strength of Superman plus all the allure of a good and beautiful woman."[17]

A sour man with lifelong pain in one leg from a childhood accident, Gaines had no objection to hiring Alice to write "Wonder Women" stories based on actual people to deepen interest in his fictional series about Princess Diana of the Amazons. Disguised as an army nurse, Diana sometimes helped her friend in army intelligence, Major Trevor, snare the enemy. Of course, they were in love.

In Marble's capacity as associate editor for *Wonder Women Quarterly*, she researched and wrote up the lives of almost twenty accomplished real-life women.

In an effort to attract readers, Alice sent a letter, dated July 20, 1942, to nurses at army bases around the country, addressed "Dear Army Nurse," accompanied by a complimentary first copy with her story about Florence Nightingale:

> *This is the story of the lady of the lamp, a wise and beautiful English girl who, like Wonder Woman, gave up the birthright of her happy and protected home to save the lives of suffering humanity. Florence Nightingale was the first of her sex to force her way, as nurse, into a British military hospital at the Crimean front and there with superhuman strength of will and purpose, she restored an entire army to health and efficiency. Wounded soldiers kissed her shadow on their pillows as she passed and today millions of men fighting for the "Four Freedoms" on war fronts all over the world bless the devoted nurses who follow the lead of the "Angel of Crimea."*

A promotional piece from the publisher showed Marble reading her inaugural effort and included her statement: "While I have always liked to read the comics and assumed that most people did, it wasn't until the last year or so, while traveling extensively throughout the country, talking to groups of young people that I began to realize what a large part comics and comic books play in the life of the average American boy or girl. Wonder Woman being my favorite comic character, I am very happy, indeed, to become associated with it."

Marble claimed to have made $50,000 for writing the life stories of Joan of Arc, Sojourner Truth, Susan B. Anthony, Helen Keller, and Clara Barton, among others. Some scholars have concluded that Marble's contributions may have been limited to lending "her name and her likeness."[18] She left the job after a year or so, but the series continued until 1954, when the publisher decided to change gears and, instead of highlighting women of historical significance with proven accomplishments, launch a new series about marriage, reflecting the times, when women were expected to find husbands and raise families.

MARBLE TURNED HER ATTENTION back to the war effort. When New York kicked off a ten-day war-bond drive with the goal of ringing the doorbell of every home in June of 1942, Marble was photographed signing a war-bond pledge.[19] A headshot of Marble, in a pert red hat, illustrated a story about a fashion show fundraiser for Russian war relief, at the Hotel Astor roof garden in the city.[20] Marble was among the big names (others were Ed Sullivan, Irene Dunne, and George Burns and Gracie Allen) advertised for "3 hours of continuous fun . . . excitement every minute!" at a victory party in late July on Fifth Avenue, sponsored by New York retailers.[21]

Mary Hardwick, still thinking of ways to send money home to England, came up with the idea of touring military camps. She invited Marble to join her. "Mary and Alice will play mixed doubles exhibition at Atlantic City and then go around the eastern camps," columnist Alice Hughes wrote, "playing any soldiers who want to take a chance of beating these mere girls."[22] Marble recalled: "The tennis courts we encountered were even more diverse than those on the pro tour. We played on the rolling decks of ships, on baked-earth courts, and in a variety of gyms, armories, and Quonset huts."[23]

In Atlantic City, at the convention hall on June 9, the two women appeared before an audience of forty-five hundred, mostly soldiers. Before the match, from the balcony, Marble sang "The Old Mill Stream" and "Girl of My Dreams." At Fort Slocum in New York, it was so hot and still that in the distance, on Long Island Sound, sailboats were motionless. Whenever players changed courts, Marble poured water on herself. They played as well in Maryland, at both Fort Meade and the US Naval Academy in Annapolis.

Marble returned to the lecture circuit, lining up several dozen appearances on her own. For the most part, she flitted from one venue to another. In the fall of 1943, in St. Louis, for example, she presented for two nights in a row, at a charge of fifty-five cents a ticket, at the Centenary Church and Webster Groves High School. Other notables in the series included Alexandra Tolstoy, Will Rogers Jr., and the Fisk Jubilee Singers.[24]

On January 28, 1944, Marble was part of the Fourth War Loan Drive at the Seventh Regiment Armory in New York. The tennis show collected $2,706,000 for war bonds, a spectacular success. *New York Times* tennis writer Allison Danzig, War Bond Tennis Committee chairman, assembled the players. All the men were in the service: Don Budge, a lieutenant in the US Army Air Forces; Lieutenant (JG) W. Donald McNeill, of the US Naval Reserve; and Ensign Fredrick Schroeder and Cadet Jack Kramer of the Coast Guard Academy. The women were Marble, Hardwick, Pauline Betz, Katherine Winthrop, and Dorothy Round Little. Marble defeated Hardwick, 6–2, cut to a single set to keep to the schedule. Among men's singles was a normally forbidden match pitting a professional (Budge) against an amateur (Kramer). But these were wartime conditions, and the USLTA, working with the War Department, agreed to a contest as long as at least one person was in the military. Budge won, 7–5, 7–5.[25]

American Lawn Tennis announced that "tennis had gone to war" when Marble and Hardwick became the first athletes allowed to travel overseas in two years. They had a challenging schedule: eleven exhibitions in the Panama Canal Zone for army and navy personnel stationed in the area, attracting an audience of ninety-two hundred military men. The two young women were told that their primary mission was to lift spirits, a charge upon which they apparently delivered, as they played tennis by day and danced with soldiers at night. "I don't know which is worse," Alice remarked years later, "the rough courts, or being trampled on the dance floor."[26]

"Everywhere they went, the soldiers and sailors accorded Alice and Mary top marks for being top entertainers," wrote Jack Miller, a navy lieutenant who covered the tour for *American Lawn Tennis*. "Always between matches, the girls would sit down with the G.I.'s and 'shoot the breeze' as the Navy says. Over Cokes and cigarettes, they would chat casually about every subject under the sun."[27] They went overboard dancing. "In fact, they jitterbugged so much that they had to call a halt because of blistered feet," according to the *Philadelphia Inquirer*.[28] The official news stayed impersonal and clean-cut, a matter of two smiling young women, their spirited sportsmanship, and hopeful songs. At one of the US Navy bases, Marble grabbed a borrowed guitar and sang for the sailors.[29]

Hardwick was certain that their tour was "a re-education for the soldiers." She told a reporter: "Most of them never saw tennis—good tennis, pardon me—before, they've heard about it, but still were convinced it was a sissy game. And it amazes them that a girl can hit as hard as we do."[30]

On March 14, 1944, Marble and Hardwick appeared at Madison Square Garden for a Red Cross fundraiser, where Marble easily defeated Hardwick, 6–3, 6–1. In a surprise, Jack Kramer defeated Budge, 6–3, 6–2—one of the "most decisive defeats ever received by the world champion."[31]

In August, Marble and Hardwick played for servicewomen at Women's Army Corps (WAC) training camps, the first tour of its kind sponsored by United Service Organizations (USO).[32] They played eleven exhibitions in eight states and stayed on the WAC bases. The three-week tour kicked off at Fort Sheridan, Illinois. At Fort Oglethorpe in Georgia, Mary Churchill, daughter of Britain's prime minister, was visiting as a member of the Women's Auxiliary Territorial Service, the British equivalent of WAC.[33]

Years later, in *Courting Danger*, Marble revealed an aspect of the tour that provides a veiled, but revealing, insight into her own sexual struggles and inclinations. She recalled frequently receiving visits from women at night, saying they were courageous as well as foolhardy to admit to such an attraction, and she offered words of support: "If you happen to fall in love with a man, the world gushes in approval. If you fall in love with a woman, you're treated like a monster. You're *not* a monster; don't ever think that you are or be ashamed."[34]

IN THE SUMMER OF 1944, the *California Eagle*, a Black-owned newspaper, announced matches of far greater import: "Alice Marble, world champion, and Mary Hardwick, English champ, both white, will play exhibition matches" at the Cosmopolitan Tennis Club in Harlem, for the twenty-seventh annual American Tennis Association tournament.[35]

The American Tennis Association began operations in 1916, after the USLTA banned African American players from competing in its tournaments. The Cosmopolitan Club, first called the Colonial Tennis Club, began in the same era, in 1915, at Convent Avenue and 149th Street in Harlem.[36]

The appearance of Marble and Hardwick was newsworthy, but there was precedence. Four years earlier Don Budge, playing as a professional, went against top-ranking Black player Jimmie McDaniel at the Cosmopolitan Club courts. The match marked when the "wall of segregation in tennis began to crumble,"[37] a sports breakthrough even before Kenny Washington joined the National Football League in 1946 and Jackie Robinson joined Major League Baseball in 1947.[38] The *Brooklyn Eagle* declared that the "'color line'"[39] was erased, at least temporarily. An estimated 2,200 spectators filled up the field and clubhouse porch, with others viewing from apartment windows and rooftops overlooking the court.

American Lawn Tennis said Budge was at "his near best" and did not "play down"[40] to his opponent, winning 6–1, 6–2. McDaniel seemed nervous, double-faulting several times in the match. His terrific net game became more obvious in doubles, during which Budge and Dr. Reginald Weir of New York divided sets with McDaniel and Richard Cohen, his doubles partner from college.

Marble and Hardwick took to the courts at the Cosmopolitan Club four years later to the same divided world. The ATA was inclusive; the USLTA was not. The two women played each other and partnered with Black female tennis players in doubles—Marble and Frances Gittens defeated Hardwick and Lillian Van Buren.[41] For the mixed doubles, Marble teamed with Robert Ryland, an army private stationed at the air base in Walterboro, South Carolina. As a top-seeded ATA player, Bob Ryland said, "The army thought it would be good publicity to send me to New York for the match. It was two black men and two white women, but we were in Harlem, so the army didn't worry about anyone getting upset. We couldn't have done that in the South, though."[42]

Ryland's father taught him tennis, and he was coached by Mary Ann Seames, nicknamed "Mother," a noted Black tennis coach and one of the founders of the Chicago Prairie Tennis Club. Ryland would go on to win the ATA men's singles championship in 1955 and 1956. While at Wayne State University, Ryland would be one of the first Black men to play in a National Collegiate Athletic Association tournament, and he would later be the first to go on a pro tour.[43] He taught tennis to Defense Secretary Robert McNamara and Arthur Ashe, and coached, for a short while, tennis legends Venus and Serena Williams.[44]

Hardwick's partner, Dr. Reginald Weir, was known as the Black Bill Tilden for his "power and versatility." He had been the City College of New York tennis team captain[45] and the ATA national champion five times.

The spectators included a young player, Althea Gibson, the ATA's national girls' champion that year, who watched Marble play. "I was mesmerized. She was beautiful. I was a young girl, about 15 or 16. She left an indelible impression upon me," said Gibson.[46]

When Marble and Ryland met for cocktails, they talked about Gibson. "Alice asked me if I thought Althea could make it in the major tournaments, and I said she definitely had the talent to do it," Ryland remembered. "I told her Althea was strong and had a good head for the game. She just lacked the experience, that's all."[47]

Their conversation would transform tennis, though not for another six years.

MARBLE AND HARDWICK continued touring stateside in August and September. They played at the new tennis center at the US Naval Air Station in Atlantic City, and then at the US Merchant Marine Academy on Long Island. At one point, when Marble needed a towel, a cadet offered his handkerchief. A towel was produced, which Marble and Hardwick shared. "You'd think the Academy could afford more than one towel, wouldn't you Mary?" said Alice, making the spectators "howl" with laughter. Helen Hull Jacobs, now a lieutenant in WAVES, watched the matches at the US Naval Training Center for WAVES in the Bronx. Another reunion occurred when French tennis champion Sylvia Henrotin (Alice's opponent when she fainted at Roland-Garros) umpired matches at the Lake Placid Club in the Adirondacks, recently taken over by the US Army and renamed the Lake Placid Distribution Center. In two sets, Hardwick won the first, 8–6, and Marble the second, 6–4.[48]

The Marble family on the steep steps of their San Francisco home. Left to right, bottom row: Dan, George, Hazel, Alice, Tim. Left to right, top row: Harry and Jessie.

Alice, the baby, intent even then.

Alice's favorite sport was baseball and she was a regular at Seals Stadium. The *San Francisco Examiner* dubbed her "Little Queen of Swat."

Seals Stadium ca. 1924.

TENNIS COURTS GOLDEN GATE PARK.   680

The tennis courts in Golden Gate Park ca. 1910s, prior to when
Alice Marble would have played there.

Alice playfully strumming her racquet as a guitar. She was musically gifted from a young age. January 1929.

Alice at seventeen: junior champion of California in 1931.

Alice with her coach Eleanor "Teach" Tennant early in their collaboration.

Alice jumping rope as part of recovering her health and spurring her comeback to competition.

Hollywood actress Marion Davies became a good friend of Alice. They met at one of William Randolph Hearst's famous parties at his estate.

William Randolph Hearst's extraordinary San Simeon estate, where Alice was an occasional guest.

French champion and expressive legend Suzanne Lenglen, whose style matched her skill on court.

American champion Helen Wills Moody in 1932. She won Wimbledon that year among her eight victories there, along with seven US Open and four French Open singles victories.

Alice Marble's powerful serve captured in sequence.

Marble receiving her first major trophy, the US Open championship in 1936, with her opponent, American star Helen Jacobs.

Marble was greeted by San Francisco mayor Angelo J. Rossi on her return to San Francisco after her US Open victory and feted as a hometown hero with a motorcade through the city and festivities at city hall.

Alice and Teach Tennant traveled widely together, here stylishly off-court in the stands at Smith College in Northampton, Massachusetts.

Alice with her Spanish teacher and friend, Tica Madrigal.

Alice with close friends and Hollywood icons Carole Lombard and Clark Gable in Los Angeles. A timely note from Lombard aided Marble in her recovery at a sanitarium when she was twenty-one years old.

Marble reaching for a volley at Wimbledon in 1939. Having been disappointed the previous two years, she won the title that year with her powerful serve-and-volley game.

Marble handily defeated British star Kay Stammers in the 1939 final, losing just two games in the process.

Marble with her regular doubles partner, Sarah Palfrey, at Wimbledon, where they won the doubles title in 1938 and 1939, and also prevailed four times at the US Open.

Alice at dinner with fellow Californian, good friend, and mixed doubles partner Don Budge, with whom she won one US Open and two Wimbledon titles.

Marble with Polish star and rival
Ja-Ja Jedrzejowska.

Alice's great friend
Mary K. "Brownie" Brown.

Alice's friend and patron Will
du Pont Jr., an accomplished
horseman.

Marble's 1946 memoir, *The Road to
Wimbledon*, was edited by legendary
Scribner editor Max Perkins, editor
of Hemingway and Fitzgerald,
among others.

Marble worked on her manuscript in New York, with her portrait by
London artist Dorothy Vicaji on the wall behind her.

Marble at a press
conference as she
enthusiastically announces
her decision to go pro.

Marble (with coat over her
arm) with her three Pro
Tour colleagues Don Budge
(to her left), Mary Hardwick
(to her right), and long-
time star Bill Tilden (to the
right of Hardwick). Teach
Tennant is to Tilden's right.

Marble modeling a jacket she promoted.

Advertisement for Marble's fashion line,
showing the many stores where it
was on offer.

Marble singing in the Sert Room at the Waldorf Astoria Hotel.
She got excellent reviews.

Her career largely interrupted by the war, Marble supported the war effort in several ways, including raising money for ambulances.

In 1941, Marble was made assistant physical director of the Office of Civilian Defense, with the goal of raising the fitness level of women across the country. Here, Olympic rower, John Kelly, her male counterpart on the OCD, sat to her right, with New York City mayor Fiorello La Guardia, director of the OCD, on her left.

Left to right: Margaret Peters, Mildred Brown, Alice Marble, Lulu Ballard, Mary Hardwick, Helen Hutchinson, and Roumania Peters at an American Tennis Association exhibition event at the Cosmopolitan Tennis Club in Harlem, 1944.

Marble and Black star Althea Gibson, whom Marble championed prior to the 1950 US Open. They are holding the Southwest Women's Singles trophy, which Marble won twice and Gibson won as well.

Alice with a youthful Billie Jean Moffitt, whom she coached, and Carole Caldwell, in 1961.

Alice admiring a display case of her trophies at the International Tennis Hall of Fame.

The Centenary Lawn Tennis Championships

1877–1977

Their Royal Highnesses the Duke and Duchess of Kent with

the Past Singles Champions

Group photograph of past Wimbledon champions during the Wimbledon centenary in 1977. Alice Marble is seated front row, fourth from the right. Other notable stars include Arthur Ashe and Stan Smith (back row, far left) and John Newcombe and Rod Laver (back row, second and third from right).

Marble returned to Wimbledon in 1984 and received a gift on-court from the Duke and Duchess of Kent, patrons of the tournament.

Later in life, Marble could enjoy the memory of being on the cover of *LIFE* magazine on August 28, 1939, photographed by the famed Alfred Eisenstaedt following her unprecedented triple victories that year at Wimbledon and the US Open.

Marble tallied up visits to three hundred bases with Hardwick over the course of almost three years. In the beginning, both women had worried their audiences would be bored: "We had learned through a very accurate poll that only about 10 percent of them had ever seen tennis and an even smaller number had ever played. We couldn't have been more mistaken in our fears; I've never had the privilege of playing before a more receptive or warmer audience."[49]

Among the thousands upon thousands of soldiers who attended her exhibition matches, Marble made a strong impression on one in Norfolk, Virginia. Willis Jefferson "Bill" Moffitt, a navy man who had shipped out ten days after his wife told him she was pregnant with their first child,[50] a daughter, was an athletic sort himself, and he admired Marble's game. Years later, when his little girl had become a tennis-playing teen and came to him with a plan to work with Marble as her coach, he gave his blessing—to Billie Jean Moffit, the future Billie Jean King.

THROUGH IT ALL, Will du Pont never flagged in his concern for Alice and her welfare. He managed her finances. "I made the $500 transfer from your Special Account and told them to notify you," he had written to her in December 1943.[51] A year later, he provided transportation: "I inclose [sic] the Pullman and round-trip railroad tickets."[52] He planned surprises. His most lavish gift, or at least most unexpected, was his purchase of the portrait by Dorothy Vicaji that Roz Bloomingdale Cowen had urged Marble to sit for in London in the summer of 1938. He found the painting for sale at a show at the de Young Museum in San Francisco and had it crated and sent to Alice at her New York apartment as a surprise. Even more than all the trophies, most of which she had given away by the end of her life, this portrait of her at her idealized best accompanied her everywhere she lived, from her apartment in New York, at 24 West Fifty-Fifth Street, after the war all the way to her final little house in the desert, where it loomed above her couch.

Toward the end of the war, interest in Alice from the press shifted from courts to courtship, with questions about romance. Headlines began to appear with some frequency suggesting she was going to settle down. Alice was responsible for the rumors. In an interview with the United Press, she said tennis was out except for recreationally and that she had "many other interests—including the matter of earning a living." She also had a mate in mind. She referred to him as "Joe" or offered, "Let's call him Joe." The details shifted as to how and when they met, but he was a "very special guy and "an army captain overseas." She did not reveal his last name.

In one version they met at a party in New York.

"The hostess asked me to 'Look after Joe,'" she said. "Well I looked after him all right. We'll be married as soon as the war is over."[53] Various newspapers ran similar stories in which the marriage was always in the future . . . soon . . . any day now.

The end of the war coincided with the final fraying of what had become the threadbare relationship between Marble and Teach. The exact nature of their partnership, and whether it went beyond mentor-mentee, had been a source of speculation over the course of many years. Was there a mother-daughter component? Were they ever lovers, despite Marble's assertion to the contrary? Publicly, Alice always framed their relationship as chaste and as crucial to her survival. As she put it years later, "Without Teach I never would have made it. I was too sunny a person."[54]

Teach later styled herself as a savior-martinet with one job, to get Alice to shape up: "Alice had perfect timing and rhythm and no inhibitions. There was a reason why she had no inhibitions. Because for eleven years she didn't have to worry about income tax or making a living, because it was my good fortune to make a home for Alice Marble. . . . All that she had to do was to go out and play tennis, take her singing lessons and enjoy life."[55]

For most of their relationship, it appears that Teach was keener to control Marble than to seduce her. Tennis historian Ted Tinling theorized that the breakup was inevitable. Teach could not handle the way in which success transformed Marble, stating, "I have always held that after winning the Wimbledon crown no one is ever the same again." Marble started to assert herself, and Teach, being an "all or nothing person," was enraged to lose power over her protégée. "Her bitterness was total," Tinling wrote.[56]

Alice also believed that when she created a life independent from Teach, which included arranging for a speaking tour with forty stops on her own, that the balance of power shifted, and Teach could not take it. The relationship came to a halt when, as she relates in *Courting Danger*, Alice told Teach, "I've lived my whole life in one dimension, the tennis court, and it's not enough anymore. I'm a person, not a trophy for you to show off."

The more clearly Marble could see it was time for her mentor to move on, to find another future champion, the more Teach resisted: "The woman to whom affection meant a pat on the head rather than a kiss finally realized that she loved me, and her desire to hold onto me ultimately destroyed our relationship." The bond had degenerated to the point where the coach, with her love of martinis, would berate her pupil when she was drunk, which was often, and then "brush off the incidents the next day, without apology, as 'yesterday's news.'" Teach accused Marble of affairs, "with anyone who came close, man or woman."[57]

Returning home to their suite at the Sherry-Netherland became a nightmare for Marble. As she inserted the key in the door, she could frequently hear Teach scrambling to take up a perch on a windowsill from which she threatened to jump. It became a sick game, with Marble begging her not to.

The only version of the final scene comes from Marble: When Teach finally admitted to herself and to Marble it was over, she demanded the new car and half their bank account (rightfully hers in light of their long-standing agreement). Marble expressed sorrow over the end of their partnership, but Teach would hear none of it. She shoved Alice so hard she fell. Witnessing the violence, a maid urged Marble to head to a park while Teach packed her bags and left on her own. As Marble bided her time on a park bench, she saw the actress Marlene Dietrich strolling with her grandchild. In the story, the athlete and the actress remembered a silly moment in which they had both stood up on a chair and showed off their legs to see whose were better. "We laughed, and I momentarily forgot my misery as we chatted," said Marble.[58]

Returning three hours later to the suite, Marble discovered that the maid and a crew had rearranged the furniture, even providing a new couch in the sitting room. The timetable of this breakup is murky, but it appears to have been at or around the end of the war, coinciding with Teach's decision to return to California. (By 1946, phone records establish Marble in the apartment on West Fifty-Fifth Steet, where she lived until she also decamped for California.)

Before the war, Marble had been hailed as the girl who had everything. Her fame had hardly diminished, her name a touchstone easily understood and referenced in the press. An army sergeant who claimed superiority at checkers said he "would no more think of playing a game with a man of inferior skill than Alice Marble would consider playing a set of tennis with Mahatma [Gandhi]."[59] A summer playground with young female tennis players was described as filled with "potential Alice Marbles."[60] If someone looked polished, she had that "Alice Marble well-pressed and well-priced look."[61] Marble even provided the object lesson in a newspaper feature about grammar: "If you think punctuation doesn't matter, try shifting the comma in that news head, 'Alice Marble, Champion.'"[62]

PART FIVE

1946–1966

CHAPTER 22

A GOOD ADDRESS

A FTER THE WAR'S END, New York City reinvented itself as the cultural capital of the world, having inherited the mantle from the European cities now in postwar recovery. Greenwich Village became the in spot for hipsters and dreamers, writers and artists. Anatole Broyard's *Kafka Was the Rage: A Greenwich Village Memoir* caught the spirit:

> *Nineteen forty-six was a good time—perhaps the best time—in the twentieth century. The war was over, the Depression had ended, and everyone was discovering the simple pleasures. A war is like an illness and when it's over you think you've never felt so well. There's a terrific sense of coming back, of repossessing your life.*
>
> *New York City had never been so attractive. The postwar years were like a great smile in its sullen history. The Village was as close in 1946 as it would ever come to Paris in the twenties. Rents were cheap, restaurants were cheap, and it seemed to me that happiness itself might be cheaply had.*[1]

Marble lived at a good address in midtown Manhattan—close to the Museum of Modern Art, Rockefeller Center, the theater district, and the New York Public Library's main branch. The Rockefeller Apartments, Marble's residence, were sunny and airy. The designers gave "15 percent more space to light and air than required by building codes." There was a courtyard, and the ground floor had doctors' offices, a restaurant, a drugstore, and a hairdresser.[2]

Marble traveled north to Columbia University and south to New York University and the New School to study "everything from Latin American culture to radio script writing and all sorts of writing courses, oh I had a marvelous time."[3]

Bookstores filled the cityscape, from "grand book emporiums" such as Brentano's and Scribner's on Fifth Avenue to the various used bookstores on Fourth Avenue.[4] The newest invention was a vending machine for twenty-five-cent paperbacks, offering fifteen titles and holding ninety-six books, installed in the Lincoln Building at 60 East Forty-Second Street.[5] Greenwich Village was home to Djuna Barnes, William S. Burroughs, e. e. cummings, Margaret Mead, Anaïs Nin, and Richard Wright, among many other authors. The most discussed books included *Hiroshima* (1946) by John Hersey and *The Naked and the Dead* (1948) by Norman Mailer, both about war and mass destruction. *The Street* (1946) by Ann Petry, the first novel by a Black woman to sell more than one million copies, was about a single mother raising her son in poverty in Harlem.[6]

Alice herself earned the title of author after yet another chance encounter. In the club car during a train ride in 1945, she met the Reverend Austin Pardue, a clergyman with a radio program, *Our Morale*, broadcast coast to coast. He had recently been named bishop of the Episcopal Diocese of Pittsburgh. An author of inspirational books, including *Bold to Say* and *Your Morale and How to Build It*,[7] he became mesmerized with the details of Alice's story.

The bishop urged her to write a book, offering access to his publisher, Charles Scribner Sr., head of the eponymous publishing house. Scribner agreed to a business lunch, upholding the company's ethos, which prided itself on conviviality, operating on a business model of publishing as a gentleman's pursuit, in which "a handshake was a deal and writers looked upon their publisher as friends."[8] He suggested she write a "typical first chapter." She was assigned to the editor Maxwell Perkins, known for his work with Ernest Hemingway, F. Scott Fitzgerald, and Thomas Wolfe. He had edited a book written by Helen Wills Moody but felt she could not write very well, and he was not generally interested in "nonliterary works."[9]

Marble provided Perkins with an outline, in which she proposed to write about her family history, her girlhood, her illness, her philosophy, tennis highlights, and the value of hard work. She acknowledged that she was in fact "very young" to sum up her life, "but everyone should live ten years ahead. Alice Marble, tennis player, is finished. Alice Marble, woman, just beginning. One door closes, another opens."[10]

On March 21, Perkins read the sample chapter "with pleasure." He wrote to Marble: "The only reason we do not now propose drawing a contract with specific terms is that the kind of book we should make, and whether it should be illustrated, and all such questions, cannot yet be determined very well, but I hope you will take this letter as an agreement on our part that we are to publish on terms mutually satisfactory."

Night after night, Marble typed away in the apartment she now shared with Mary Hardwick, who nudged her along. The portrait by Vicaji hung in the living room. It took six months of working three hours a day at her desk—purposely turned toward the wall to avoid distractions—to complete the manuscript.

In a handwritten note on sky-blue paper, with her name and address in all caps on two lines, no city, Marble happily announced to Perkins on September 5 that she would be handing in the finished product: "Please forgive the hurried note without benefit of typewriter. I am in the country and asking a friend to mail this for me in town. It is just to say that I am sending my material to you just as soon as it has been typed . . . by Monday or Tuesday of next week."

W. L. Savage,[11] a junior editor, sent Perkins a memo about "a number of instances where she refers to people without giving much information about who they are." He also pointed out that some of the final chapters were thin, an opinion Perkins passed along to Marble on November 7, 1945:

> It seems to me that your book would be improved by the omission of a number of the chapters close to the end, and perhaps you could insert two or three other chapters in other positions. These last chapters, as is common in an autobiographical book, tend to become desultory and topical, and make an anti-climax after the direct narrative. The ones I suggest omitting are "Among Friends," "The English Way of Doing Things," and "U.S.A." and it seems to me that "Amateur Tennis," "Blueprint for Competition," "What It Means to be Champion" and "Strategy," might be worked in at appropriate places earlier in the book so that they would not come so close together. If you approve of this, we could immediately send the manuscript to the printer.

On March 14, 1946, Margaret Treadwell, the ghostwriter on the project, dispatched to Perkins a "full, new, correctly punctuated and typed, copy of the Alice Marble mss." She apologized to Alice for any delay: "Believe me, nothing could distress me more than holding you up, or falling down, for I want you to give me more writing."

With its descriptions of hardship (the challenges of farm life, the death of her father, and the time in the sanatorium) alternating with rosy tributes to the "westward ho" spirit, Marble's *Road to Wimbledon* is less in the tradition of Perkins's celebrated male heavyweight authors than in that of Willa Cather's *O Pioneers!* and Laura Ingalls Wilder's *Little House on the Prairie*. As Marble wrote, "'Pioneer' is not just a word to me. It has all the tall, strong body, broad shoulders, brown hair and steady brown eyes of my father, Harry."[12] Perhaps in finding the rousing language to describe real-life Wonder Women, Marble also discovered, with help from Perkins and Treadwell, the template for how to frame her own story.

The book so moved its typesetter that afterward he took the time to send Marble a letter of gratitude in care of Scribner's, dated March 28, 1946.

> *Dear Miss Marble:*
>
> *I have just finished setting up the type on your book* The Will to Win[13] *and for one of the few times in my many years of typesetting I feel that I actually owe an author a note of thanks. It is not only because the typewriter job on the final draft was among the best I have ever worked from, but also because the story itself rang true as a bell and stayed in my mind. I am not the least bit interested in tennis, yet I found myself with you every page of the way!*
>
> *In my opinion—and I have read millions of words—your story besides being entertaining has sound moral value, and I sincerely hope it will attain the wide distribution it certainly deserves.*
>
> *If it is not asking too much, I would be ever so happy to have a copy inscribed by you: "To Ronald Pollett who enjoyed setting up the type.—Alice Marble." Please write that on the inside title page and have Scribner's send me the book C.O.D.*
>
> *Again I say I enjoyed being with you!*[14]

Margaret Treadwell suggested "Little Queen of Swat," "That Sissy Game," and "Scrambling for Shots" as titles. Perkins came up with *The Road to Wimbledon*.[15] On April 9, 1946, Marble expressed her top pick to Perkins: "After much thought and the gathering of reactions from friends in regard to the title, 'The Road to Wimbledon' is an overwhelming favorite. So with your approval, I would like to settle on it. It seems to me that while 'That Sissy Game' is flashy it seems a little derogatory to tennis and I don't want to take that chance." The title stood, and the aspect that makes it remarkable in retrospect is that the book makes only glancing reference to Wimbledon in just the first two pages. The final pages of the book are devoted to a quick rundown of the first national championship win in 1936, a short discussion of amateur versus professional tennis, and a sketch of her singing at the Waldorf, in which she confessed that disappointed fans thought she had deserted the "clean sports world for one of smoky night clubs filled with drunken people."[16] In the book's second to the last page, she described meeting and falling in love with Joe, and on the last page he has died. "Life was over, or so it seemed . . ." The final words are a vow to win at the most important game of all, the game of life.

While Marble busied herself with the book, she experienced another loss, this time from afar, when Bill Johnston died suddenly of a heart attack on May 1 at his home in San Francisco at the age of fifty-one. The tribute in *American Lawn Tennis* called him a "greatly beloved figure whose sudden passing grieved the entire lawn tennis world."[17]

On June 24, 1946, Wimbledon reopened, featuring players from thirty-two nations. In London, the Grosvenor House Hotel, where Alice had attended the Wimbledon Ball, welcomed back its regular clientele. The establishment had had what was called a good war, spared any damage to its structure; the dining rooms had been conscripted as mess halls for the troops.

The tennis courts at Wimbledon had received a reprieve from their early duty as a mortuary, when far fewer citizens of the city lost their lives than initially feared: 150 at the final count, as opposed to more than 40,000 civilian Londoners killed between September 1940 and May 1941. For a time, the facility even became a pasture for pigs, part of an attempt to build up the country's waning food supply. Although several more years would pass before all the structural damage was repaired, spirits were high at the courts' reopening: "Never before had the players from overseas been so eager to get here and never has their enthusiasm reached such a pitch. Many of them have had to overcome great difficulties in making this journey. Never before have countries shown themselves to be such ardent lovers of the game as they have now by raising public subscriptions to meet their players' expenses in order that their country might be represented."[18]

The press in England hailed the return to tennis as a "tangible and poignant symbol of peace" and touted the prospects of two brilliant women, Pauline Betz and Margaret Osborne. Alice Marble was on hand, in a new role as a reporter for the International News Service. Her credentials appeared in parentheses beneath her byline: "Former United States and Wimbledon Tennis Champion." Seven years had passed since she won Wimbledon, and she was about to turn thirty-three. In her pre-tournament newspaper commentary, Marble appraised the contenders, picking Jack Kramer to win the men's singles. Instead, Frenchman Yvon Petra defeated Australia's Geoff Brown in the finals. In the women's, Pauline Betz defeated Louise Brough. Alice played a practice match with Kay Stammers, who showed "marked improvement" since 1939.

Reflecting, Marble wrote: "To me this is a thrill of a lifetime, to roam around these familiar grounds again, seeing old faces, and remembering seven long years ago when I played three final matches on the center court with all the glamor of success. So I come back to Wimbledon to watch them play for . . . titles I held or shared—the women's singles, the women's doubles and the mixed doubles."[19]

While she was there, she received a chatty letter from Will du Pont dated July 1, 1946, sent to the Dorchester Hotel on Park Lane: "I am sorry to see in last night's papers that Kramer was out. I assume his hand was the problem. One might think, with the little tennis he has played in the last 4 or 5 years that he would hardly get blistered."

He told her, "I have been very busy breaking my yearlings and with various different things which go on here, but I have missed having our usual game. I note that you will let me know what time you will be getting back on the 11th. That will be my usual Thursday and I hope we can have a welcome-home party. We won't be able to see you come winging in past the Statue of Liberty as you will most probably just be coming out of a cloud!!"

Just as Wimbledon was ending, in a letter dated to Perkins July 10, 1946, Treadwell explained that she had asked Alice to "include in the book a brief credit of a line or two including my name. . . . I hope that you did not regard this as brash or inappropriate on my part but of course I am very happy to rest upon your views in this matter. I enjoyed doing the writing on 'The Road to Wimbledon' and I want to do more."

She also liked the kind of work she had done with Alice, describing "the excitement of matching your vocabulary to that of your subject in a biography and expressing what you want to with those words, either with or without that person."

On July 11, 1946, Perkins had disappointing news for Treadwell: "We would not put your name anywhere in or on the book without Alice Marble's approval, and for that matter we never asked. Both a publisher and an author do prefer to conceal the fact that there was a ghost.

"It does not seem quite honest, and it often troubles me, but the truth is a book sells better when the fact is concealed. As to other work, I cannot think of anything steady, and there is nothing at the moment. . . . I can only promise to be on the lookout."

Shortly after *The Road to Wimbledon* came out, Marble shared her impressions on becoming a writer with the readers of *American Lawn Tennis*:

> *If I had thought that tennis required mental discipline, writing required even more. I could think of a hundred reasons for not sitting at the typewriter. Yes, I even preferred sewing on buttons or washing my kitchen floor. But there was always that driving force—the thought that I would someday see my book,* The Road to Wimbledon *in the shop windows; where, incidentally, it is now. I feel a sense of achievement almost as great as winning the championship at Forest Hills. It goes to prove just once more—that you can succeed in spite of handicaps in the most important game of all—the game of life.*[20]

Marble's rousing prose supports the impression that she had internalized the rhythms of Teach's familiar approach, in which bravura was the default mode.

To promote her book, Alice hoped to secure the services of Russell Birdwell, Carole Lombard's former publicist and the most prominent practitioner in his field at that time. The only hitch was his hefty price. Alice turned to her favorite banker. Will du Pont Jr. responded favorably, in a letter dated August 7, 1946.

> *Dear Alice:*
> *I enclose my check for $1500, the loan I arranged for you to pay the man to push your book.*
> *It is worth the gamble and I hope it will turn out most successfully.*

Birdwell's specialty was to create a drumbeat for a product, preferably through a stunt. In what was then a pioneering move, he staggered ads for a movie over a five-and-a-half-mile-long road in Culver City, California. He invented the "search for a star" approach by orchestrating a three-year-long quest, in which fifteen hundred actresses gave auditions, before Vivien Leigh was finally cast as Scarlett O'Hara in *Gone with the Wind*. He forged merchandizing tie-ins by marketing copies of her wedding dress from the movie at department stores at the time of the movie's release.

Birdwell also launched the pinup, which began with his promotion of the 1943 movie *The Outlaw*. He hired a photographer to take photographs of Jane Russell, then unknown, literally rolling in the hay. He wanted one perfect image, emphasizing her plunging neckline, allowing him to declare: "Her breasts hung over the picture like a summer thunderstorm spread out over a landscape."[21]

With Marble, Birdwell adopted a family-friendly posture, appealing to every "clean" and "right-thinking" boy and girl in the country as this letter to Marble's old patron, William Randolph Hearst, demonstrates. He began it "Dear Chief."

Infrequently as you know, I have come knocking at your door with an idea which I feel may be good for the largest number of people who seek and find inspiration in the reading of your newspapers. It is my good fortune to be representing in publicity, Alice Marble, the tennis champion, who has written a book entitled "The Road to Wimbledon," the biography of a girl who was born in the backwoods of Plumas County, California, doomed to an illness which most doctors said would be lifelong, and who began playing tennis in public parks and rose to be champion of the world through having the driving spirit of an American, a true American pioneer. You were once her host at San Simeon, and on that occasion she met your great Arthur Brisbane, who wrote of her. . . .

In the midst of international chaos, in the midst of national juvenile delinquency, Alice Marble and her great true story shines out as an inspiration to all other young Americans. I wire you in the hope that you will ask your editors and editorial writers to help point up and point out this truly inspirational story of a typical American girl so that mothers and fathers as well as young people facing the problems of life in this uncertain period can be reminded that the Horatio Alger story can happen over and over again but only in the American way of life. Alice Marble tells me that Mr. Brisbane in encouraging her to write the story of her life once said: "It would be an inspiration to every clean, right-thinking boy and girl throughout the country." Feeling that you and Mr. Brisbane were the ones mostly responsible for this great American girl putting down her simple and rich story in "The Road to Wimbledon," it is my hope that you may go one step further and bring it to the attention of as many people as possible in this country as a lesson in clean living, clean thinking, and most of all, pointing out that the American way of life is still the best way.[22]

Birdwell took out ads in various newspapers, reprinting the letter, as if to give readers an inside scoop on personal correspondence to no less a personage than William Randolph Hearst.

Following a list of names provided by Marble, Scribner's sent complimentary copies of the book to at least two dozen potential readers, including Bishop Pardue, *American Lawn Tennis* editor Merrihew, several representatives of Wilson Sporting Goods, Brownie, Claire Arkell, Arthur Loew, Perry Jones at the Los Angeles Tennis Club, and Howard Kinsey at the California Tennis Club. Also on the list was Eleanor Tennant, in care of the Beverly Hills Tennis Club, indicating that the two women, despite their differences, were able to maintain a cordial, if distant, relationship.

The book, which retailed for $2.75, received acclaim for its wholesome message as much as for its literary value upon its publication in the fall of 1946. The *Boston Traveler* praised the "lively story of a determined girl, born on the wrong side of the tracks, who, through hard work, ability and the will to win, did win and tasted the joyous fruits of success in her chosen field."[23] The *Hartford Courant* said of it: "Simply and unaffectedly written, this typically American story is both easy and instructive summer reading."[24] However, *The Road to Wimbledon* was not the financial success that Alice had hoped for, as the following two letters indicate.

On January 9, 1947, Scribner wrote,

Enclosed is an accounting of the sale of your book to date. I fear that you will be rather shocked at learning that the sales are not larger. You are very kind in saying that you have enjoyed working with our organization, but perhaps you will not think so highly of them after this report. All we can hope is that the sales will continue and that in the end you will not be disappointed. For my own part, I am very happy at having the book published if it does not mean that you are disgruntled.

And then, on July 16, 1947, Perkins wrote,

As we told you that it would our trade department has made a special effort to see that at every bookstore our salesmen visited the buyers should be reminded [sic] about "The Road to Wimbledon" as a title which should be popular during the summer months. This effort has produced noticeable results—nothing on an enormous scale—but during the months of May and June the book has been reordered to the number of one hundred and fifty copies and now has a total sale of approximately three thousand.

I think the fact that "The Road to Wimbledon" is still being reordered so many months after its original publication is encouraging. I realize that you were worried that all sales might stop and the book expire in this country. Although there does not seem to be any indication of a tremendous total sale, it does seem likely that the book may go on selling for some time to come. We shall do our best to see that these sales continue.

The book added a halo to Marble's previously established credentials as an inspirational speaker. Represented for a time by the Charles Pearson Lecture Management Agency, she took in between $70 and $400[25] per appearance after she paid a 30 percent agency fee, barnstorming from civic centers to college lecture halls, giving speeches titled "Focus on the Horizon" and "The Will to Win." She knew how to flatter an audience. At Randolph-Macon Woman's College in Lynchburg, Virginia, Marble played to the crowd by mentioning how much the surrounding hills reminded her of San Francisco. She lectured at Earlham College in Richmond, Indiana; at the YMCA in Rockford, Illinois; and in Alabama, where the *Greenville Advocate* reported that adults paid fifty cents and children under the age of twelve twenty-five cents to hear her explain what she called "the basic rules of successful living: self-discipline, physical and mental fitness, a pleasant voice, ability to hold enjoyable conversations, absence of worry, and good habits." She assured the members of the women's club of central Kentucky, "If you want anything badly enough, you can get it." Sometimes she ended her lectures by breaking out her guitar, part of her repertoire since those first early days in the desert, leading the audience in a sing-along. Her command of the guitar was like her ability to speak Spanish and her expertise in fashion: a self-learner, she picked it up along the way. She saved compliments. The thank-you notes confirmed her success, preserved by Marble in well-ordered scrapbooks that chronicled the public aspects of her life.[26] Margaretta Stevenson, vice principal, Alexander Hamilton High School in Los Angeles, observed after

Marble gave a speech during Girls' Week: "We paid her thirty-five dollars and felt it was the most worthwhile girls' activity we had in a long time."

The press promoted a globe-trotting version of Alice Marble—even during an innocuous shopping trip:

> *Christmas shoppers in downtown Indianapolis may not have recognized the tall, attractive young woman in wintry guise as she visited department stores Monday. Her beaver coat, her smart suit of black wool . . . her heelless pumps were a far cry from the abbreviated white garb in which she flashes about the world's great tennis court[s]. But blond, hatless, as full of verve as her best serve, the fair Alice strode briskly from a parking garage to "do" the stores.*
>
> *She expects to fly to England and Sweden in February for her second journey to Europe since the war's end. An invitation was extended to her and Mary Hardwick by King Gustav of Sweden to play a series of exhibition matches. They will play both in Sweden and England, as well as give tennis lessons.*[27]

On January 18, 1947, she confirmed to a reporter at the *San Francisco Examiner* that she and Hardwick planned to keep what she called a "date I've been trying to make for years: an appointment to give a command performance tennis exhibition before King Gustav in Sweden. I was always too busy to go although the idea of flying to Sweden was exciting enough to give me dream-material for months."

That year also marked the official end of any dreams du Pont had of marrying Alice. Aware that his devotion was not reciprocated, he told her he intended to marry someone else, another tennis player, Margaret Osborne, and sought her approval. She thought it would be a good match, believing that his intended's even-keeled manner would help her tolerate du Pont's unusual habits. Alice Marble, four years older, had known Margaret since she was thirteen. Margaret had always impressed her favorably; Alice wrote in one of her columns: "She is short but resembles Princess Elizabeth, with thick dark brown hair, brown eyes with little crinkly sun lines around them." On the courts, Osborne was a natural athlete, but Marble cautioned that sometimes people with innate talent have to "work harder than 'made' players because the games come too easily to them."

On November 26, 1947, du Pont and Margaret Osborne married at the Wilmington, Delaware, city hall. He was fifty-one, she was twenty-nine.

Like Alice, she grew up in San Francisco, came from a working-class family—her father was a garage mechanic—and started her tennis career playing on the courts at Golden Gate Park. Earlier that year, she had won the women's singles championship at Wimbledon.

ALSO IN 1947, Marble joined *American Lawn Tennis*, still carrying its stately subtitle, *The Illustrated Magazine of the Game Founded in 1907 by S. Wallis Merrihew*. Previously, she had shown up in the magazine as the subject of articles and in advertisements for tennis shorts, shirts, and dresses. Now she was hired to write a column, titled As I See It, in which she had free rein to express her many opinions on the sport.

The magazine was both staid and progressive. Merrihew considered his life to be a "daily campaign for the betterment of tennis," but years before, he had ended the magazine's official connection with the USLTA over the organization's rule forbidding amateur tennis players from writing about tennis when they played the game competitively, saying it was "unwise, unfair and aimed specifically against one player—the champion Tilden." He had data on his side, arguing that none of the twenty-five or more nations that participated in Davis Cup play had ever adopted such a restriction. To the contrary, those countries actively encouraged their players to write about tennis. For example, the Australian Lawn Tennis Association had urged Pat O'Hara Wood, a member of its 1924 Davis Cup team, to write accounts of the matches he both played and observed. To Merrihew, there was an obvious distinction between playing tennis and writing about it, and he did not see how writing about it should have any bearing on one's amateur status. In separating the magazine from the USLTA, Merrihew, otherwise held in the highest esteem in the tennis world, earned the everlasting wrath of Julian Myrick, who said, "Mr. Merrihew had done a great deal for tennis," adding, nastily, "but I think he has made a comfortable living out of it."

Merrihew's magazine never missed its goal of fifteen annual issues from 1907 through 1950. In a larger format, between thirty-two and sixty-four pages, each issue was packed full of information. Believing "pictures are the answer" to every good story, Merrihew promoted the use of photographs, even though they added to his costs and sometimes crowded out the stories. Covers, he believed, were for the readers, and he refused to sully his with ads or a table of contents.[28] The revenue for the magazine came from subscriptions as well as tennis-based ads mixed in with pitches for posh vacation destinations. There were no ads for liquor, chewing gum, or cigarettes.

In addition to reporting on tournaments, the pages of *American Lawn Tennis* examined controversies over foot faults, offered advice on the proper way to string a racket, and debated the height of the chairs of umpires and linesmen. A service component characterized articles such as "How to Cure Tennis Ills," published on July 20, 1932: "If your feet are badly blistered and have much pain in them, soak them in hot water in which tannic acid powder has been added. This will remove the soreness and cause the feet to heal much faster."

The overall tone was one of cheerleading: "It is becoming increasingly difficult to realize that lawn tennis was once looked upon as a sissy game, and even yet is thought by many to lack the blood and iron qualities that go to make games for 'he men.' . . . Ours is a game of brawn and brains, of strategy and tactics, demanding the best the player has. Weaklings have no place in championship tennis, and he who would scale the heights must be clad in armor of plate and equipped with weapons sharp and staunch."[29]

In one significant way, the magazine defied the tennis establishment and society itself. For years it had reported on the scores and participants in matches played by members of the American Tennis Association, the oldest Black sports organization in the United States, founded in 1916 by businessmen, professors, and doctors, in reaction to the USLTA's ban on Black players. Starting in the 1890s, students at historically Black colleges and universities played tennis on their own campuses. Philadelphia's Chautauqua Tennis Club hosted the first invitational tournament for Black players in 1898. The first national championship sponsored by the ATA took place at Baltimore's Druid Hill Park in August 1917. The early ATA National Championships were held at various campuses including Hampton Institute (now Hampton University) and Morehouse College. Mindful that Black Americans would be barred from most hotels, the organizers chose those venues for their ready housing. The national competition attracted a large following in the Black community, and soon, auxiliary events contributed to the sense of festivity, including fashion shows and dances.[30]

On August 20, 1935, under the headline "A Visit to Harlem," *American Lawn Tennis* sent a reporter to the Tennis and Allied Sports Club in New York City: "Like almost all courts located in the city, where land is at a premium the four Harlem courts lack an ample amount of back space, but in every other respect they afford pleasurable playing conditions. The clay surface is particularly fine and the courts well-oriented and protected from wind by a high fence and apartment houses on three sides and a small clubhouse and stands on the fourth. The atmosphere of the place was one of real love for tennis and keenness to improve both in the playing and management of the game."

The piece then took on the air of a scouting report: "Curiosity regarding the standard of play among the colored people was satisfied to a degree, despite the lack of any direct competitions with players whose ability could be taken as a standard."

Even so, the magazine was hardly free from the taint of prejudice. The full-page promotion for Victor strings in the August 20, 1938, issue depicted ceramic-looking statues of a tall white man in tennis attire on one side of the net, gleefully examining his racket, towering over a much shorter Black man in a striped polo shirt, holding a ball. The latter speaks from what is said to be "the ball boy's angle" in offensively stereotyped dialect, "Wen de ball's got zip to it like it's alive, Ah know it's VICTOR Strings that win."

Merrihew served as editor, writer, and publisher until his death in 1947. Fortunately for Alice, Merrihew's successor as editor subscribed to his convictions about fair play and fair pay. She flourished in her column As I See It. Some of her prose was anodyne, alternating pleasantries with gossip of a benign sort. "Alice Marble is with idea" begins one column dedicated to a discussion of ways to make the public more tennis-conscious, formulated at a dinner party. In another, she came out against the restrictive nature of the eight weeks' rule, named for the short interval in which amateur players could accept expense money, which kept them from tournaments that would enhance their standing but that they could not afford to attend.

She gave her old friends support, even when they were in big trouble. In November 1947, two days before Thanksgiving, Tilden had been pulled over on Sunset Boulevard by Beverly Hills police. In the driver's seat, a fourteen-year-old boy steered the athlete's capacious Packard Clipper. For years, the tennis establishment had lived in fear that Tilden would be outed, looking the other way in the hope that at least he found his partners outside the world of tennis. Police observed Tilden with one arm draped around the boy's back and the other on his lap. Four buttons of the child's fly were undone. Tilden was arrested for contributing to the delinquency of a minor.

The news was not widely covered in the mainstream press, where sexual matters were often ignored in favor of discretion. Repercussions were felt elsewhere. His old childhood clubhouse, the Germantown Cricket Club in Philadelphia, removed all images and mention of him, and Dunlop Sport severed its association, ending the manufacture of a racket that bore his name and retiring the slogan used to sell it, "You may not be able to fill Tilden's shoes, but you can play with his *Racket!*"

American Lawn Tennis writers omitted him from their coverage, the exception being Marble, who wrote a June 1947 column titled "The King of Tennis," in which she defended Tilden not for his misdeeds but for his continual kindness toward her and others. She thanked him for championing her after seeing her play as a teenager at the California Tennis Club. During her "play for pay" professional tour with Tilden, Mary Hardwick, and Don Budge, she said he was always a gentleman, ready with a kind word, especially when someone's play was off.

"Four people in close quarters covering sixty-five cities can get on each other's nerves," she wrote, "but Bill was always the model of decorum, extremely considerate, and made sure that Mary and I had comfortable rooms in the various auditoriums, arenas, and gymnasiums." Marble appreciated the way he made a point of watching the women in their matches, and how no matter how overmatched he was by Budge, he fought back.

Marble urged sympathy for "Bill, the temperamental, strange man whom nobody really knows; the genius of the courts, the man who has done so much to inspire young and old." She asked the public to suspend judgment and to join in wishing him every success in this his most difficult battle.

Tilden appeared in court in January 1948, where he was put on five years' probation, with nine months to be served in prison. The judge had little sympathy for Tilden, despite his slumped shoulders and tearful demeanor, rebuking him: "You have been the hero of youngsters all over the world. Many adults have admired you for your sportsmanship. It is a great shock that you are involved in an offense like this."[31]

Tilden was released from prison after serving seven and a half months.[32] He wrote a book, called *My Story*, which Marble praised in a subsequent column, admiring what she called his humble appeal to the public when he wrote, "I was just one more guy in jail, which was what I deserved to be, and what I wanted to be. Now all that is past. All I ask is the chance to prove that

I have learned my lesson, that I have paid my debt, and that I am intent on resuming life as an honorable member of society."[33] Good intentions aside, he would face the same charges a few years later and serve further jail time.

Marble gave Bobby Riggs a sympathetic nod in a column when his book *Tennis Is My Racket* was published in 1949: "When I stop to think of the tough road he had to hoe, living in the shadow of a great champion, Don Budge; scrapping to prove his worth before the officials and the public, I can only take my hat off to this great little battler."

Alice dropped more than the names of tennis players. "I was sitting with Academy Award winner Humphrey Bogart, a tennis fan of long-standing," she wrote in one column. She asked Bogart his opinion about tennis players who turn professional: "Pro tennis or pro football means the best in sports," the actor said. "They are the people who have proved themselves tops in the amateur game. I'm frank to admit that I like class in anything, especially sports."

Sometimes she thrilled readers with true stories from tennis matches of yore, as in her account of the finals at Forest Hills in 1920 between Tilden and Bill Johnston:

> The doughty rivals have split sets, Tilden leading 3–1 when a small plane buzzed the stadium. As Big Bill walked back to the baseline, the plane's engine stalled and it plummeted to earth within five hundred feet of the old west stand, carrying to their deaths the pilot and the newspaper photographer who was his passenger.
>
> As the shocked and stunned gallery, some ten thousand strong, made a nervous movement, Umpire E. C. Conlon realized that only quick action would avert a stampede which might kill or injure scores of others. "Can you go on?" he asked Johnston.
>
> "Yes," Bill answered, moving into position to receive service.
>
> "How about you, Bill?"
>
> "I'm ready," Tilden said and turned to receive the balls from the waiting ball boy.
>
> The immediate resumption of play, for all its apparent callousness, steadied the spectators, brought them safely over the thin margin that separates excitement from hysteria, and fewer than fifty people of those thousands left the stands for the macabre scene of the wreckage.

A full-page ad in the magazine promoted Alice's career as a public speaker with Charles S. Pearson as her exclusive manager: "Alice Marble believes that if you want anything badly enough you can have it. Make that your philosophy, add an equal amount of faith and serve it up with plenty of hard work and there's your guaranteed not-to-fail recipe for championship." The ad quoted a paper in Knoxville: "Alice Marble is tall, trim, sincere, very gracious. The liking of her large audience was reflected in the spontaneous applause with which they greeted her talk."[34]

WHILE WORKING AT THE MAGAZINE, Marble found time to traverse the country with her message of personal betterment. At a February 1, 1949, lecture at a college in Louisiana she told women that they can't have their cake and eat it too if they expect to be tennis winners.

No one witnessing her speak onstage or reading her quick comebacks and ardent opinions in the pages of *American Lawn Tennis* would ever guess that her health was a concern, but her lungs, never completely recovered from the illness of years ago, had become more compromised by a lifelong smoking habit. Her breathing was so ragged she sought medical attention.

The doctors had bad news. One lung was so infected that she was given a choice: surgery, with a fifty-fifty chance of survival, or the life of an invalid. She chose the first.

Her hospitalization that September attracted the attention of Walter Winchell, the most prominent radio commentator and gossip columnist in his day, known for inventing his own patois. A couple getting married "middle-aisled it." If later they divorced, they were "RENO-vated." Ellipses were invented for Winchell's clipped style, while he trademarked the newsman's look of a hat draped over the eyes and a loosened tie along with a tendency to issue bon mots from the side of one's mouth. On September 21, 1949, Winchell sandwiched his news flash about Alice between political news and a dart aimed at the new hit musical *South Pacific*, which had opened on Broadway on April 7. His staccato was as unmistakable in print as on the air: "Insiders hear that if Truman steps aside (in '52) he will boom Defense Secy. Louis Johnson for that job. . . . Ambassador Lewis Douglas is here for his fourth operation on his injured orb. . . . His resignation's been on the President's desk for weeks. . . . Alice Marble, the tennis star, is very ill in a midtown hosp. . . . Everything about 'South Pacific' is expensive. The ice cream parlor at 47th and B'way features a 'S. Pacific sundae' at $1.50."[35]

After three days of shots of penicillin in the hospital ("My rear felt like a pincushion"), Alice awakened post-surgery to find two ribs and a lobe of one lung had been removed, replaced by a twelve-inch scar under her right breast. When she threated to sue her doctor if her "bosom was lopsided,"[36] he congratulated her on her fighting spirit.

Winchell's bulletin sent out such a strong message of impending mortality that Marble lost money when an upcoming speaking tour was canceled, a loss she did not lightly countenance once she recovered. At least she did not have to worry about the cost of the medical care. When asked to underwrite the procedure, du Pont did not hesitate. On September 6, 1949, he addressed a short note to "Pinkie," a pet name bestowed on her years ago by Hearst at his castle and invoked by du Pont, who loved nicknames. He sent her a check to cover the operation and inquired the name of the hospital where the procedure was taking place so he and Margaret could be in touch. The note was signed "Love."

CHAPTER 23

A VITAL ISSUE

NOTHING IN MARBLE'S career as a commentator rivaled the impact of her July 1950 column in *American Lawn Tennis*, which galvanized the tennis establishment into taking a long overdue step in the direction of racial justice. When she wrote the column, her most famous, about the African American player Althea Gibson, she had a following predisposed to respect her views. The magazine showed its support by publishing a profile of young Althea by another writer in the same issue. The story and the column combined to create a one-two punch for readers, so there would be no ambiguity about where the magazine stood regarding this up-and-coming athlete and the proper future of the game.

Marble's strong views on racial equality were many years in the making. She ascribes her awakening to the disconnect she witnessed firsthand in her prospects as a young white athlete playing on public courts in contrast to the fate of her Asian American peers: "There were dozens of Chinese and Filipinos with whom I played as a youngster. Several years later when I went to dinner parties, I found many of these same boys working as butlers or houseboys. And I shocked my hosts and hostesses by carrying on lengthy conversations on tennis with the boys as they served the dinner."[1]

Althea Gibson was born in 1927 on a five-acre farm in South Carolina. With little chance of creating a livelihood, her sharecropper father decided to move the family to New York, where he got a job working in a garage for ten dollars a week. Like Alice, who described herself as a "healthy well-cared-for scrap of humanity"[2] as a baby, Althea was born sturdy, weighing eight pounds, referred to as a "big fat one" by her mother. She loved basketball above all, and for a time her father nursed the dream that she could be a prizefighter. Paddle tennis, played on the streets, preceded her career as a tennis player. A musician named Buddy Walker saw her play and introduced her to the

Harlem River Tennis Courts at 150th Street, where her admittedly wild and untutored strokes won admiration. In response, neighbors contributed to a fund to pay for her training at the Cosmopolitan Club. Like Alice, Althea resisted the sport at first, but then, "After a while I began to understand that you could walk out on the court like a lady, all dressed up in immaculate white, be polite to everybody, and still play like a tiger and beat the liver and lights out of the ball. I remember thinking to myself that it was kind of like a matador going into the bullring, beautifully dressed, bowing in all directions, following the fancy rules to the letter, and all the time having nothing in mind except striking that sword in the bull's guts and killing him as dead as hell."[3]

Althea received her first tennis racket at age fifteen, in 1942, and won the all-Black American Tennis League's girls' division championships in 1944 and 1945. She lost in the adult women's tournament in 1946, but by the time she was profiled in *American Lawn Tennis* she had won the women's title every year since 1947 (and would continue to until 1957). The article shared images of Gibson serving a ball, studying at a desk at Florida Agricultural and Mechanical College in Tallahassee, playing table tennis, playing the saxophone, and bearing flowers and wearing smiles next to Nancy Chaffee, a white player to whom she had recently lost in a US National Indoor Championship tournament, and projected as a wholesome well-rounded young woman. Officials from the American Tennis Association, while expressing the hope that she would be able to play in the US National Championships at Forest Hills in 1950, made it clear that they did not wish to create a stir. The USLTA was leaving the matter up to the organizers of the tournament, who placed the burden to decide on a thirty-six-member committee. Mary Hardwick gave Gibson an endorsement: "Althea is a charming girl, a fine sportswoman, and an excellent representative of both her race and her country."[4]

Hamilton Chambers, a correspondent for *American Lawn Tennis*, assessed her abilities:

> She has a terrific forehand drive, but she cannot handle speed. In second rate company, where the ball is set up for her, she is dynamite. Against a retriever, she can get set for the shot and drive at will to score on placements. Her serve is adequate and sufficient in pace, but insufficient as regards her ability to place it. Against a hard hitter, and once on the defensive, she is lost. With a ball coming back to her with pace, she is undecisive. . . . Yet,

*she has the makings of a very fine player although she looks to be at least
two years away from big-time tennis.*[5]

But for now, Forest Hills was off-limits to Gibson because of her race.
When someone asked her how she would feel about playing there, she said,
"Huh! Who you kidding?" She assumed her interrogator already "knew
I would give my right arm to play against the white girls, and he knew that
I knew that he knew it. I had talked about it often enough, although never as
a genuine possibility, just as something that rankled and ate at me."[6]

Gibson was tall, slender, powerful. She was also realistic. She had grown
up expecting to encounter prejudice, in the Deep South and in Harlem. She
didn't like it when she got on a bus and was told to sit in the back, although
the closest she came to rebellion was to sit as far away from the back as her
oppressors would allow. She understood that at a lunch counter, she could
buy a hot dog but would have to consume it off the premises. She anticipated
that she might be forced to yield her path on a sidewalk to a white person.
She hated how at the movies "the ushers practically knocked us colored down
making sure we got up to the back balcony, which is the only place in the
whole theater we were allowed to sit."[7] She knew about the Ku Klux Klan
and lynching. She was grateful in her own life to have evaded the worst.

"I have never regarded myself as a crusader," she later reflected.

*I try to do the best I can in every situation I find myself in, and naturally
I'm always glad when something I do turns out to be helpful and important
to all Negroes—or, for that matter, to all Americans, or maybe only to all
tennis players. But I don't consciously beat the drums for any special cause,
not even the cause of the Negro in the United States, because I feel that our
best chance to advance is to prove ourselves as individuals. That way, when
you are accepted, you are accepted voluntarily, because people appreciate
you and respect you and want you, not because you have been shoved down
their throats. This doesn't mean I'm opposed to the fight for integration of
the schools or other movements like that. It simply means that in my own
career I try to steer clear of political involvements and make my way as
Althea Gibson, private individual.*[8]

Gibson received word that if she submitted an entry form to the Eastern
Indoor Championships, a tournament held annually in February on hard

courts at the Seventh Regiment Armory on Park Avenue in New York City, she would be allowed to play, so she filled out the proper application for the 1950 competition. Gibson believed most of the tennis community was composed of decent people and would surely approve, as any right-minded person would. She made it to the quarterfinals. After her last match, she was asked to enter the US National Indoor Championships the following week, where once again she made it to the quarterfinals—both respectable performances, if not record-breaking.

Gibson had every reason to hope that the United States Lawn Tennis Association would extend her an invitation to play in the 1950 summer grass-court events, including Forest Hills. The hitch was that a player could not qualify for Forest Hills unless she had played in the earlier tournaments, scheduled at all-white clubs, an invitation for which was not forthcoming. Gibson began to doubt her prospects when, "without any warning at all, a powerful champion struck a blow in my behalf."[9]

As a teenager, Gibson had seen Alice Marble play in the 1944 exhibition match billed as "genuinely mixed doubles with a white and a black player on either side" at the Cosmopolitan Club in the Sugar Hill section of Harlem.[10] Gibson could not keep her eyes off Marble.

> I can still remember saying to myself, boy, would I like to be able to play tennis like that! She was the only woman tennis player I'd ever seen that I felt exactly that way about. Until I saw her, I'd always had eyes only for the good men players. But her effectiveness of strike, and the power that she had, impressed me terrifically. Basically, of course, it was the aggressiveness behind her game that I liked. Watching her smack that effortless serve, and then follow it into the net and put the ball away with an overhead as good as any man's, I saw the possibilities in the game of tennis that I had never seen before.[11]

Gibson had been too young to join the subsequent social hour, but Marble had stayed after the match and had a drink at the club; the casual mingling carried its own strong message. In her outreach in this regard, Marble followed the example of fellow Californian Don Budge.

Marble had not yet met Gibson when she unleashed her finest rhetoric, taking dead aim at the tennis establishment. Marble's column, titled "A Vital

Issue," appeared in *American Lawn Tennis* on July 1, 1950, preceded by an endorsement from her editor:

> American Lawn Tennis *is privileged to turn its editorial columns to Miss Alice Marble. Miss Marble's column this month deals with an issue of such importance to the game that we felt that its rightful position was on a page specifically devoted to opinion. We hope on future occasions to carry editorials by other outstanding tennis personalities. At times we may disagree with their opinions, but in this case* American Lawn Tennis *wishes to go on record as wholeheartedly supporting the sentiments and opinions expressed by Miss Marble in the following editorial.*

In the column, Marble laced into the tennis establishment for setting up a classic can't-win situation: Gibson was welcome to apply to play at Forest Hills, but first she had to play in all the tournaments leading up to the US National Championships, which were invitational and to which she was not invited. Marble accused the USLTA committee of putting Miss Gibson over a "cunningly-wrought barrel," of which Marble hoped her "one lone opinion" might loosen a few staves.

"I think it's time," wrote Marble, "we faced a few facts."

> *If tennis is a game for ladies and gentlemen, it's also time we acted a little more like gentlepeople and less like sanctimonious hypocrites. If there is anything left in the name of sportsmanship, it's more than time to display what it means to us. If Althea Gibson represents a challenge to the present crop of women players, it's only fair that they should meet that challenge on the courts, where tennis is played. I know those girls, and I can't think of one who would refuse to meet Miss Gibson in competition. She might be soundly beaten for a while—but she has a much better chance on the courts than in the inner sanctum of the committee, where a different kind of game is played.*

Marble made it clear that based on having seen her play at one of the indoor championships, she could not say whether Gibson had it in her to be a champion. Marble did not know if Gibson possessed that indispensable elusive quality of athletes who rebound even when the chips are down. Perhaps she would turn out to be "one more youngster who failed to live up to her initial promise." That would be something Gibson had to live with. But if she were refused the chance to show her skills on the basis of her skin color, it would be an "uneradicable mark against a game to which I have devoted most of my life, and I would be bitterly ashamed."

Marble said she believed the inclusion of Black players was only a matter of time. If her own generation did not make the change, perhaps the next generation would follow the example of such other sports as baseball, football, and boxing. Eventually it would happen. There was too much talent. Why not now?

"Speaking for myself," she concluded, "I will be glad to help Althea Gibson in any way I can. If I can improve her game or merely give her the benefit of my own experiences, as I have many other young players, I'll do that. If I can give her an iota more of confidence by rooting my heart out from the gallery, she can take my word for it: I'll be there."

Not long afterward, the thirty-six members of the USLTA championship committee held a meeting to ponder Gibson's fate. In the end, they opened the door and ducked at the same time. The male and female champions of the ATA Nationals would play at Forest Hills. Success in the summer's grass-court tournaments would no longer be required to qualify, which meant that "integrating the grass-court tournaments held at exclusive clubs would not be necessary."[12]

The rank and file welcomed Gibson far more than the governing body. Marble was not the only white player to step up to welcome her. Once it was clear that Gibson would be permitted to play in the US National Championships, Sarah Palfrey Cooke made a point of pressing the owners of the West Side Tennis Club, where she was not even a member, to allow her as a former champion to escort Althea to the courts. The two women were able to practice together, which according to Gibson helped settle her nerves.[13] This kind of ambassadorial gesture from a Boston blueblood helped Althea's cause and, by corollary, helped spread an image of tennis as an enterprise interested in fair play. Cooke always downplayed her actions as a routine act of hospitality. Perhaps it was routine to her, reflecting her gratitude for a privileged upbringing in which she had been given opportunities.

Much of the press stood at the ready to ratify the points made in "A Vital Issue." A *New York Herald Tribune* editorial, titled "Alice Marble Calls a Turn," said that tennis was no different from any other sport, and it should welcome any competitor with proven ability. It was a question of simple fairness: "Let the girl show what she can do."[14]

In November 1950, Marble dedicated a column to the reactions she experienced after writing "A Vital Issue." Under the title "An Open Letter to Althea Gibson," Alice began by congratulating Gibson on making history: "quite a burden of honor for twenty-three-year-old shoulders to carry." She praised her for playing some "remarkably good tennis," especially considering that Gibson had played on grass only three times previously. Alice also urged Gibson to keep her first appearance at Forest Hills in perspective. She had played an admirable second-round match against Louise Brough but did not win. From Marble's point of view, the odds of a newcomer beating a proven champ like Brough were slim to none: "Winning Wimbledon three times against very strong fields is scarcely within the realm of coincidence." Alice said some people erroneously credited her with Gibson's good showing: "It's kind of your fans to include me in your moral triumph, but I can't take any credit for your performance. As Ogden Nash said, 'I'm a stranger here myself.'"

Alice cautioned Gibson against the hangers-on who attached themselves to her at the competition. Baseball great Ted Williams, she said, called such opportunists "front runners," people who don't help you on the way up but who want a piece of you when it suddenly appears convenient and lucrative.

Warning against the distractions of these "newfound oracles," she wrote: "If they had your natural ability, they'd be playing at Forest Hills; since they haven't, they should not be allowed to capitalize on yours at the risk of destroying you." She urged Gibson to heed the counsel of her "proven friends," rather than opportunistic newcomers.

Reflecting on those who had turned on her after "A Vital Issue" appeared, Alice wrote:

> *I am long past competitive tennis, and I still don't know who my friends are. I only know, after this year at Forest Hills, who my friends aren't. . . . People who fell all over their feet to entertain me when I was champion greeted me very formally this September. People who had called me "Champ" since 1938 suddenly remembered I was "Miss Marble." People who had taken ostentatious advantage of our kissing acquaintance gave me a chilly handshake or failed to notice my approach or glared which was even funnier. Kids I had known as Juniors, whose weak shots I had helped to correct, kids I had plugged as championship material who now have national rankings—they*

forgot how much more I had done for them than I ever did for you. They only remember a terrible article I wrote, saying that a good tennis player named Gibson ought to play in the Nationals. Things are tough all over, aren't they?

Finally, she offered Gibson encouragement, praise, criticism, and a call to arms:

I've never seen a combined service and forehand hit with better style and force than yours, unless it is that of Doris Hart. On the other hand, literally, I think that your backhand could stand quite a bit of attention this winter; from where I sat, it did not look as sound as your other strokes.

So . . . the summing up, Althea. You were blessed with more natural ability than any woman on the courts today; you're a bold player and you have that rare spark. Without discounting the years you have given to this labor of love, I tell you now that you must work even harder to gain the mechanics, the fundamentals, to harness those assets and direct them into the proper channels in order to become a champion worthy of the name.

Forget the people. Forget your almost-upset of Miss Brough, which is past history. Concentrate on learning and playing the very best tennis of which you are capable, and that's fine tennis, indeed. Don't bother to tell 'em who you are; prove it, instead. See you in 1951. On the center court, I hope.

In February 1951, Gibson was given her own podium in the magazine to respond to Marble, which she did in a spirit of feisty gratitude. She expressed her sorrow to Marble over the false friends who forsook her when they did not like her stance.

"Miss Marble," she wrote, "If you find things really tough, imagine how I find them. . . . I am a poor girl from a family not able to support or help me."

She apologized for her own hangers-on who made matters difficult at Forest Hills, and she expressed the hope that no matter, whites and Blacks would find more and more chances to compete against each other.

"We do not want to socialize but we do want to improve our tennis. Again I say not a single player participating at any tournament has voiced any objection to playing against a colored player. To the contrary they have been most pleasant, very good sports and seemed to have enjoyed their matches, whether won or lost."

Alice's column helped open the door, and Althea Gibson eventually took full advantage as her game matured. In 1956 she won the French Championships; she followed with a spectacular 1957 season, during which she won the Australian Championships, Wimbledon (over Louise Brough), and the US National Championships, and was ranked number one in the world. She then repeated her Wimbledon and US wins in 1958.

Later, Gibson was the first Black woman to appear on the cover of *Sports Illustrated* and *Time* magazines, and she was also the first player to whom Queen Elizabeth II personally bestowed a trophy. Gibson's own mother said, "I didn't think a Negro girl could go that high."[15]

Among the letters she received was a congratulatory note from President Dwight Eisenhower right after her first Wimbledon victory, which she said was "best of all":

> *Dear Miss Gibson,*
>
> *Many Americans, including myself, have watched with increasing admiration your sustained and successful effort to win the heights of the tennis world. Millions of your fellow citizens would, if they could, join with me in felicitations of your outstanding victory at Wimbledon.*
>
> *Recognizing the odds you face, we have applauded your courage, persistence and application. Certainly it is not easy for anyone to stand in the center court at Wimbledon and in the glare of world publicity and under the critical gaze of thousands of spectators, do his or her very best. You met the challenge superbly.*[16]

"Shaking hands with the Queen of England," said Gibson, in a comment that deserves its own trophy for understatement, "was a long way from being forced to sit in the colored section of the bus going into downtown Wilmington, North Carolina."[17]

CHAPTER 24

THIS IS YOUR LIFE

S OON AFTER SHE WROTE THE COLUMN welcoming Althea Gibson into tennis competition at the highest levels, Marble sat back and contemplated, with a sharp focus, what the game had meant to her.

On one matter, she never stopped being outspoken: the dilemma of how to support oneself as a tennis player. It had never been easy, and even now, after the war, amateur players still had to wing it in terms of food and lodgings. Usually, the two top players in a tournament would be given hotel rooms, and if inclined, they invited others who placed less favorably to pile in, sleeping in the bathtub, if need be, and sharing meals consisting of bananas (ten cents for three) and a loaf of bread and jar of peanut butter.[1] And yet the pro circuit was no guarantee of financial security or even a good experience. Marble recollected her professional tour with mixed feelings in an article in *American Lawn Tennis* in which she addressed the newest pros:

> *It's no fun to make one-night stands, to be asked to play your best on inadequate courts, to be away from home and family for months on end, to keep in shape as best you can on unimaginative restaurant meals. It's tiring and tiresome and seems, toward the end of the tour, like the worst possible way to make a living. You play an occasional bad match and you mind, because you're still a tennis player. When you play your best match, you're always in a tankwater town where there's nobody to appreciate your splendid performance. Things get lost, important letters fail to arrive, favorite rackets break—and it's still tennis and you love every minute of it and you swear you'll never tour again. At least that's the way Mr. Budge, Mr. Tilden, Miss Hardwick and I played it.*

I wish the present troupe good luck. Good luck, soft beds, tender steaks,
adequate lighting, and a comfortable amount of space behind the baseline.
I hope they all make a million dollars.[2]

Marble expressed equally strong views in a January 11, 1953, article in the *Los Angeles Times* called "Alice Marble Believes Pro Future Dark for Gals," focusing on her disappointment in the disparity between the prospects of women and men who went pro: "I'm not knocking the sport which has been good to me. But the facts speak for themselves. Gussie Moran's pro tour [in 1950], with some of the greatest advance publicity in sports, failed to pay off. Jack Kramer expects to gross $200,000 on his [1953] tour with Frank Sedgman, with not a woman in the picture. I've heard him say that as long as he is promoter, he can't afford the risk of presenting women players. For women, this is a one-tour deal, if that."

Marble believed that the public had no interest in paying money to watch women's tennis. In 1941, when Mary Hardwick and she had toured with Budge and Tilden, the two women had been the warm-up act, always playing first. Even Marble had to admit that the women's tennis seemed like "a slow-motion picture compared to the blazing action of the men."

Tilden, she said, had color.

That is something women since Suzanne Lenglen have lacked. However,
the major obstacle is that there has never been a feminine "natural."

When I turned pro, there was no one of my caliber to compete against.
I won 68 matches to Mary Hardwick's 3. . . . If Maureen Connolly turns
pro in a few years—as she probably will—whom will she play? She eclipses
the field now.

Marble pointed out that it was hard to settle into the tedium of teaching, partly because as amateurs "we are a little spoiled." On the circuit, there's "glamour, excitement, homage." In her heyday, Marble had been an honorary member of sixty tennis clubs throughout the world. She was "a celebrity whose friendship was coveted."

After turning pro, her status diminished almost overnight to the point of near collapse: "In the space of 24 hours, I suddenly became not nearly so nice a person."

Clubs where she had received a hero's welcome in the past now acted as though she were "hired help," to the point of showing her the back door. One exclusive club in New York, which she declined to name, would not allow her to join. The only reason she regained her membership in the All England Club at Wimbledon was because she had voluntarily helped young English girls during a visit in 1947.[3]

During a conversation at Forest Hills during the US National Championships in 1947, Pauline Betz, who had made the leap to pro, complained to Marble about being snubbed.

Alice told her, "If people don't make as much over you now that you're a pro, they weren't loyal in the first place."

She saw the dilemma with clarity: "But it is hard. After your one big tour, what do you do? Fade into oblivion? Twelve years later, I'm still living on my reputation as an amateur."

Marble's solution, at least for a while, was to remain in the public eye as a commentator. Many readers praised her in letters to the editor:

> *Gentlemen:*
>
> *For many years I have thoroughly enjoyed your progressive maga-zine. After looking through all the pictures, the first article I read is one by Miss Alice Marble. It is always so authoritative and most interesting. She is such a great credit to the game both as a writer and player—a truly great sportswoman.*[4]

Some readers took issue, forcing Marble to stand up for herself and choose her words with precision. In January 1951, Ike Shynook, who identi-fied himself as a tennis writer with the Rochester *Democrat and Chronicle*, criticized Marble's write-up of Gussie Moran's play in a pro tournament that had also featured Jack Kramer, Bobby Riggs, and Pauline Betz Addie. In his letter to the editor, he claimed to detect "the faint aroma of sour grapes in Miss Marble's voluble but vapid" coverage, and he suggested the magazine would be well served to do without the "tarnished comments of this inept observer." He attacked Marble personally, saying it was "not so long ago that she too toured the provinces in quest of a 'fast buck.' How well she succeeded is perhaps reflected in her sudden demise from the national tennis scene."[5]

Alice responded with a speedy volley that attests to her growing strength as a writer. From the timid prose in *The Road to Wimbledon* with its reliance on homily and the implicit goodwill of the reader, the voice in her reply could not be less sentimental or more direct:

> Obviously I turned professional for the purpose of earning money. The people who taught me tennis had devoted a number of years and a great deal of effort to making me a champion, and I had no other way to repay them; it's no disgrace to have been poor. My "sudden demise from the national tennis scene" was, however, precipitated by an international incident called World War II. I chose a dollar-a-year job as United States Director of Physical Fitness rather than embark on another tour while the country was at war. "How well I succeed is perhaps reflected" by the fact that I was able to accept a dollar-a-year job after touring one season. If Mr. Shynook cared, he could also learn that still later I toured military installations here and abroad with my erstwhile professional rival, Mary Hardwick, for the purpose of playing exhibitions for the Armed Forces. Does that explain my "sudden demise" sufficiently, Mr. Shynook?[6]

She refused to offer the public apology this same nettlesome critic demanded she make to Gussie Moran. Marble felt Moran had misused her talent as a tennis player and made a clown out of herself with stunt-driven photographs that included standing on her head. In 1949, Moran lost in singles in the first round but made it to the finals in doubles at Wimbledon. Of greater note, at least within the world of tennis, if not fashion, was her attire. Designer Ted Tinling created a short dress paired with underwear decorated with two-inch bands of lace. The "widely mentioned unmentionables" were visible whenever "Gussie races across the court or leaps for a high shot," the New York Times said. Photographers reportedly scrambled to get the most revealing pictures. Headlines such as one in the June 22, 1949, Indianapolis News were common: "Gussie Wins Match, 20,000 See Panties." The chairman of the All England Club was not amused. Tinling was castigated for drawing "attention to the sexual area." The overseers of Wimbledon felt that Tinling's offensive frilly creation had brought "sin and vulgarity into tennis."[7] Concern was expressed toward the royal family and its sensibilities, and the matter was considered of sufficient moment that it was addressed in Parliament.

Afterward, Moran earned the lifelong nickname "Gorgeous Gussie." Tinling, a long-time Wimbledon master of ceremonies, was banned from the event for thirty-three years. Moran said she was so mortified, she threw the offending garment in a trash can as soon as she could. Decades later, she felt her nickname was a misnomer: "I was embarrassed because they were putting so much adulation on the character, 'Gorgeous Gussie.' You know, I was really never anything to write home about. I was a plain girl. But *Life* magazine ran a picture calling me 'Gorgeous Gussie,' and the British picked it up and did a real job with it. Then people would see me, and I'd hear them say, 'I've seen better looking waitresses at the hot dog stand.' I just went to pieces. Emotionally, I couldn't handle it."[8]

Marble did not see anything playful or appealing in Gussie's antics. Responding further to Shynook's criticism, she declared:

> As a player schooled in the finest traditions of the game, I would have preferred that this sort of thing not be associated with tennis. When I "too, toured the provinces in quest of a fast buck," I was billed as a tennis player, dressed for tennis, and played the best game I knew how. The known success of that tour seems to have justified my doing so. . . . One other thing, since we're being personal. Your letter characterizes my writing both as satiric, which Webster's defines as "cutting, caustic, poignant, ironical, bitter, reproach-ful, abusive," and as vapid which the same reference sets down as "having lost its life, spirit or zest."

Marble told Shynook he needed to choose: her writing could not be both at the same time. "Come, come, Mr. Shynook, perhaps you ought to take up my game, which is tennis, and leave writing to us tennis players."

INCREASINGLY CONCERNED ABOUT HER own health after the lung surgery, Alice realized it was time to regroup. Even du Pont was worried about her. After he learned in the summer of 1951 that she had recently broken her hand, he expressed sympathy in a letter dated August 10: "I have broken my collarbone several times in hot weather and I know how uncomfortable and itchy you feel in the cast." In a more expansive and pensive tone than usual, he employed an equine analogy to describe how he saw her future:

> Many people have farms just for broken-down racehorses, but I am seriously considering having one for broken-down tennis players. Margaret still has a pulled muscle and is not going to play any more this year. Broughie's elbow

is out and whether it will be any good I really don't know. . . . Miss Thelma
Long of Australia is staying with us, fell in London and broke her arm
which is just out of the cast. So I think my farm will have a grand start
and afterwards you most probably would have to be kept in a glass case
marked "fragile."[9]

Not much later, Marble announced that she was making a huge change in her life. "After ten long and lovely years in New York," she told readers in March 1952 in the *Racquet*, "I have finally made a very necessary concession to health and taken up residence in Los Angeles."

By her reckoning, she had given more than fifteen hundred lectures and clinics since before the war—"a blur of one-night stands, driving three hundred miles a day and forgetting what town I was in."

Alice reassured her audience that it was "wonderful to be home—I hadn't realized how much I missed the outdoor life while I was in New York. Now I miss the theatre, of course, and the symphony and, most of all, the friends I left behind. But there is compensation. There is the sun, the conviction I grow stronger and healthier every day. There's the sound of a tennis ball being hit well, which has always been music to my ears."

Years later she wrote, even more directly, in her memoir: "I realized I couldn't stand it anymore."[10]

She sent out announcements with her new address in Los Angeles, including one in her perfect handwriting, postmarked October 27, 1952, to Will du Pont.

In a subsequent note that made it clear that Alice was on friendly terms with both Mr. and Mrs. du Pont, she informed them that the house was little, with a small patio, cost half the rent of what she paid in New York, and was in a good location. She hoped the du Ponts would pay a visit, and she sent "a special greeting to young William!"

Du Pont responded, "We expect to come out with William III around the end of January for a while, though I will have to come back and not spend too much time there as I am very busy this year."[11]

The move to California put Alice back in touch with Hollywood. Though her previous screen tests had been less than successful, she finally appeared in a movie in 1952, playing herself in *Pat and Mike*, directed by George Cukor and starring Katharine Hepburn and Spencer Tracy. The film follows an athlete (Hepburn) whose fiancé wants her to quit golf, so she connives with a shady but good-hearted promoter (Tracy) to continue to pursue her dreams. The movie was written by Garson Kanin and Ruth Gordon as a vanity project to highlight Hepburn's talents in golf and tennis, showing her in competition with real-life athletes like Marble, golfer Babe Didrikson Zaharias, Gussie Moran, and Don Budge. *Time Out* observed: "Hepburn gets to show off her considerable athletic talents as the bright, upper middle class sporting all-rounder; Tracy gets to be gruffly loveable as the rough-diamond promoter-manager who finally becomes her protector. There are far too many shots featuring real-life sports stars."[12]

With that moment on the silver screen, the fantasy of a career in film finally died, though as time went on Marble herself acknowledged that it was not her realm. In an interview much later in life, she gave a more detailed and less positive account of that 1937 screen test:

> *It was more convenient for Clark to set it up at MGM than for Carole to do it at Paramount for some reason. So I went and I made some tests. The first thing they did—I had a rather low voice—was to dress me like Helen Morgan [a torch singer] in a spangled black dress with a black wig and I sat on the piano and sang, "And along came Bill" [sings in a low, deep voice]. And here I am the outdoor girl of the world and here I am doing this and I just hated it. I felt terribly self-conscious. I hated the little oily assistant director who kept chasing me in the corners and the reason that Carole learned to swear was because this is what happened to her. She really had to go out and support her mother. These guys would try to get her in bed and she called them a God damn fucking son of a bitch. This is how she learned . . . [to] keep them away. I never resorted to this because I'd always resort to saying, "OK, buster, I've got a tennis racket in my hand."[13]*

In 1953, du Pont bought Point Happy Ranch in La Quinta, California, twenty-five miles from Palm Springs, nine from Palm Desert, in the Santa Rosa Mountains, a property rich with date palms and fig, pecan, avocado, and citrus trees. It also boasted a history of horse breeding, initiated by a previous owner who believed the climate provided the perfect conditions for the raising of Arabian horses. Originally home to the Cahuilla people, the spot was protected by the Santa Rosas, offering shelter from sandstorms and flash flooding.

Du Pont had been scouting many locations, looking for a vacation spot, according to Alice: "He tried Europe, and he tried Jamaica, and he tried the islands." Finally, she said to him, "Why don't you try Palm Springs?"[14] Du Pont envisioned a compound, a "ranch with a plantation of fruit and citrus trees, houses for rent, a house for his family to stay in during the winter months, a horse arena, and tennis courts."[15] He had other ideas for the property that he would reveal to Alice in the upcoming years.

THE PUBLICITY MACHINE set in motion by Teach so long ago continued to crank out attention in Alice's favor. On February 3, 1954, she was the focal point of the popular television show *This Is Your Life*. The concept behind the show, an early version of reality TV, was to subject an individual to a walk down memory lane in front of a studio audience. The guest of honor sat onstage while people from the past—family members, former teachers or coaches, clergy, school pals, professional associates—offered tributes. When the show concluded, everyone surrounded the guest—one big happy family—who then received prizes and a copy of the show. The program vacillated between well-known guests like Rock Hudson and Buster Keaton, and subjects with personal valor but little to no fame, including a nurse from the Philippines and a Holocaust survivor. By that time in her life, Alice occupied neither category; she was now famous for having once been famous.

Ralph Edwards, the emcee, known for his warm chuckle and folksy manner, explained to the studio audience: "Our principal subject is somewhere here in our audience, not suspecting that the thunderbolt of surprise is about to strike. Now I'm aiming it right now, it's about to fall on someone who came here with a friend just to enjoy the show."

The camera focused on Alice, who shook her head and smiled.

It could not have been a surprise. The tennis star looked smart in a dress with dark stripes, and she carried gloves and a short-handled handbag. She also happened, by apparent good fortune, to have an aisle seat, all the better for jumping up to the stage where Edwards beckoned, wiggling his hand enthusiastically, as if casting a spell. The producers of *This Is Your Life* had been courting members of Alice's circle for months beforehand in preparation for the evening. About five weeks before the event, Hazel's son—the child of her early short-lived marriage—died, in his twenties, in a car accident. The Marble siblings had mixed feelings about whether an appearance on the show would be good for Hazel's emotional well-being and finally decided in favor of it.[16]

"Tonight, this is your life, Alice Marble of Los Angeles. Yes, Alice Marble, come on dear, a champion who revolutionized the game of tennis for women, simultaneously held six world tennis titles. This is your life. Come on, wish her well, ladies and gentlemen, here she is. Take your richly deserved chair of honor . . ."

Reading from a script as if it were an ancient tablet, Edwards began: "The High Sierras [snowcapped mountain photo comes on screen] looked down on your happy girlhood on a small cattle ranch in Northern California, right? You're the fourth of five children" [Marble family photo comes on-screen]. Alice knew the drill. It fell on her to project delight, graciousness, and pangs of sorrow in a cascade of alternating emotions, depending on what memories the host presented from the past.

The show mostly covered well-trod territory, but it did yield a few insights. In spite of the gap in their life experience and any estrangement that might have ensued as a result, all of Alice's siblings showed up. Dan got the speaking role. His discomfort was obvious as he stared off into space, reading stiffly from cue cards. "I pushed her into many tournaments," he said in a halting voice, to which she responded, with a bit more pep, "That I could have killed him for."

Edwards announced a new guest: "Someone else who entered your life at a turning point. Who is it Alice?"

Alice, hearing a voice offstage, grins. "This is one of America's best athletes, Mary K. Browne." Brownie and Alice then relived the moment when they stood up to the tennis establishment, and proved Alice was healthy enough to play in the 1936 Nationals.

Brownie: "Alice, you were determined. You were determined as the dickens. . . . The committee voted three to two in favor of Alice, and she had the right to play again. Your birthright, Alice, because you were born to be a champion."

Marble: "God bless you, Brownie."

The host stressed the usual biographical shards: the death of Marble's father, the racket from Dan, the heat at Maidstone, the ignominy of collapsing on the court in Paris, the stay at the sanatorium, Myrick's refusal to permit her to play in the East, the death of her mother, the triumphant string of wins.

Music cued a new chapter.

Edwards plowed ahead: "Again, you take up the broken pieces of your dreams to live again, usefully and bravely. In 1949 and 1950 you're writing a column for the *American Lawn Tennis* magazine."

The next offstage voice made Marble smile: "My story is an example of how much Miss Marble has done for fair play in sports. I'm sure I would have given up tennis had it not been for her encouragement."

Edwards perked up. "You recognize that voice?"

Alice smiled. "Oh, yes, Althea Gibson."

Edwards spoke with enthusiasm: "It's someone you benefited greatly in your efforts for democracy on the courts. Here from Jefferson City, Missouri, is the seventh-ranking woman tennis player in America, Althea Gibson, ladies and gentlemen."

Alice's eyes lit up upon the arrival of Gibson, who spoke first: "You know, Ralph, it sure helped the way Miss Marble stood up for me in fair play in sports. The tennis association treated me fairly based on my qualifications as a player. But naturally some people made it rough for me. I was embarrassed and got very discouraged. Miss Marble helped to break down the racial barrier to give me and others like me a fair chance at tennis. . . . She came up to me on the courts and said, 'Have courage. Remember, you're just like all the rest of us.'"

Of all the people Edwards gathered from Alice's past, the most mesmerizing was Teach. Edwards gave her a rousing introduction: "Yes, one of the foremost tennis authorities in America, maker of champions . . . your friend, coach, and manager for many years, Eleanor Tennant, ladies and gentlemen."

Teach bounded onto stage. Alice greeted her mentor with enough warmth to deflect any rumors of tension between the two women. Teach spoke of the past in a brisk tone: "Well, Alice, as you know, I had faith in you, and you became my pupil. If you remember I painted kind of a strict picture. It was a matter of no dates with boys but a lot of dates with tennis. . . . It was no drive-ins, no movies, just playing tennis, more tennis. As a matter of fact, I think you're the only person that can tell what great sacrifices you had to make for greatness."

When it was time for Teach to exit, Alice extended her right arm and latched onto Teach's forearm. A viewer looking for visual clues as to their relationship could detect her nudging Teach off center stage. It appeared in that slight but telling gesture that the once mutually beneficial relationship had outlived its utility.

Edwards ended with a surprise for Alice: "We've heard a lot about the inspiring lectures you give before our American youth and colleges . . . but we know it's seasonal work and sometimes bookings are few and sort of far between. . . . Now, you've been driving the same car for years to and fro on these long trips, that old car has about played its last match."

Edwards dangled a set of keys to a "brand-new 1954 Mercury" in front of Marble, saying, "Alice, we hope many more lecture bookings come in from schools and colleges from around the country, so their young people can hear from your own lips one of the most heroic stories in American sports, from one who played the game of tennis and life like a champion. Good night, God bless you."

The show made it clear: Alice, at the age of forty, was at the point where the pressure was on to continually press "repeat." Nothing in Alice's present was as exciting as her past.

CHAPTER 25

THE HOMESTRETCH

A S TENNIS CAME TO PLAY less of a role in her life, Alice began
to ponder what it had meant to her to not be able to pursue her true
athletic love, baseball. She even held it against her parents for saddling her
with the wrong gender: "I never quite forgave my mother and father for the
mean trick they pulled on me: That I was a girl and girls never play in the big
leagues!"[1] One time she showed off several fingers that had been permanently
bent from throwing the ball, to a sportswriter who apparently questioned
her throwing prowess.

"Did I ever play? Look at these. And it wasn't softball either. I could
throw from centerfield to home plate. Was in a throwing contest once but
didn't realize you have to get some elevation on the ball to get distance.
Smead Jolley showed me how though."[2]

She established her affinity for baseball beyond doubt in an August 1955
article in the *New York Times Magazine* titled "A Love Letter to Baseball."

"If there has to be a reason, baseball is still my favorite sport because
it was my first, unforgettable love," Marble wrote. In the piece, she revealed
what happened when the San Francisco Seals adopted her as their mascot.
Her family looked at her photo in the *San Francisco Examiner*, decided she
had "outgrown the cute phase," and corralled her into taking up the "more
genteel" game of tennis.

"Tennis," she wrote, "is what I *did*, but there is a difference in the way
I love it. When I'm watching the finals of a tournament and someone asks
the inevitable, 'Don't you wish you were playing this match?' my answer is
a sincere negative. Not when I suffer so much as a spectator. My palms per-
spire, my handkerchief is shredded in sympathy for the player on the short
end of the score, remembering as I do what a lonely place the center court
is when you're losing."

Even the names of the baseball players resonated for her. "I love the names they give each other right out of Damon Runyon—Sad Sam, Leo the Lip, Harry the Cat, Sal the Barber, the Yankee Clipper, the Splendid Splinter, the Little Professor, Rabbit, the Junkman, the Scooter, the Octopus, the Whip, the Thumper, Snuffy, Suitcase, Shotgun . . ."

She admired how hitters stand and relished the feeling of being on the field.

> *The ones who are big in terms of greatness have something in common: they don't fall away from the close ball unless it's a low-bridge. . . . I still itch to be down there on that field, and failing that, I love to watch a ball game. There is something poetic in the symmetry of the white of the lines, the green of the outfield, the grace of relaxed, conditioned athletes warming up.*
>
> *Having seen it once, I will always have a picture of Williams' big hands bruising a bat handle and the ripple of his swing. Of Musial in that unlikely crouch. Of Snider going effortlessly up the wall for an impossible catch. Of Yogi Berra's slue-footed [sic] trudge out to the mound.*[3]

Alice prepared for a major life adjustment. She needed a full-time job. The lecture circuit had lost its appeal: too many long hours on the road, too many overnights in strange places. She always considered herself open to any work she could find: "I did all the menial things when I was a kid, depression days." She would work as a "gift wrapper, and soda jerk and fry cook and babysitter . . . just name it."[4] Propitiously, Alice secured three new income streams at roughly the same time.

The first came courtesy of Will du Pont, who wanted to start construction on his property in Palm Desert. On lush land, filled with "date palms and avocado, orange, fig, pecan, apricot, mulberry and grapefruit trees, row crops and sugar cane," he planned to build a house for himself and, to the southwest of the palm grove, a home in the Spanish colonial style for Marble.[5]

He even devised a way of making her part of the process, sending her a check for $1,000 to "cover necessities you talked about." Whether this sum would cover past expenses or new ones is not clear, as she helped oversee construction, visited the construction site, and checked in with the work crews, taking photographs and "describing the progress of projects," as their correspondence made clear.

Alice was thrilled to be on board, writing to du Pont on March 10, 1956, "My spirits are sky high for the first time in ages." A few days later, she added, "I remember the houses and set-up at Belmont and can see that you have a wonderful imagination and talent for creating unusual homes."[6]

The second income stream came her way thanks to yet another fortunate encounter, this time with Dr. John Bach, a member of the Los Angeles Tennis Club, who suggested she train as an assistant in a doctor's office. The opportunity appealed in part because her mother had been a nurse, and so she felt it was a family tradition. After a two-and-a-half-month course at night school, she received an offer of employment, from Dr. Bach himself in his two-person practice on Ventura Boulevard. She wrote to du Pont, "I can still go down on Saturday afternoons and return on Sunday. I look forward to the job very much but the chores are a little foreign; injections, blood counts, electrocardiograms, urinalysis besides typing, filing, making out statements and keeping the two doctors and patients happy."[7]

At first her friends thought she "had gone mad," she told a reporter. "To work six days a week, reporting to the office at 8 a.m. on Saturday," not only assigned to medical tasks but also "keeping books, filling out insurance forms, making appointments, quieting down whimpering babies and nervous mamas. 'That's not for you, Alice,' they predicted. But it is. I love it."[8] She discouraged any allusions to her former celebrity status. The adult patients of Dr. John Bach, an obstetrician, called her by her first name, and the child patients of Dr. William Misbach, a pediatrician, called her "Nursie."

Her third occupation was typing scripts for Rod Serling of *Twilight Zone* fame, with whom she later claimed to have enjoyed a romantic involvement: "He was married, but we were drawn to each other, and began an affair that lasted for years. . . . Ulcers made him perpetually grim-faced. . . . Rod would sometimes sit all evening at a party and not say a word. Yet he loved the theater with a passion, and the crew on his show thought highly of him. So did I. He had a marvelous mind, and we got along well. I often typed his scripts for him, and if I changed one comma, he would notice, and tell me he didn't need an editor."[9]

Despite the hope of moving to the desert in a dream house provided by du Pont, she relished her current circumstances, a home at 5210 Nestle Avenue in the town of Tarzana, a suburban community with its own show business connection. Given her love of Hollywood, it must have been appealing to live in a place named for a character in a movie. Edgar Rice Burroughs, author of *Tarzan of the Apes*, had owned a tract of land on which much of the town was built. The Tarzan series, though fictional, was banned by the state of California in 1929 on the grounds that it set a bad example because its jungle hero and his female partner, Jane, lived together but were not married.

The house was only five minutes from her job. She wrote to du Pont on July 31, 1956, asking for a clarification of her schedule: "I am interested to learn from you, Will, if you want me to do anything more right now. Wilsons have booked me for clinics for the next two Sundays and want to know if they can continue to do so until the kids return to school in September. I told them I would have to ask you first. They pay me for the clinics and naturally the money comes in handy now that I am a proud house owner."[10]

Already, she was experiencing homeowner anxiety over a huge backyard with no shade, which ensured that the house was hot, especially at night. In the summer, with its inland location, Tarzana has a Mediterranean climate. Alice wondered: Would bamboo on the perimeter cool things down? She asked du Pont's advice, "I know if you were here you could think of something to do in five minutes." She decided to learn how to tend to the yard herself rather than pay the Japanese gardener who wanted "fifty dollars just to clean up the back yard."

A year later, after a visit in March, du Pont thanked her for showing him her new home and the "breakfast with all the trimmings which went with it."

That October, she wrote to him asking for an advance. She said she would be happy to visit his property at Point Happy:

> *When you are ready for me to go, you'll tell me. I expect this is true, Will. But, I need some money, if you will be so kind (even if I haven't earned it). The reason is that I ordered a new refrigerator-freezer, since my old one is old, too small and needs repairing. Since I don't get home until so late at night, I have no time to shop. I needed a freezer compartment, so I need only to shop once a week. It's a dandy Philco, and I would like to have the appliance man send it out, but I have to pay for it first.*

Less than a week later, he responded: "I enclose check and hope that it will take care of everything satisfactorily."

Finally, on January 9, 1958, it appeared her services in the desert were needed, and she drove down in order to file a progress report.

A few months later, she shared the news with du Pont that her brother Tim had paid her a visit: "It's mighty good to have some company. He is starting to play tennis and after only about six sessions he can hit the ball well enough for me to get some exercise. We have a very nice private court at our disposal, which saves driving to the L.A. Club."

Du Pont responded with tennis news of his own: at the age of forty, his wife, Margaret Osborne, was preparing to play on the 1958 Wightman Cup team and perhaps also compete at Wimbledon again. During her glittering tennis career, she had already won thirty-four major tournaments, including the Wimbledon women's singles in 1947, the year she was ranked number one in the world, and an astonishing twenty-seven women's doubles and mixed doubles titles. In the 1958 US Nationals, she would win the mixed doubles with Neale Fraser.

The following year, du Pont sent Alice a "check for $1,000 to cover your swimming pool and a few odds and ends you desire." In June 1959 he sent a check for $2,800 to pay off the mortgage on her property. By October she was asking him for more cash: "I have a big project for Christmas with some forty kids and would like to start getting some of their presents. We do have such a good time and, while I spend too much money, it is worth it to see how happy the kids are." She appeared to be constantly living somewhat beyond her means and not shy about turning to du Pont for a bailout.

WHILE WORKING AT THE DOCTOR'S OFFICE, Alice also supported herself by teaching tennis on the weekends. At one point she claimed to have fifteen regular students "with 450 on the waiting list," almost all girls and women, teaching them on a private court owned by Walt Disney's daughter.[11]

The Los Angeles tennis scene was small enough that she inevitably ran into Teach, who asked Alice to work with Maureen Connolly on her serve. Jack Kramer put Alice in touch with Darlene Hard, and Alice's simple suggestion, a change in her forehand grip from continental to eastern style, improved her game immensely. Hard later praised Alice for much of her success, which included twenty-one major titles of her own.

Nonetheless, two pupils from the Tarzana era stand out above the others.

Sally Ride, the future astronaut, was a young tennis prodigy, and Alice began coaching her at age ten, in 1961, at the Deauville Country Club near

Alice's home. Her natural talent aside, Ride ultimately frustrated Alice, who could not get her to decelerate and work on technique. Alice had to ask her to stop hitting the ball so hard, pleading age as an excuse: "I'm fifty years old!" Alice was not the only one who found it hard to control Sally. Her own mother, Joyce, stopped playing with her daughter when she realized, "I wasn't seeing the ball go by."

"Alice's penchant for hyperbole—or her frustration with the independent-minded preteen whose athleticism she admired—seemed to grow in retrospect," according to Sally Ride biographer Lynn Sherr. Years later, Marble told Sherr that Sally would deliberately try to hit her head: "I had to duck like crazy. It wasn't that she mis-hit the ball. She had perfect aim. I was terribly amused she was chosen to be an astronaut. . . . I think she probably had these aggressive feelings all her life."[12]

Alice's relationship with the other pupil, a chunky working-class kid with a big smile and bad eyes (20/400) named Billie Jean Moffit, also ended on a rocky note, though it lasted longer and had far greater impact in the world of tennis.[13]

Like Marble, Billie Jean[14] did not come from a "rich family," as she revealed in her memoir. "We didn't have money for racquets. Much less for proper tennis dress. The first time I was supposed to be in a group photograph was at the Los Angeles Tennis Club during the Southern California Junior Championships. They wouldn't let me post because I was only able to wear a blouse and a pair of shorts that my mother made for me. All the other players were photographed."[15]

Like Marble, Billie Jean excelled at baseball and softball as a child, switching to tennis at age eleven, because her family felt she should engage in a more ladylike sport—echoing Alice's experience with her brother Dan. Billie Jean learned on public courts, hers in Long Beach, as Alice had three decades earlier in San Francisco.

She was already a player to watch in her mid-teens when a Wilson Sporting Goods salesman suggested she take lessons with Alice. Billie Jean's father, a firefighter, was on board right away, having seen Alice play on the navy base in Norfolk, Virginia, during the war and remembering her as "a good jock." As a matter of etiquette, Billie Jean made sure her then coach Clyde Walker was in accord. Alice had been impressed when she saw Billie Jean play in the Pacific Southwest Championships in 1959.

Billie Jean recalled no anxious hovering. Her parents, who lived about forty miles away in Long Beach, would drop her off at noon on Saturdays, when Alice finished up work at the doctors' office, and then repeat the trip to pick her up late the next day. Billie Jean, age sixteen in the fall of 1959, would spend the night at Alice's house.

Billie Jean knew that her coach worked hard at her day job and "would be exhausted from the week, but luckily, she found the time for me." Alice's fatigue did not show itself on the court, despite smoking while instructing her pupil, coughing as she issued corrections and tips.

"Alice was a tough woman," Billie Jean remembered. "It became clear pretty quickly that she thought I was too soft. She could be encouraging but intense at the same time, and her demanding approach was just what I needed. I was in awe of her."[16]

The first time out, Alice subjected her new student to an arduous drill in which the two players stood across from each other in the front court while the champion pounded balls at the teen. Years later, Billie Jean King (who took her husband Larry's last name after their 1965 marriage) compared it to what Jimmy Connors's mother did to him, goading him to excel, "Get your tiger juices flowing, Jimmy."[17] At one point she made a show of walking Billie Jean from the baseline halfway up the court, pausing to say "this is the service line, right?" Billie Jean assented as her teacher waved her racket in the midcourt, before imparting valuable information: "Billie Jean, this is where most matches are won or lost. It's the players who miss these—the easy ones, the gimmes—that lose."[18]

Billie Jean recalled that she "walked around pretty fast. There was a sense of purpose when she walked. She didn't dilly-dally." Billie Jean also recalled that Marble told her, in a statement that still amazes her, "Your backhand volley is better than mine." The younger tennis player's reaction at the time was an interior swoon expressed in the teen lingo of her era: "Holy kamoley!"

In the evenings, Alice would bring out what Billie Jean remembers as her "precious scrapbooks," the carefully assembled news clips that stuck to the public highlights, headlines about tennis, old photographs of Marble in an evening dress, performing her music, and more. Mostly, Billie Jean listened. "Alice would talk about Don Budge, Bobby Riggs, Helen Hull Jacobs, Helen Wills Moody, and the other great players of her era. Just being around her and hearing her talk about what it was like to play championship tennis under pressure, about winning Wimbledon and Forest Hills, really rubbed off and gave me a sense of what it would be like for me when the time came—as I was getting to know it would."[19]

Sometimes Alice would play the guitar and sing in Spanish.

"Boy, did I eat it up. I was in seventh heaven," Billie Jean recalled.[20]

Alice told Billie Jean "and anyone else who would listen about how she had secretly worked in Army Intelligence" and that she had been "shot in the back while escaping a Nazi double agent during a mission in Switzerland."[21]

Billie Jean King said it was hard for her as a teen to make sense of Marble and her life. "I would ask her questions. I asked if she was ever married. I was just a teenager. I didn't know that might be something you didn't ask. I was struck by what a glamorous life she led in the thirties. She could sing, she could speak some Spanish, she was so hungry for an escape. She talked about Teach. The story she told over and over was about how 'I won Wimbledon and afterwards Teach wouldn't let me have a cookie.' That cookie came up a whole lot."

At night, while trying to sleep, Billie Jean could hear Marble in her bedroom coughing. "She had only one lung. She should not have been smoking." To make matters worse, she also had an oxygen tank nearby. "I am a firefighter's daughter. Even then, I thought this can't be a good idea." In addition to the constant cough, Billie Jean could hear the clink of ice, observed in a glass earlier in the evening.

Daytime told a different story. The highly focused coach, King wrote in an early memoir called *Billie Jean*, "kept explaining to me how to do things right. She helped me a lot technically. She took up where Clyde had left off on the fundamentals and worked hard on the advanced aspects of shot-making, and she spotted a lot of little flaws in my game."[22]

In a later memoir, King reflected: "Alice and I thought alike. The funny thing is she helped me most with my groundstrokes. We could relate to each other in our whole style, so that we could understand each other well in any detail in the mosaic. She kept rasping at me that I was too close when I hit a groundstroke, that almost all players stood too close, because they were insecure and afraid to move away. I was lucky. I knew baseball well, and so I could envision hitting a ball over the far corner of the plate."[23]

"Alice," continued Billie Jean, "taught me things that you can only learn from someone who's been best in the world."

Marble also demonstrated good manners. Billie Jean observed that whenever Marble had reason to express gratitude to someone, she did not hesitate to write a personal thank-you note, a habit that Billie Jean later imitated. On Sundays, before heading for home, King would play tennis with the man who lent them his court for the lessons, Mickey Goldsen, or his children. It was a way of saying thank you to a tennis host, something that Alice always emphasized.

However, their relationship ended abruptly, not long after it began.

One day, Alice asked, "What is your goal in tennis?"

Billie Jean didn't hesitate. "I want to be the best player ever."

It might have been the right answer for Billie Jean, but Alice appeared to take it as an insult. She was not eager to be dethroned.

Billie Jean "knew immediately she wasn't going to be able to handle that. Because what I was really saying was that I wanted to be a better player than Alice Marble, even."[24]

The lessons stopped not much later, after Alice called to cancel due to a bout of pneumonia, and Billie Jean offended her coach by failing to express any sympathy, a lapse she now credits to youthful obtuseness. Alice took it as a sign of her pupil's ingratitude and used it as the pretext to end the lessons. Billie Jean remembers a two-month partnership, lasting from November to December 1959; other sources say four months.

Two more significant numbers are not in doubt. Billie Jean came to Alice ranked number nineteen nationally by the USLTA, and she was number four by the subsequent summer. She was selected as a member of the Junior Wightman Cup team the following spring. In her extraordinary career, she would win thirty-nine Grand Slam titles, and become, arguably, the most admired female tennis player of her time.

EVEN IF ONE GRANTS that Billie Jean saw Marble through the eyes of a young, inexperienced adolescent, her impression of Marble's consumption of tobacco and presumably of spirits, the hair-trigger sensitivities, the brooding by night, and the constant coughing indicate that beneath the surface, all was not well.

Alice acknowledged her physical struggles in a letter to du Pont dated July 19, 1960, while also underplaying them: "Things are okay here except that I have a little more of the bronchial trouble, for which I had the operation ten years ago. We're just trying new medicines now to go with my oxygen tank and hope to avoid more surgery. I can do anything I want, but now must stay at home pretty much and avoid foggy weather. This puts a crimp in vacation plans, but I'll do anything to avoid being cut up again. I feel fine really and don't mind having a cough occasionally except that it is harming my one poor tired lung."

In August 1963, a month before her fiftieth birthday, Marble had a curious interview, in which she laid claim to a tragic loss, a loss she appears never to have mentioned again and for which there is no documentation. The exchange with the reporter began on a congenial note. Marble said she had been recently "asked by a 15-year-old boy who does some work for me 'How's it feel to be a half century old?'"

"No big deal," was her answer to the boy and to journalist Jack Hawn when he posed the same question.

"Alice's charming personality is refreshing perhaps even stimulating as she talks with the vigor and enthusiasm of a young carefree girl who still is living on Cloud Nine," Hawn wrote, but then he added: "The truth of the matter is Alice Marble has been plagued by tragedy."[25] Alice's brother Dan had died days earlier at the age of fifty-six, having suffered a heart attack on Monday, August 26, while on vacation at Camp Mather, about 150 miles east of San Francisco. In announcing the funeral service for that Friday, the *San Francisco Examiner* said Dan was considered "one of the cleverest handball strategists and shot-makers of all time. He made the national finals twice in his playing career, losing to Joe Platak in 1936 and to Jack Clements in 1942. He was three times Pacific Coast champion. Survivors include his wife, Eleanor[26]; sons, Dan Jr., and Bill; sisters, Alice and Hazel, and brothers, Tim (ex-Coast League ballplayer) and George. Interment will be at Cypress Lawn Memorial Park."[27]

In the midst of talking about this sad event, she referenced what must have been read as a bombshell, trumpeted in the article in bold typeface with the headline: "Death Claims Son." Alice told the reporter that a boy that she and her husband had adopted at age five died in a car accident earlier that year. "'He was in medical school at Harvard when he was killed,' she sadly reported." There appears to be no other mention of such a person in any other context in a life filled with encounters with interviewers. The admission appears tossed off; she then went on to another tragic story, the death of husband Joe in World War II.

After sharing these two strands of information, she abandoned them both and appeared to brighten. "'I'm still looking (for a new mate),' she cracked, quickly changing the mood of the conversation, realizing apparently such talk naturally is uncomfortable for those who want to express their sorrow but don't quite know how.

She soon reverted to the topic that prompted the story: Alice's appointment as the Lake Encino Racquet Club director. The article ended on a cheerful note: "Alice spoke with a burning enthusiasm eager to begin work."[28]

The country club aspect of the enterprise and the promise of an opportunity to coach turned out to be a fake. Her real job was to entice famous people to buy into the development. Marble claimed to have success with "Efrem Zimbalist, Charlton Heston, Robert Stack, even Mary Pickford," but even if so, she lost her bait-and-switch job to Gussie Moran, because in Marble's opinion, the owners could get her cheaper, a humiliation that rankled.[29]

LETTERS TO AND FROM Will du Pont came and went with some frequency. Most were mundane, businesslike, monetary in flavor. Some concerned the feasibility of whether Alice could bring a houseguest to Point Happy. She shared the news that two front teeth had been pulled. He hoped that she got to play some golf. They tell a story, if nothing else, of du Pont's unflagging ardor.

On October 2, 1963, precise and banker-like as always, he asked Alice for her birth year: "I told you that I was going to set up a trust so that you would receive money in the event I die. I know September 28 is your birthday, but I have forgotten the year? I will brief you in with the details when we are all set."

A few weeks later, he shared the details:

October 18, 1963

Dear Alice.

Well, this is the day we finally got around to setting up a trust for you—$6,000.00 per year or $500.00 per month.

(1)   You will receive your first check for $500.00 on November 1, 1964.

(2)   I am letting the fund accumulate for one year in order to have a cushion so that if the bonds didn't come due monthly they have the money to advance you on a monthly basis. The investment is set up in municipal bonds and $500.00 will be free from Federal Income Tax but might be subject to State Income Tax.

(3) *While our aim is $6,000.00 or $500.00 per month, at Christmas time they might send you a little bit additional as whatever the principal paid, they would forward it to you outside of the amount they keep the first year for the cushion.*

(4) *They might not be able to replace the municipal bonds when they come due at exactly the same rate; hence, the cushion in the first year, or it may be unlawful to have it in tax free bonds of any kind. With that in view, they would invest in higher yielding securities so as to give you more money per month which you would receive for income tax that you might have to pay on it. The present rates would take about $1,000.00 to pay the tax on $6,000.00.*

(5) *The principal at the time of your death goes to another trust that is for my grandchildren.*

In a letter ironically dated February 14, 1964, Valentine's Day, du Pont wrote to Marble about his pending divorce from his second wife. "Margaret will be in Reno as she wants a divorce. She hasn't found the reason yet except that I am doing the same things as usual—foxhunting, shooting, and racing. Since she quit playing major tennis, she has taken up squash, table tennis and runs with a different group so our paths seem to have separated."

In 1947, du Pont had confided his marriage plans to Marble, who was glad that the fifty-one-year-old banker would have a tennis player as a wife. Twenty-two years younger than du Pont, Margaret was at the height of her powers as a player when they wed. Over the years, Marble saw them together on many occasions, but she worried about whether Margaret was happy, as she noted in *Courting Danger*: "Will was the master of the household. That meant that he and his wife never stayed to celebrate after tournaments, catching the train home to Wilmington instead, so Will would be there for business the next day." He refused to let Margaret play in the Australian Open, preferring she be by his side in California during the winter when the dry air was therapeutic.[30] Marble thought the relationship suited Osborne, who "had lived as so many of us on the circuit did, never having a penny to our names. The lifestyle provided by Will was worth some sacrifice."[31]

In the same letter, he confided that he had health problems of his own, including varicose veins, "so I haven't been doing too much since last June." He was also experiencing a shortness of breath that he worried could be heart trouble.

Alice was not in the best shape either. In June, she wrote back to him, complaining of "violent headaches." She got checked by an eye doctor, who diagnosed "very bad eye strain from teaching and facing the sun for so many hours during the day." She decided to quit giving lessons, at least for the time being, "A person gets to a certain age where this much physical activity is impossible. I'm not a natural loafer—so I don't know how long I can stand not doing something."

In October, du Pont shared the good news that the trust had been activated, and although he sent the first check himself, future installments would arrive directly from the bank.

ALICE DID NOT LIKE to emphasize her health issues in public, but she was obligated to reveal her struggles when she confirmed plans to attend her induction into the International Tennis Hall of Fame in Newport, Rhode Island, in August 1964. (She would be following in the footsteps of her friend Brownie, who had been inducted in 1957.) In a letter to the committee dated July 22, 1964, she specified that she would need a large (seventy-cubic-foot) oxygen tank with a regulator, indicating it was a standard item, easily rented from any hospital supplies shop, and that she would bring her own aerosol medication. "I know this all sounds dramatic but . . . I play tennis and golf regularly. The oxygen is only to keep my old lung clear."

Before she left, Marble's friends in the Deauville Women's Golf Auxiliary threw a farewell party for her. Giving herself plenty of lead time, Marble departed for the East Coast ten days before the ceremony. Her plans included a stop in New York to visit friends and go to the theater and the world's fair, which had opened that spring.[32]

What awaited Marble in Newport, Rhode Island, was a mix of salt air, summer mansions, and a well-established tennis colony. The first US National Championships were held there in 1881, attended by a "large number of fashionable spectators."[33] While the championships had moved long ago to Forest Hills, the Newport Casino Invitational tournament was held the week of the induction, a men's only grass-court event, won that year by American Chuck McKinley.

The other honorees in the hall of fame's class of 1964 included George T. Addee, former president of the USLTA, and four players. Sidney Wood, in 1927, at the age of fifteen, had set the record for youngest Wimbledon competitor up to that time, a tournament he then won in 1931, when fellow American Frank Shields defaulted. In his later years, Wood invented Supreme Court, a playing surface used for indoor courts. Fellow inductee Frank Shields, also an actor, was ranked in the top ten players eight times, reaching number two in 1930 and number one in 1933. George Lott was considered the best doubles player up to that time, having won the US National Championships five times with three different partners. Finally, most celebrated of all and fittingly paired with Alice, was Don Budge, Marble's pal from the 1941 pro tour.

Before the ceremony on August 15, the hall of famers played a one-set exhibition match, with Marble and Budge teamed against George Lott and Sidney Wood. Frank Shields was the referee.[34] The match was "very satisfying," according to the *Newport Daily News*; the article added that Marble was "operating on only one-and-a-quarter lungs."[35]

The ceremony was held at the center court at the Newport Casino. James Van Alen, president of the hall of fame, inducted the honorees, aided, ironically for Alice, by none other than Julian Myrick.

Alice left Newport after the ceremony to pay a visit to du Pont. He arranged for a chauffeur to pick her up and bring her to his estate in Wilmington, Delaware. By now the two old friends were both frail.

A few weeks later, she sent a note thanking the organizers for all the "complimentary remarks." In response to a request for objects to display in her honor at the Hall of Fame, she said, "I have but one National Singles trophy left and I'm sending it off to you. Sorry I have no old racquets or other mementoes. All but just a few trophies (of the 750 I won) have been spread around the world to friends and family." She explained that she had often given her winning trophies to her hosts at the great mansions as an acknowledgement of their hospitality. She made the oft-repeated point that her per diem from the United States Lawn Tennis Association meant she could not afford to buy anything commensurate with their hospitality as a way of thanking them for sharing their homes.

During the next year, the house at Point Happy came to completion. Brownie would be moving in with Marble, after her recent divorce. There was never any outward indication that the two women were any more than dear old friends who now shared in the good fortune of du Pont's largesse. In his old age, du Pont desired the consolation of having people he cared about and who cared for him nearby, and he could afford to make it happen. Over the years du Pont had frequently commissioned Brownie to create portraits of his beloved animals, and now he would supply her with a studio with a northern exposure so she could continue to paint. Alice's bedroom looked out on a pool just outside her window and a tennis court on the other side. The thick stucco walls guaranteed the interior of the house would be cool. Alice had only one complaint, a common lament in the valley: "The only thing that was bad, it was right under the mountains, so the sun went down at three o'clock."[36]

On October 26, 1965, du Pont sent what appears to have been his last letter to Alice, according to his own files. He wrote that he hoped to be able to spend a lot of time with her when he came out to the desert in the winter, adding, "I have been very busy as usual, so I have not had very much time to write." He did not specify the ways in which he was "very busy," and it may have been a bit of a euphemism, meant to downplay grievous health struggles of his own.[37]

In November Alice wrote again to express her gratitude and enthusiasm, "I know you are going to be very proud of the house, Will. It is truly a show place. I have been looking at Spanish houses since May and I have never seen one as beautiful. I am the luckiest person alive." She located some Spanish tiles, which she called "beautiful," to put around the living room fireplace. Her cheerful, forward-looking patter indicates she had no idea how sick her long-time friend and loyal patron was.

Alice and Brownie moved in with all their belongings on December 29, 1965.

That same day, Will du Pont's daughter sent Alice a letter requiring her signature upon receipt:

Dear Miss Marble:

Due to the critical condition of Wm. du Pont, Jr., who is in the hospital, we think that no changes should be made with respect to any of his property.

Consequently, this is to advise you that we cannot permit you or Mary K. Browne to occupy house #7 on the Point Happy property until further word from the undersigned who are acting as attorneys in fact for Wm. du Pont, Jr.

Very truly yours,
Jean Ellen McConnell
William S. Potter

Two days later, on December 31, 1965, at the age of sixty-nine, du Pont died at the Wilmington Medical Center from complications after surgery. It was the same holiday, New Year's Eve, on which Alice's mother had died, and the day before the holiday when her father had breathed his last.

Jean Ellen du Pont McConnell blamed Alice for the breakup of her parents' marriage, fairly or unfairly, and now she had the perfect opportunity to exact her revenge.

When asked: "Why don't you sue the family?" Marble said, "I can't sue the family of the man who set up a very generous trust fund for me."[38]

It's also possible she was realistic enough to know that the du Pont family had the means and the will to fight her. As one old friend of du Pont put it, "One of his boys shouted at the reading of the will, 'I'm rich. I'm rich.' That's the kind of kids they were. Not very nice."[39]

1966–1990

CHAPTER 26

ONCE A CHAMPION

MARBLE MAY HAVE BEEN the queen of the court, but she was also queen of the pivot. In later years, she spoke of the eviction in almost lighthearted terms: "We had a marvelous kitchen. I remember it cost me $75 to line the cabinets. And that's the thing I got most annoyed [about] . . . that I have to leave my seventy-five dollars' worth of stickum paper."[1]

Alice and Brownie had enjoyed approximately forty-eight hours in their dream house. They found lodging at the Palm Desert Country Club and on May 23, Marble was back in San Francisco, being honored as the queen of the international tennis world in the "decade before World War II," as she presided over the dedication of public courts named in her honor at Lombard and Hyde Streets.[2] In remarks to a reporter, she praised her housemate for getting her to pick up a golf club. The *Palm Desert Post* reported on July 21 that Marble and Browne had a housewarming party—"with 14 of the gals and boys playing 9 holes of golf in an invitational tournament in the afternoon and 20 of their closest friends gathering for cocktails and a potluck supper later. The new home seemed to echo a welcome to its new inhabitants sensing there will be many, many fun activities there in the future."

The two old friends, Marble and Brownie, lived together for two years at the Palm Desert Country Club.

Alice liked to make it sound as if she were set for life with what she airily called a "very generous trust fund," but it was not large enough to sustain her without other sources of income. Alice supplemented the annuity by teaching tennis at the club, though sometimes she instructed young people free of charge. "I talked to the [club's] tennis pro about it," she said. "I couldn't tell whether he was for it. I'm not trying to get in the way. But $25 a half hour is steep. A lot of kids can't afford it."[3]

She even tended bar, a skill she had acquired during the first of her desert years. She remembered people from the past, men she called her suitors, by their preferred libation, as she told a reporter: "Fernando, an artist, drank hot port in the winter and cold port in the summer; Charlie, a Yale grad, drank Tom Collinses; Jerry drank Manhattans."[4] Years later, when she let her bartender's license expire, she worked without pay. All she required in return was that her customers donate either to the International Tennis Hall of Fame or treat her to dinner at the restaurant of her choice.[5]

When Brownie decamped for Laguna Beach, where she planned to spend her time painting and playing golf, Alice was on her own once again. In 1969, she accepted an appointment as social director of the Palm Desert Country Club; she immediately announced festive plans for a "box lunch dinner and song fest by the pools, a 'Night in Las Vegas,' and an unusual costume party."[6] As part of her job, she would be the face of the club, pictured in the paper bestowing the Desert Cup to winners at interclub tournaments. She became a homeowner again, buying a modest house at the Palm Desert Resort and Country Club. The property held less charm than the one du Pont had hoped to provide, but the price was right: $21,000[7] when she purchased it in 1971—the same year in which Brownie died, at the age of eighty. Marble praised her friend in The Net Set, her column in the *Palm Desert Post* on December 16.

"Our lives crossed many times," she wrote. In addition to thanking Brownie for standing up to the tennis establishment when it tried to keep Alice out of the competition, Alice reminded readers of her old friend's impressive career: "Mary Kendall Browne was a legend in tennis, having won her first National Championship in 1912. She was the first of the women to volley; she was, with Suzanne Lenglen, the first to go on a pro tour in 1926. In 1924 Brownie was a [semi-]finalist to Helen Wills at Forest Hills. Two weeks later she defeated Glenna Collett Vare to move into the finals of the National Amateur Golf Championship in Providence, Rhode Island."

Alice also gave a personal portrait of Brownie, calling her "the most patriotic person I have known." Marble continued:

> She taught tennis at Lake Erie College in Ohio for many years, wrote seven
> books on tennis and metaphysics. . . . In 1957 she was elected to the Tennis
> Hall of Fame where she met an old high school chum and at the age of 67,
> married for the first time. It was an odd sight to see Brownie 5 feet one
> inches with Kenneth at 6'3". Browne had lived a country club life for years

with cocktails and bridge after golf. Kenneth was the son of a minister and an elder in the church. He was forever trying to reform her from swearing and drinking. One day I was visiting them and heard Kenneth trying to convince Brownie to go to a religious retreat with him. . . . . After the divorce, Brownie and I moved to the Palm Desert Country Club and shared a house for two years. She celebrated her 75th birthday here and played to a 9 handicap. She left to resume her painting in Laguna Beach and had done 26 watercolor portraits. A week before her eightieth birthday, she suffered a massive stroke and died on August 19 of this year. The night before she was stricken, she called to say, "I'll be down tomorrow for some golf and bridge with you." . . . The world has lost a wonderful human being and I have lost a dear, dear friend.

It helped that Marble enjoyed the limelight as a desert favorite, and thanks to the area's strong celebratory impulse, she received many honors. "Alice Marble Night," held in 1974 at the Balboa Bay Club/Indian Wells, with its elaborate name, featured a dinner, a dance, the "presentation of Alice to the audience," and a showing of an old short black-and-white film of Alice called *Tennis in Rhythm*.[8] She was given a "sheaf of red roses."[9] As much as tennis remained Alice's main claim to fame, movies held her heart even more. One evening she watched a televised tribute to the old film stars. She was so compelled that when somebody interrupted with a phone call, she said, "The hell with you. I'm not going to be interested in another tennis tournament until I get over this program."[10]

The losses—of old friends and family, mentors and tormentors—kept piling up. Two and a half hours southwest, Marble's old coach and nemesis, Teach Tennant, having faded into obscurity, faced her final days. Crippled by arthritis and nearly blind, she succumbed on May 11, 1974, in her home in La Jolla, at age seventy-nine.

After the split with Alice, Teach had spent the rest of her life trying, in vain, to find another young female player she could mold as she did Marble. The closest she came was with Maureen Connolly, a child prodigy from San Diego. In her usual no-nonsense way, Teach set about retraining Connolly, a natural lefty, to play right-handed mostly by playing catch with her endlessly, throwing ball after ball to be caught with her right hand.

When Connolly became the national champ at age sixteen in 1951, Marble congratulated her in her column, "As I See It: Meet the Champ,"

published in the inaugural issue of *The Racquet* in November 1951, replacing
American Lawn Tennis to embrace more sports.

Marble took the opportunity to add some reflections about Teach:

> *She has mellowed since I studied with her, though; she even asked my opinion
> on some matter of technique this year. In the old days I had no opinions.
> I did what I was told every hour of the day. I ate and jumped rope, played
> tennis and went to bed according to schedule, and Teach was always there
> to see that I did so. Now she dictated only the court strategy of her champion.
> Young Maureen actually went to the theatre one night during the U.S.
> National Championship and she stayed at the Forest Hills Inn, while Teach
> was lodged with friends out on Long Island.*

Soon, though, Teach's overbearing personality caused a split with Connolly. Unlike Alice's mother, who ceded control of her daughter's tennis destiny to Teach, Connolly's mother saw her "daughter as a child being dragged
out of her natural age group and pushed relentlessly toward stardom."[11] "Little
Mo," as she became known, asserted her independence at Wimbledon in
1952. Teach had urged her not to compete, as her shoulder was hurting, and
Connolly insisted on playing. After winning her first match while Teach
was out of town, she called a press conference to announce that she had
broken off her relationship with her coach: "She does not represent my views.
Anything she says is without my authority."[12] At the Wimbledon Ball that
followed Connelly's ultimate victory in the singles championship, her first
of three consecutive Wimbledon triumphs before her career was abruptly
ended by an accident at nineteen, Connolly and Teach avoided each other.
In contrast to the gala in 1939, when Marble in her red chiffon dress made a
point of addressing Teach and thanking her for all she had done, Teach sat
by herself, unacknowledged.

The press hailed Teach in death by naming the people whose paths
she had crossed in life, from the usual Hollywood suspects (Groucho Marx,
Bing Crosby, Charlie Chaplin, Joan Crawford, Marlene Dietrich, and Carole
Lombard) to Alice Marble, whose game she improved by taking it away from
the baseline; Maureen Connolly, whose game she improved by stressing
the similarity between pitching in baseball and serving; and Bobby Riggs,
who resisted her advice but prospered anyway. Given his lifelong ability to

hog the limelight, he got more than his share of attention in the Associated Press obituary.

IN 1977, Alice returned to England for the one hundredth anniversary of Wimbledon, which happened to coincide with Queen Elizabeth's silver jubilee, celebrating her twenty-five years on Britain's throne. Alice realized she could not afford to pay her own way, owing to some unanticipated expenses, so she accepted donations. "Everything had gone to pot. The swimming pool, the air conditioner, the garbage disposal," she said to a reporter. She tapped a variety of sources to get the money. Hazel gave her plane fare, a party at Indian Wells Racquet Club added to the fund, and she accepted two dollars handed to her in a supermarket by a child she did not know. Marble did not mind accepting charity. She saw it as a favor to those who wanted to show their generosity.

"I sent a lot of young tennis players to Canada (for training) in my day, and I always felt part of their trip," she explained. "I knew people who contributed to me would feel the same way."[13]

The most refreshing change at Wimbledon was that for the first time, ball girls were permitted to assist with the play.

Alice later told her audiences back in the desert, "The best part was when the Duchess noticed my needlepoint bag" and, next best, when an autograph-seeking child asked, "Are you anyone important?"[14]

The press back home in the desert faithfully noted her achievements and sightings in bouncy dribs and drabs. She was pictured serving on the welcoming committee that gave reigning champion Martina Navratilova the keys to the cities of Palm Springs and Rancho Mirage, and she was featured on the USA Network's *Greatest Sports Legends* hosted by Tom Seaver, the great New York Mets pitcher. Alice addressed groups such as the Palm Springs–Palm Desert division of the California Retired Teachers Association; their chosen topic was "Reminiscing with Alice Marble."[15]

One press notice stood out: Alice Marble's trip home to San Francisco in September 1979 for her first family reunion in eleven years. Brother Dan's widow would be there and "her son Danny and wife Katie, also son Bill and children, plus Alice's sister Hazel and husband Sam. . . . Ages of the merry-makers ranged from her brother George at 71 . . . to ten-month-old baby Clark."[16] The gathering was hosted by George and his wife, Bernice.

A Marble descendant, her grandniece Linda Marble McCrory, remembered the occasion well. In addition to the usual whirlwind of tourist-type activities, "visits to the beach, a trip to attend the King Tut exhibit, a production of *Evita* at the Orpheum, to Candlestick Park to take in a ballgame,"[17] her great aunt had gathered with the family, by whom she was treated like visiting royalty.

> She was the prize child. Everything went into her. The family made sure she had her favorite cocktail and got to sit in the seat she preferred. She would be smoking, and she would tell the naughty stories, especially about Clark Gable. Her brother Dan became a very hard drinker. . . . They all drank, except for my grandfather, George. I don't know why he didn't pick up the drink. Uncle Tim was the worst. I only remember him as a very dirty, sloppy bum. He would pass out in bushes. It was a really sad story. My grandfather took care of him. Grandmother did not want him in the house. Their hardship made them all so driven.[18]

McCrory was a child when she interacted with her famous relation, and the memories are not as expansive as she might wish, but the impression was of a strong colorful woman whom the others seemed to regard as a family hero.

Indeed, Marble remained driven as she sought a new career even in 1981, when she accepted a position at the Palm Desert Resort and Country Club as adviser to the tennis facility. "The atmosphere here is great, and the facilities are excellent," she told a reporter. "We have 16 night-lighted courts and see a lot of night play as well as daytime use."[19] In the desert, the retired teachers were not the only ones asking Alice to reminisce. Feature reporters, and in one case, an earnest young oral historian armed with a tape recorder and scripted questions, showed up at Marble's house with some frequency. Some of the taped interviews share the same background noise: ice rattling in glasses, matches being struck, and a cough that kept earning apologies. The findings of the interrogators reveal a woman who was still trying to rule a room. The reporters took note of the small pool big enough for a quick dip, a Ping-Pong table on the patio, and an autograph wall where she urged company to sign their names. One reporter observed a "gallery of photographs" of Marble with Ronald Coleman, Jack Dempsey, Babe Ruth, and John Wayne—"as well as a comfortably dog-eared décor." Cat-eared might be more like it: Marble professed endless patience for Friskie the cat and his apparent crusade to shred as much furniture as possible. "'When I can't stand it,' Marble says, 'I go to another garage sale.'"[20]

Looming over it all was the imposing portrait of her painted in 1938, with its showy beauty. Whenever Marble was asked about it, which was frequently— Will du Pont's color-drenched gift saturated the room—she would issue a terse, "Oh, that," followed by a shrug. "It looks like me on the best day I never had."[21] The self-deprecating comment was a crowd-pleaser even if the crowd consisted of just one interviewer. When she was asked how such an ambitious rendering came to exist in the first place, she would usually answer, "Now that's a story in itself."

A story in itself: if it wasn't Marble's favorite phrase, certainly it was one of her most employed ones.

The tale that followed was what her admirers liked to call "pure Alice" in that it involved a posh location, a well-heeled benefactor, improbable good luck, and a touch of intrigue. Since she could not afford the painting at the time of its composition in 1938, it soon faded into just another fond memory—until, "fourteen years later, I was in the middle of a Spanish lesson in my New York apartment when the doorman knocked and said he had 'a treat' for me. An enormously wealthy ex-suitor of mine had seen the painting in an exhibition. He purchased it and had it delivered to me as a gift."[22]

Omitting du Pont's name, even in death, suggests that was she was protecting him from the two scourges that dog the extremely wealthy: gold diggers and gossip.

She told another reporter that when she was young, she possessed "good features and such beautiful teeth," but that surgery at the age of thirty-six to remove part of her right lung had aged her quickly.

"'I got old looking, terribly fast,' she said, lapsing into baby-talk as she addressed the cat. 'But they're not wrinkles, are they, Frisk? They're character lines.'"

As for regrets: "If I had it to do over again, I'd have half-a-dozen kids and animals."[23]

Tennis had changed, in her opinion, and not entirely for the better. She decried the tendency of some players to throw tantrums, believing a fine would not be enough deter them, only a complete ban. Without naming names, she said that in her era, "We had a very promising young college boy who got into the same kind of mood as the guys today. He berated the umpire; the police took him off and he never played again. I think that's an excellent idea. Some people want to come out and see the players act badly but I just duck under my chair. I'm no angel and I've thrown a few rackets in my lifetime but only until I saw how ugly it was. I had a temper, but it turned into determination."[24]

She had seen the game go through radical changes during her lifetime: "Well, it's no longer a country club sport . . . it's a money game now. When Open Tennis began [in 1968], we had 12 million tennis players, as of right now we have 34 million. I belong to a club with eight courts. I had a date to play at three o'clock, and we can't get a court."[25]

Health challenges kept adding up. In 1981, diagnosed with colon cancer, Marble had three surgeries at the Eisenhower Medical Center in Palm Springs, resulting in a colostomy bag, followed by two more procedures that eradicated the need for it. She told one reporter that not only had she "battled back from TB" and had "pneumonia 18 times, pleurisy 11 times," she also said she had "five major surgeries" and had been in "12 car crashes."[26]

While suffering from the pain, she received news that her old friend Tica Madrigal was dying of throat cancer. Just before her death, the Spanish teacher and the one woman with whom Marble acknowledged a sexual relationship mailed Marble signed copies of her instructional books and a cigarette case Marble had made for her, using one of her championship medals as an inset.

Alice had lived long enough to see some of her old tennis records being broken. In 1978, Chris Evert became the second woman in tennis history, after Marble, to hold the number-one ranking by the United States Tennis Association for five years in a row. In 1982, Evert won her sixth US Open.

In one of her long-ago articles for *American Lawn Tennis*, Alice cited a headline in the *New York Times* about an upcoming contest between two aging prizefighters: "And in the third corner, Father Time."

The final decade of Marble's life might well be called one long middle Sunday, such as they had at Wimbledon, when play was suspended for twenty-four hours to give the grounds a break. Life was not as uneventful as waiting for the grass to recover but not bursting with fireworks either.

CHAPTER 27

QUEEN ALICE

E VEN WITH MARBLE'S physical challenges and the deaths of so many people who had been dear to her, some moments stood out for their welcome cargo of happiness. The desert continued to greet her with its version of open arms: a lifetime membership in the Palm Springs Racquet Club,[1] cocktail parties in her honor, and the kind of local fame that keeps the notion of a more far-reaching one afloat. She always said she loved where she lived: "It's just super. Wonderful people. Wonderful climate."[2] Her upbeat attitude was embodied in one of her favorite quotes, borrowed from her friend and desert neighbor Bob Hope: "Life may be a headache, but it is never a bore." Hope's wife, Dolores, and actress Carol Burnett added the luster of their names to the Girls Club of Coachella Valley, where they served as honorary members along with Marble.[3]

When Alice visited San Francisco in February 1984 to attend a ceremony at the Bay Area Sports Hall of Fame to welcome new members (Helen Jacobs as well as golfer Ken Venturi, swimmer Mark Spitz, basketball coach Pete Newell, and football coaching legend Pop Warner), she greeted a newspaper columnist with a kiss on the cheek and the gleeful information: "Guess what! I'm into Ping-Pong."[4] She had told reporters in the past that she refused to call the game "table tennis" because it would be an insult to real tennis to associate it with such a lesser endeavor, but she did credit it with improving her mobility and eyesight.[5]

The columnist at the hall of fame celebration gave Marble what amounts to a reporter's version of a clean bill of health, "She moves about A-OK. Her spirits are high. She's as conversational as the proverbial jaybird." Accepting the award on behalf of Helen Jacobs, who lived in Connecticut and could not travel due to a bad back, the ever-affable Don Budge told a reporter what it was like to play doubles with Marble as a partner when an opponent hit a lob: "Alice would shove me aside and shout 'I'll take it.'"[6]

Marble received her own star turn at her induction a year later.[7]

In the valley, as a guest speaker at lunches, desirous of being trim, Alice could not help but decry the rich food served at these events in the middle of the day, contrasting them to her standard lunch when she was in training: "lean roast beef, sliced tomatoes with French dressing, and fruit." Her audience nodded its polite low-calorie approval, but a matron at one of those clubs advised Marble to go light on the inspirational spiels about health and nutrition saying the audience was too old to worry about all the health stuff and urged Marble to stick to stories about the kings and queens.

Alice could summon plenty of moldering gossip about royalty along with captains of industry and show people, all trusty standbys in her grab bag of topics: King Gustav, Queen Mary, William Randolph Hearst, Marion Davies, Carole and Clarke. She did not even have to dig all that deep to come up with a tale about a curly-haired dimpled darling: "One time I was hitting with a pro and a little girl came up on her bicycle, and said, 'Bet you can't play tennis on a bicycle.' The pro got the PR lady to come with the photographer and take a picture of me playing tennis on a bicycle. The little girl was Shirley Temple."

Alice noticed that this story pleased elderly conventioneers, a demographic "old enough so they know who I am which is nice." And if they did not recognize her, if they looked befuddled, she professed not to care: "I've had all the fame I need. I'm even a dummy in a wax museum in San Francisco."[8]

She liked to mention her photographic memory, bragging that she shopped for groceries without a list, proof that she was still with it, a miracle of cognitive prowess, even if it was nestled inside a crumbling body—its own source of dilapidated pride.

At 130 pounds, Alice struck Beverly Beyette from the *Los Angeles Times* as tanned and trim, good-humoredly giving her height as "5 feet 7 and shrinking." Marble sold herself to Beyette as a bundle of energy, saying she played Ping-Pong on a regular basis from three to four in the afternoon and liked to dip in and out of her pool where she would "jog like crazy, twist and kick run against the water once an hour." She could still hit a tennis ball well but, she said, "I have no mobility" on the court.[9]

She went to church every other week, and she often bartended at parties thrown by friends. She enjoyed the occasional cigarette and a gin and tonic from time to time, she volunteered, but that was it.

She also said, "I don't live in the past. I reminisce when people ask me"—perhaps not as true as she may have wished. She seemed to spend much of her time recalling the old days, in particular growing more and more expansive about a moment that she had kept under wraps when it was unfolding—the story of the love of her life. As she aged, Joe graduated from just a beau, as he was in *The Road to Wimbledon*, to a husband. They married, she would say, in 1942, and he died in Germany, in the line of duty, not long after she had miscarried their child in an automobile accident. In the expanded version, she became pregnant during the time she was in Panama, and he was able to pay a secret visit. Sometimes he died in December 1944; sometimes the following spring. "I had a long war. I lost my husband the last two weeks of the war."

There would be other suitors, including du Pont and "a bearded painter who didn't like people,"[10] but none who caught on to the same degree. She kept a photo of herself with a man, dancing. Toward the end it too became cracked and rickety. She liked to say it was of her and Joe.

Even though she claimed not to live in the past, the pressure from outsiders created the opposite effect.

Marble was lured back to Wimbledon again in 1984, joining sixteen other former female singles champions to mark the one hundredth anniversary of the first Wimbledon game in which women competed. (Maud Watson beat her sister Lilian for the singles title in 1884.) The Duke and Duchess of Kent presented each woman with a commemorative piece of Waterford crystal, going from youngest to oldest. Eighty-eight-year-old Kitty Godfree, the winner in 1924 and 1926, was the last to be honored. An official photo of the champions shows Marble seated in the front row, patriotically attired in a navy suit, white blouse, and red sandals, hands folded in her lap, her neutral gaze turned dutifully in the direction of the camera.

Reporters kept requesting interviews, asking her to play the same old song, over and over, the same high notes, the same low notes, the same refrain. One such encounter stood out as different from the others, as an extreme unveiling.

Stan Hart, an author and bookstore owner and a former editor at the publishing house Little, Brown, had an idea for a book about tennis that would use a popular approach known as "participatory journalism." Practiced most colorfully by the founder of the *Paris Review*, George Plimpton, writers would take on the role of their subjects to get a deeper sense of their lives. Plimpton, for instance, boxed with three greats, served as backup quarterback for the Detroit Lions, played hockey goalie for the Boston Bruins, did stand-up comedy at Caesar's Palace in Las Vegas, pitched part of a post-season exhibition game at Yankee Stadium, and performed with the New York Philharmonic—by no means an exhaustive list. Hart's idea was to play tennis with and interview as many former tennis greats as he could find. Among his partners on what he called the "Eastern Swing" would be Pauline Betz Addie, Althea Gibson, Sarah Palfrey, Gardnar Mulloy, and Don Budge. In the "Wild West" Hart would square off against Gussie Moran, Ellsworth Vines, Jack Kramer, Louise Brough, Margaret Osborne du Pont, and Bobby Riggs, among others. Early on, Hart informed his readers that Marble was the Holy Grail, the brass ring he was grabbing for to make the journey a success.

Hart said he underestimated his naïveté when he undertook the project. The chapter title, "Alice Marble: Queen Bee," is a tipoff to his subsequent misgivings. He made an appointment to see the seventy-year-old Marble at her home in Palm Desert, calling her "Queen Alice" in addition to "Queen Bee."

Before the interview, flooded with admiration, Hart spent the breakfast hour by himself reviewing Marble's impressive records. He considered her ability to throw a ball as far as the best outfielders to be "superhuman, when you consider she was a girl, and not a large-boned masculine girl but wiry and of average height."[11]

When Hart called to confirm the appointment, the voice that greeted him could not have been more agreeable. Upon arrival, he was taken aback by the modesty of her lodgings: "Alice Marble made quite a bit of money [he was clearly misinformed], although when you look at her small home, its walls made of poured concrete, and the miniscule front yard on a road laid down in a housing grid, you might not believe it."[12] Surely, he thought, the annuity set up by du Pont would have provided for something more sumptuous. He was taken aback by her looks as well. "She is still wiry, and hard as a knot in a redwood tree. Her hair is cut so short she looks like a woman who is supposed to wear a wig, but that is not the case. It is broiling hot in Palm Desert, and her short hair makes sense."[13]

Hart's tape recorder didn't work that day, so Marble urged him to take notes in longhand. She said she hadn't written much of anything about her life in recent years beyond the text for a five-by-seven-inch Wheaties pamphlet, printed on flimsy stock, titled "Want to be a Tennis Champion?"—though that was years ago, in 1945.

Readers who mailed ten cents and a star printed on the top of a Wheaties package to a place called the Wheaties Library of Sports in Minneapolis could have the thirty-page pamphlet shipped free to their home address.

Hart's initial impression of Alice was favorable. He found her to be "energetic" and "gracious," talking "rat-a-tat at me, recalling things from her past, not bothering to watch her language, as open as a brilliant Palm Desert star-filled night." He had not known until she mentioned it that she had been married or that her husband had died, as she told him, in the last two weeks of the war.

Hart and Marble left her house in the late morning to visit her club and to rally before playing. On the way, she mentioned her bout with colon cancer and how the colostomy bag had interfered with her game at one point: "I was forever keeping my backhand close to my hip to protect that damn sack from being struck by a ball."

On the court, Hart observed how Marble "pounced along the baseline like a jackrabbit, and once she rushed the net as she had done in the old days." She suggested they play singles, with Hart doing the serving: "Since her shoulder was lame, I agreed at once. But this posed a problem for me. I knew that I could not sting her with fast shots," but he also didn't "want to play pat-a-cake either."

She proved to be a generous opponent: "She had played with me only for the purposes of my book . . . so I could say that I had once played the great Alice Marble, because she knew I was a fan and was living a fantasy." They played four games and stopped when it was "clear she could not run well." In the clubhouse, Marble made many merry introductions of Hart to other club members, and they paused to admire a glass case containing photos of her. At lunch she ordered a drink—and then drinks. The plan for the afternoon was that she would go home, and Hart would play some pickup games and call when he was done. Marble would return to pick him up, and they would continue the interview into the evening.

When he contacted her again at five thirty or so, she was a different person. She said she could not come get him and that he had better get a ride as soon as he could to collect his "junk"—a word that rankled him.

Nonetheless, he entered her house "all smiles," only to find his hostess in an uproar: "I want you to know I wouldn't wait two hours for Gary Cooper, much less for the likes of you. It just so happens that I had nothing planned this afternoon, so I just sat here. Otherwise, I would have gone and thrown your crap out on the front lawn."

Hart now assumed he had been discourteous in planning to play tennis socially with others in the afternoon, and his mind "grasped at straws" as he concocted an explanation: Was she jealous that he had played tennis with another woman? Did she think she owned him?

While he waited for a taxi, she said: "A long time ago, I was having trouble with a man, and I went to a psychiatrist. You know what he said? He said, 'Look, Alice, you are a champion, and you don't need to take crap from anybody.'"

At that point, Hart said she pointed at him.

"And that means you."

He was stunned by the change from the "scrappy, good-natured woman" of earlier in the day.

And she didn't attack just him. Sportswriters also took a licking: "They are parasites. They cling to athletes that play the game they cannot play. Egocentric, conceited bastards like you." Hart protested, saying he was not a sportswriter. He was "a writer who happened to be a sports fan." The distinction made no dent in her fury.

Later he tried to explore what he might have done to make matters worse. "I admitted that I had made an error. Indeed, I had. I should have gone directly home with her after lunch and done my work before I went off to play. I always knew that you should get your work done first—then goof off if you want to. It was a rule I had violated. Yet—and this was my excuse—it was she who got me into the game."

Had she turned into a harridan, or was Hart himself a cad, out to defrock the deity he claimed to so admire? Was his version true, or was it character assassination? Hart had struggled for years to be more self-aware and personally responsible. At some point in his life he made a pact with the universe to be as honest as possible and to abjure alcohol. In this light, his enduring memory of the encounter with Marble, which hit him so hard, is poignant: "I remembered the drink in her hand."

And he remembered one unsettling sound, when Marble started hissing, "Gusssie-eee." Marble's voice was taunting, contemptuous. Gussie Moran was one of the many tennis players Hart planned to profile in his book, and Marble objected to being lumped in the same category as "Gusssie-eee."

Hart concluded: "I had offended her sense of being Alice Marble; her well-earned regal disposition had not been deferred to. I had taken her as a pal, a regular woman, a good egg. I had taken her as she appeared to be prior to our lunch."

In contrast to the interview with Hart, published in book form in 1985, the always adulatory local press continued to present a peppy version of Marble, applauding her presence at Tiempo de los Niños, the children's support group at Desert Hospital, at a buffet brunch and fashion show in the Capra Room at La Quinta Hotel.[14] The *Desert Sun* radiated positivity: "Like fine wine, Alice Marble improves with age. Bright and intelligent, she speaks her mind and is a delight. When she was informed . . . that she was to be this year's official honoree . . . she quipped, 'What happened. Did you run out of men?'"[15] Bob Hope gave her a humanitarian award at a fundraiser held at the Palm Springs High School to benefit Angel View Crippled Children's Hospital, the Braille Institute, and the American Cancer Society.

More and more, Marble added details about her past that had not surfaced previously. She told one reporter that she lamented the show-biz career she did not have, indicating that because her father had been a professional songwriter and singer, she may have missed her destiny.

"Remember 'It's a Lovely Day Tomorrow?' That was one of his."[16]

The words are filled with uplift and hope.

The sudden introduction of her father's talent as a musician was curious for two reasons. While the sentiment of the lyrics may be true—it may be indeed lovely in the morrow—their author was not Harry Marble, who had been dead for eighteen years when the song was written in 1938, by Irving Berlin.

On February 21, 1985, Alice went to the St. Francis Hotel in downtown San Francisco, where guests paid seventy-five dollars[17] to watch her be inducted into the Bay Area Sports Hall of Fame along with Baltimore Colts defensive end Gino Marchetti, San Francisco 49ers tackle Leo Nomellini, jockey Johnny Longden, and the 49ers' late first coach, Lawrence T. "Buck" Shaw. This was the sixth awards ceremony for the organization, which did not have a building (its slogan: "The Hall Without a Hall"), deciding instead to raise money for youth sports.[18] A reporter asked Alice to name her "big moment." She chose a match that happened three years before her triumph at Wimbledon. Marble had been on her quest to reenter tennis after her illness when, in 1936, she beat Carolin Babcock at the Palm Springs invitational tournament. For Alice, the victory was a turning point. "It wasn't an easy road back. I had to diet to lose 45 pounds and regain my stamina and strokes," she said. "The win at Palm Springs convinced me that my dreams of a comeback would be realized."[19]

And even though many days stood out when a sunny moment claimed the light, darkness descended as well. May 22, 1985, marked another hard loss, the death of Alice's brother George. Now there were three, only she and Hazel and Tim, left living.

Still, interviewers showed up and politely waited while she mined old memories. "I was impressed by Althea at the National Indoor Tennis Finals," Marble told one reporter in May 1986. "But they [tennis officials] wouldn't let her play on the eastern tour. They said she hadn't proved herself. I wrote a scathing article in which I called them hypocrites. That gave her a little push."[20]

Then she added a new twist. While "fiddling with a neck chain that has broken, causing a medallion engraved with Greek letters to fall in her lap," Marble suddenly recalled yet another feather in her cap: the honorary degree in journalism she had received from Harvard University for the article she wrote about Gibson in *American Lawn Tennis*.[21]

In November, Alice joined forces at a Veterans Day lunch with Ruth Monroe, a former member of the Women's Army Corps, and the local paper slipped in another new element of Alice's story, claiming that she was "in a way . . . a veteran, having received a bullet wound for undercover work in Europe, and having played over 500 tennis exhibition matches to entertain World War II troops."[22] The five hundred tennis matches were old news. The bullet wound added a new element to the public Alice, war hero, and showed she was now willing to discuss publicly a chapter from the wartime years she had kept under wraps for so long. Reporters hoping to find a congenial subject sometimes did, especially if they caught her early enough in the day and ended the chat in a timely fashion. When she suddenly lost steam, almost sputtering along, she would shoo visitors out, muttering, "Bye, bye, bye."

For his part, Stan Hart joined the procession of visitors who, after taking leave of her, were left to ponder the mystery of what it must have been like to be Alice Marble at the end, living inside a palace of memories with walls of poured concrete.

CHAPTER 28

TAKING A CHANCE
ON LOVE

W HEN ALICE RECEIVED A REQUEST to attend an event at the International Tennis Hall of Fame in Newport, Rhode Island, in the spring of 1986, twenty-two years after her induction, she sent her regrets to Ms. Jane G. Brown in a letter dated May 16, 1986: "I always promised myself that I would once again get to Newport. However, this year is impossible. . . . I have an interesting project for the summer. ABC is doing a television program of my life, so I must be here to go wherever it is necessary." It must have tickled Alice to experience the joy of rejecting a terrific invitation because something even better had come along. Procter & Gamble planned a TV series of biographical tributes titled *Great American Women*. Rita Mae Brown, writer, athlete, and former partner of Martina Navratilova, was hired to write the screenplay for the first segment, about Alice.

Brown made her literary debut in 1973, at the age of twenty-nine, with the publication of *Rubyfruit Jungle*, considered a groundbreaking lesbian coming-of-age story. When a little-known feminist press named Daughters Inc. published the book, expectations were low. Nevertheless, the book sold so well it paved the way for Brown's subsequent illustrious career.

As a teenager in Florida, Brown had known of Alice and had watched her play tennis at an event organized by Jimmy Evert, Chris Evert's father, as part of a Fort Lauderdale city tournament. Evert often arranged for pros to play each other and sometimes, as a courtesy, the pros would deign to play the kids who were on their way up. Brown watched not only Alice but also Maureen Connolly, Darlene Hard, and Pauline Betz. She was impressed by Alice: "Her ground strokes, classic, sent the ball back to you flat and hard. Just when you got used to the pace she'd change up."[1]

Brown said that Alice had a perfect tennis body: "She was a medium-sized girl. She could move well and be powerful. Well proportioned. Nothing out of whack."[2]

When Brown and Marble first met at a restaurant in Beverly Hills in 1986, Alice had no memory of her from Fort Lauderdale, but she did recall the tennis courts and Jimmy Evert.

"Everyone loved Jimmy," Brown wrote in a subsequent account of the meeting. Alice "regaled the assembled" with stories from the "golden era of talkies. Alice's stories were liberally spiced with innuendo. She was funny. She also had a hollow leg. The girl could drink."[3]

The two women hit it off: "Once Alice started talking, you couldn't not listen. If there was a chip on her shoulder, I never found it."[4]

Brown understood that it was "painfully obvious all Alice could do was relive past glory. But what a glory it was. As beautiful as a movie star in her high days, she attracted male and female alike. She frolicked with them too. In me she found new ears, yet someone who had also known her at the end of her career. I hadn't seen her at her peak, but when I did see her in the early 1960s, she was damned impressive. She still blew me off the court in her seventies."[5]

In the story Alice now shared, more details of her life emerged.[6] This would be the story that Rita Mae mined for multiple drafts of her screenplay and which she would share with Dale Leatherman, whom she convinced to become Alice's collaborator on her second memoir, *Courting Danger*, in which the escapade provided the centerpiece.

Alice gave "let's call him Joe" a full name, Joseph Norman Crowley. He had graduated from college in Ohio and been a Rhodes scholar and studied at the Sorbonne before joining the service. In this telling, he and Alice met at the Stage Door Canteen in New York City sometime after the establishment opened on March 2, 1942, in the basement of a theater on West Forty-Fourth Street. They could not have picked a more symbolic place, a pop culture icon in its day. The New York club inspired the 1943 movie *Stage Door Canteen* and *This is the Army*, both the 1942 Broadway musical and its 1943 film adaptation, with songs by Irving Berlin, including "I Left My Heart at the Stage Door Canteen."

From the start, the Stage Door Canteen was a huge hit, filled with "dancing, singing, talking and laughing," the *New York Times* reported.[7] Patrons danced the night away—the jitterbug, Lindy hop, conga line. Cigarettes were free, no alcohol was served, and milk was the "favorite tipple."[8] Young women, wearing red, white, and blue aprons, served food and non-alcoholic beverages. In the story of how she met Crowley, Marble took to the microphone and sang an old standby, "Taking a Chance on Love." The rendition won instant favor with a handsome young army pilot who had grown up on a farm in Kansas. The attraction was mutual. They played Ping-Pong at the canteen, had a drink back at her apartment, and made a date to see each other when he was next back in town.

When Crowley reappeared three months later, he made it clear he meant business, proposing marriage to Alice. They spent the night at the apartment she shared with Teach, who was conveniently out of town. The next morning, Alice awakened to the smell of coffee and pancakes and the dreamy conviction, "There *had* been a man in my bed."[9] Teach was not so thrilled when she discovered the duo a few hours later, and once again Alice reported a tug of wills—only this time, she says, she stood up for herself.

Crowley went off to war, and Marble continued her contributions to the war effort, playing exhibition matches at military bases and on "the rolling decks of ships."[10]

They wed, in one account, aboard a naval ship on the Hudson River with plenty of sailors "in dress whites" as witnesses but none of Marble's family or friends.[11] She said the reason no one in her circle ever met Crowley was that his work in the military involved espionage and required him to keep a low profile, in part to protect her from becoming a target. They had a quick honeymoon during one of many tours, then a pregnancy, and then she lost the baby in a car accident while he was serving overseas. As she recovered, she envisioned a quiet Christmas Eve in 1944 with Teach, Brownie, du Pont, Madrigal and her lover. Instead, a knock at the door announced a messenger with the telegram conveying the tragic news that Joe Crowley had been killed in action when his plane was shot down over Germany. In the aftermath, her grief led to a suicide attempt. Alice never would have recovered without her friends at her side. Clark Gable sent three dozen roses and a note, "If I can do it, so can you," employing the message that Lombard had written to Alice when she was at the sanatorium.

A few months later, still living in New York City and grieving the death of her husband, Alice set forth on a spring day in 1945, wearing a dress she had designed for Best and Company under a polo coat, for a lunch date at the 21 club with Teach and Brownie, unable to shake the creepy conviction that she was being followed. Before the other women arrived at the restaurant, a man in uniform intercepted Alice and asked her if they could speak privately. He produced identification showing that he was an army intelligence officer, and she agreed that he could be in touch later. The three women enjoyed a soused lunch thanks to complimentary champagne supplied by the venue. The next day, "Captain Al Jones" called Marble at her home. (As in many of Alice's most dramatic stories, she employed a pseudonym rather than the man's real name.)

She believed his interest was routine; probably an invitation for a game of doubles "with some fat general."[12] Picking her up in midtown Manhattan, Captain Jones took her to a warehouse in Brooklyn. On the way, he made insinuating and gratuitous comments about liking to watch girls play tennis, and for a moment, Marble recoiled from his lewdness. But he appeared genuine when he introduced her to another officer, "Colonel Linden," who had a proposal. Had not she once been in love with the dashing Swiss banker Hans Steinmetz? The romance had been short-lived, and they had not been in touch in the intervening years. Whatever lingering feelings she may have once entertained had evaporated when she fell for Joe Crowley.

The colonel explained that the United States government suspected Hans of collaborating with the Nazis and smuggling plunder out of Germany and into Switzerland, to be used after the war by war criminals to set up their lives elsewhere, naming South America as a possible destination.

The colonel softened the blow a bit by saying Hans might be just a sympathizer rather than a Nazi, and he might not even possess any loot, but intelligence units believed that in a secret room in his home he had documents in which he recorded financial transactions. Would she, in service to her nation, pretend to rekindle the flame so she could visit him in his castle, with the purpose of documenting his vault? The government would set up tennis clinics and exhibitions for her so well publicized that Hans would inevitably take notice and, if the gamble paid off, get in touch with her. Marble pondered the offer for a few days and then told the colonel she would do it. After all she had nothing to lose. He disagreed: "You do. Your life."

"I'll take that chance."

For the next few weeks, as Marble recounted to Brown and later to Leatherman, she maintained a busy routine: tennis in the morning and espionage training in the afternoon in the warehouse in Brooklyn, which included instruction in the use of a .25 caliber automatic pistol, target practice, combat training, and lessons in map reading, safecracking, and photography and in how to disarm explosives and silence alarms. She was schooled in the details of the likely interior of Hans's castle and given a contact in Geneva, a goldsmith to whom she gave another pseudonym, Franz Regenbogen. Her task was to take pictures of the contents of the vault and to deliver the film to him, using a compact spy camera, "perfected by Kodak for undercover work."[13] Should she get into trouble, he would help with a quick getaway.

She arrived in Switzerland in April 1945 with the avowed purpose of giving tennis clinics. It took Hans only three days to take the bait, inviting her to dinner. Their mutual attraction was rekindled.

By night two, they were dining at Hans's château, with silent servants sidling into the room with exquisite dishes. A tour of the wine cellar and passion in a four-poster bed followed. At this point in the story, Marble confessed to misgivings about the morality of the venture. She spent three days apart from Hans, wrestling with her conscience and refusing to take his calls or to respond to his notes. When she finally called him and made plans to return to the castle, she was all business, her suitcase containing not just the usual items but also "my gun, camera, and tools."[14] That night, Marble and Hans attended a party at the Argentine embassy, but first he gave her a gift: "a necklace of diamonds and sapphires, glittering like ice in the sunlight."[15]

At the dance, Alice could not help but wonder: "Hans, the place is full of Germans. Why are the Argentines being so hospitable?"[16]

The answer was pure math. The Swiss were rumored to have more than three hundred million German marks in their banks. The Argentines wanted that money to divert to their coffers after the war. Hans admitted he had German money in his bank but acknowledged no scruples: "I'm a banker. I don't worry about where money comes from."[17]

Later that night, at the castle, Hans nearly consumed a magnum of champagne on his own while he bragged about how he had the Nazis "by the balls."[18] First, he took their money, then he charged them interest for watching over it, and when the war was over and they were imprisoned in their homeland, he would take their savings and live in high style. In his drunken gabbiness, he also let on that the only way to open the vault was with a key, and that key just happened to be "hidden in a radiator knob, where nobody would think to look."[19]

Pretending to be sick, Marble sent Hans off to socialize on his own while she waited for the quiet of nighttime to overtake the castle. Her mind made up, she retrieved the key, got her gun, and inched her way down the stone steps to the cellar with racks filled with wine. A heavy wooden door swung open to reveal the safe. She knelt down in front of it, trying over and over to crack it, when "finally, the tumblers in the locking mechanism clicked into place,"[20] revealing paintings, gold bars imprinted with swastikas, and jewels. The biggest find was a leather-bound ledger containing names and numbers of all the financial transactions. She aimed the lens of the camera at the columns upon columns of deposits.

Then she heard footsteps and had only seconds to act. Hans always left the keys in his car, so she made a quick dodge to the Mercedes. She fired it up and careened down a dark, narrow mountain road. Soon a car in pursuit loomed in the rearview mirror, approaching fast. It passed her, then halted, creating a roadblock. Forced to stop, she got out of the Mercedes and was relieved to see Al Jones, her initial contact from the army, the man who drove her to the Brooklyn warehouse on that first day. But he turned out to be a double agent.

"Stop wasting time on that bitch. Get the film," shouted a sidekick in his car. "Kill her! Hurry!"[21]

Marble's gun was sitting in the Mercedes where it was of no use. With no choice but to run, that was what she did, only to be shot in the back.

As luck would have it, Colonel Linden had begun to suspect Al Jones's perfidy, and he somehow found a way to rescue Marble and to get her hospitalized. Under Colonel Linden's orders, American operatives cornered Jones and his partner and killed them both. Al Jones's final act of treason was to open the camera and expose the film so that all of Marble's stealthy documentation would be lost forever, but Marble's much-vaunted photographic memory came to the rescue. Frail and bandaged, she was able to relate the contents of the pages that she photographed to an army stenographer at her side. She arrived back home, on May 7, 1945, the day before the war was declared over in Europe. She recovered at a base hospital, telling Teach and others that she was recuperating from a far more plebian procedure, the removal of a cyst from her back.

The story combined glamour with suspense with derring-do, and at its center was a beautiful, young lovelorn woman versus more than one bad guy.

How could Hollywood resist?

The story was perfect to lead P&G's new television-movie series *Great American Women*. The correspondence between Brown and various partners in the process is a case study in how a film gets shelved despite the best intentions of those involved.[22]

The project began on a note of exuberance with a letter from Brenda Friend, director of development at Twentieth Century Fox, dated January 2, 1986, announcing that major talent was already on board: "Linda Evans is attached, so the picture would more than likely shoot during her hiatus from 'Dynasty' in May and early June." The producers sought a strict focus on Marble's "ill-fated marriage" and her time as a spy. Her career in tennis would be "supplemental, but on a secondary level."[23]

Rita Mae Brown would be paid $50,000 for a screenplay that would run two hours, plus bonuses and profit participation. Brown would travel first class and receive a generous per diem if called upon to consult in person in California. From the beginning, Brown communicated with the producers about the progress of her work, seeking advice on elements of plot and character development. On February 5, 1986, Brown sent what she considered "not a scene-by-scene breakdown" but rather a "rough cut of structure." By late February, Brown felt the work was going well enough to merit "story approval" from the producers, meaning "more monies are forthcoming from you [the producers] to me [Brown]—always a happy state of affairs as far as I'm concerned."

Brown paused in her negotiations to ask whether the producers were cutting Alice "a fair deal." She added, "I wish somebody would buy that old girl a new car. I don't think she's terribly bright about money and even though Willy invested money for her I doubt seriously, if she gets more than $10–15,000 off of it." (In the margin, the words "per annum.") Brown ended the note, "It's none of my business, but she's become quite dear to me."

On March 12, 1986, Brown acknowledged the producers' misgivings about the truthfulness of Marble's account, writing to them: "My worry, the same as yours, is that Alice is not quite accurate. I'll go over to Palm Springs Monday night so I can get up at the crack of dawn. It's the best way to get clarity from her." Brown liked to talk to Marble early in the day: "You can't get much from her after lunch but attention means so much to her."

Brown wrote: "If Alice is lying, sorry to be blunt, she's not going to cough up anything to be cross-checked. She may be garrulous and fond of her spirits but she isn't dumb." Brown ended again with a declaration of affection: "I like her very much." She also suggested that the producers schedule a meeting with the executives from ABC: "It isn't that I consider ABC an enemy but my experience with network people is that they're there because they aren't tough enough to be independent producers. . . . They'll quibble and waver long before any of us will. I like us to present a united front. Up to you."

Then, a note from Brenda Friend arrived on April 29, saying a team from ABC had scheduled a trip to the desert so they could question Marble directly. Friend urged Brown to conduct her own investigation and thus put the network executives at ease.

The Department of Broadcast Standards and Practices at ABC had rigorous guidelines for docudramas, defined as "programs based on actual events . . . [that] range from major historical happenings involving public figures to projects based on the personal memoirs of private individuals." The goal was to "enable such dramatization to be presented within the bounds of authenticity, as a fair interpretation of the facts, within the time limits of the dramatic form, and in such a manner as not to mislead, deceive or be untruthful to the facts or events as presented to the viewer."

ABC composed a five-page single-spaced document with one stickler of a question after another: Did Alice really have TB? Were her "three brothers in the service, as scripted"? In the script Joe is "an Air Force pilot. For 'The Road to Wimbledon,' wasn't he a captain in the Army Intelligence Service?" Can they confirm the nature of her spy work? "Is it accurate that a warehouse in Brooklyn was the army intelligence headquarters?" "Did Alice run tennis clinics in Switzerland as a cover?" "Please confirm the scripted detail about the key to Hans' safe being in a radiator cap and that 'Hans' told Alice this detail." "What was made of the information from the safe? How was it used?"

In the end, the files reflected the only evidence Marble had produced, an undated, handwritten, not entirely grammatical note allegedly from Tica Madrigal:

Muy Querida Alicia,

While your [sic] risking your foolish neck in Switzerland, perhaps you'll keep up your Spanish lessons by reading my book. You're loco, loco, loco! *Switzerland is for mountain climbing and sightseeing, not undercover work. You've been through so much with Joes' [sic] death and* mi amor. *I don't want to lose you—come back safely.*

Rita Mae Brown thought the producers were being unduly diligent. Referring to the head of the OSS (Office of Strategic Services, the US intelligence agency during World War II), she observed, "Wild Bill Donovan . . . wasn't noted for his filing habits." She considered William J. Donovan a bit of a cowboy and not much of a director. As far as Brown was concerned, ABC should just go ahead and make the movie: "What did it matter? Everyone involved was dead."[24]

ABC thought otherwise, and in the end, the project fell apart in a multipage memo filled with one niggling question after another that could not be resolved to the network's satisfaction.

Even without the movie to unite them in a common cause, and despite an age difference of thirty-one years, the friendship between the two women flourished. Brown relished playing tennis with Marble: "I never short-shotted her. That would have been dirty pool. I stayed in the backcourt, where she'd destroy me with glee." Alice paid her tennis partner a big compliment: "If only I could have coached you when you were a kid."[25]

With Brown on the East Coast, visiting the desert once a year or so, the two women spoke on the phone and maintained a lively long-distance correspondence from 1986 on. The letters give a picture of Alice still connecting with the world, still maintaining a bright presence, with social excursions outside the house and wry asides about some of the people in her social landscape. Throughout, a flirtatious subtext is evident, indicating perhaps something more between the two women, or the wish for it, at least on Alice's part.

"You remind me of my first favorite teacher," Alice wrote an undated letter to Brown at some point during their correspondence between 1986 and 1990, referring to Miss Coyne,[26] who "tried without success to take up tennis for me. She was my first love and just a word from her would set me up for days. You do the same for me. I read your books, your letters and dream. It's a very special bond I feel. Warm and spiritual. Thanks for assuring me that you 'felt something' or my ego would have been wounded."

Alice filled Rita Mae in on family news: "I'm sad today as I talked with my brother-in-law last night and my sis is doing very badly. . . . I hate to lose her as we have become very close the last few years." Even worse, "my oldest nephew's wife—age 42—and mother of two honor students, is dying of throat cancer; just two lovely people who love each other deeply."

Alice shared updates on her life, including her gratitude that a male companion named Bob Prestie escorted her to a "great Thanksgiving Day with our friend Dr. Toote and her family." About Prestie, Alice wrote, "My 'romance,' as you put it is one of the sweetest experiences I've had. It's a touching, loving one with no sex. Bob is a very spiritual man, thoughtful and devoted. He is the perfect escort."

Alice never acknowledged, at least in the letters to Brown, that she understood that the challenges to the veracity of her story were the real reason the project got shunted aside. Instead, she focused on the traditional Hollywood excuse for why something sinks or swims: they could not find a star to attach to the project. To Brown she wrote, affecting a tone of insider ennui, "I'm happy that I don't have to make my living in the TV field. Everything is so 'hurry up and wait.'"

CHAPTER 29

LULLABY AT NIGHT

R ITA MAE BROWN ONCE OBSERVED that Martina Navratilova and Alice Marble shared "strong performer personalities. Remove the limelight and they wander about."[1]

Restore it and, in Alice's case, a miracle of rejuvenation occurred. Invitations to speak at luncheons and other functions in the desert still found their way to Alice, despite her increasing frailty. Just when those in her orbit might have thought *game over* in private, she surprised them in public when a reflexive graciousness kicked in. The well-mannered facade had the force of armor. Her voice, now dry and raspy, thanks to age and cigarettes, was reinvigorated. It would increase in volume thanks to the microphone. For a moment, time's burdens appeared to vanish, or at least recede. She would unwilt.

If any occasion stands out above all others in her waning years, it was the dedication of Alice Marble Center Court at the Palm Desert Resort and Country Club on April 11, 1987, when not even the weather, which was broiling, could ruin the feeling of goodwill.

Two stalwart souls stood next to each other at the podium, Marble and Althea Gibson, who had made a special trip to the desert to honor her old friend. Gibson delivered an emotional tribute, speaking of the "barriers in the way" for her as an African American to play in the US National Championship.[2]

"Alice Marble wrote an open letter to USLTA that finally opened the door," she said, stepping up to tell the old story one more time. Gibson said that when she received her first trophy, she felt "like I feel right now. I had a tear in my eye and a prayer in my heart for Alice Marble, my idol, who showed me the way. Alice, may God continue to bless you."

After turning the podium over to Alice, Gibson stepped aside and wiped her eyes.

Alice, for her part, acknowledged all the work that went into organizing the ceremony, and then said: "And so, ladies and gentlemen, the only thing I can say is, I'm proud to have this honor. I appreciate your coming. I'm sorry it was hot." She added: "I'd like to say with all my heart, God bless you and thank you."

Gibson, almost a head taller, hooked her arm over Alice's shoulder, a protective, gentle gesture. The plaque was unveiled. Red, white, and blue balloons were released, tumbling toward the sky. Marble paused to ponder something. She was, as she once wrote, "with thought." Bouncing back to the podium, to applause, she shared her insight: "I've already made up my mind. This is going to be the women's challenge court." She meant it as a quip. Of course, men would be playing on the court, but the cause of women and their prospects as athletes was never far from her mind. In that millisecond, Alice appeared crisp and tingling as in the days of yore.

Marble's physical reserves were easily depleted, and the excitement of the dedication caused her to overdo it. The next day she rested, but the following morning she golfed. That night, dinner was delayed. At ten o'clock, on an empty stomach, she found herself sitting alone, away from the partygoers. A man, a seeming Good Samaritan, approached her and tried to get her to stand up, but then they both slipped on the wet patio. She broke an arm, a kneecap, and several ribs.

News of her injuries spread quickly. The president of the Women's Club of the Desert informed members at an otherwise festive midday luau. A newspaper account predicted a happy outcome: "Sidelined from her Ping-Pong table and golf course, Alice remains undaunted and optimistic, and plans to be back tending bar for the Women's Club when the new season starts in the fall. Who has more friends than the unflappable Alice? They have seen her volley with misfortune on many a previous occasion. Adversity is always outmatched by this classy lady who emerges as the true champion she is."[3]

On July 4 and 5, Marble felt well enough to host the "Breakfast at Wimbledon" at the Palm Desert Resort and Country Club for two mornings in a row from eight to eleven. The festivities included a buffet with strawberries and cream, live television, activities, and prizes. Her job was to watch the matches with the guests and to repeat anecdotes from long ago—what it had been like in England right before the war, to beat the elegant Kay Stammers, to meet the queen, and to receive a transatlantic phone call from Lombard and Gable congratulating her on her win.

Despite the injuries, Alice consented to a filmed interview on July 25, 1987, with a local tennis player, Courtney Gebhart, for an oral history project sponsored by the Palm Springs Public Library.[4] Gebhart, twenty-three, hoped to launch an acting career.[5] She addressed her subject with enthusiastic sincerity, claiming Marble was more than just a tennis star: "She's also a singer, a writer, a lecturer, sports announcer, clothes designer, and she was even a spy."

Alice appeared limp and bruised. In her zeal, the young interviewer launched the session with a compliment that had no objective basis in fact: "You look terrific."

Bandaged, moving gingerly, Alice cast a skeptical side-eye at Gebhart, who charged ahead. "We're going to discuss some special memories with Alice Marble."

The conversation bounced around a bit, balls on an uneven surface. From Alice, the usual gambits are heard on the tape and in a subsequent transcription in which there are a few minor discrepancies. Even so, the gist of the story that Alice shared that day contains the same broad strokes she had been reciting as soon as she was old (and prominent) enough to frame her backstory as a quest and not a mere résumé:

> *I was born on a farm, believe it or not, five miles from a town of ninety-eight people. . . . [My grandfather] come from Maine when he was sixteen around the Horn to make his fortune in gold, and he didn't. . . . My dad was one of six children. . . . I learned to milk a cow when I was four years old and think I could still do it. . . . A little house on top of a high hill in San Francisco . . . sixty steps . . . we were on the second of two long hills so I think that's where I got the strong legs from . . . a seven-letter girl in high school . . . Dan was kind of the papa . . . Carole was, well, like an older sister. When I had TB and I was in the sanatorium . . . she wrote me a letter and said, 'If I can do it, you can' . . . she followed every kind of cult every kind of religion you can imagine, astrology, numerology, psychics and all this sort of thing. Big blow when Carole was killed because she had been such a person in my life.*

One of the special memories that Alice wished to relive was of recent vintage, the dedication of Alice Marble Center Court, telling Gebhart, as if this could not be more impressive, "All the mayors attended." She pointed out that she received notes of congratulations from Billie Jean King and President Gerald Ford. Best of all, Althea Gibson flew in from New York. She shared her version of the accident: "And this guy came and sat next to me, and he got up and he sort of gave me his hand," after which, she remembers, "He slipped on the marble terrace and fell on top of me and broke my ribs and broke my arm and broke my leg."

Alice told Gebhart about the upcoming movie based on her life, saying that a "very famous writer" named Rita Mae Brown had written the script. Then she rattled off a list of the potential stars that had been bandied about to play her. It was a typical Hollywood wish list in that the names would be proffered and canceled in the same breath. First the producers thought they had actress Linda Evans, but no, she had another commitment, and then they hoped to have . . . here Alice hesitated while the name escaped her, apologizing, "talk about my good memory—the *Moonlighting* girl."

Gebhart came to the rescue: "Cybill Shepherd."

Yes, yes, Cybill Shepherd, but she wanted much more money than the producers wanted to pay. Next came Cheryl Ladd from *Charlie's Angels*, but maybe she wasn't well enough known anymore.

The name of Cheryl Ladd caused Marble to pause and give Gebhart an appraising look: "You look a bit like her . . . we should get you."

Gebhart did not hesitate: "I'll do it."

When Gebhart asked whether a photo in Alice's house was of her husband, Alice replied that it was indeed Joe, adding, "I'm so sorry the frame broke."

In this version of the story,

He dated me, and we got married, much to my teacher's annoyance. But that's beside the point. A nice guy—he was a scratch golfer, Ohio State. He was an engineer. He was in the Air Force Intelligence. He was—do we have a lot of time or not? I met Joe, and then he was off to the Pacific, and then he was off to Europe, and then he was all over the place. And he came back. He called me up and said, "I'm coming home." I didn't particularly want to get married, but he did, and so—you know, people were leaving, and I didn't think it was right. Anyway, that picture happens to be in Panama, because he was—I was playing exhibitions for the troops, and Joe was piloting a general, which he hated. He wanted to get in the fighting. But we got married, and we sort of had a honeymoon in Panama.

The story then gets a bit confusing. Joe told her, "I'm coming home, and I've got tons of money, 'cause I haven't been able to spend it."

The next portion of the interview verges on stream of consciousness:

> *And I'd worked for a restaurant during World War II called Le Pavillon, which was a very famous place on—I did publicity during the war for Henri Soulé, the owner. He had a restaurant at the fair. And then he opened one on Fifty-Seventh Street in New York, so it was my favorite place. So I made a reservation, and Henri was so excited to meet my husband. We were sitting there—by this time I had learned to drink some wine. I had never drunk anything, but Joe introduced me to wine, and three quite famous people came in, and spotted me with this good-looking—I guess Joe was a lieutenant then—Mary Pickford, Gloria Swanson, and Carole Lombard.*
>
> *They all came into the restaurant and spotted me and said—oh, with a male escort, Gus Schirmer, who is head of the big music company[6]—he said, "Join us." And Joe said, "I'm not that loaded." And I said, "Don't worry. Mr. Schirmer will help out." So he said, "I'll never get a word in edgewise all evening long." They kept asking Joe questions. You know, they thought he was kind of cute, and he was. And only one person came up and said, "Miss Marble, we're just finished dinner. I don't want to spoil your dinner, but I just wanted to say how much I enjoyed watching you play."*
>
> *And Joe said, "And she is my wife."*

Joe, "a movie buff," then endeared himself to the three famous actresses by displaying his familiarity with their work, which, according to Alice, is "always a tremendous hit" with stars.

The story Marble told of Joe and their romance went through many permutations as it was recounted to various people, though in most, she stressed the secrecy of their love for each other. In this version the relationship was public, with Hollywood royalty witnessing it, a trio no less. Mary Pickford and Gloria Swanson both lived to ripe old age, though whether they were in New York that day is not known. Surely Carole Lombard too would have loved being part of the party—if she had not already been dead for years.

ALICE STILL HOPED for a second book based on her life, "a very different autobiography, a decent one. About me."[7] She did not clarify what had been

not decent about the first effort, or what it had been about if not about her.
But something about the first volume rankled. Perhaps she wanted to dig
deeper, and certainly there was more she could add. *The Road to Wimbledon*,
curiously, makes a brief opening reference to Wimbledon itself on page one
that extends halfway through page two and then the topic recedes altogether.

On October 7, 1987, Marble wrote to Rita Mae Brown,[8] first telling her
about the big day with Althea Gibson, giving a concise version of the events
and her accident. Employment, as had been the case all her life, remained a
concern: "Last week the Resort was sold and I am out of a job, enough gloom."
On a happier note, while she was laid up, Alice's thoughts had turned more
insistently to a second memoir: "During the months at home I cleaned every
cupboard, drawers, files and found so much material for a book. My love,
what would you suggest? I would love to have a writer like George Vecsey
of the *N.Y. Times* or Frank Deford of *Sports Illustrated*. . . . Would you call
me or drop a line? I love you and always will. Thank you and let's meet in
the next life."

Brown agreed that Alice's life story deserved a fresh turn. She appreciated Alice's long history in the spotlight and at its outer edges. "She knew
everyone, even Ronald Reagan. She loved to dish but not in a cruel way. She
was a nonvicious Truman Capote."[9]

In a new book, the telling should be less prim than *The Road to Wimbledon*, more confessional and racier, in keeping with the mood of the era,
which not only encouraged intimacy but required it in the increasingly hot
memoir genre.[10]

Marble asked Brown whether she would be willing to write it with her,
an "as told to," but Brown said, "It's not my thing." Still, she had someone in
mind who might be a good fit. She contacted a riding friend, Dale Leatherman, a journalist in her forties, who covered and participated in a variety of
sports, including golf, equestrian events, and race-car driving. She was also
a member of the Society of American Travel Writers.[11]

Testing the waters, Brown asked Leatherman whether the name Alice
Marble meant anything to her. It didn't, so Brown gave a quick pitch.
Alice had been a tennis champion in her day. She had been a secret spy for
the United States during World War II, a story she had kept under wraps for
security reasons for many years but was now willing to share more openly.
Leatherman's interest was piqued. She had only a superficial understanding of tennis and had never written anything this ambitious before, but she

was not fearful about having to learn something new, and she was used to meeting deadlines.

Brown even reviewed Leatherman's initial proposal to the publisher, based on conversations with Alice, and offered some tips in a letter to her: "Put the photographic memory up front so it doesn't jump out of the blue later. . . . Mention the greats of her era, Tilden, Budge, Gottfried Von Cramm (once had a match interrupted by a phone call from Hitler, great story). . . . Be clear in the Swiss section about why the Nazis are funneling out money: because they know they're going to lose and they're feathering their nest elsewhere: South America. This has a perverse, romantic appeal to people. . . . You've got glamour, glitter, and the gutter. Can't lose."[12]

"It's going to take patience," Brown warned, but she thought it would be worth it in the end. "I think you need to get to know her. This project will change your life."

It ultimately earned Leatherman the distinction of being one of the people closest to Marble in her final years. Leatherman said it was tough writing through someone else's eyes even if that person possessed a photographic memory. After all, Marble could only remember what she saw. On all those trips to Europe, she would not likely be staring out the windows of her hotel rooms. She would be concerned only with tennis. Leatherman gathered photos of the places where she wanted to recreate scenes. "Fortunately, in Europe, a lot of things stay the same," Leatherman said. "I did the best I could with the tools that I had at the time. My editor was shocked when I got the manuscript in on time."[13]

The book advance, as well as any future royalties and earnings from film deals, were to be shared fifty-fifty by Leatherman and Alice. The money did not support extensive travel. "Did I go to Geneva to try to get the layout of the city and a sense of how the spying could have occurred? No. There was no budget for that," Leatherman said. She did travel occasionally to California to interview Alice in person. The cigarette smoke caused her to sneeze incessantly. The only relief was to take breaks every couple of hours for a quick dip in the pool. From her home in the East, Leatherman called her subject with a list of questions a couple of times a week. Alice would take down the questions and later, speaking into a recorder, tape the answers on mini-cassettes that she would then drop in the mail.

Leatherman stayed in the guest room of Alice's small house. Together, they pored over photographs and news clips in the old albums from the time of Alice's greatest prominence.[14] On one frantic day, Marble started ripping items out, pressing them on Leatherman, who stymied the rampage before too much damage was done.

Leatherman observed how profoundly alone Marble was. The dish drainer in the kitchen featured one cup, one plate, one knife, one fork, and one spoon. Every time she witnessed the simple sight, she was struck anew by the singularity of each item.

On some nights, Alice sang. "It was disconcerting," Leatherman remembered in an in-person interview in May of 2018, "to get a lullaby."

> She was now spending a lot of time by herself when during so much of her life she was surrounded by fans. It was not just sports people who admired her. It was everyone. She had accomplished so much. It was hard to be with her, to sit there and see a woman who had done so much with her life, experience such a lonely old age, with that painting staring down at her, that portrait of her in the prime of life. Maybe the lesson is: don't grow old.
>
> Alcohol played its part. At my party school, I used to able to keep up as a beer drinker with the best of them, but Alice was way out of my league. She was sitting there in this house by herself thinking back on her career and all she had lost. Your life is truly behind you, and you are waiting for it to end. Yeah, drinking would be in the cards. She started drinking at noon. Vodka, always vodka. Never gin.

Just before the holidays in 1987, a Christmas gift of sorts arrived, a letter from the All England Lawn Tennis and Croquet Club with an invitation to attend the tournament festivities at the championships to be held the following year, from June 20 to July 3, at which the organizers wanted "to recognize your extraordinary achievements of the late 1930s." The many activities included the Lawn Tennis Association Ball on June 25, a reception with His Royal Highness the Duke of Kent, and a champions dinner at the Savoy Hotel on the final Sunday. Airfare would be paid in advance, and should she so desire, she would be given a complimentary room at the Rembrandt Hotel.

On January 2, 1988, Marble wrote to Rita Mae Brown, telling her the good news about Wimbledon, and that she had received a "special request" from the chairman: "I guess they figured I might not last until 1989 which will be my fiftieth anniversary," she observed. "My dentist and his wife are going as I'm not sure I could make this trip alone." She was able to give them the two complimentary tickets she received because this time she had a special third invitation.

Before she left for Wimbledon for the 1988 season, the *Palm Desert Post* wrote: "The Duchess of Tennis, Palm Desert's very own Alice Marble is going to be there again this year accompanied by her friends and desert residents Oscar and Lee Breyer of Indio."[15] A photograph at Wimbledon of Marble with Martina Navratilova shows the two great attacking players looking chummy and radiant. Alice did not report a great deal about the event except that her ancient, disobedient bones made it impossible for her to curtsy.

In a letter to Rita Mae Brown dated December 12, 1988, she indicated that her greatest energies were being devoted to her new memoir, *Courting Danger.* Work on the book was progressing: "Dale keeps in touch, and I have sent her some tapes, which she says are very helpful. It was difficult at first because I am so self-conscious talking into the little machine. . . . She even talked me into writing about my romance with Tica Madrigal, my Spanish teacher, my first and only romance with a woman."[16]

Marble also told Brown that despite her injuries she was walking almost two miles a day, though she confided that a nasty letter from Hazel she received when she was flat on her back didn't help their relationship, which was back to being less than positive: "She is bossy and sneaky and sometimes I don't like her at all but she is my sister."

Midway through 1989, Alice committed some memories to paper to help Leatherman with her work. The seven-page handwritten document appears to have been written in several sittings. At times, the penmanship flags as if it has laryngitis, and then it picks up again in a strong hand, spilling out to the edges of the pages. The prose jumps around in time and place. It begins with a story about how, if it hadn't been for Friskie, Alice surely would have died.

The near tragedy occurred on a typical evening. She invited some new neighbors for a swim and cocktails. The precise date is not clear. After they left, Alice ate dinner, did the dishes, and noticed a spark when she started the garbage disposal. Making a mental note to contact a neighbor the next day so he could check it out, she dozed off, awakening when the cat scratched and bit her. The kitchen was in flames. She grabbed Friskie, ran into the bathroom, and threw him out the window. She screamed for help. Someone called the fire department, and a firefighter forced her to squirm out a small bedroom window, cracking her ribs. There was a hole in her shorty pajamas, and someone was able to grab her a robe. The blaze was extinguished.

In the aftermath, Friskie was fine, "chasing butterflies," but while giving a tennis lesson to a brother and sister from Los Angeles, Alice realized, "The more I talked, the more I coughed up black. The dad was an opera singer and he told me how to breathe and get out the smoke."

She moved in with neighbors for two weeks while repairs were done on her house. Her boss badgered her to get back to work. People came by, "some out of curiosity, others, to help."

In the memo she prepared for Leatherman, Marble took inventory of some of the objects in her house, mentioning the portrait by Dorothy Vicaji: "[She had] painted all the Bloomingdale Cowen boys. Ros insisted I pose. Miss Vicaji obviously annoyed." There was a copy of a painting by Vladimir Tretchikoff, given to her by Hazel after she had admired it, a portrait of a woman who is "very black with a gold turban, gold necklace and gold bracelet." It reminded Alice of Tallulah Bankhead's former maid, who wound up as a caterer in Hollywood and who often worked for Teach in the days when she invited movie stars to dinner.

"I realized why I wanted the painting so badly," she wrote. "Teach was such a slave driver that [the maid] was the buffer. I remember what she said to me when Teach was pushing me too hard: 'I'm angry with everyone but Miss Marble and Blackie,' the half dachshund and half Scottie that Carole Lombard had given me."

Under "treasures," she wrote, "I look around the living room and see a few trophies—about ten—I won over 750 in my lifetime. Tennis and golf. Many are in private homes, wealthy people mostly, who put us up when we lived on $12 per diem. I gave Carole Lombard many silver trays, which were lost when she died. There is a statue of a tennis player done by a sixteen-year-old, made out of soft wood from California. A picture of Aunt Josephine taken in 1910 (married Dr. Gere.) A palm frond with a face by a ten-year-old boy . . ."

She traveled back a year or so in time, including to when she fell at the cocktail party on the treacherous patio and broke several bones. She found the alarm expressed by some of her friends when they saw her confined to a wheelchair, and their eagerness to get her out of it, to be hypocritical and irksome. "The fact that I had had cancer didn't matter," but the notion that "'Champ Marble' might be 'crippled for life' did."

She wrote that after the fall, when she was finally able to get to church, she put on a bright face, thanking everyone for their prayers and their get-well cards, and even cracked a joke, "Just one comment. The better I feel the younger my contemporaries get."

She also wrote, "My neighbor calls me a Pollyanna. I am an optimist. My mother always said when asked, 'I am fine, thank you.'"

Leatherman says it was her idea to end the book on a high, if bittersweet, note, with Alice starting over, as she had done so many times in her life. "After that turning point, when she and Teach parted company, I could not see another high note to end on. Oh, sure, she accomplished many things after that, and coached a lot of young stars, but the lung surgery ended her competitive career. Then Will died. Then Brownie. Then Tica. Then she had cancer. Tennis was her life, and she had become a 'has-been,' her accomplishments forgotten. Sports are cruel that way. Hell, life is cruel that way."

Courting Danger closes in 1945, with Marble at the top of her global game, saving the world from Nazis. An epilogue condenses the final forty-five years of her life into eleven pages. The last words express appreciation: "The memories. I'm grateful for the wonderful mosaic of memories—of tennis, of being famous, of serving my country, of loving and being loved. Every night, I end my prayers with one my mother taught me: 'God bless and angels keep.' . . . My prayer has been answered many, many times in my life."[17]

Leatherman found herself moved by Alice and her circumstances. "Nobody came to see her. She was considered a cranky old coot by most of the neighbors, who kind of liked her and kind of tolerated her. They would see her in her big old tank of a car, likely going out to the liquor store and back, probably scaring the whole neighborhood, that car."

She was most impressed by how Alice could surprise a person and rise to the occasion in front of an audience, coming back to life: "I saw it myself, saw the transformation from this hard-smoking hard-drinking kind of embittered person who essentially felt she had been forgotten. I saw her take on the role of guest speaker at one of the clubs where they had major tennis matches. More than once, I saw her change before my very eyes. She acted so composed. She would dress in a clean, tidy outfit and look ten years younger. I saw the steeliness that was always in her. She was like an old warhorse heeding the call of a bugle."

CHAPTER 30

IRON LADY

W HEN THE TIME COMES," Alice was quoted as saying, "I just want to be ground up and thrown on some tennis court."[1]

In December 1990, a worried neighbor—one of the few who really seemed to care about her, according to Leatherman—noticed that Marble had not left her house in days. The woman contacted the journalist on the East Coast, and they agreed it would be wise to call the police right away about a wellness check. Leatherman felt there was no close family to call for help, saying, "Hazel was the only sibling still alive, and she was not in real good health. The children of her brothers didn't visit, didn't appear to know much about her."[2] (Tim was alive, but leading a marginal life, hardly able to care for himself. He died in 1992.)

The neat, modest house was in shambles. It was obvious to the emergency crew that came to take her to the hospital that for days Marble had lived in a combination of chaos and filth. Leatherman was able to obtain her number at the hospital: "I called and called and called. The nurses held the phone up to her ear, but no matter what I said to her, she refused to utter a word in return. Alice was furious with me. She must have had it in her head that it would be better to stay there in the house and just starve to death. I had taken that choice away from her, and she was real mad. She didn't want any more surgeries. She didn't want to die in the hospital. The ambulance was the ultimate betrayal. Wouldn't even say hello." Leatherman thought of her as "Iron Lady."

Marble was in the hospital with pernicious anemia, succumbing on December 13, 1990, according to the obituary in the *New York Times*.[3] Her physician, Dr. Cecil Jones, gave cancer as the cause.[4] The immediate aftermath of Alice's death was a time of confusion, made worse by people traipsing in and out of her house, perhaps even plundering. Leatherman recalled that "she had a silver cigarette box that she tried to give me, but I told her she should keep her things while she is still alive. I have no idea what happened to that, and I don't know where the trophies are. The painting ended up with a relative, from what I understand, but he is a bit of a recluse. I would love to see it again someday."

Leatherman said it always bothered her that there was no service, no orderly procession of speakers, no formal event commensurate with her status, or at least her former status. The women's club to which Alice had been a member for twenty-six years pledged that "henceforth all scholarships will be given in her name."[5] On April 28, 1991, at the Palm Desert Country Club, where she had worked and played tennis for about twenty years, her memory was honored with a commemorative plaque, and the main lounge was dedicated in her name. Her friend Bob Corwin led a sing-along featuring Alice's favorite songs. The attendees were told they could look forward to reading *Courting Danger*, to be published the following month.[6]

Dreams of a comeback died with Marble, much to Leatherman's sorrow: "I wanted her to survive. I wanted her to see the book, wanted us to go on tour. I wanted her to go back to Wimbledon in triumph, waving the book there and at the US Open. I wanted her to have a last hurrah."

Among the nods Marble missed was a review by the critic Jonathan Yardley of the *Washington Post*:

> *Suzanne Lenglen, Helen Wills Moody, Helen Jacobs, Alice Marble—they were the great players of the earliest years of women's tennis, international figures in their day but largely forgotten now by the general public and, less forgivably, by the hugely successful players for whom they laid the groundwork. We think of them, if we think of them at all, as genteel ladies in skirts; in reality they were tough women whose lacy costumes did not fully disguise the grit it took to succeed at their demanding game.*
>
> *Arguably the most celebrated of them was Alice Marble. . . . She died late last year at the age of 77, but before her death had completed work with Dale Leatherman on* Courting Danger, *the story of a life that really was more interesting off the court than on.*[7]

On April 15, 1991, *Publishers Weekly* declared there was "nary a dull moment in this fast-moving glamorous tale." On June 9, 1991, the *New York Times Book Review* praised Marble's account in the book for its "remarkable lack of self-pity, displaying the courage, candor and wit that made her a winner." On May 15, 1991, *Library Journal* predicted that "Marble's hair-raising exploits as a spy" and the "inherent melodrama of this remarkable woman's life" would appeal to "lovers of romance."

A writer named Jeff Brown in the July 29, 1991, issue of *People Weekly* offered a rare skeptical opinion about the "high-stakes spying," saying it "strains credulity," as related by Marble. "Can we believe all this? And that plucky Alice—having learned to shoot, fight dirty and open safes—takes off for Geneva, where the banker does turn up? The rest is as weirdly dramatic— and implausible—as any Hitchcock thriller. After such a tale, Marble's concluding comments on today's tennis players are monumentally anticlimactic. 'Martina Navratilova,' she says modestly, 'would have wiped me out.' Probably right. On the other hand, Martina has never shown the slightest ability to outfox Nazis, crack safes or dodge bullets."

One final document survived Marble: her last will and testament, originally filed on May 30, 1975.

In the will, Marble wrote, "I declare myself to be the widow of Joseph N. Crowley; that I have no children, living or deceased."

Marble left 10 percent of her cash assets to the United Church of the Desert in Palm Desert, a sum of $1,568.25, and the remainder of the estate originally to her siblings Hazel and George but now exclusively to Hazel, with George deceased and Tim a marginalized member of the family.[8] Marble's house sold for $84,800, and her 1975 Mercury Cougar for $600. After Hazel took possession of any personal items she wished to keep, she donated some property to the International Tennis Hall of Fame and sold the rest at auction. She directed that no memorial or funeral service be held in her sister's honor.

"She wanted her ashes scattered at Wimbledon," said Leatherman. "I called, but they said no. They sounded horrified. 'We can't have ashes scattered on the grounds.' My memory from 1990 is they were never claimed. I hope I'm wrong. I hope she's spread out somewhere that she loved, perhaps across the [San Francisco] Bay."

Alice Marble lives on, in the places that bear her name and in the memories of those who were touched by her because they either knew her or knew of her.

The Alice Marble Tennis Courts on Russian Hill, owned by the San Francisco Recreation and Parks Department, with their view of the bay and the Golden Gate Bridge, are considered gems. The International Tennis Federation launched the Alice Marble Cup for women in the sixty-plus age category in 1988. Marble's name comes up in college courses. Dr. Ashley Brown, an assistant professor in the Department of History at the University of Wisconsin–Madison, includes Marble in her lecture to undergraduates in a sports-history survey course. She explained the inclusion as part of an ongoing email correspondence and occasional phone call with the author:

> *I remind students that, while "heroes" are constructed figures made by the times in which they live and to suit the needs of interested publics, people can live, work, and use their prominence in ways to inspire and affect change. I place Marble in a broad overview that includes the reasons Joe DiMaggio, Joe Louis, and Hank Greenberg were considered heroes to various groups during their times. I draw upon the material in my article, "Swinging for the State Department," to link Marble to the concept of the hero/heroine because of her volunteer service during World War II, the admirable standing that she had among American sportswomen, and the sympathetic ear that she gave lesbian servicewomen that she encountered during the war. I also mention her friendship with Bill Tilden.*

The sleepy desert town of Palm Springs that nurtured Marble back to health in the 1930s is now the site of major tennis tournaments, over a hundred golf courses, an international film festival, an annual event called Modernism Week, the Coachella music festival, and pilgrimages to Joshua Tree National Park for premium stargazing, thanks to the dark sky and lack of light pollution. Palm Springs, which sat the first all-LGBT city council in the nation, is considered one of the most gay-friendly cities in America.

Contemporary visitors to the Coachella Valley are often amused by the bombardment of famous names strewn throughout, many with ties to old-time Hollywood: Bing Crosby Drive, Gene Autry Trail, Jack Benny Road, Bob Hope Drive, Burns and Allen Road, Kirk Douglas Way. Elvis Presley honeymooned in Palm Springs; Sinatra is buried nearby. As Alice put it, "Everybody in the world comes to Palm Springs, even Prince Charles."[9] Commemorating her are Alice Marble Lane and Alice Marble Hall, the recreation room of the homeowners' association in the development where Marble last lived. A small display of artifacts hanging on the wall at the entrance was created after Marble's death: ten photographs, two newspaper articles, one book excerpt, five proclamations, and the cover of the August 28, 1939, issue of *Life* magazine.[10]

Osamu Funato, who currently lives in Alice Marble's childhood home in San Francisco, keeps slippers by the front door for guests and readily brews tea for visitors. It is very much the same modest house the Marble family filled with music and poker games and big breakfasts. When he reviewed the list of previous owners of his house and saw the name Marble among them, he was thrilled. "It makes no sense," says Funato, wondering how a championship tennis player who achieved such stature during her lifetime, on and off the court, could appear to be so little heralded in death. The first-floor bedroom contains a collection of black-and-white photos of the tennis star from her glory years, purchased on eBay, as well as a copy of the *Life* magazine with Marble on the cover.

The house is set back from the street, unusual in a neighborhood where every inch counts. In the front yard are a garden and the sixty steps to the front door. The views north include Golden Gate Park and the Golden Gate Bridge and Marin County, where Alice and her siblings enjoyed daylong Sunday hikes years ago. Funato feels the house is filled with a "good spirit." In front of their home, visible to a passerby, Funato and his wife have posted a grayish-green marble plaque surrounded by succulents with the street numbers and the word "Alice" engraved in gold in a dancing script that echoes her real signature, including her round, generous, assertive *A*.

Born in 1913. Peaked in 1939. Carried on until 1990. History never favored Marble. Not after she became the most decorated woman in tennis in her time—just as the whole world went dark, and the pursuit of athletic distinction became a detachable luxury easily jettisoned in a world gone mad. After the war ended, people were so eager to create shiny futures—superhighways, space exploration, the baby boom—they did not want to look back. It was as if the war had swallowed up everything that came right before it. Marble entered middle age in the 1950s. It was an era known for discouraging mature self-expression and worldly success in women outside the home. Cry hard enough on televised contests such as *Queen for a Day*, and a Maytag dishwasher just might be yours. The years drifted by, with fewer high points to distinguish them. Just as she was about to reenter the public arena with *Courting Danger*, scheduled to come out in the following spring, death in December denied her one last star turn.

"She gloried in being the center of attention," Rita Mae Brown put it. "She missed her curtain call."[11]

Today Alice's living relatives, first- and second-generation descendants of her brothers, share a 50 percent ownership of the royalties from *Courting Danger*, both the book and any potential film deals. Her estate was small. The trophies had almost all been distributed over the course of her lifetime. A set of Wimbledon trophies had gone to a friend in the women's club at a dinner dance on the friend's eightieth birthday, Alice's mark of "esteem and affection for the honoree."[12] As for the others, they also were, like so much else, gone with the wind, as Alice acknowledged years ago in a letter dated September 4, 1964, in response to a friend, addressed only by his first name, Henry: "I have but one National Singles trophy left and I'm sending it off to you . . . All but just a few trophies (of the 750 I won) have been spread around the world to friends and family."

The trust fund set up by Will du Pont reverted to his grandchildren immediately upon Alice's death.

Courtney Gebhart, the interviewer for the Palm Springs Public Library's historical project, believes Marble was ahead of her time.

What bothers me is that all these women before us who paid the price like Marble are disappearing. No one remembers who they were. Maybe it is about to change. This time where we are right now, . . . I want to think it's a huge turning point. I don't feel as if we ever know in the moment that we are in a trailblazing time, but I feel it now. Even Serena going back after having a baby . . . It's exciting to see tennis open up. I studied the players way back, the crazy cool characters: Nastase, McEnroe, Chrissie. It lulled out for a while, but then, thanks to Serena with her outfits, and others, it's come back in. When someone brings who they are to the sport, the game is so much more exciting to partake in or even watch, even as a spectator. Marble brought who she was to the endeavor. She might not have started that trend, but she pushed it along. She has my respect forever.[13]

Linda Marble McCrory, granddaughter of Alice's brother George, is the self-appointed keeper of the Marble family flame, eager to learn anything new she can about her great-aunt Alice to store along with some distant memories of when, as a young child, she saw Marble visit her grandparents and granduncles and grandaunt from time to time.

As I have gotten older, I have been trying to learn more and to appreciate more about what she went through to get to where she did. Even though I was born in San Francisco, I had never driven by her old house, which I did a few years ago on my sister's birthday. We followed the walk she took to the courts. It was a straight shot, but it was a hefty walk, not a hop, skip, jump. We took photos where she would have practiced. In some of the photos from when she got old, you would never guess she had been a great athlete. But there is this one video from the late seventies. She is on the courts, coming toward the camera, swinging her racket. I remember watching her and thinking, She looks more hardcore at that age than even when she was young. . . . Oh my God, she is still a badass.[14]

Billie Jean King remembers Alice best as the coach from when she was sixteen and spent Saturdays overnight at her home in Southern California. In the evenings, after grueling workouts, Alice would spin tales from the past. "When we first met, I was just a kid. You couldn't tell if she was telling the truth."

Billie Jean is not sure Teach did Marble any favors in the long run: "Teach never let up. She was so tough. She made it about her instead of the pupil."

Nonetheless Billie Jean identifies Marble as the first "*female* sports-activist": "Sure, there had been a few sportswomen who became sensations—Suzanne Lenglen, Alice Marble, Althea Gibson, and Maureen Connolly in tennis; the golfers Patty Berg, Mickey Wright, and Kathy Whitworth; the figure skater Peggy Fleming; the sprinter Wilma Rudolph; and the all-around athlete Babe Didrikson Zaharias. But none of them was overtly political except for Alice, through her advocacy for Althea's inclusion. Alice was a feminist too. She used to talk at length about how every woman athlete owes a debt to the women before her."[15]

Star athletes die twice, first when they give up their sport at the highest level, and then they die again, in the fullness of whatever earthly time has been allotted. Between the first death and the second, their job is to content themselves with life on a different level, filled not so much with big public wins as smaller personal ones—ordinary happiness, good relationships, purposeful work. They must make peace with what Alice had in another context so aptly called "the dull, unadventurous earth."[16]

Billie Jean King tells current players, especially the ones who have achieved great heights, that their time in the sun will not last forever. She dispenses advice about managing their money: "You have to be really care-ful about this. At some point, those days are gone. When you are finished playing, don't expect anything. Keep moving and have a life and help others."

Billie Jean is, finally, filled with admiration for her old coach. "She changed my life for the better. She just had that extra something. She was a champion. She had it in every way; she had a presence; she was articulate. She was so colorful and so wonderful in so many ways."[17]

"Even a starlet has a better chance at a future than a jock," said Rita Mae Brown. "Alice, by refusing to marry Will du Pont, essentially screwed herself," adding that when Mary K. Browne died, Alice was "up shit creek."[18]

The last time Brown saw her friend was a happy quiet occasion at Marble's home sometime during the year before her death. Alice had a "rapt audience" in Brown, who remembers Alice "floating in her pool drink in hand, regaling me with a tale about Spencer Tracy making a pass at her and saying, 'Kate and I have an understanding.'"[19]

Brown had her own understanding of the complicated business of being Alice Marble: "There wasn't much Alice couldn't do except make sense of her own life."[20]

CHAPTER 31

GAME, SET, MATCH . . . AND QUESTIONS

FOR A WOMAN WHO LIKED to portray herself as a simple farmer's daughter with a straightforward, uplifting story of betterment based on the will to win, Marble managed to lead a convoluted life, made more so by a tendency to gild the lily, to embellish where none is necessary.

Her life overflows with stunning victories and verifiable accomplishments, as an athlete but in other spheres as well. She did pal around with movie stars, she did design clothing, she did sing in public, she did write columns demanding long overdue changes in tennis and getting them. But, it appears, sometimes her imagination outran the facts.

Perhaps it is petty to accuse Marble of what might be called hyperbole, one of the basic tools of storytelling, beloved of poets and hucksters alike. Is it such a sin, the desire to take a good story and make it better? And what about the external pressure brought to bear on Marble by the press with its impulse toward hagiography when it comes to athletes? So much of Marble's life was led out loud, in interviews in which she was routinely pictured as larger than life.

Some of the inconsistencies in her story are more than understandable. Marble always claimed her father died on Christmas Eve, making a woeful loss more woeful, yet the death certificate indicates he died on January 1 and was cremated two days later. It seems likely that the uncelebrated Christmas holiday and the actual date of her father's death conflated in Marble's six-year-old mind, and her grown-up mind never managed to correct the misconception.

Over the years, the saga of "The Little Queen of Swat" received upgrades. The original article had no byline, but Marble liked to claim that

Curley Grieve had written it, adding a layer of prestige. Grieve eventually earned great stature as the sports editor of the San Francisco Examiner, but Marble's version of his résumé is off the mark. Born in 1902 in Belleville, Illinois, Grieve worked for the *Salt Lake Tribune* and the *Rocky Mountain News*, and at the time the article about Marble appeared, he was listed, under his formal name, Vernon Grieve, as "sports editor News" in the Denver, Colorado, 1927 city directory. He did not join the *San Francisco Examiner* until 1931. During his editorship, he did interview Marble and members of her family many times, so perhaps she mixed up the original interview with one of those interactions.

Of that fateful day when she first tasted fame, Marble often claimed, "My hero, Lefty O'Doul, asked me to shag flies for him." There is no mention in any of the original accounts that Lefty O'Doul himself summoned her onto the field that day, though she did meet him in person as the years went on. She also told Dale Leatherman, and others, that Joe DiMaggio, beside her in center field, "yelled encouragement."[1] At that time, DiMaggio was a child even younger than Alice. He joined the Seals for the last three games of the 1932 season, when he subbed for another player as a shortstop. (For the record, DiMaggio was discovered by Lefty O'Doul—who took little credit, saying he was just smart enough to leave him alone.)

Two childhood incidents described in *Courting Danger* (and earlier in this account) defy verification, traumas not previously reported in her innumerable retellings of her saga. The first—witnessing the death of a playmate named Billy run over by a trolley—occurred in the same year that her father died: "I'd seen my father and my best friend put into the ground in less than a year."[2] An examination of San Francisco papers from the time frame when the incident would logically have occurred in 1920, at around the time of her father's death, did not yield corroborating data. That doesn't mean it didn't happen, just that if there is proof, it is hard to find, especially since Marble identified the victim by only his first name. However, if one expands the time frame, a report in the *Fresno Bee* on February 15, 1923, may have provided the inspiration for the story, the details of which Marble later changed. The headlines read:

TRAILER KILLS 7-YEAR OLD BOY
LAD FALLS FROM BICYCLE AND UNDER WHEELS OF VEHICLE

The story said, "Billie Hockelberg 7, of 2522 Browley Avenue, was fatally injured when he fell down from a bicycle between a truck and a trailer and a wheel from the trailer passed over his body. The truck onto which Billie was hanging was driven by Harold Dickenson, 635 Stafford Street." Could it be the same Harold Dickenson who introduced Marble to Teach? Born in 1902, he would have been twenty-one years old at the time of the accident. Employed by Dyas, a Los Angeles sporting-goods retailer, his duties required going on the road as a salesman. The 1920 and 1930 census both have him living at home in Los Angeles; there is no one by that name living in Fresno in the same census years. The address in the Fresno paper may not have been his full-time residence, but a boarding or rooming house in which he stayed while there on business. If it is indeed the same Harold Dickenson, perhaps he shared this tragic story with Marble, and changing some elements, she repurposed it, folding it into her repertoire.

As for the rape that occurred as she was leaving the tennis courts at Golden Gate Park, it was common practice to hide sexual assaults in those days, so the absence of any official record is not a surprise. Assuming it did happen, Marble's decision to conceal the crime from her mother to spare her an added burden must have added to the lonely horror of the experience.

Contemporary accounts of Marble's calamity at the tournament at the Maidstone Club on Long Island indicate that she lost twelve pounds on July 31, 1933. As time went on, the weight loss climbed from twelve to thirteen to fourteen pounds and stayed there. In her telling, the temperature also climbed at least four degrees higher than the highest temperature reported during the long heat wave, to 108 degrees—one for each game played. Whatever her inconsistencies here, all can agree: it was beastly hot that day.

Time proves elastic more than once. In an interview with Beverly Beyette of the *Los Angeles Times* on June 22, 1983, the four-and-a-half-month-long pro tour with sixty-one stops became "seven months of one-night stands in seventy cities." She stretched out her stint in the wartime role of official government spokeswoman from nine months to two years.

Marble's life was filled with celebrity sightings and friendships, but sometimes it appears she upped the ante, with phantom sightings and friend-ships. Did she really meet George Bernard Shaw at the Hearst mansion, and did Shaw really say, "Young lady, I admire the moles on your back"? Photos from the castle show Shaw with his host and hostess and prancing in his elfin style around the grounds. There appear to be none with Marble.

As for the moles, what happened to them as time passed? When she bared her back after the war to show the effects of bullet wounds, Dale Leatherman and others noticed scars. Such disfigurements can be caused by gunshots, but they are also a common result of surgical excisions.

At a party in a mansion after losing during the 1937 US National Championships at Forest Hills, Marble said she had spent part of the evening chatting with the elderly Felix Moritz Warburg and that he was found dead the next morning. She recalled that his grieving family implored her to remember everything he had said to her the night before.[3] This story, while touching, does not jibe with facts. The tournament at Forest Hills took place from September 2 to September 11, the period Marble was staying with the Warburgs on Long Island. The *New York Times* wrote that the older man's death occurred about five weeks later, on October 20, in New York City, attended by his wife and their five children.[4] He died at one in the afternoon after having been bedridden for several days.[5]

Marble shared memories in *Courting Danger* of how she led the parade at the opening of the Golden Gate Bridge: "Senator Phelan invited me to be the first person to cross the bridge. Again, I was treated to a convertible ride, a cheering crowd (San Franciscans love parades), and a ribbon-cutting ceremony at the end of the bridge."[6]

If Alice was at the bridge, she joined a cast of thousands upon thousands celebrating the modern marvel on May 27, 1937. Senator James D. Phelan could not have escorted her, as he had died seven years earlier, in 1930, and had ended his career in public office in 1921. In an era that loved a stunt, the actual opening was for pedestrians only, with many individuals vying to set records to be the first to, for example, tap dance across its forty-two-hundred-foot span, walk it backwards, cross it by a unicycle, or proceed on stilts. The most convincing evidence against her being there is that on May 27, 1937, she advanced to the women's singles semifinals at the Middlesex championships in England.[7] On May 29, Anita Lizana defeated Marble, 9–7, 9–7, in the Middlesex women's singles final.[8] Shortly after, Alice won Wimbledon's mixed doubles title with Don Budge.

Whenever Marble mentioned attending the premiere of *Gone with the Wind*, she specified the legendary December 15 opening in Atlanta, but exhaustive press accounts do not document her presence there. It seems she mentally got herself invited retroactively to a party she never attended. However, her name was linked to the opening in Los Angeles later that month, on December 28, a celebration that overflowed with stars flaunting fabulous garments, including Vivien Leigh in a fuchsia soufflé gown sprinkled with sequins.[9]

Marble had a gift for summoning celebrities at a moment's notice, as in her version of the dramatic breakup with Teach, which Marble indicates occurred shortly after the war ended. This is a harrowing story and must have been devastating for both women. Banished to the park to cool her heels while Teach angrily packed her belongings in their shared apartment, no less a light than Marlene Dietrich happened to come by, at least in Marble's star-studded memory, her grandchild in tow, sharing a happy memory. Once again, the timetable is muddled. Dietrich did not become a grandmother until several years later, June 28, 1948, earning her the title, "World's Most Glamorous Grandma."

Marble often began the story of her stay at the Pottenger Sanatorium in Monrovia with the not-quite-accurate phrase, "When I had TB . . ." When she tried to join the service during World War II, she said she was rejected when she told the recruitment officers of her history of TB—instead of the more accurate diagnosis of pleurisy with effusion.

Even accomplishments about which there is no doubt invited filigree. Yes, she wrote a "scathing article" about Althea Gibson and how the tennis hierarchy refused to let her compete on the eastern tour. Yes, she called them hypocrites, and the piece had the effect of shaming them into eventually changing their policies. Her further claim that Harvard awarded her an honorary degree in journalism has no basis in reality. Harvard does not give degrees in journalism, honorary or otherwise. The institution did not give its first honorary degree to a woman until 1955, to Helen Keller.[10]

Any student of Marble's life must weigh the veracity of certain alliances. Was Rod Serling really a lover? Yes, if you read *Serling: The Rise and Twilight of Television's Last Angry Man*, a biography by Gordon F. Sander. Maybe not, when you realize that Sander's only source was Marble herself in *Courting Danger*.

AT A CERTAIN POINT, the habit of inflation became so ingrained as to be reflexive. One could charitably argue that many of the inconsistencies cited here are minor inventions, and in any long life, events and dates merge and muddle and morph, but two interlocking narrative threads pose more riddles than they unravel. The first is her marriage, about which she offered vague and contradictory details over the years, and the second is her time as a spy, filled with as many alleged twists and turns as the chase scene at its hair-raising finale. They pose the deepest challenges to crafting a full and accurate account of Marble's life, however much they add to her mystique.

The press began printing rumors of an upcoming marriage before the war ended, such as the report in the *Albany Democrat-Herald* (Albany, Oregon) on January 24, 1944: "Alice Marble, queen of the world's tennis courts, revealed today that she will be married as soon as the war is over and that she is through with competitive tennis. Her husband-to-be is a 'very special guy' named Joe, an army captain overseas, she told the United Press in an exclusive interview. But she refused to reveal his last name. She said their romance began a year and a half ago when they met at a party in New York."

In Marble's 1946 memoir, the Joe Crowley who died in the war was a fiancé and not a husband. Marble introduced the story of Joe on the second-to-last page of *The Road to Wimbledon*. In that telling, they met when she was performing one evening for servicemen with a little three-piece orchestra, and she noticed him walk into the room: "He was brown-haired, and stocky, not terribly tall."

> *Joe was a captain* [though sometimes he changed rank to lieutenant] *in the army intelligence service, and soon we were spending every moment we could together. I found myself waiting for his telephone calls, waiting all evening at home hoping he would come in. Joe was in the intelligence* [sic] *because of his ability to speak five languages. He came from Kansas, had educated himself at Ohio State College, graduated as an engineer, and was on his way to big things when the war came. It maddened me that he couldn't talk about his job, for I wanted to know everything he thought, everything he did. But it was wonderful just to be with him, sometimes for only a half hour of talk, other times when we rode up and down on the Fifth Avenue bus or went to dinner at some small restaurant with sawdust on the floor.*

She said she didn't want to marry him immediately: "It just didn't seem right." She had seen "so many girls make hurried decisions about marrying their soldiers."

Her account continues:

One night a week before Christmas, when I had pressed my clothes, packed my bag and at nine o'clock was leaving for another tour, the telephone rang. It was Joe's commanding officer. The Colonel's voice trembled when he said that a report had just come in that Joe and six other officers had crashed and died in a flight over Germany.

On Christmas Eve I opened a small box to find a bottle of my favorite perfume, and a letter from Joe written two weeks before.

In that moment she concluded, "Life was over, or so it seemed to me." And yet, as she wrote, in an amazingly quick recovery, on paper if not in fact, she had overcome being a loser in the past and she hoped she would overcome this loss as well. The book ends with a pep talk: "I know that everyone is endowed with the qualities of the champion and can succeed in spite of handicaps in the most important game—the game of life."

By the time Dale Leatherman heard the story, as it is recounted in *Courting Danger*, the plot had thickened. Marble eventually claimed to her and others that she and Joe had married in a ceremony, on the Hudson River, officiated by a navy chaplain, and the only witnesses were hundreds of smartly dressed sailors sworn to secrecy. It had to be that way—his sensitive military assignment required it. She presented Joe as a paragon: "Joe had been Mr. Right for me. After he was gone, he was too hard to duplicate."[11]

In some versions, Joe had managed to get leave and visit her in Panama during her WAC tour. That story begins with a car accident. A GI chauffeur charged with getting Marble to her matches skidded off the road onto a precipice with a fifty-degree angle. Twenty feet away, the mountain dropped into a valley one thousand feet below. She crawled her way out of the vehicle. For two weeks she was out of commission while her hands, which took the brunt of her injuries, healed. Fortunately, Joe was able to fly in, and finally they had a honeymoon. When Marble returned to New York, she realized she was pregnant.

In the account shared with Leatherman, Marble had not only secretly married Crowley but also suffered a miscarriage—caused by another car accident, this one on Long Island, while he was serving overseas. A drunk driver crossed over to her side of the road and forced her into a ditch. Teach and Brownie flanked her hospital bed so they were her first sight when she opened her eyes and asked, "The baby?" Marble vowed to tell Joe about both the baby and its loss all at once, when he came home for Christmas.

Brownie answered, "But you're okay. You and Joe will have another chance to start a family." Neither Teach nor Brownie was still alive to confirm this account.

While recovering from that trauma, Alice told Leatherman, she was informed of her husband's death, in an even more dramatic way than in earlier accounts: "Christmas has never been a joyous occasion for me, not with the memory of my father's death on Christmas Eve, but this year was different. I had recovered from the miscarriage, physically if not mentally, and I knew everything would be all right when Joe came home."

She described being at a party with Teach, Will du Pont, and Tica Madrigal. In the midst of the partygoers' caroling, the doorbell rang, and a man, in uniform, delivered a telegram. The guests, oblivious, continued singing "God Rest Ye, Merry Gentlemen" while Marble read the missive: "We regret to inform you that Joseph Crowley was killed in action when his plane was shot down over Germany."[12]

Next, in *Courting Danger*, readers learn about a suicide attempt, that very evening, with pills, from what she described as a "nearly full prescription" for sedatives she had for treating insomnia while on tour.

In every account, whether fiancé or husband, Joe Crowley died toward the end of the war, though not always in the same month or even year. In a 1981 interview, she gave the latest date for his death, saying he was shot down over Germany on a reconnaissance flight in late April 1945, two weeks before the war with Germany ended. This time frame negates her motive for the spy mission in the first place: a kind of long-term uncontrolled grief that needed to be sublimated into meaningful action.

As for a motive, if she was making Joe up, some have suggested that he was a convenient mock-up character to cover for Alice's lesbian predilections, at a time when Alice was marketing herself, and homosexuality was not easily accepted. The marriage records of New York City reveal no official document for Joseph Norman Crowley and Alice Irene Marble between 1943 and 1944. No searchers have been able to locate his military record either.

Did Joe Crowley even exist, or was he concocted by Marble to give her the mantle of heterosexual respectability and a built-in excuse for why she was not married? (Or remarried: it is hard to imagine any subsequent suitor living up to such a paragon.) It was not unheard of for gay men and women to enter heterosexual alliances or to make up a partner of the opposite sex to survive in a hostile social environment. Yet in Marble's own inner circle, she had examples of same-sex relationships. Helen Jacobs, who went by Jake, had commenced a partnership in 1934 with Louisville heiress Henrietta Bingham, which lasted until 1943, and neither woman tried to hide it. After her marriage to du Pont broke up, Margaret Osborne du Pont had an intimate relationship with their friend Margaret Varner Bloss, also an athlete, who had worked as her husband's social secretary and their son's tutor. The two women moved to El Paso after du Pont died, where they operated a ranch and gave their horses tennis-themed names: Tennis Star, Super Set, Court Shot, and Net Effect.[13]

Much skepticism also exists about Marble's days as a secret agent, on similar grounds: lack of evidence. One observer in an online history group posted a common-sense question: "Would Army Intelligence have recruited a woman who had just had a miscarriage, lost her husband and attempted suicide all in the space of about 7 months to be a spy?"[14]

Dale Leatherman, on the other hand, believes Alice's story, as recounted to her at the end of Alice's life, in one of many interviews with the author:

> She had no reason to make it up. She had already gotten as much attention as she craved. Never got the sense that she was craving a return to the spotlight. I got the sense that her life had been completed. A done deal, and she didn't need to do more. She could rest on her laurels. Also, it seemed to be something she wanted to talk about while she still could. Everything I asked her about the incident, she had an answer. It was just there. And when I repeated the same questions in a different way, it all came out the same. It would be so difficult to fabricate the details. No reason. No incentive. She really didn't care. Finally, what motive was being served by lying at this point in her life?

When there was still hope that a movie would be made, Leatherman sent a fax[15] explaining to Anne Hopkins at Marian Rees Productions on April 18, 1985, sharing her theory of Hans's identity:

"The most compelling verification I have is a conversation I had (and taped) with Mary Bancroft, author of *Autobiography of a Spy*. Bancroft was the mistress of Allen Dulles, director of the OSS bureau in Switzerland during World War II."

Bancroft indicated she had a "good idea of who 'Hans' was, but wasn't willing to say."

Leatherman's own sleuthing led her to conclude that the obvious candidate was Baron de Blonay. Leatherman said he was known by other tennis pros in Switzerland. He came from a prominent family, and he loved sports. Baron de Blonay was allegedly on hand at Roland-Garros when Marble collapsed, and might have been the person she had the brief affair with while in France.

Leatherman argued that the "skeptics of Alice's spy story don't realize how easy it was to become a spy in the 1940s." She wrote to Hopkins that the OSS operated "storefronts in Washington, New York, and other cities where people could just walk in off the street and say, 'I want to be a spy.'" Prior to World War II, this country had no need for an intelligence service. The OSS came into being at that time, and all branches of the service trained and deployed their own agents.

She ended her letter vouching for Marble's integrity:

"In light of the spy stuff we see today, Alice's spy story seems so simple, but that was the reality of the day. I must add that I personally witnessed her incredible memory, and saw the scar from the bullet wound in her back.

"Though she was a heavy drinker during the time I knew her, Alice never contradicted any aspect of her story. I think she was a woman of uncommon integrity and patriotism."

It is true that amateurs were recruited to work for the OSS during World War II and that the organization had an improvisational quality, channeling young men, many from Yale and Harvard, into its initial higher-level ranks.[16] Women generally worked as secretaries. Most had to fulfill OSS director William Donovan's checklist for a desirable pedigree: "The right type of office worker was a cross between a Smith College graduate, a Powers model, and a Katie Gibbs secretary."[17] Marble scored two out of three: She had had training with John Robert Powers (the man who shared the secrets of charm with women and is credited with inventing the concept of the supermodel), and she knew how to type. Donovan called the women who patiently organized the paperwork for the OSS its "invisible apron strings." A very few broke free of those ranks to work in map making and cryptography. Not many went overseas, and fewer still had a dramatic non-clerical posting.[18] Marble's assignment, as she narrated it to Leatherman, fell into the "fewer still" percentage of those both going abroad and working an operation, though in neutral Switzerland, not enemy territory.

It is also true that the United States had its eyes on Switzerland and potentially fraught financial dealings, as embodied in the US government's Project Safehaven, created "to make it impossible for Germany to start another war." One strategy was "to prevent Germany from sequestering assets in neutral countries." Switzerland's role was significant, according to the CIA: "Swiss banks acted as clearinghouses whereby German gold—much of which was looted from occupied countries—could be converted to a more suitable medium of exchange." The project started in late 1944, and the OSS eventually became involved.[19]

The OSS indeed recruited from the ranks of Americans who might not be suspected to be spies: a chef, an actor, athletes. The most well known is Julia Child who, when she interviewed with the OSS, was called "pleasant, alert, capable, very tall."[20] Her background was tailor-made for OSS females: Smith graduate, moneyed family, proficient typist. Her first assignment was research assistant, working for Donovan, typing "thousands of names on little white note cards, a system that was needed to keep track of officers during the days before computers."[21]

Among the more famous of the recruited athletes was Moe Berg, a Major League Baseball catcher. Berg spoke several languages, devoured newspapers and books, and attended the Sorbonne, Princeton University, and Columbia Law School. He was the kind of person who could talk to Albert Einstein or be the butt of a joke. A teammate, when told Berg could speak in seven languages, retorted: "Yeah, I know, and he can't hit in any of them."[22] Closer to Alice, her old friend and rival Helen Jacobs also worked in espionage during the war.

In the early days of the Cold War, the CIA recruited tennis player Fred Kovaleski, who played tennis with a KGB Russian defector, priming him to spill information. In an article in the *Washington Post Magazine*, Kovaleski's son, Serge, said of the two secret agents: "My father could easily have upstaged the Russian on the court, but instead he focused on building rallies so [Yuri] Rastvorov had a hard workout. 'I never hit a winner against him,' he said. 'The idea was to make him feel better about himself, to soothe his ego. And I think the tennis was real therapy for him.'"[23]

Yes, women worked as spies during World War II, but rarely in the field. Yes, athletes joined the list of government recruits. But did Marble? Her passport, issued on February 15, 1944, lists her occupation as "tennis player and lecturer." Stamps indicate permission to land in Kingston, Jamaica, on February 21 and to visit Guatemala on March 17 and Panama on July 26, that year; to visit England in June and Ireland in July 1946; and England again and Sweden in 1947. As far as the United States government is concerned, she did not leave the country in 1945.

The timetable of her own account of her work does more than strain credulity. It flatly contradicts her spying claims. She said she had four weeks in Switzerland, followed by time in an army hospital recovering from the bullet wound. If she returned to the United States as she said, on May 7, 1945, she would have been on her mission throughout much of April. Clearly this was not true, since she was documented in several places in the United States midway through April.

The *Minneapolis Star-Journal* reported that Marble had arrived on the University of Minnesota campus on Thursday, April 19, 1945, for a talk: "Alice Marble, former American women's tennis champion, came to Minneapolis sans tennis rackets and luggage. It wasn't an oversight, the tennis queen said. She finds it's easier to travel light these days."[24] That afternoon about a thousand people watched Marble play an exhibition match at the university's field house with coach Phil Brain and another with Norm MacDonald, a Minneapolis amateur player.[25] A few days later, on April 22, Marble was in Chicago on WGN radio during its *Distinguished Guest Hour.* Her announced topic was "Physical Fitness and the Will to Win."[26] The following day, she was a guest on WBBM's *Melody Lane* sharing her beautiful voice, in songs like "People Will Say We're in Love," "Blue Skies," "Smoke Gets in Your Eyes," and "Beautiful Lady."[27] On April 26, 1945, the *Springfield Leader and Press* in Missouri wrote that Marble delivered a "stereotyped speech" about "following the rules" for health at Drury University. But in a question-and-answer session after, she loosened up, conceding to smoking cigarettes ("a filthy habit") and not getting enough sleep or eating the "right food." Moreover, while on the road, she shortchanged exercise except jumping rope, a "daily must." Alice was well dressed: black skirt, white blouse with a green tie, a "natty" jacket tucked at the waist. She had a full day's schedule: lunch on campus, tennis demonstration at O'Reilly Hospital, afternoon faculty tea, and an evening event at the hospital.[28]

One comment in Marble's story to Leatherman may further understanding about whether her spy story has credibility. She said the authorities planned to send her to Switzerland for some well-publicized clinics and exhibitions, and then let Hans find her.

The key phrase here is "well-publicized." News stories about Marble in Geneva at that time would lend credence to the tale, but there is no mention of a series of exhibition matches in any issues of *American Lawn Tennis* during the time frame in question, the winter and spring of 1945. The magazine prided itself on casting a wide net. In the same general time frame of the alleged exhibitions in Geneva, the magazine featured headlines such as "India Holds National Chps."[29] and "Jack Kramer in New Guinea."[30] With its stated mission of saturation coverage of the world of tennis, the magazine would surely have kept tabs on exhibition matches in Switzerland featuring Alice Marble.

At least one detail in Marble's account has a basis in fact. Marble said in *Courting Danger* she was given a spy camera, and it was a "snap to use." Eastman Kodak did manufacture spy cameras for the OSS during World War II. The camera, designed to fit inside a European-style matchbox, was about two and a quarter inches long and two and three-quarter inches high. It used sixteen millimeter film and produced half-inch-square photos. The camera was intended for spies and not available to the public.[31] A concrete detail of that sort could have come from any number of sources, including from her old friend Helen Jacobs, who along with only four other women, achieved the rank of commander in the US Navy Intelligence during World War II.

ALICE MARBLE SEEMED to believe in what happened and what might have happened with equal fervor. Was there a pattern to her prevarication? Did she take something with a basis in fact and pump it up, to make herself sound either less isolated or more heroic? Why was enough not enough?

Perhaps being famous in her teens and twenties meant belonging to others in a way that didn't allow her a chance to belong to herself. Perhaps deficits from a childhood in which she suffered the loss of a parent left her less equipped for the fray as she got older. During the span of Marble's most intense fame, in the 1930s, she submitted to the kind of mythmaking usually associated with movie stars, shape-shifters in the service of story, paid to become, in the camera's glare, someone else. As early as 1936, not yet twenty-three, she had expressed an odd feeling of disassociation to a reporter (noted earlier), right after winning the US Nationals: "I told my story of ill-ness, despair, and comeback so many times, I began to feel as if I were talking about someone else, some fictional character."[32]

There is also the matter of the degree to which the press, with its bar-rage of extravagant language and intense attention, distorted Marble's idea of her place in the world and her value to humanity. She had become a product almost before she had a chance to be a person. Did her vast and early fame made her ill equipped to handle changing fortune, the slow, grinding loss of her athletic talent, and the diminutions of age? What happens to a person used to the limelight when all that scrutiny and sycophancy vanishes and migrates to the next new thing?

Absent absolute proof, but armed with convincing evidence, one can acknowledge that the life of Alice Marble had an extraordinary overstory with easily documented highs and lows, one filled with real pain and real glory. It also had an understory, written by a shadow self, filled with imagined pain and imagined glory. Someone inclined to judgment might call her a liar. Those who acknowledge nuance might consider calling her a fabulist or an unreliable narrator. Every life is a mystery in which some facts fail to fit neatly together. Perhaps hers was a more extreme case. Examined in that light, the alternative narrative does not negate the verifiable one so much as perfume it, heighten it in the way of Technicolor. Only someone drenched in the culture of movies could possibly have concocted a spy saga that resembles such a plot-heavy thriller, bursting with melodrama, mountainous roads, Nazis, plunder, champagne, and dialogue so bad it is almost good. Marble liked to surprise the guests at Hearst Castle with her arcane knowledge of stars and their movies, and how she was able to name every silent star and the roles they played. "When I was a child, ten cents let me into that magic world. I saw every movie that came to town," she told Dale Leatherman.[33] She supported her movie-going habit with a series of gigs: "I was a fry cook, I was a soda jerk, gift wrapper, babysitter so I could make enough money to go to the movies."[34]

Of all the possible figments, the disturbing story about the boy she and her husband adopted at age five, who died in 1963 in a car accident while he was in medical school at Harvard, appears to have been the least discussed, reported to one interviewer and no one else. What may be most telling is the timing of this disclosure. She had just turned fifty; her brother Dan had died days before, and she was working as a medical helper, chain-smoking while she gave tennis lessons, breaking it off with at least one promising pupil in a most destructive and self-defeating way. After so many years of proceeding through life like the child in the "Little Queen of Swat" photo, full steam ahead, it appears the ride had turned bumpy.

In the end, the instincts of two women with outstanding résumés of their own offer valuable perspective of a former coach on the one hand and a beloved friend on the other.

Billie Jean King, with whom Marble parted in such a volatile fashion, remembers how she and Marble "touched base from time to time as life went on. I saw her in Palm Springs and different places." It became increasingly clear to King that Alice could be "harsh in some ways. She was not one hundred percent emotionally, and she never got any help. She could have been bipolar, maybe depressed. By now in my life, I've done so much therapy myself, I might have recognized it better, but when we first met, I was just a kid."[35]

As for Alice's marriage and her derring-do: "You couldn't tell if she was telling the truth. I never knew what the truth was about loving Joe. The spy story, come on!"[36]

Rita Mae Browne visited "Champie" about once a year in the final decade of Marble's life, and she wrote or spoke to her two or three times a month. Brown recalled: "She told me she loved women as well as men. How she hid it. How she hated herself for hiding it. I think Alice wanted me to absolve her. It's not in my power to do that for anyone but I would say, 'You did what you thought was best. It was a different time.'"[37]

Brown wrote that she "loved Alice despite her drinking."

I should note here I am not remotely tolerant of alcohol or drug abuse, and if you're loaded, I will excuse myself. I simply can't stand it.

But I could stand it in Alice because I saw her fragility, her vanity. Eroded as her body was by the booze and by her various afflictions, she could still hit a tennis ball with precision and power.

And she knew tennis. I especially enjoy learning from someone as great as Alice, who changed the women's game forever. She upped the aggression with her net play and she introduced glamour . . . She could play on any surface.[38]

Later Brown reflected, "She was not a well-educated woman, but she absorbed everything. She was not born to be a housewife or a mother. She really was a buccaneer: she was unique and wild and a creature of the moment. I loved her. I really did."[39]

In her memoir, Brown had quipped, "Alice had a million stories, few of them true."[40]

It appears that in the beginning, Marble needed the fantasies in order to succeed. In her later years, she needed them in order to survive.

ACKNOWLEDGMENTS

W RITING A BOOK is both a solo endeavor and a team sport. I have many to thank for helping me bring this work to completion. Librarians rank high on the list. The unfailingly pleasant Penny White, Reference Librarian, Albert & Shirley Small Special Collections Library, University of Virginia, provided the Rita Mae Brown files. Lucas R. Clawson, Reference Archivist / Hagley Historian, Manuscripts and Archives Department Hagley Museum and Library, Wilmington, Delaware, provided William du Pont Jr. material and a research room overlooking the museum grounds, and readily gave assistance and insights into the Du Pont family and its amply documented history. Meredith Richards, Librarian, The Museum at the International Tennis Hall of Fame, Newport, Rhode Island, provided access to Alice Marble's scrapbooks as well as fascinating Hall of Fame interviews with tennis stars from Alice Marble's era. Ymelda Laxton, Manager of Research and Education, located valuable images of Marble and her peers. Marilee Colton of The Historical Society of Palm Desert in Palm Desert, California, responded to requests for material concerning Alice Marble's latter years, sending newspaper stories and a transcript of a 1980 interview, part of the society's oral history project. AnnaLee Pauls, Photoduplication Coordinator/Reference Assistant, Department of Special Collections, Princeton University Library, Princeton, New Jersey, was so capable and so efficient in sending Scribner's Alice Marble, Helen Wills, and Maxwell Perkins correspondence that her work deserves to be highlighted in stories about how to operate under pandemic restrictions. Paving the way was Adrienne Rusinko, Special Collections Assistant, and Will Noel, the John T. Maltsberger III '55 Associate University Librarian for Rare Books and Special Collection. Michael Spellmon, assistant director of the Groton Public Library in Connecticut, shared his expertise.

A special note of gratitude to Jeffrey L. Monseau, College Archivist, Archives and Special Collections, Springfield College, Springfield, Massachusetts, a touchstone throughout, providing the complete set of *American Lawn Tennis* and *The Racquet*, helping with scanning pages, and setting a rigorous pace.

As I tried to capture Marble in the round, I kept in mind the words of filmmaker Luis Bunuel: "You have to begin to lose your memory, if only in bits and pieces, to realize that memory is what makes our lives. Life without memory is no life at all."

I believe in conducting a geographical inventory of my subjects whenever possible, and I wanted to visit in person some of the key places that lived on so vividly for Alice Marble. I began my research on Alice Marble by visiting the places that defined her, first Palm Desert in California where she spent the final quarter century of her life and then further north in San Francisco where I toured her childhood home, a dwelling that its current owners believe is filled with a "good spirit." The San Francisco Room of the public library across from City Hall yielded many treasures, including Marble's high school yearbook, an oral history of her neighborhood, and a trove of black-and-white photos. Of the many locales dear to her heart, Wimbledon in the suburbs of London ranked near the top, and I felt a jolt as I passed through the various stops the tube makes along the way to the All-England Lawn Tennis and Croquet Club: "Gloucester Road . . . Earl's Court . . . West Brompton . . . Fulham Broadway . . . Parsons Green . . . Putney Bridge . . . East Putney. . . . Southfields Station." If Wimbledon is indeed church, the obvious altar is Centre Court, where ghosts gather on an apparently routine basis. I found my own place of worship, the small shipshape library presided over by Robert McNichol, who shared copious records from Marble's heyday. In April 2022 while visiting London as a member of the Jane Austen Book Group Tour, Lucie Tate at the Grosvenor House Hotel provided a gracious tour of a storied building where Marble experienced a heady celebration on July 8, 1939, never again rivaled in her life.

Thanks also to novelist James W. Hall for putting me in touch with tennis great Donna Fales. She, along with Judith Dixon, longtime coach of the women's tennis team at the University of Massachusetts and Professor Guiliana Davidoff, professor emerita at Mount Holyoke College, offered insights into the challenges women who choose tennis as their sport face. Rick Grand-Jean, a historian by inclination, encouraged a deep dive into the early days of a game he clearly loves. Suzanne Spencer was a boon companion at several US Opens. On a day almost hot enough to rival July 31, 1933, Patty McCormick drove me to the doorstep of Maidstone on Long Island so I could witness its magnificence in person. My brother-in-law Christopher W. Katzenbach helped with a crucial legal question. Retired FBI agents John and Sue Mencer weighed in with insights regarding the plausibility of Marble's spy mission. John Bertolini, professor emeritus at Middlebury College, offered insights into G. B. Shaw. Dr. Jonathan Mueller of San Francisco emphasized the significance of tennis in the Bay Area at that time when Marble began her quest. University of Massachusetts alum Isaac Simon is an excellent research librarian in the making. Amherst College emeritus professor and poet David Sofield brought his combined tennis and linguistic prowess to an early reading of this work. Nancy Coiner, Holly Davis, Jean Kuhn, Kathy Mullin, Julie Stanton, Karin Winter, and Janis Wolkenbreit provided support at key junctures. The historian Professor Ashley Brown shared her take on Althea Gibson's role in the history of the game, making it clear that behind every great tennis player in another great tennis player. Susan Trench, Susan Johnson Banta, and Susan Rothchild are born guides, and Greta Wilcox can add professional sleuth to her résumé.

I am grateful to Les Standiford, director of Writers in Paradise at Eckerd College in St. Petersburg, Florida; Leslie Rubinkowski, director of the Goucher College MFA in Nonfiction program in Towson, Maryland; and Victoria Larrea at Rancho La Puerta in Tecate, Mexico, for sponsoring presentations of the work in progress.

My colleagues in the Journalism Department at the University of Massachusetts in Amherst, especially Professor Karen List, supported this endeavor as did Melissa McIntosh and James Kelly at the W. E. B. Du Bois Library on campus.

Dale Leatherman offered insights with generosity, good humor, and an obvious affection and deep respect for her former collaborator. Rita Mae Brown is a buccaneer in her own right, and Billie Jean King has clearly spent her life growing in insight and grace.

This project would never have gotten off the ground, not to mention seen completion, without my agent Andrew Blauner and the always amazing staff at Grove Atlantic, including Justina Batchelor, Julia Berner-Tobin, Emily Burns, Natalie Church, Ian Dreiblatt, Amy Hughes, Brett Keener, Cassie McSorley, Deb Seager, and Andrew Unger. Thanks, as always, to Morgan Entrekin and his amazing leadership.

Most significantly, I have two individuals to thank above all for their laborious behind-the-scenes stitching and unstitching: my sister Jacqueline, editor, reporter, teacher, a twin at heart if not in fact, and executive editor George Gibson at Grove, as wise as he is patient. Their handiwork is behind anything of merit in this book.

I am beyond grateful to my husband, John Katzenbach; my children and their partners, Nick Katzenbach and Rebecca Borbe, and Justine Katzenbach and Ryan Brown; and my grandchildren, Genevieve and Adrian Brown.

APPENDIX

A Vital Issue

BY ALICE MARBLE

American Lawn Tennis, July 1950

W HEN OLIVER REA, the new publisher of ALT, gave me the green light on this article, I couldn't have been happier. The subject has been on my mind for some months, and I consider the opportunity to speak my piece a privilege. Moreover, the willingness of the magazine to take a stand, to examine as honestly as possible, all the salient points of an issue important to tennis, please me enormously. Whether its views coincide with my own is not the relevant factor; that it doesn't choose to emulate an ostrich seems awfully important.

On my current lecture tours the question I am most expected to answer is no longer "What do you think of [Gussie's] panties?" For every individual who cares if [Gussie] has lace on her drawers, there are three who want to know if Althea Gibson will be permitted to play in the Nationals this year. Not being privy to the sentiments of the USLTA committee, I couldn't answer their questions, but I came back to New York determined to find out. When I directed the question at a committee member of long standing, his answer, tacitly given, was in the negative. Unless something in the realm of the supernatural occurs, Miss Gibson will not be allowed to play in the Nationals.

He said nothing of the sort, of course. The attitude of the committee will be that Miss Gibson has not sufficiently proven herself. True enough, she was a finalist in the National Indoors, the gentleman admitted—but didn't I think the field was awfully poor? I did not. It is my opinion that Miss Gibson performed beautifully under the circumstances. Considering how little play she has had in top competition, her win over a seasoned veteran like Midge Buck seems to me a real triumph.

Nevertheless, the committee, according to this member, insists that in order to qualify for the Nationals, Miss Gibson must also make a strong showing in the major Eastern tournaments to be played between now and the date set for the big do at Forest Hills. Most of these major tournaments—Orange, East Hampton, Essex, etc.—are invitational, of course. If she is not invited to participate in them, as my committee member freely predicted, then she obviously will be unable to prove anything at all, and it will be the reluctant duty of the committee to reject her entry at Forest Hills. Miss Gibson is over a very cunningly-wrought barrel, and I can hope to loosen a few of its staves with one lone opinion.

I think it's time we faced a few facts. If tennis is a game for ladies and gentlemen, it's also time we acted a little more like gentlepeople and less like sanctimonious hypocrites. If there is anything left in the name of sportsmanship, it's more than time to display what it means to us. If Althea Gibson represents a challenge to the present crop of women players, it's only fair that they should meet that challenge on the courts, where tennis is played. I know those girls, and I can't think of one who would refuse to meet Miss Gibson in competition. She might be soundly beaten for a while—but she has a much better chance on the courts than in the inner sanctum of the committee, where a different kind of game is played.

I can't honestly say that I believe Miss Gibson to be a potential champion; I don't know. In the Indoors she played under tremendous pressure, but there were moments when she exhibited a bold, exciting game that will doubtlessly improve against first-class competition. Whether she can achieve championship status here or abroad depends no more on her lovely strokes than on what Althea Gibson finds within herself when the chips are down. If she can do it, a proud new chapter will have been added to the history of tennis. If she cannot, we will have seen nothing more and nothing less than one more youngster who failed to live up to her initial promise. But if she is refused a chance to succeed or to fail, then there is an uneradicable mark against a game to which I have devoted most of my life, and I would be bitterly ashamed.

We can accept the evasions, ignore the fact that no one will be honest enough to shoulder the responsibility for Althea Gibson's probable exclusion from the Nationals. We can just "not think about it." Or we can face the issue squarely and honestly. It so happens that I tan very heavily in the summer—but I doubt that anyone ever questioned my right to play in the Nationals because of it. Margaret duPont collects a few freckles—but whoever thought to omit her name for such a reason? The committee would have felt pretty foolish saying, "Alice Marble can't play because of that tan," or "We can't accept Margaret duPont; she gets freckles across her nose." It's just as ridiculous to reject Althea Gibson on the same basis—and that's the truth of it. She is not being judged by the yardstick of ability but by the fact that her pigmentation is somewhat different.

If the field of sports has got to pave the way for all of civilization, let's do it. At this moment tennis is privileged to take its place among the pioneers for a true democracy, if it will accept that privilege. If it declines to do so, the honor will fall to the next generation, perhaps—but someone will break the ground. The entrance of Negroes into National tennis is as inevitable as it has proven to be in baseball, in football, or boxing; there is no denying so much talent. The committee at Forest Hills has the power to stifle the efforts of one Althea Gibson, who may or may not be the stuff of which champions are made, but eventually she will be succeeded by others of her race who have equal or superior ability. They will knock at the door as she has done. Eventually the tennis world will rise up en masse to protest the injustices perpetuated by our policy-makers.

Eventually—why not now?

I am beating no drums for Miss Gibson as a player of outstanding quality. As I said, I have seen her only in the National Indoors, where she obviously did not play her best and was still able to display some lovely shots. To me, she is a fellow tennis player and, as such, deserving of the same chance as I had to prove myself. I've never met Miss Gibson but, to me, she is a fellow human being to whom equal privileges ought to be extended.

Speaking for myself, I will be glad to help Althea Gibson in any way I can. If I can improve her game or merely give her the benefit of my own experiences, as I have many other young players, I'll do that. If I can give her an iota more of confidence by rooting my heart out from the gallery she can take my word for it: I'll be there.

PHOTO CREDITS

Image 1.1	Courtesy of the International Tennis Hall of Fame.
Image 1.2	Courtesy of Dale Leatherman.
Image 1.3	Courtesy of Dale Leatherman.
Image 2.1	FoundSF.org
Image 2.2	San Francisco History Center, San Francisco Public Library.
Image 3.1	Courtesy of the International Tennis Hall of Fame.
Image 3.2	*The Road to Wimbledon* by Alice Marble.
Image 3.3	AP Photo
Image 3.4	Courtesy of the International Tennis Hall of Fame.
Image 4.1	Library of Congress, Prints and Photographs Division.
Image 4.2	National Archives at College Park - Still Pictures.
Image 5.1	Courtesy of the International Tennis Hall of Fame.
Image 5.2	Courtesy of the International Tennis Hall of Fame.
Image 5.3	Library of Congress, Prints and Photographs Division.
Image 6.1	AP Photo
Image 6.2	Fang family *San Francisco Examiner* Photograph Archive Negative Files, BANC PIC 2006.029—NEG box 650, sleeve 094040_01, © The Regents of the University of California, The Bancroft Library, University of California, Berkeley.
Image 7.1	Courtesy of the International Tennis Hall of Fame.
Image 7.2	Photograph by Frank Nothaft. Courtesy of the International Tennis Hall of Fame.
Image 7.3	Getty Images
Image 8.1	AP Photo/Len Puttnam
Image 8.2	AP Photo/Len Puttnam
Image 9.1	Courtesy of Dale Leatherman.
Image 9.2	Courtesy of the International Tennis Hall of Fame.
Image 10.1	Photographer D. Stuart. Courtesy of the International Tennis Hall of Fame.
Image 10.2	Courtesy of Dale Leatherman.
Image 10.3	Series I. Correspondence, Box 91, Folder '1923-1926 S', William du Pont, Jr. papers (Accession 2317.II), Manuscripts and Archives Department, Hagley Museum and Library, Wilmington, DE 19807.
Image 10.4	Library of Congress, Prints and Photographs Division.
Image 11.1	*American Lawn Tennis Magazine*, October 1946. Courtesy of Springfield College Library.
Image 11.2	Author collection.
Image 11.3	Photograph by Fred G. Chase. Courtesy of the International Tennis Hall of Fame.
Image 12.1	Courtesy of the International Tennis Hall of Fame.
Image 12.2	Courtesy of the International Tennis Hall of Fame.
Image 12.3	Courtesy of Dale Leatherman.
Image 13.1	AP Photo
Image 13.2	AP Photo/Tom Sande
Image 14.1	Courtesy of the International Tennis Hall of Fame.
Image 14.2	World Tennis Magazine Archive. Courtesy of the International Tennis Hall of Fame.
Image 14.3	Courtesy of Dale Leatherman.
Image 14.4	Courtesy of Dale Leatherman.
Image 15.1	Courtesy of Dale Leatherman.
Image 16.1	Photograph by John Russell. Courtesy of the International Tennis Hall of Fame.
Image 16.2	Courtesy of Dale Leatherman.

NOTES

Preface: Sixty Steps

1. "Behind the Scenes at Wimbledon," *Daily Sketch* (Manchester, UK), June 16, 1939.
2. John R. Tunis, "A Reporter at Large: Wimbledon," *New Yorker*, July 5, 1930.
3. Alice Marble, interview by Courtney Gebhart, July 25, 1987, Prickly Pears: Portraits of Historical Palm Springs (local history project), vol. 48, Palm Springs Public Library, Palm Springs, CA.
4. Charlotte Himber, *Famous in Their Twenties* (New York: Association Press, 1942), 41.
5. *Click: The National Picture Monthly*, October 1939, 6.
6. Mel Heimer, "The Comeback" *Professional Tennis Tour Official Program*, season 1941.
7. Bill Plunkett, "Pioneer in Women's Tennis Dies," *Desert Sun* (Palm Springs, CA), December 14, 1990.
8. Thomas Rogers, "Alice Marble, 77, Top U.S. Tennis Star of 1930's," *New York Times*, December 14, 1990.

1. The Little White House on the Hill

1. Marble's *The Road to Wimbledon* (London: W. H. Allen, 1947) is the major source of the detailed picture of her childhood presented here and in the following chapter, although she shared elements of the story in other formats over the course of many years, including in interviews and speeches. There is no way to ascertain the truthfulness of the account—these are, after all, her childhood memories. The book had a ghostwriter, who may have shored up some of the narrative to make it more exciting. For instance, the story of Harry Marble's visit to San Francisco when he met his wife indicates that he hoped to see some of the ruins of the earthquake ("Travelers coming to Plumas County told harrowing stories of flood and fire and famine"), but that event occurred a year later, after Marble's parents had met and married and moved to Plumas County.
2. Marble, *The Road to Wimbledon*, 5.
3. Ibid., 6.
4. The legacy of James Beckwourth was preserved by chance because he shared his story, of being a fur trader adopted into the Crow tribe, with a justice of the peace named Thomas Bonner. Beckwourth's account appeared under the title *The Life and Adventures of James P. Beckwourth, Mountaineer, Scout, and Pioneer and the Chief of the Crow Nation of Indians* in 1856. His reputation continued to grow after his death, as shifts in society broadened beyond white men to include others in the cast of characters acknowledged for their contributions to history. In 1994 a postage stamp was issued in his honor, and in 2015 Beckwourth's story influenced the movie *The Revenant*.
5. Marble, *The Road to Wimbledon*, 8.
6. Ibid., 9.
7. Ibid.

8. Ibid.
9. Ibid., 10.
10. Ibid., 11–12.
11. Ibid., 9–10.
12. Ibid.,15.
13. The figure was purposely minimized to downplay the disaster, arrived at by conveniently excluding many victims, especially Asian Americans, from the count. Modern estimates give the number of dead at up to three thousand.
14. Julia Cooley Altrocchi, *The Spectacular San Franciscans* (New York: E. P. Dutton, 1949), 287.
15. "Panama–Pacific International Exposition," Wikipedia, accessed September 9, 2022, https://en.wikipedia.org/wiki/Panama–Pacific_International_Exposition. The Wikipedia entry cites: "Liberty Bell Attracts Crowd in Greenville during 1915 Stop," *Greenville Advocate*, July 3, 2007; Doug Nye, *The United States Grand Prix and Grand Prize Races, 1908–1977* (Garden City, NY: Doubleday, 1979), 32–33; Esther McCoy, *Five California Architects* (New York: Reinhold, 1960), 6.
16. "Influenza Not to Close Down City Schools," *San Francisco Chronicle*, October 11, 1918.
17. "Health Board Closes Public Meeting Places; Schools, Churches, Theaters and Dance Halls to Be Shut Today," *San Francisco Chronicle*, October 18, 1918.
18. "San Francisco, California," *Influenza Encyclopedia: The American Influenza Epidemic of 1918–1919*, University of Michigan Center for the History of Medicine and Michigan Publishing, University of Michigan Library, accessed November 10, 2021, influenzaarchive.org.
19. "Health Board Giving Battle to Influenza," *San Francisco Chronicle*, October 21, 1918.
20. "San Francisco, California," *Influenza Encyclopedia.*
21. "Here Is the Text of City Mask Ordinance; Violation Incurs Fine or Imprisonment," *San Francisco Chronicle*, October 25, 1918.
22. "Health Board Giving Battle to Influenza," *San Francisco Chronicle*, October 21, 1918.
23. "San Francisco, California," *Influenza Encyclopedia.*
24. Alfred W. Crosby, *America's Forgotten Pandemic: The Influenza of 1918* (New York: Cambridge University Press, 2003), 106.
25. "Public Schools of City Reopen This Morning," *San Francisco Chronicle*, November 25, 1918.
26. Crosby, *America's Forgotten Pandemic*, 111–12.
27. Marble, *The Road to Wimbledon*, 19.
28. "Ford Model T," Wikipedia, accessed September 9, 2022, https://en.wikipedia.org/wiki/Ford_Model_T. The Wikipedia entry cites *Henry Ford and the Model T* (John Wiley and Sons, 1996).
29. "Driving a Model-T Is a Lot Harder Than You'd Think! We Tried It," Bloomberg QuickTake, January 21, 2016, YouTube video, accessed February 26, 2022, https://www.youtube.com/watch?v=MLMS_QtKamg.
30. Marble, *The Road to Wimbledon*, 20.
31. Ibid., 21.
32. Lorri Ungaretti, *Stories in the Sand: San Francisco's Sunset District 1847–1964* (San Francisco: Balangero Books, 2012), 3.
33. Ibid., 46.
34. Marble, *The Road to Wimbledon*, 21.

35. Alice Marble, interview by Lyn Tornabene, March 23, 1974, in Palm Desert, CA, Clark Gable collection compiled by Lyn Tornabene, Margaret Herrick Library, Academy of Motion Picture Arts and Sciences, Beverly Hills, CA.

36. Ted Tinling, with Rod Humphries, *Love and Faults: Personalities Who Have Changed the History of Tennis in My Lifetime* (New York: Crown, 1979), 154.

37. Marble, *The Road to Wimbledon*, 21–22.

38. Ibid., 23.

39. Ibid.

40. Alice Marble, with Dale Leatherman, *Courting Danger: My Adventures in World-Class Tennis, Golden Age Hollywood, and High-Stakes Spying* (New York: St. Martin's Press, 1991), 2–3. A perusal of San Francisco newspapers from the time frame Marble indicates for this incident shows no evidence of a matching event.

41. Ibid., 23.

42. Ibid., 35–36.

43. Alice Marble, interview by Courtney Gebhart, July 25, 1987, Prickly Pears: Portraits of Historical Palm Springs (local history project), vol. 48, Palm Springs Public Library, Palm Springs, CA.

44. Marble, with Leatherman, *Courting Danger*, 31.

2. "Atta Boy, Alice"

1. Alice Marble, *The Road to Wimbledon* (London: W. H. Allen, 1947), 24.

2. "1920s Cost of Food," The People History, accessed November 10, 2021, http://www .thepeoplehistory.com/20sfood.html.

3. Linda Marble McCrory (Alice Marble's grandniece), telephone interview by author, July 13, 2019.

4. Marble, *The Road to Wimbledon*, 25.

5. Ibid., 32.

6. Ibid.

7. Ibid., 33.

8. Jerry Flamm, *Good Life in Hard Times: San Francisco in the '20s and '30s* (San Francisco: Chronicle Books, 1999), 60–61.

9. Charlotte Himber, *Famous in Their Twenties* (New York: Association Press, 1942), 43.

10. Harry Grayson, "Only Marble Can Beat Marble in English Tourney," *Cumberland Evening Times* (Cumberland, MD), May 27, 1939.

11. "Coughlin Wins Junior Class Tennis Title," *San Francisco Examiner*, October 17, 1926.

12. Himber, *Famous in Their Twenties*, 45.

13. Ibid.

14. Many details of Lenglen's life are commonly circulated, but anyone seeking a deep look at her life and legacy should read Larry Engelmann, *The Goddess and the American Girl: The Story of Suzanne Lenglen and Helen Wills* (New York: Oxford University Press, 1988), the remarkably thorough source for this synopsis of her life story. Lenglen still shows up in the popular culture from time to time. On May 24, 2016, on the 127th anniversary of her birth, Google Doodles honored her with the following citation: "Back in the day, tennis was a rigid affair. Amateurs couldn't compete with pros, and participation fees for important matches were astronomical. Then Suzanne Lenglen came along." Less than a year later, on March 8, 2017, Google honored her on International Women's Day.

15. Engelmann, *The Goddess and the American Girl*, 24.
16. Alan Little, *Suzanne Lenglen: Tennis Idol of the Twenties* (London: Wimbledon Lawn Tennis Museum, 1988), 26.
17. "Helen Wills Moody Roark, Biography," International Tennis Hall of Fame, accessed January 22, 2022, https://www.tennisfame.com/hall-of-famers/inductees/helen-wills -moody-roark.
18. United Press, "Suzanne Lenglen Likes America but Not Prohibition," *Sacramento Bee* (Sacramento, CA), December 1, 1926.
19. "Scanning the Field," *Monrovia Daily News* (Monrovia, CA), December 2, 1926.
20. Louise Landis, "Suzanne Enjoys Life as a Net Pro," *San Francisco Examiner*, December 7, 1926.
21. "Famous French Champion Opposes Mary K. Browne," *San Francisco Examiner*, December 7, 1926.
22. Harry M. Hayward, "Suzanne Wins before Net Fans," *San Francisco Examiner*, December 8, 1926.
23. Ibid.
24. Ibid.
25. Marble, *The Road to Wimbledon*, 26.
26. Ibid., 33.
27. "Park Net Tourney to Start Sunday," *San Francisco Examiner*, January 8, 1927.
28. Wilson O'Brien, "Miss Brohm Victor in Tennis Play," *San Francisco Examiner*, April 10, 1927.
29. Abe Kemp, "Averill's Homers Give Seals Two Games," *San Francisco Examiner*, August 8, 1927.
30. Marble, *The Road to Wimbledon*, 28.
31. Ibid., 29.
32. Dennis Snelling, *Lefty O'Doul's Forgotten Ambassador* (Lincoln: University of Nebraska Press, 2017), 11.
33. Ralph Berger, "Ping Bodie," Society for American Baseball Research, accessed November 11, 2021, sabr.org/bioproj/person/ping-bodie.
34. "Atta Boy, Alice," *San Francisco Examiner*, July 12, 1927. Marble references the article in *The Road to Wimbledon*, but she quotes slightly different verbiage, perhaps from memory. For the purposes of keeping the record straight, the article reproduced in this volume is in its original form.
35. Snelling, *Lefty O'Doul*, 51.
36. Marble, *The Road to Wimbledon*, 35.
37. Ibid., 34.
38. Ibid., 35.
39. Ibid., 37.
40. Ibid.
41. Don Caswell, "Alice Marble Welcomed Home to Play in S. F.," *Californian* (Salinas, CA), March 5, 1941.
42. Marble, *The Road to Wimbledon*, 38.

3. Where It Is Always June

1. Elizabeth Wilson, *Love Game: A History of Tennis, from Victorian Pastime to Global Phenomenon* (Chicago: University of Chicago Press, 2016), 20, 21, 22.
2. Heiner Gillmeister, *Tennis: A Cultural History* (New York: New York University Press, 1998), 174.

3. Warren F. Kimball, *The United States Tennis Association: Raising the Game* (Lincoln: University of Nebraska Press, 2017), 4.
4. Ibid., 4.
5. Gillmeister, *Tennis*, 174.
6. David Berry, *A People's History of Tennis* (London: Pluto Press, 2020), 26.
7. Wilson, *Love Game*, 11.
8. Ashley Brown, "Swinging for the State Department: American Women Tennis Players in Diplomatic Goodwill Tours, 1941–59," *Journal of Sport History* 42, no. 3 (Fall 2015), 289–309.
9. Bud Collins, *The Bud Collins History of Tennis: An Authoritative Encyclopedia and Record Book*, 2nd ed., Canada: New Chapter Press, 2010, 6. Today's four Grand Slam events got their start in that era: Wimbledon (1877), US Open (1881), French Open (1891), and Australian Open (1905).
10. Richard D. Sears, "The First American Championships," in *The Right Set: A Tennis Anthology*, ed. Caryl Phillips (New York: Vintage, 1999), 23.
11. Billie Jean King, with Cynthia Starr, *We Have Come a Long Way: The Story of Women's Tennis* (New York: McGraw-Hill, 1988), 12–13.
12. Larry Engelmann, *The Goddess and the American Girl: The Story of Suzanne Lenglen and Helen Wills* (New York: Oxford University Press, 1988), 63.
13. Ted Tinling, with Rod Humphries, *Love and Faults: Personalities Who Have Changed the History of Tennis in My Lifetime* (New York: Crown, 1979), 159.
14. Engelmann, *The Goddess and the American Girl*, 64.
15. Marble never lost an opportunity to thank California for being the breeding ground it was for her and so many others. Writing in *American Lawn Tennis* on July 1, 1947, she laid out the facts: "Here are a few statistics: California men have won ten National Singles Championships in the past twenty years. . . . California women have won the championship sixteen times. . . . I think it's a crying shame that more opportunities are not made for tennis aspirants in other states."
16. Engelmann, *The Goddess and the American Girl*, 66.
17. Alice Marble, As I See It, "The Tennis Fathers," *American Lawn Tennis*, September 1, 1949.
18. Much of the background information on Helen Wills Moody Roark comes from Engelmann, *The Goddess and the American Girl*, an invaluable resource in documenting the tennis scene, especially in Northern California at the beginning of the twentieth century.
19. King, with Starr, *We Have Come a Long Way*, 33.
20. Engelmann, *The Goddess and the American Girl*, 336.
21. Ibid.

4. High Hat

1. Alice Marble, *The Road to Wimbledon* (London: W. H. Allen, 1947), 38.
2. Ibid.
3. Ibid., 35.
4. Ibid., 40.
5. Alice Marble, interview by Bud Lessor, March 11, 1975, Oral History Collection, International Tennis Hall of Fame, Newport, RI.
6. Marble, *The Road to Wimbledon*, 44.
7. Francis B. O'Gara, "Holman Loses to Stratford in Net Play," *San Francisco Examiner*, June 17, 1929.

8. Francis B. O'Gara, "Bob Seller Wins Coast Net Singles at Berkeley," *San Francisco Examiner*, June 24, 1929.
9. Marble, *The Road to Wimbledon*, 44.
10. Ibid., 45.
11. Ibid.
12. Ibid.
13. "Lawn Tennis in San Francisco," *Daily Alta California* (San Francisco), September 8, 1884.
14. Nancy Barr Mavity, "Helen Jacobs Forced to Limit by English Girl Court Star in International Team Matches," *Oakland Tribune* (Oakland, CA), September 16, 1929.
15. "Alice Marble Wins Net Title," *San Francisco Examiner*, September 22, 1929.
16. "Girls Net Play on This Morning," *San Francisco Examiner*, October 19, 1929.
17. "Misses McCoy and Hunt in Net Finals," *San Francisco Examiner*, November 10, 1929.
18. "Cranston Holman Win Tennis Title," *San Francisco Examiner*, November 18, 1929.
19. "Holman Placed First in Western Tennis Rankings," *San Francisco Examiner*, December 8, 1929.
20. "Girls' Tennis to Start Tomorrow," *San Francisco Examiner*, January 17, 1930.
21. "Miss Maxwell Wins Tennis Event," *San Francisco Examiner*, February 9, 1930.
22. "Alice Marble Triumphs in Girls Park Tennis," *San Francisco Examiner*, March 23, 1930.
23. "Alice Marble Wins over Helen Hannah," *San Francisco Examiner*, May 4, 1930.
24. "Becomes Finalist," *Fresno Morning Republican* (Fresno, CA), June 14, 1930.
25. "Champions Are Crowned at Berkeley," *Oakland Tribune*, June 16, 1930.
26. "Championship Flight in Women's Net Play," *San Francisco Examiner*, June 27, 1930.
27. "Alice Marble Wins Park Net Honors," *San Francisco Examiner*, June 30, 1930.
28. Larry Engelmann, *The Goddess and the American Girl: The Story of Suzanne Lenglen and Helen Wills* (New York: Oxford University Press, 1988), 412.
29. Alice Marble, with Dale Leatherman, *Courting Danger: My Adventures in World-Class Tennis, Golden Age Hollywood, and High-Stakes Spying* (New York: St. Martin's Press, 1991), 6.
30. Ibid., 6–7.
31. Ibid., 8.
32. Ibid.
33. Alice Marble, As I See It, "The State of the Tennis Union," *Racquet*, March 1953.
34. Marble, *The Road to Wimbledon*, 46–47.

5. Three Crisp Twenty-Dollar Bills

1. Alice Marble, *The Road to Wimbledon* (London: W. H. Allen, 1947), 52.
2. Ibid., 52–53.
3. Federal Writers Project of the Works Progress Administration, *San Francisco in the 1930s: The WPA Guide to the City by the Bay* (Berkeley and Los Angeles: University of California Press, 2011), 110. The cited passage is: "The Nation-wide financial crisis did not immediately check San Francisco's building boom, and public improvements continued. In 1930 its population passed the 634,000 mark. The great Hetch-Hetchy dam in the high Sierras was nearing completion and pending availability of its resources of light and power the city augmented its public utilities by purchasing the Spring Valley Water Company.... Even the onslaught of the depression which struck the city in 1932, while it brought about a decline in shipping and industry and threw some 70,000 workers out of employment, delayed only for another year the initial construction of the San Francisco–Oakland Bay

Bridge. The city's sound financial and business structure enabled it to emerge with losses less serious than those of any other major American city."

4. "Visiting Players in Front," *Vancouver Sun* (Vancouver, BC), July 18, 1930.
5. "Harrison in Three Jericho Tennis Finals, Beats Brawn in Singles—Prusoff Downs Gove, Alice Marble Stars," *Province* (Vancouver, BC), July 19, 1930.
6. Marble, *The Road to Wimbledon*, 55.
7. "American Girls in Junior Final, Alice Marble and Carolyn Fringess put out B.C. Tennis Hopes," *Province* (Vancouver, BC), July 24, 1930.
8. Associated Press, "Gove, Harrison Battle Tennis Final Today," *San Francisco Examiner*, July 26, 1930.
9. "Harrison Stars in Play for Western Canada Net Titles," *Vancouver Sun* (Vancouver, BC), July 28, 1930.
10. "Bob Johnson Beats Victoria City Champion," *Province* (Vancouver, BC) July 29, 1930.
11. Marble, *The Road to Wimbledon*, 57.
12. Francis B. O'Gara, "Mrs. Moody Wins State Title," *San Francisco Examiner*, October 6, 1930.
13. Marble, *The Road to Wimbledon*, 58.
14. Marble, *The Road to Wimbledon*, 59.
15. Ibid.

6. "Teach"

1. Alice Marble, *The Road to Wimbledon* (London: W. H. Allen, 1947), 60.
2. Nancy Spain, *"Teach" Tennant: The Story of Eleanor Tennant; The Greatest Tennis Coach in the World* (London: Werner Laurie, 1953), 15.
3. Spain, *"Teach" Tennant*, 10.
4. Alma Whitaker, "Feminine Athlete Finds Instructor Career Profitable," *Los Angeles Times*, November 2, 1934.
5. "Los Angeles, Wealthiest County of the West," *Los Angeles Daily Times*, January 1, 1913.
6. Nancie Clare, "How Fame Came to Beverly Hills: Why Old Hollywood Moved In," *Hollywood Reporter*, March 29, 2014, https://www.hollywoodreporter.com/news/how-fame-came-beverly-hills-690925.
7. Alma Whitaker, "Feminine Athlete Finds Instructor Career Profitable," *Los Angeles Times*, November 2, 1934.
8. Spain, *"Teach" Tennant*, 24.
9. Ibid., 25.
10. Associated Press, "Eleanor Tennant, Who Taught Many Tennis Notables, Dead," *New York Times*, May 13, 1974.
11. Spain, *"Teach" Tennant*, 30.
12. Lisa Fogarty, "What Getting a Divorce Was Like Every Decade since the 1900s," *Redbook*, April 11, 2017, www.redbookmag.com/love-sex/relationships/g4275/divorce-throughout-history/#sidepanel.
13. Spain, *"Teach" Tennant*, 31.
14. Alma Whitaker, "Feminine Athlete Finds Instructor Career Profitable," *Los Angeles Times*, November 2, 1934.
15. Alice Marble, "Meet the Champ" Column in the *Racquet*, November 1951.
16. Ted Tinling, with Rod Humphries, *Love and Faults: Personalities Who Have Changed the History of Tennis in My Lifetime* (New York: Crown, 1979), 158.

17. Spain, *"Teach" Tennant*, 25–26.

18. Ibid., 38.

19. Ibid., 39.

20. Marble, *The Road to Wimbledon*, 60.

21. Ibid.

22. Ibid., 43–44.

23. *Pygmalion* has enjoyed subsequent iterations as the musical *My Fair Lady* and the movie *Pretty Woman*.

24. "California Tennis Championships Start Tomorrow at Berkeley Club, Eleven Titles to Be Placed in Competition, Mrs. Helen Moody Looks Likely to Win Women's Title, with Good Entries in Men's Events," *San Francisco Examiner*, June 5, 1931.

25. "Mrs. Moody Out of Tennis Tourney," *San Francisco Examiner*, June 6, 1931.

26. "Alice Marble Captures Women's State Tennis Title, Vines Upsets Bud Chandler to Take Men's Singles Crown," *San Francisco Examiner*, June 15, 1931.

27. Marble, *The Road to Wimbledon*, 63.

28. Lucius Beebe, *The Overland Limited* (Berkeley, CA: Howell-North Books 1963), 30.

7. Precarious

1. Frances D. McMullen, "Soft Spots in the Hardened City's Heart," *New York Times Magazine*, January 11, 1931.

2. "Apple Vendors Will Be Put off Streets, New York Police Decide They Obstruct Traffic," *Democrat and Chronicle* (Rochester, NY), April 3, 1931.

3. "Furniture Taken from the Victoria," *New York Times*, August 26, 1931.

4. "Starving Man Collapses," *New York Times*, August 17, 1931.

5. "Frees 22 Park Sleepers, Magistrate Gottlieb Then Gives Them $2 Each," *New York Times*, July 25, 1931.

6. "Breadline Is Longer," *New York Times*, June 7, 1931.

7. Mary Day Winn, "Daughters of the Depression," *Washington Evening Star: Sunday Star Magazine*, August 9, 1931.

8. "Warns Idle Girls Away," *New York Times*, August 3, 1931.

9. Tunnels to the Biltmore, Roosevelt, and Commodore Hotels, Yale Club, and the Graybar and Chrysler Buildings operated out of Grand Central Station until the early 1990s, according to Jen Carlson, "Inside the Subterranean Passageway that Once Linked Grand Central to the Roosevelt Hotel," *Gothamist*, April 21, 2015.

10. Alice Marble, *The Road to Wimbledon* (London: W. H. Allen, 1947), 65.

11. Allison Danzig, "Doeg Double Victor in Seabright Tennis," *New York Times*, July 28, 1931.

12. Marble, *The Road to Wimbledon*, 66.

13. Alice Marble, interview by Bud Lessor, March 11, 1975, Oral History Collection, International Tennis Hall of Fame, Newport, RI.

14. Marble, *The Road to Wimbledon*, 67.

15. Associated Press, "Lost Entry of Alice Marble Causes Redraw for Women's National Tennis Tournament," *Press and Sun-Bulletin* (Binghamton, New York), August 13, 1931.

16. J.P. Allen, Special by Wire to the *Tribune*, "Marble's Loss Hit Tourney Body's Moves," *Oakland Tribune* (Oakland, California), August 18, 1931.

17. Marble, *The Road to Wimbledon*, 66.

18. Ibid., 69.

19. Associated Press, "Girl Tennis Players from West Feature," *St. Louis Globe-Democrat*, September 8, 1931.
20. Dora Lurie, "Ruby Bishop Wins Junior Net Crown," *Philadelphia Inquirer*, September 13, 1931.
21. Mrs. Shippen Lewis, "Notes on Girls' Play in Philadelphia," *American Lawn Tennis*, September 20, 1931.
22. Ibid.
23. Marble, *The Road to Wimbledon*, 68.

8. Cannonball

1. Nancy Spain, *"Teach" Tennant: The Story of Eleanor Tennant; The Greatest Tennis Coach in the World* (London: Werner Laurie, 1953), 39.
2. Ibid.
3. Associated Press, "Howard Kinsey, 66, A Tennis Champion," *New York Times*, July 28, 1966.
4. Bill Tobitt, "Bud Chandler, Alice Marble Win State Singles Titles," *Oakland Tribune* (Oakland, CA), June 27, 1932.
5. "Exhibition Net Matches Saturday," *San Francisco Examiner*, July 14, 1932.
6. "Mrs. Wightman Will Play in Exhibition," *Oakland Tribune*, July 15, 1932.
7. Frank Reil, "Matron Beats Coast Girl in Tennis Match," *Brooklyn Eagle*, August 8, 1932.
8. George Currie, "Alice Marble Adds to Tennis Complexity," *Brooklyn Eagle*, June 7, 1933.
9. Henry R. Ilsley, "English Stars Gain Net Quarter Finals," *New York Times*, August 18, 1932.
10. Allison Danzig, "Miss Babcock Wins from Mrs. Harper," *New York Times*, August 20, 1932.
11. Billie Jean King, with Johnette Howard and Maryanne Vollers, *All In: An Autobiography* (New York: Alfred A. Knopf, 2021), 46.
12. "Young Girls Have Their Day," *American Lawn Tennis*, July 5, 1932.
13. Advertisement, *American Lawn Tennis*, October 20, 1932.
14. Spain, *"Teach" Tennant*, 40.
15. Alice Marble, interview by Lyn Tornabene, March 23, 1974, in Palm Desert, CA, Clark Gable collection compiled by Lyn Tornabene, Margaret Herrick Library, Academy of Motion Picture Arts and Sciences, Beverly Hills, CA.
16. Spain, *"Teach" Tennant*, 40.
17. Alice Marble, *The Road to Wimbledon* (London: W. H. Allen, 1947), 87.
18. Alice Marble, with Dale Leatherman, *Courting Danger: My Adventures in World-Class Tennis, Golden Age Hollywood, and High-Stakes Spying* (New York: St. Martin's Press, 1991), 22.
19. Marble, *The Road to Wimbledon*, 87.
20. Ibid., 89.
21. Styles of play go in and out. Due to the decline in grass surfaces and the increase in hard surfaces, the old-style western grip is back in favor now, partly because it creates better topspin. This observation is courtesy of Donna Fales, ranked number five in the United States women's singles in 1960 and 1962 and ranked number two in doubles in the United States three times in 1960, 1963, and 1967. A former captain and player on the Wightman Cup team, she reached number one in the International Tennis Federation

World rankings in 2010 women's 70s singles. Donna Fales, interview with the author, March 14, 2018, Coral Gables, FL.

22. Marble, *The Road to Wimbledon*, 89.
23. Spain, *"Teach" Tennant*, 74–75.
24. Marble, with Leatherman, *Courting Danger*, 19.
25. Marble, interview by Tornabene.
26. Spain, *"Teach" Tennant*, 41.
27. Alice Marble, interview by Marie Nay, "Tennis at the Hilltop," Hearst San Simeon State Historical Monument Oral History Project (San Simeon, CA), Guide 1, June 4, 1977, 19.
28. Marble, with Leatherman, *Courting Danger*, 65–66.
29. Ibid., 19–20.
30. Ibid., 20.
31. Alice Marble, interview by Bud Lessor, March 11, 1975, Oral History Collection, International Tennis Hall of Fame, Newport, RI.

9. A Little Hideaway

1. Alice Marble, with Dale Leatherman, *Courting Danger: My Adventures in World-Class Tennis, Golden Age Hollywood, and High-Stakes Spying* (New York: St. Martin's Press, 1991), 32.
2. Alice Marble, interview by Marie Nay, "Tennis at the Hilltop," Hearst San Simeon State Historical Monument Oral History Project (San Simeon, CA), Guide 1, June 4, 1977, 2. Marble gives 1932 as the year of her first visit, but she also indicates she met G. B. Shaw on her first visit, though he did not come to the estate until the following year. During the interview, she acknowledged that there were aspects of the first visit that were hazy, "I can't remember—it's been too many years." Ample documentation attests that Marble and Teach made many visits over the course of the early 1930s, so some confusion is inevitable.
3. Nancy Spain, *"Teach" Tennant: The Story of Eleanor Tennant; The Greatest Tennis Coach in the World* (London: Werner Laurie, 1953), 42.
4. Victoria Kastner, *Hearst Castle: Biography of a Country House* (New York: Harry N. Abrams, 2000), 10.
5. "Pat on the Back: Eleanor Tennant," *Sports Illustrated*, January 13, 1958.
6. Alice Marble, interview by Marie Nay, "Tennis at the Hilltop," Hearst San Simeon State Historical Monument Oral History Project (San Simeon, CA), Guide 1, June 4, 1977, 2.
7. Kastner, *Hearst Castle*, 20.
8. Brendan Gill, foreword, in Robert MacKay, Anthony K. Baker, and Carol A. Traynor, *Long Island Country Houses and Their Architects, 1860–1940* (New York: Society for the Preservation of Long Island Antiquities; W. W. Norton, 1997), 13.
9. Orson Welles would base the character of Charles Foster Kane in *Citizen Kane* on Hearst, in part. Hearst, in turn, did what he could to block the success of the movie when it was released in 1941, including a ban on reviewing it in all of his publications. With Hearst fulminating in the background, the film had mediocre box office success when it opened, but after being rediscovered in the 1950s by foreign critics, it has attracted universal praise. The American Film Institute has featured it on its list of one hundred best movies ever made, twice at number one.
10. David Nasaw, *The Chief: The Life of William Randolph Hearst* (Boston: Mariner Books, 2001), 340.

11. Marble, with Leatherman, *Courting Danger*, 33.
12. Alice Marble, interview by Marie Nay, "Tennis at the Hilltop," Hearst San Simeon State Historical Monument Oral History Project (San Simeon, CA), Guide 1, June 4, 1977, 9.
13. George Plimpton believes he would have found the house rules to be "irksome"; foreword, Kastner, *Hearst Castle*, 10–11.
14. Kastner, *Hearst Castle*, 125.
15. Marble, *The Road to Wimbledon*, 109.
16. Kastner, *Hearst Castle*, 127.
17. Spain, *"Teach" Tennant*, 44.
18. Alice Marble, interview by Marie Nay, "Tennis at the Hilltop," Hearst San Simeon State Historical Monument Oral History Project (San Simeon, CA), Guide 1, June 4, 1977, 8.
19. Ibid., 10.
20. Marble, with Leatherman, *Courting Danger*, 38.
21. Alice Marble, interview by Marie Nay, "Tennis at the Hilltop," Hearst San Simeon State Historical Monument Oral History Project (San Simeon, CA), Guide 1, June 4, 1977, 19.
22. Photos of these and other costume-wearing movie stars at parties hosted by Hearst can be found in Marion Davies, *The Times We Had: Life with William Randolph Hearst* (New York: Ballantine Books, 1979).
23. Marble, with Leatherman, *Courting Danger*, 40–41.
24. Maybe not quite so final an authority. See last chapter.
25. Alice Marble, interview by Marie Nay, "Tennis at the Hilltop," Hearst San Simeon State Historical Monument Oral History Project (San Simeon, CA), Guide 1, June 4, 1977, 5.
26. In Lita Grey Chaplin, *My Life with Chaplin* (New York: Grove Press, 1966), 214–15, Davies shared with Chaplin's second wife a candid take on her relationship with Hearst: "God I'd give everything I have to marry that silly old man. Not for the money and security—he's given me more than I'll ever need. Not because he's such cozy company, either. Most times he starts jawing, he bores me stiff. And certainly not because he's so wonderful behind the barn. No, you know what he gives me? Sugar! He gives me the feeling I'm worth something to him—he snores, and he can be petty, and has sons about as old as me. But he's kind and he's good to me and I'll never walk out on him."
27. Alice Marble, interview by Marie Nay, "Tennis at the Hilltop," Hearst San Simeon State Historical Monument Oral History Project (San Simeon, CA), Guide 1, June 4, 1977, 9.
28. Alice Marble, interview by Marie Nay, "Tennis at the Hilltop," Hearst San Simeon State Historical Monument Oral History Project (San Simeon, CA), Guide 1, June 4, 1977, 11–12.
29. Alice Marble, interview by Marie Nay, "Tennis at the Hilltop," Hearst San Simeon State Historical Monument Oral History Project (San Simeon, CA), Guide 1, June 4, 1977, 6.
30. Nasaw, *The Chief*, 389. Hearst and Shaw eventually parted ideological ways. Hearst had started out as a populist and became an anti-FDR conservative by the end, especially after his enterprises imploded in the late 1930s, leaving him close to financial ruin.
31. Ibid.
32. "Shaw Bests Army of Interviewers: They Run out of Questions at San Francisco as the Dramatist Snaps Back Answers," *New York Times*, March 25, 1933.
33. Alice Marble, interview by Marie Nay, "Tennis at the Hilltop," Hearst San Simeon State Historical Monument Oral History Project (San Simeon, CA), Guide 1, June 4, 1977, 6.
34. Alice Marble, interview by Marie Nay, "Tennis at the Hilltop," Hearst San Simeon State Historical Monument Oral History Project (San Simeon, CA), Guide 1, June 4, 1977, 6.
35. Marble with Leatherman, *Courting Danger*, 40.
36. Ibid.

37. "Text of George Bernard Shaw's Address Before Throng of 3,500 at Metropolitan Opera House," *New York Times*, April 12, 1933.
38. "Tilden Raves after First Peek at Alice Marble, New Net Ace," *San Francisco Examiner*, March 16, 1933.
39. Marble, *The Road to Wimbledon*, 99.
40. Ibid., 100.

10. Heat Wave

1. Alice Marble, with Dale Leatherman, *Courting Danger: My Adventures in World-Class Tennis, Golden Age Hollywood, and High-Stakes Spying* (New York: St. Martin's Press, 1991), 25.
2. Marble, with Leatherman, *Courting Danger*, 25.
3. Marble, with Leatherman, *Courting Danger*, 26–27.
4. Larry Engelmann, *The Goddess and the American Girl: The Story of Suzanne Lenglen and Helen Wills* (New York: Oxford University Press, 1988), 412.
5. Engelmann, *The Goddess and the American Girl*, 412.
6. Frank Deford, *Big Bill Tilden: The Triumphs and the Tragedy* (New York: Simon and Schuster, 1976), 139.
7. Marble, with Leatherman, *Courting Danger*, 25.
8. Deford, *Big Bill Tilden*, 110.
9. John J. A O'Neill, "Weather Paralyzed! Can't Cool Itself Off," *The Brooklyn Daily Eagle*, August 1, 1933.
10. Nancy Randolph, "Shebas of Tennis Swelter, but 400 Sticks to Seats," *Daily News* (New York), August 1, 1933.
11. "Short on Shorts," *Ogdensburg Journal* (Ogdensburg, NY), August 1, 1933.
12. Nancy Barr Mavity, "Shorts Win Favor at State Meet; Alice Would Like to Wear Them as Pat Does," *Oakland Tribune* (Oakland, California), June 25, 1933.
13. Allison Danzig, "Miss Nuthall Wins at Maidstone Club," *New York Times*, July 31, 1933.
14. Marble, with Leatherman, *Courting Danger*, 26.
15. Bud Collins, *The Bud Collins History of Tennis: An Authoritative Encyclopedia and Record Book*, 2nd ed (Canada: New Chapter Press, 2010), 49.
16. Marble, with Leatherman, *Courting Danger*, 26.
17. Alice Marble, *The Road to Wimbledon* (London: W. H. Allen, 1947), 102.
18. "Woodin Challenge Cup Won by Miss Betty Nuthall in Maidstone Final," *East Hampton Star* (East Hampton, NY), August 4, 1933.
19. "Visitors Win at Maidstone," *American Lawn Tennis*, August 20, 1933.
20. Nancy Spain, *"Teach" Tennant: The Story of Eleanor Tennant; The Greatest Tennis Coach in the World* (London: Werner Laurie, 1953), 48.
21. As a designer, Tinling created tennis outfits worn by Martina Navratilova and Billie Jean King as well as the bridal gown worn by Chris Evert when she married John Lloyd.
22. Spain, *"Teach" Tennant*, 48.
23. Alice Marble, *The Road to Wimbledon* (London: W. H. Allen, 1947), 103.

11. Hello, Venus

1. Ted Tinling, with Rod Humphries, *Love and Faults: Personalities Who Have Changed the History of Tennis in My Lifetime* (New York: Crown, 1979), 160.

2. Bud Collins, "Death Finally Separates Two of Tennis' Great Rivals," *Los Angeles Times*, June 8, 1997.

3. Paul Gallico, "Moody by Kayo," *Daily News* (New York), August 20, 1933.

4. Mary Heely, Associated Press, "Betty Nuthall Turns Back Alice Marble by Sensational Rally," *Miami Herald*, August 20, 1933.

5. "Sport: Wightman Cup," *Time*, August 14, 1933.

6. Alice Marble, with Dale Leatherman, *Courting Danger: My Adventures in World-Class Tennis, Golden Age Hollywood, and High-Stakes Spying* (New York: St. Martin's Press, 1991), 42.

7. Linda Marble McCrory, telephone interview by author, July 13, 2019.

8. Marble, with Leatherman, *Courting Danger*, 42.

9. Alice Marble, interview by Marie Nay, "Tennis at the Hilltop," Hearst San Simeon State Historical Monument Oral History Project (San Simeon, CA), Guide 1, June 4, 1977, 8.

10. Curley Grieve, "Sports Parade, Tilden Lauds Vines, Greatest in History, Tour Huge Success, About Miss Marble," *San Francisco Examiner*, January 27, 1934.

11. Curley Grieve, "Auto Promised Alice Marble If She Wins," *San Francisco Examiner*, February 16, 1934.

12. Quoted in Marble, with Leatherman, *Courting Danger*, 44.

13. Ibid., 44–45.

14. John Lardner, "Bill Tilden's Troupe Chagrined No Little," *Nebraska State Journal* (Lincoln, NE), May 11, 1934.

15. "The Wightman Cup Players Sail," *American Lawn Tennis*, May 20, 1934. In the end, the doubles players for the American team for the 1934 Wightman Cup were Carolin Babcock, Josephine Cruickshank, Helen Jacobs, and Sarah Palfrey.

16. Marble, with Leatherman, *Courting Danger*, 45.

17. Ibid., 47.

18. In 2020, the official store at the stadium sold the Roland-Garros Mini Suzanne Lenglen Cup, 2¾ by 2¾ inches, packaged in a cardboard box, made in China, for about $60.

19. Marble, with Leatherman, *Courting Danger*, 48.

20. Alice Marble, *The Road to Wimbledon* (London: W. H. Allen, 1947), 118.

21. Marble, with Leatherman, *Courting Danger*, 48.

22. Ibid.

23. Helen Jacobs, *Gallery of Champions* (New York: A. S. Barnes, 1949), 56–57.

24. Marble, with Leatherman, *Courting Danger*, 49.

25. Jacobs, *Gallery of Champions*, 57.

26. Marble, with Leatherman, *Courting Danger*, 53.

27. Nancy Spain, *"Teach" Tennant: The Story of Eleanor Tennant; The Greatest Tennis Coach in the World* (London: Werner Laurie, 1953), 50.

28. Tinling, with Humphries, *Love and Faults*, 165–66.

29. Spain, *"Teach" Tennant*, 50.

30. Ibid.

31. "Miss Marble Is Back," *American Lawn Tennis*, July 5, 1934.

32. Curley Grieve, "Alice Marble Arrives Home; Plans Six Months' Rest, Young Tennis Ace May Quit Play for Year," *San Francisco Examiner*, July 7, 1934.

33. Marble, with Leatherman, *Courting Danger*, 55.

34. Grieve, "Alice Marble Arrives Home."

35. Spain, *"Teach" Tennant*, 16.

12. "You Don't Know Me, But . . ."

1. Alice Marble, *The Road to Wimbledon* (London: W. H. Allen, 1947), 124.

2. The brochures for the Pottenger Sanatorium claim that it is only sixteen miles out of the city, but Marble gives it as twenty-five miles in *The Road to Wimbledon*. In later years, Marble told interviewers that Teach would visit her daily at 150 miles a day round trip, inflating the distance first a bit and then a bit more.

3. F. M. Pottenger, "The Pottenger Sanatorium for Diseases of the Lungs and Throat, Monrovia, California, U.S.A.," *British Journal of Tuberculosis*, July 1911.

4. Thomas M. Daniel, *Captain of Death: The Story of Tuberculosis* (Rochester, NY: University of Rochester Press, 1999), 89.

5. Ibid., 91.

6. Even today, tuberculosis is not eradicated. In "We Know How to Conquer Tuberculosis," September 26, 2018, the *New York Times* editorial board cautioned: "Tuberculosis remains the world's leading infectious disease killer, by far. It infects some 10 million people around the world every year, killing roughly 1.5 million. That's some 4,000 deaths per day. By comparison, Ebola killed four people in 2017. America's opioid epidemic kills about 115 people a day."

7. Francis M. Pottenger, *The Diagnosis and Treatment of Pulmonary Tuberculosis* (New York: William Wood, 1908), 126, 127.

8. Ibid., 136–37.

9. Ibid., 128.

10. Marble, *The Road to Wimbledon*, 125–26.

11. "Alice Marble, in Sanatorium, Hopes to Play Tennis in '35," *The San Francisco News*, September 11, 1934.

12. Alice Marble, with Dale Leatherman, *Courting Danger: My Adventures in World-Class Tennis, Golden Age Hollywood, and High-Stakes Spying* (New York: St. Martin's Press, 1991), 61.

13. Marble, *The Road to Wimbledon*, 127.

14. Larry Swindell, *Screwball: The Life of Carole Lombard* (Brattleboro, VT: Echo Point Books and Media, 2016), 50–51.

15. "Suit over Scar on Girl Settled," *Los Angeles Times*, October 15, 1927.

16. Marble, with Leatherman, *Courting Danger*, 59.

17. Nancy Spain, *"Teach" Tennant: The Story of Eleanor Tennant; The Greatest Tennis Coach in the World* (London: Werner Laurie, 1953), 53–54.

18. Spain, *"Teach" Tennant*, 52.

19. Marble, with Leatherman, *Courting Danger*, 59.

20. "Miss Tennant Tells Secret of Success to Eager Vassar Tennis Enthusiasts," *Vassar Miscellany News* 23, no. 5, October 15, 1938.

21. Marble, *The Road to Wimbledon* 135.

22. Noel F. Busch, "A Loud Cheer for the Screwball Girl," *Life* magazine, October 17, 1938.

23. Marble, quoted in Lyn Tornabene, *Long Live the King: A Biography of Clark Gable* (New York: G. P. Putnam's Sons, 1976), 218.

24. "'Tomboy' Lombard Earned 2,000,000," *Los Angeles Times*, January 18, 1942.

25. Swindell, *Screwball*, 177.

26. "'Tomboy' Lombard Earned 2,000,000."

27. Marble frequently referenced people whose names needed no elaboration in her time, but some have faded from the spotlight. Louise Macy appears to have been a fashion

journalist and socialite who married Harry Hopkins from Pasadena, a trusted adviser to FDR.

28. Marble, *The Road to Wimbledon*, 134.
29. Alice Marble, interview by Courtney Gebhart, July 25, 1987, Prickly Pears: Portraits of Historical Palm Springs (local history project), vol. 48, Palm Springs Public Library, Palm Springs, CA.
30. Alice Marble, interview by Lyn Tornabene, March 23, 1974, in Palm Desert, CA, Clark Gable collection compiled by Lyn Tornabene, Margaret Herrick Library, Academy of Motion Picture Arts and Sciences, Beverly Hills, CA.
31. Ibid.
32. Ibid.
33. "Chic off Court, She Also Serves with Glamour," *Courier-Journal* (Louisville, KY), September 10, 1939.

13. Starry Nights

1. Alice Marble, interview by Courtney Gebhart, July 25, 1987, Prickly Pears: Portraits of Historical Palm Springs (local history project), vol. 48, Palm Springs Public Library, Palm Springs, CA.
2. Toward the end of his career, Charles Farrell played Vern Albright on the television show *My Little Margie*, and Ralph Bellamy's last film appearance was in *Pretty Woman*, with Julia Roberts and Richard Gere.
3. Renee Brown, "Racquet Club Attracted Hollywood to Area," *Desert Sun* (Palm Springs, CA), July 3, 2016.
4. Jamie Lee Pricer, "Valley's Tennis Heartland," *Desert Sun*, March 9, 2009.
5. Marble, interview by Gebhart.
6. Alice Marble, with Dale Leatherman, *Courting Danger: My Adventures in World-Class Tennis, Golden Age Hollywood, and High-Stakes Spying* (New York: St. Martin's Press, 1991), 70.
7. Marble, *The Road to Wimbledon*, 140.
8. Marble, with Leatherman, *Courting Danger*, 74–75.
9. Ibid., 75.
10. Ibid.
11. Mark Kelly, "Tennis Committee Hit for Ignoring Miss Alice Marble," *San Francisco Examiner*, July 5, 1935.
12. Marble, *The Road to Wimbledon*, 144.
13. The *Los Angeles Times* and United Press reported Marble and Casey lost the doubles, but the *Desert Sun*, International News Service, *Illustrated Daily News*, and subsequent news accounts give them the victory.
14. "Budge, Mako and Other Net Stars at Racquet Club," *Desert Sun*, March 13, 1936.
15. Bernard Brown, "Alice Should Make Successful Comeback," *Brooklyn Times Union*, April 15, 1936.
16. Sparky Salduna, "Budge in Easy Net Win over Tidball," *Illustrated Daily News* (Los Angeles), March 9, 1936.
17. United Press, "Budge Beats Shields," *News-Pilot* (San Pedro, CA), March 24, 1936.
18. Marble, with Leatherman, *Courting Danger*, 72.
19. United Press, "Don Budge Again Wins Palm Springs Tourney," *Los Angeles Times*, March 30, 1936.
20. Marble, with Leatherman, *Courting Danger*, 73.

21. International News Service, "Alice Marble Denied Place on Wightman Team," *Fresno Bee* (Fresno, CA), March 31, 1936.
22. Wallace X. Rawles, International News Service, "Alice Marble, Health Back, Eyes World Net Title," *Des Moines Tribune*, April 24, 1936.
23. Bill Henry, "Riggs Beats Carr to Capture Tennis Title, Junior New Net Champ Alice Marble in Title Win," *Los Angeles Times*, May 11, 1936.
24. "Alice Marble Travels East," *Los Angeles Times*, May 24, 1936.
25. Marble, *The Road to Wimbledon*, 62.
26. "Star Feminine Netter to Play Matches Here," *Salt Lake Tribune*, May 24, 1936.
27. "Alice Marble Thrills Fans in Salt Lake," *Salt Lake Tribune*, May 25, 1936.
28. "California Net Star Plays Here," *Omaha Bee-News*, May 27, 1936.
29. Nate Cutler, "On Comeback Trail—California Net Star Plays Here," *Omaha Bee-News*, May 28, 1936.
30. Marble, with Leatherman, *Courting Danger*, 78.
31. Mrs. Penrose Lyly, "Play Tennis for Beauty," *San Bernardino County Sun* (San Bernardino, CA), June 26, 1938.
32. Marble, with Leatherman, *Courting Danger*, 78.
33. Phil Gundelfinger Jr., "Marble Rolling Right Along," *The Pittsburgh Press*, June 24, 1936.
34. Marble, with Leatherman, *Courting Danger*, 78–79.
35. Ibid., 79.
36. Ibid., 80.
37. Ibid.
38. Nancy Spain, *"Teach" Tennant: The Story of Eleanor Tennant; The Greatest Tennis Coach in the World* (London: Werner Laurie, 1953), 60.
39. Ted Tinling, with Rod Humphries, *Love and Faults: Personalities Who Have Changed the History of Tennis in My Lifetime* (New York: Crown, 1979), 168.
40. Marble, with Leatherman, *Courting Danger*, 81.
41. Ibid.

14. And Then . . . She Kissed It

1. Monica Randall, *The Mansions of Long Island's Gold Coast* (New York: Rizzoli, 1987), 246.
2. Alice Marble, with Dale Leatherman, *Courting Danger: My Adventures in World-Class Tennis, Golden Age Hollywood, and High-Stakes Spying* (New York: St. Martin's Press, 1991), 82.
3. "Life as a Boy Made Kahn Arts Patron," *New York Times*, March 30, 1934.
4. Randall, *The Mansions of Long Island*, 246.
5. Stammers, a pilot, drove ambulances during World War II and married twice. Her second marriage, to an American, brought her to Louisville, Kentucky, where she ran annual steeplechases for charity. She traveled to Wimbledon every year until physically unable to do so.
6. Marble, with Leatherman, *Courting Danger*, 82.
7. Larry Engelmann, *The Goddess and the American Girl: The Story of Suzanne Lenglen and Helen Wills* (New York: Oxford University Press, 1988), 405.
8. Marble, with Leatherman, *Courting Danger*, 72.
9. Alice Marble, "Eye-Poppers," *News-Herald* (Franklin, PA), April 10, 1944.
10. Marble, with Leatherman, *Courting Danger*, 85.
11. Ibid.
12. Ibid., 86.

13. Marble, with Leatherman, *Courting Danger*, 87.

14. Ellsworth Vines, American Newspapers, Inc., "Alice Will Make Great Champion," *San Francisco Examiner*, September 13, 1936.

15. Art Rosenbaum, "Helen's Mother Phones Mrs. Marble," *San Francisco Chronicle*, September 13, 1936.

16. Curley Grieve, "Dan Marble Attacks Acts of Net Moguls; Brother of New Champion Blames Myrick for Her Collapse during '34," *San Francisco Examiner*, September 13, 1936.

17. Marble, with Leatherman, *Courting Danger*, 90.

18. Carolyn Anspacher, "She Won't Talk; Alice Marble, Mum, Arrives in S.F.," *San Francisco Chronicle*, October 18, 1936.

19. Curley Grieve, "Alice Marble Arrives for Net Match Today," *San Francisco Examiner*, October 18, 1936.

20. Marble, with Leatherman, *Courting Danger*, 91.

21. Ibid., 93.

22. Ibid., 90.

23. Ibid., 92.

24. Harry B. Smith, "Alice to Prepare for Wimbledon Net Invasion," *San Francisco Chronicle*, October 23, 1936.

25. Marble, with Leatherman, *Courting Danger*, 92.

26. Grace Wilcox, "Christmas Comes to Hollywood," *Democrat and Chronicle* (Rochester, NY), December 20, 1936.

27. John Robert Powers, with Mary Sue Miller, *Secrets of Charm* (Philadelphia: John C. Winston, 1954), vii.

28. Ibid., 56–57.

29. "The Mayfair Ball," Dear Mr. Gable: Clark Gable Archive, accessed December 6, 2021, dearmrgable.com.

30. Louella O. Parsons, "'Stepping Toes' to Be Next Astaire-Rogers Dance Film," *San Francisco Examiner*, October 13, 1936.

31. Dick Williams, "How the Girl Weakling Became Champion," *Physical Culture: The Personal Problem Magazine*, January 1937.

32. Associated Press, "New Row Is Started by Tennis Rankings," *Akron Beacon Journal* (Akron, OH), January 4, 1937.

33. Associated Press, "Alice for Films, Miss Marble Starts Her Plans," *San Francisco Examiner*, February 7, 1937.

15. The Heart of Their Universe

1. Virginia Vale, "Star Dust," *Comstock News* (Comstock, NE), February 4, 1937.

2. Associated Press, "Alice for Films, Miss Marble Starts Her Plans," *San Francisco Examiner*, February 7, 1937.

3. Dick Charnock, "National Net Queen Splits Sets in Duel," *Pasadena Post* (Pasadena, CA), March 9, 1937.

4. "Alice Marble Defeats Dorothy Workman," *Los Angeles Times*, April 6, 1937.

5. Louella Parsons, "March Will Play La Fitte in DeMille's 'Buccaneer,'" *San Francisco Examiner*, April 13, 1937.

6. Alice Marble, with Dale Leatherman, *Courting Danger: My Adventures in World-Class Tennis, Golden Age Hollywood, and High-Stakes Spying* (New York: St. Martin's Press, 1991), 93.

7. Davison Obear, "Weinstock to Play Women's Champion in Tennis Match," *St. Louis Post-Dispatch*, April 16, 1937.

8. Davison Obear, "Alice Marble Breaks Even with Two Set Exhibition Tennis Match with Robert Weinstock," *St. Louis Post-Dispatch*, April 20, 1937.

9. Associated Press, "Last Coronation Ships Sail from United States," *Boston Globe*, May 5, 1937.

10. Associated Press, "Alice Marble Boards Ship for England and Wimbledon Meet," *Indianapolis News*, May 4, 1937.

11. "Alice Marble, Babe Ruth in Sports News," May 1, 1937, Paramount, Pathe Newsreels, Sherman Grinberg Film Library, Los Angeles, CA.

12. Marble, with Leatherman, *Courting Danger*, 94.

13. Ibid., 92–93.

14. Our London Correspondent, "Miss Marble in England," *American Lawn Tennis*, June 20, 1937.

15. Alice Marble, As I See It, *American Lawn Tennis*, October 1947.

16. Judith Dixon, former tennis coach at the University of Massachusetts, Amherst, interview by author, spring 2015.

17. Christopher Benfey, Andrew W. Mellon Professor of English at Mount Holyoke College and author of *If: The Untold Story of Kipling's American Years* (New York: Penguin Press, 2019), in interview by author, September 15, 2018, explains what Kipling likely meant by the two imposters: "Kipling experienced what many might consider triumphs (world famous in his early twenties, Nobel Prize winner at age forty-two) and disasters (farmed out with a sadistic English foster-mother at the age of five, he endured beatings and psychological humiliation for six years; his beloved daughter, Josephine, died of the flu at age eight; and his son was blown to bits in World War I). I think he wanted stronger words than mere success and failure, hence triumph and disaster. He seemed to be warning his readers not to view their lives as high melodrama. A tennis player might think something like this: How should I look at winning and losing? A win—even a major tournament win—has to be kept in perspective. It doesn't mean 'I'll always win.' And a loss, well, it's not a disaster; I've got to forget it and move on. Tomorrow, as someone else said, is another day."

18. Stanley N. Doust, "So Nervy She Even Forgot Her Bow to the Queen," *Daily Mail* (London), June 28, 1939.

19. Don Budge, *A Tennis Memoir* (New York, Viking Press, 1969), 51–52.

20. Bud Collins, *My Life with the Pros* (New York: E. P. Dutton, 1989), 240, 244.

21. This quote appears on pages 116–17 in one of the most remarkable books about tennis ever written, *A Terrible Splendor: Three Extraordinary Men, A World Poised for War, and the Greatest Tennis Match Ever Played* (New York: Crown, 2009), by Marshall Jon Fisher, which takes readers to a 1937 Davis Cup match, played at Wimbledon, with Don Budge, number-one player, going against Baron Gottfried von Cramm from Germany, number two. The life-and-death stakes were hidden from most of the spectators and even most tennis insiders. Thurber made the comments in a piece titled "Budge and Television," originally published in the *New Yorker*.

22. Bruce Harris, "Players to Watch at Wimbledon To-day: Finding the Women Semi-finalists," *Evening Standard* (London), June 29, 1937.

23. A. Wallis Myers, "Miss Round in Wimbledon Final," *Daily Telegraph* (London), July 1, 1937.

24. Marble, with Leatherman, *Courting Danger*, 100.

25. Don Budge, *A Tennis Memoir* (New York, Viking Press, 1969), 166.

26. Associated Press, "American Entries Advance in Tennis in Wimbledon Play," *Daily Press* (Newport News, VA), June 23, 1937.

27. "Miss Marble Back from Play Abroad," *New York Times*, July 14, 1937.

28. Associated Press, "Polish Net Queen Picks Up Slang," *Brooklyn Daily Eagle*, July 30, 1937.

29. Allison Danzig, "Miss Marble Beats Miss Jedrzejowska in Thrilling Final at Seabright Net," *New York Times*, July 31, 1937.

30. Our Alice Is Out for Revenge!" *The Daily News* (New York), August 15, 1936.

31. Allison Danzig, "Polish Ace Victor Over Miss Marble in Straight Sets," *New York Times*, August 15, 1936.

32. United Press, "Polish Girl Scores Straight-Set Triumph over Alice Marble in Rye Final," *Pittsburgh Press*, August 15, 1937.

33. United Press, "U.S. Needs One Match to Keep Wightman Cup," *Detroit Free Press*, August 21, 1937.

34. Bill King, Associated Press, "Von Cramm, Henkel Defeat Budge, Mako in Finals," *Salt Lake Tribune*, August 31, 1937.

35. Allison Danzig, "Miss Bundy Dethrones Miss Marble as National Net Queen," *New York Times*, September 9, 1937.

36. Gene Ward, "Champion Marble Beaten by Bundy," *Daily News* (New York), September 9, 1937.

37. Marble, with Leatherman, *Courting Danger*, 108.

38. Ibid., 110.

39. Ibid., 112.

40. Ibid.

41. Ibid., 115.

42. Ibid., 117.

43. Alice Marble, interview by Bud Lessor, March 11, 1975, Oral History Collection, International Tennis Hall of Fame, Newport, RI.

44. Advertisement, "Alice Marble Enters a New Field," *Los Angeles Times*, December 28, 1937.

45. "Getting in Trim," *World* (Coos Bay, OR), February 23, 1938.

46. Curley Grieve, "Miss Marble Now Is Style Expert," *San Francisco Examiner*, March 2, 1938.

47. "Hunt, Wood Lead Entries," *Los Angeles Times*, April 5, 1938.

48. Bill Henry, "Alice Marble, Don Budge in Mixed Doubles Victory," *Los Angeles Times*, April 17, 1938.

49. Bill Henry, "Wood Captures Tennis Title," *Los Angeles Times*, April 18, 1938.

50. "Alice Marble in Net Exhibitions Here," *St. Louis Star-Times*, April 30, 1938.

51. Associated Press, "Alice Marble Leaves on Trip to Wimbledon," *Miami News*, April 25, 1938.

52. "Today's Features," *Chicago Tribune*, April 27, 1938.

53. "Alice Marble to Open Class for Juniors Today," *Chicago Tribune*, April 28, 1938.

54. June Provines, "Big City Sights," *Chicago Tribune*, April 30, 1938.

55. Davison Obear, "Alice Marble, Top-Ranking Woman Tennis Star, to Play Here Today," *St. Louis Post-Dispatch* (St. Louis, MO), April 30, 1938.

56. "Marble at Tops," *Daily News* (New York), May 6, 1938.

57. Harold Parrott, "Pick up the Marbles, Hunter Prefers Wills," *Brooklyn Daily Eagle*, May 6, 1938.

58. Budge, *A Tennis Memoir*, 108.

59. Beatrice Oppenheim, "Lack Time to Be Ourselves," *Brooklyn Eagle*, March 31, 1929.

60. Marble, with Leatherman, *Courting Danger*, 120.
61. Ibid., 121.
62. Larry Engelmann, *The Goddess and the American Girl: The Story of Suzanne Lenglen and Helen Wills* (New York: Oxford University Press, 1988), 415.
63. Associated Press, "Alice Misses on Crucial Shot," *San Francisco Examiner*, July 1, 1938.
64. Marble, with Leatherman, *Courting Danger*, 121.
65. Ibid., 122.
66. "Helen Moody Sets Record with 8th Wimbledon Title," *San Francisco Examiner*, July 3, 1938.
67. Marble, with Leatherman, *Courting Danger*, 123.
68. "The Editor's Talk with His Readers," *American Lawn Tennis*, July 20, 1938.
69. "Miss Sketch's' Diary," *Sketch*, July 13, 1938.
70. "Suzanne Lenglen, Tennis Star, Dies," *New York Times*, July 4, 1938.
71. "Mlle. Lenglen," *New York Times*, July 5, 1938.
72. Maurice Blein, "Wimbledon Whimsy," *American Lawn Tennis*, July 20, 1938.
73. Alfred Bloomingdale is known as the father of the credit card and served as an adviser in Ronald Reagan's "kitchen cabinet." His love life always seemed to be an issue. When he died in 1982, his thirty-year-old paramour of twelve years sued his estate for posthumous lifetime support, which Bloomingdale had supposedly promised and his widow mostly blocked.
74. Marble, with Leatherman, *Courting Danger*, 127.
75. Ibid., 131.
76. Ibid., 132.
77. Allison Danzig, "Brilliant Triumph Enables Miss Marble to Retire Seabright Bowl," *New York Times*, August 1, 1938.
78. Harold Parrott, "Tennis Scene Shifts to Two Local Fronts," *Brooklyn Daily Eagle*, August 1, 1938.
79. "The Ladies at Rye," *American Lawn Tennis*, August 20, 1938.
80. Associated Press, "Alice Marble Wins Singles, Doubles Titles," *Salt Lake Tribune*, August 21, 1938.
81. Allison Danzig, "Unseated Player Upsets Bromwich," *New York Times*, September 24, 1939.
82. Wynne's wins spanned sixteen years (interrupted by World War II), during which time she won twenty major titles, all in Australia, a record eventually beaten by Margaret Court, with twenty-one titles.
83. Warren Hill and Pam Stockley, *Nancye Wynne Bolton: An Australian Tennis Champion* (Burwood East, Victoria: Memoirs Foundation, 2009).
84. "Miss Marble Makes a Come-back," *American Lawn Tennis*, September 20, 1938.
85. Associated Press, "Alice Marble Gives Secret of Keeping Trim in Figure," *Greenville News* (Greenville, SC), May 8, 1938.
86. Grieve, "Miss Marble Is Now Style Expert."
87. Babette, "Alice Marble Shows Her New Style Designs Here," *San Francisco Examiner*, March 4, 1938.
88. Mary Hampton's Column, *Santa Cruz Sentinel* (Santa Cruz, CA), March 10, 1938.

16. Debut Tonight!
1. Alice Marble, *The Road to Wimbledon* (London: W. H. Allen, 1947), 161.
2. William Alan Morrison, *Images of America: Waldorf Astoria* (Charleston, SC: Arcadia, 2014), 45.

3. Frank Farrell, *The Greatest of Them All* (New York: K. S. Giniger, 1982), 33, 112, 118.

4. Lucius Boomer, *Hotel Management* (New York and London: Harper and Brothers, 1931), 13.

5. Ibid., 375.

6. Ibid., 377, 378.

7. Ibid., 379.

8. Ibid., 481.

9. Morrison, *Images of America*, 110.

10. Langston Hughes, *The Big Sea: An Autobiography* (New York: Hill and Wang, 1993), 321.

11. Farrell, *The Greatest of Them All*, 36, 37.

12. "Death Toll in Storm Exceeds 50; 40,000 Clearing Streets in City," *New York Times*, November 26, 1938.

13. Gene Lube, "Question and Answer, A conversation with . . . Alice Marble," *Desert Sun* (Palm Springs, CA), July 27, 1981.

14. International News Service, "Tennis Champion Goes Glamouring," *Leader Telegram* (Eau Claire, WI), November 27, 1938.

15. "Ted Straeter, Band Leader, Dies in Florida," *St. Louis Globe-Democrat*, April 3, 1963; Alice Marble, with Dale Leatherman, *Courting Danger: My Adventures in World-Class Tennis, Golden Age Hollywood, and High-Stakes Spying* (New York: St. Martin's Press, 1991), 135.

16. Beverly Beyette, "Wimbledon Puts Alice Back in Wonderland," *Los Angeles Times*, June 22, 1983.

17. The description of where Alice performed is courtesy of *The Unofficial Palace of New York: A Tribute to the Waldorf-Astoria*, ed. Frank Crowninshield (New York: Hotel Waldorf-Astoria Corporation, 1939). The section cited is "The Sert Room," from the essay, "The Murals of José Maria Sert," by Royal Cortissoz, 90.

18. Beyette, "Wimbledon Puts Alice Back in Wonderland."

19. Marble, *The Road to Wimbledon*, 163–64.

20. "Miss Marble Sings," *American Lawn Tennis*, December 20, 1938.

21. Alice Hughes, "A Woman's New York," *Star Press* (Muncie, IN), December 7, 1938.

22. Inez Robb, "The Singing Athlete," *St. Louis Post-Dispatch*, December 1, 1938.

23. Marble, *The Road to Wimbledon*, 164.

24. Barbara Klaw, "Queen Mother of Tennis," *American Heritage*, August 1975, www.americanheritage.com/queen-mother-tennis.

17. July 8, 1939

1. Harry Grayson, "Only Marble Can Beat Marble in English Tourney," *Cumberland Evening Times* (Cumberland, MD), May 27, 1939.

2. Nancy Spain, *"Teach" Tennant: The Story of Eleanor Tennant; The Greatest Tennis Coach in the World* (London: Werner Laurie, 1953), 63.

3. Ted Tinling, with Rod Humphries, *Love and Faults: Personalities Who Have Changed the History of Tennis in My Lifetime* (New York: Crown, 1979), 163.

4. "German Jews Face a Crushing Task," *New York Times*, July 8, 1939.

5. "Behind the Scenes at Wimbledon," *Daily Sketch* (Manchester, UK), June 16, 1939.

6. *News Chronicle* (London), June 26, 1939.

7. Stanley N. Doust, "10 You Ought to Know," *Daily Mail*, June 26, 1939.

8. *Daily Sketch*, June 30, 1939.

9. "Alice Marble at Best for Wimbledon Event," *San Francisco Examiner*, June 11, 1939.

10. Don Budge, *A Tennis Memoir* (New York, Viking Press, 1969), 84.

11. Beverly Beyette, "Wimbledon Puts Alice Back in Wonderland," *Los Angeles Times*, June 22, 1983.
12. "Wimbledon, Greatest Lawn Tennis Tournament in the World, Opens Today," *Daily Mail* (London), June 26, 1939.
13. "Queue Out, Queue In," *Daily Herald* (London), July 8, 1939.
14. Will Swift, *The Kennedys Amidst the Gathering Storm: A Thousand Days in London, 1938–1940* (New York: Smithsonian Books; Collins, 2008), 32.
15. Alice Marble, with Dale Leatherman, *Courting Danger: My Adventures in World-Class Tennis, Golden Age Hollywood, and High-Stakes Spying* (New York: St. Martin's Press, 1991), 143–44.
16. Beyette, "Wimbledon Puts Alice Back in Wonderland."
17. "Saturday, July 8," *American Lawn Tennis*, July 20, 1939.
18. Joan Goldthrop, "Alice Beats Kay—and the Doctor," *Weekly Dispatch* (London), July 9, 1939.
19. "Lawn Tennis, The Championships, A Wimbledon Fairy Tale," *The Times* (London), July 10, 1939.
20. Marble, with Leatherman, *Courting Danger*, 144.
21. Associated Press, "English Title to Coast Miss," *Lincoln Star* (Lincoln, NE), July 8, 1939.
22. "Star's Conscience Comes First: Boxer's Come-back Bid," *The Daily Mirror*, July 10, 1939.
23. Associated Press, "English Title to Coast Miss."
24. Marble, with Leatherman, *Courting Danger*, 145.
25. Ibid.
26. Ibid., 146.
27. "Saturday, July 8," *American Lawn Tennis*, July 20, 1939.
28. James Reston, Associated Press, "Alice Marble Wins Wimbledon Title, Downs Kay Stammers," *The Philadelphia Inquirer*, July 9, 1939.
29. "The L.T.A. Ball," *Birmingham Daily Post* (Birmingham, UK), July 10, 1939.
30. Roy McKelvie, "America Triumphs at Wimbledon," *Sphere* (London), July 15, 1939.
31. Spain, *"Teach" Tennant*, 73.
32. Marble with Leatherman, *Courting Danger*, 149.

18. Swing High, Swing Low

1. Frances O'Rourke, "Great Irish Tenor's Dublin Home for €3.6 M," *Irish Times*, February 3, 2016.
2. "Alice Marble's Success, Girl Beats Man at Lawn Tennis," *Belfast Telegraph*, July 14, 1939.
3. Associated Press, "Alice Marble Has New Prof.—McCormack," *Courier-Journal* (Louisville, KY), July 15, 1939.
4. International News Service, "Alice Marble Earns Contract in Hollywood," *Tribune* (Scranton, PA), July 12, 1939.
5. "'Marvellous Time' Says Miss Marble," *Leicester Daily Mercury* (Leiscester, UK), July 19, 1939.
6. *Rapport de voyage du paquebot Champlain (CGT 1932), juillet 1939*, © Collection French Lines, 1997 004 4963.
7. William H. Miller, *Picture History of the French Line* (Mineola, NY: Dover Publications Inc., 1997), 29, 30.
8. Associated Press, "Films May Woo Her but Her Heart Belongs to Tennis," *Detroit Free Press*, July 28, 1939.

9. Alice Marble, with Dale Leatherman, *Courting Danger: My Adventures in World-Class Tennis, Golden Age Hollywood, and High-Stakes Spying* (New York: St. Martin's Press, 1991), 152.

10. Alice Marble, The Net Set, *Palm Desert Post* (Palm Desert, CA), December 16, 1971.

11. Marble, with Leatherman, *Courting Danger*, 152.

12. Eisenstaedt's enduring images include one of a headwaiter on skates at St. Moritz balancing a bottle and glasses on a tray; Hitler in his last public appearance, garbed in civilian clothing; a sailor kissing a woman in Times Square, scooping her up in his arms, on August 14, 1945, to celebrate the end of World War II; children at a puppet theater in the Tuileries Garden in Paris in 1963, wide-eyed and focused on a peaceful present; Marilyn Monroe in a black turtleneck and white capris, with her prominent mole, the defect that threw her perfection into even greater relief.

13. Alfred Eisenstaedt, *Eisenstaedt on Eisenstaedt: A Self-Portrait* (New York: Abbeville Press, 1985), 116.

14. "U.S. Publishers, Who Flew the Atlantic, Return with Assurances of Peace," *Life*, July 24, 1939, 18.

15. Anne Fadiman, *The Wine-Lover's Daughter* (New York: Farrar, Straus and Giroux, 2017), 43–44.

16. *Look*, May 7, 1940.

17. Gayle Talbot, Associated Press, "Alice Marble's Play Brilliant," *Fort Worth Star-Telegram*, September 13, 1939.

18. Allison Danzig, as quoted by Bud Collins, *The Bud Collins History of Tennis: An Authoritative Encyclopedia and Record Book* 2nd ed., Canada: New Chapter Press, 2010, 66.

19. Harry Grayson, "She Also Serves," *San Bernardino County Sun* (San Bernardino, CA), October 1, 1939.

20. *Illustrated Sporting and Dramatic News* (London), September 22, 1939.

21. Grayson, "She Also Serves."

22. Marble, with Leatherman, *Courting Danger*, 156.

23. Beverly Beyette, "Wimbledon Puts Alice Back in Wonderland," *Los Angeles Times*, June 22, 1983.

24. Steven Slosberg, "Margarita Madrigal—Dedicated to Being Extraordinary," *New London Day* (New London, CT), March 6, 1978.

25. Whitney Bolton, "Glancing Sideways," *Cumberland Evening Times* (Cumberland, MD), August 12, 1963.

26. Marble, with Leatherman, *Courting Danger*, 156.

27. Ibid., 154–55.

28. Ibid., 155.

29. Dorothy Kilgallen, "Outstanding Women of 1939 Selected by Women Writer," *The Morning Post* (Camden, NJ), December 30, 1939.

30. Bob Considine, "Sweet Alice Hid Killer Instinct," *San Francisco Examiner*, December 28, 1939.

19. $100,000 on the Table

1. Mark Bowden and Clea Benson, "The Prince of Newtown Square," *Philadelphia Inquirer*, February 4, 1996.

2. "William du Pont of Fair Hill," *Wilmington Morning News* (Wilmington, DE), January 5, 1966.

3. Red Smith, "Paradise for Horse-Players," *Saturday Evening Post*, June 29, 1957.

4. William du Pont Jr. papers, Manuscripts and Archives Department, Hagley Museum and Library, Wilmington, DE.
5. Alice Marble, with Dale Leatherman, *Courting Danger: My Adventures in World-Class Tennis, Golden Age Hollywood, and High-Stakes Spying* (New York: St. Martin's Press, 1991), 158–59.
6. Ibid.
7. Du Pont to Tennant, March 8, 1940, William du Pont Jr. papers.
8. Du Pont to Tennant, April 4, 1940, William du Pont Jr. papers.
9. Marble, with Leatherman, *Courting Danger*, 163.
10. William du Pont Jr. papers.
11. "Sport Roundup," Eddie Brietz, *Marshfield News-Herald* (Marshfield, WI), August 12, 1940.
12. "Tennis Fans See Fine Exhibition," *Shreveport Times* (Shreveport, LA), May 6, 1940.
13. "Alice Marble Thrills 2,500 at Clinton," *Greenville News* (Greenville, SC), May 14, 1940.
14. Charlie Roberts, "Alice Marble Plays Virginia Wolfenden in Women's Finals," *Atlanta Constitution*, May 19, 1940.
15. Charlie Roberts, "Marble, Grant Win Net Titles in Finals Here," *Atlanta Constitution*, May 20, 1940.
16. "Alice Marble Gains Victory," *Akron Beacon Journal* (Akron, OH), June 3, 1940.
17. Jack Guenther, United Press, "California Needs Help to Carry Tennis Load," *Wisconsin State Journal*, June 6, 1940.
18. "Town Planning Advantages Cited by Seaford Speaker," *Wilmington Morning News*, June 15, 1940.
19. Turfman, "Delaware Park Notes," *Wilmington Morning News*, June 7, 1940.
20. "National Net Champions in W.C.C. Exhibitions," *News Journal* (Wilmington, DE), June 10, 1940.
21. "Greentree Stable's Piquet Victor in Delaware Oaks," *Wilmington Morning News*, June 14, 1940.
22. Dorie Lurie, "Men Have Last Word at Nets," *Philadelphia Inquirer*, June 12, 1940.
23. Associated Press, "Riggs Falls before McNeill," *San Francisco Examiner*, June 25, 1940.
24. "Tennis Notes," *Evening Sun* (Baltimore), July 16, 1940.
25. Paul Menton, "Alice Marble Is Star Attraction," *Evening Sun* (Baltimore), July 18, 1940.
26. Associated Press, "M'Neill Tops Kramer for Baltimore Crown," *News and Observer* (Raleigh, NC), July 21, 1940.
27. "Alice Marble Trims Pauline Betz in Maryland–Middle Atlantic Tennis," *Baltimore Sun*, July 22, 1940.
28. Associated Press, "Marble Enjoying 'At Home' Season," *Evening Sun* (Baltimore), July 22, 1940.
29. Associated Press, "Alice Marble Dominates Women's Play," *Courier-News* (Bridgewater, NJ), July 29, 1940.
30. Allison Danzig, "Alice Marble Tops Miss Jacobs at Net," *New York Times*, August 11, 1940.
31. Henry McLemore, United Press, "Alice Marble Just Too Good for Her Women's Net Foes," *Buffalo Evening News*, August 19, 1940.
32. Sarah Palfrey divorced her first husband, Marshall Fabyan, on July 29, 1940, and married Elwood Cooke on October 2, 1940.
33. Allison Danzig, "Kramer-Schroeder Beat Mulloy-Prusoff for National Doubles Tennis Crown," *New York Times*, August 26, 1940.

34. Lawton Carver, International News Service, "U.S.A. Tennis Has Sad Slump, Alice Marble from West Coast Only Headliner in Game Today," *Lincoln Star* (Lincoln, NE), August 23, 1940.

35. Monica Randall, *The Mansions of Long Island's Gold Coast* (New York: Rizzoli, 1987), 40–44.

36. Marble, with Leatherman, *Courting Danger*, 165.

37. Bud Collins, *The Bud Collins History of Tennis: An Authoritative Encyclopedia and Record Book* 2nd ed. Canada: New Chapter Press, 2010, 68.

38. R. W. Apple Jr., "James Reston, for Many Years a Nonpareil among American Journalists, Dies at 86," *New York Times*, December 7, 1975.

39. Allison Danzig, "The Pigs at Fair Wimbledon," in *The Greatest Sports Stories from* The New York Times*: Sport Classics of a Century*, ed. Allison Danzig and Peter Brandwein (New York: A. S. Barnes, 1951), 527.

40. Burton Benjamin, "Alice Marble Still Serves—For U.S. Navy," *Coshocton Tribune* (Coshocton, OH), May 13, 1942.

41. Marble, with Leatherman, *Courting Danger*, 160.

42. "Alice Marble: WNEW Hires Tennis Champ to Comment on Football," WNEW 1130 AM, accessed June 2, 2022, https://www.wnew1130.com/sports/staff/alice-marble.

43. Adelaide Kerr, Associated Press, "These Women!" *Kingston Daily Freeman* (Kingston, NY), November 23, 1940.

44. "Girl Football Guesser with Alice Marble," *Variety*, October 30, 1940.

45. "Alice Marble Becomes First Lady Football Announcer," *Brooklyn Daily Eagle*, October 11, 1940.

46. Marble, with Leatherman, *Courting Danger*, 170.

47. In today's dollars this would amount to a payday of about $1 million each for Alice and Teach.

20. Sixty-One Stops

1. Don Budge, *A Tennis Memoir* (New York: Viking Press, 1969), 129.

2. Frank Deford, *Big Bill Tilden: The Triumphs and the Tragedy* (New York: Simon and Schuster, 1976), 182–184. Details of Tilden's early life are a synopsis of information attained in this excellent volume.

3. Deford, *Big Bill Tilden*, 205–6

4. Ibid., 163.

5. S. W. Merrihew, "The Editor's Talks with His Readers," *American Lawn Tennis*, July 20, 1938.

6. Budge, *A Tennis Memoir*, 128.

7. Ibid., 127–28.

8. Ibid., 125–26.

9. Ibid., 123–24.

10. Billie Jean King, with Cynthia Starr, *We Have Come a Long Way: The Story of Women's Tennis* (New York: McGraw-Hill, 1988), 40–41.

11. Ibid.

12. Trevor Wignall, "Wimbledon Is a Farce—'Open' Wanted," *Sunday Dispatch* (London), June 25, 1939.

13. "Alice Marble Signs Pro Contract," *American Lawn Tennis*, November 20, 1940.

14. Joan Younger, "Alice Marble Now Feels Like a Millionaire," *Brooklyn Citizen*, November 14, 1940.

15. Ibid.

16. The final list of venues, in the order of when events were held: New York, Chicago, Minneapolis, Cincinnati, Detroit, Milwaukee, St. Louis, Kansas City, Cleveland, Boston, Buffalo, Pittsburgh, Philadelphia, College Park (MD), Hershey (PA), Baltimore, Chapel Hill (NC), Charlotte (NC), Havana, Nassau (Bahamas), Miami Beach, New Orleans, Houston, San Antonio, Fort Worth, Austin, Los Angeles, San Francisco, Portland (OR), Seattle, Vancouver (Canada), Fresno, Phoenix, Tucson, Dallas, Little Rock (AR), Memphis, Louisville (KY), Maywood (IL), Rockford (IL), Moline (IL), Des Moines, Omaha, Champaign (IL), Indianapolis, Toledo (OH), Columbus (OH), Youngstown (OH), Syracuse (NY), Montreal, Toronto, Rochester (NY), Providence (RI), Northampton (MA), Atlantic City, White Plains (NY), Hartford (CT), Trenton (NJ), Clinton (SC), Atlanta, Birmingham (AL).

17. International News Service, "Glamour Girls Fill Tennis Lists in the U.S.," *San Francisco Examiner*, December 29, 1940.

18. Allison Danzig, "Garden Tennis Slated Tomorrow Night; Miss Marble Set for Debut as Pro," *New York Times*, January 5, 1941.

19. Janet Owen (from *New York Herald Tribune*), "Alice Marble Gets Advice from Mary K. Browne," *Dayton Daily News* (Dayton, OH), December 26, 1940.

20. "Alice Marble in Stage Debut at Loew's State," *Brooklyn Eagle*, December 28, 1940.

21. "Vaudeville Reviews, State, N.Y.," *Billboard*, January 4, 1941.

22. "New Acts in Theatres," *Variety*, January 1, 1941.

23. "Vaudeville Reviews, State, N.Y.," *Billboard*.

24. "New Acts in Theatres," *Variety*.

25. "State, N.Y.," *Variety*, January 1, 1941.

26. "New Acts in Theatres," *Variety*.

27. "Society to Watch Tennis," *New York Times*, January 1, 1941.

28. E. C. Potter Jr., "Alice Marble Makes Pro Debut," *American Lawn Tennis*, January 20, 1941.

29. Allison Danzig, "Garden Tennis Slated Tomorrow Night; Miss Marble Set for Debut as Pro," *New York Times*, January 5, 1941.

30. E. C. Potter Jr., "Alice Marble Makes Pro Debut."

31. Deford, *Big Bill Tilden*, 166.

32. Alice Marble, with Dale Leatherman, *Courting Danger: My Adventures in World-Class Tennis, Golden Age Hollywood, and High-Stakes Spying* (New York: St. Martin's Press, 1991), 172.

33. Robert Morrison, "'It's Fun,' This Pro Tennis," *St. Louis Post-Dispatch*, January 17, 1941.

34. Associated Press, "Tilden Unable to Perform," *Salt Lake Tribune*, January 19, 1941.

35. Herbert Ralby, "La Marble Beaten in Garden Match, Mary Hardwick Hands Alice First Defeat in Three Years," *Boston Globe*, January 24, 1941.

36. "'Business as Usual' And 2 Parties Mark Roosevelt Birthday, President Gets 7 Cakes; Congratulations Pour in on 59th Anniversary," *Evening Star* (Washington, DC), January 30, 1941.

37. "January 30th, 1941," Franklin D. Roosevelt Day by Day, Pare Lorentz Center at the FDR Library, www.fdrlibrary.marist.edu/daybyday/daylog/january-30th-1941.

38. "Tilden Ready for Net Tilt Here He Shows at Pittsburgh; Takes Set from Budge; Woman Stars in Big D.C. Social Events," *Evening Star* (Washington, DC), January 29, 1941.

39. "Tennis Clinic at Tech Precedes Marble's Pro Tussling; Mrs. Roosevelt, British Embassy to Entertain Alice, Mary Hardwick," *Evening Star* (Washington, DC), January 30, 1941.

40. "Marble's Debut Here Fails to Obscure Colorful Tilden," *Evening Star* (Washington, DC), January 31, 1941.

41. "Hardwick Able to Test Marble at Net, but Tilden's Weak Eyes Make Him Easy for Budge," *Evening Star* (Washington, DC), February 1, 1941.

42. "Tennis Stars Entertained by Mr. and Mrs. Osborne," *Charlotte News* (Charlotte, NC), February 7, 1941.

43. "Miss Hardwick to Play before the Duke," *Birmingham Gazette* (Birmingham, UK), February 12, 1941.

44. "Tilden Scores Upset over Don Budge," *Fort Worth Star-Telegram*, February 24, 1941.

45. Deford, *Big Bill Tilden*, 26–27.

46. Beth Stephenson, "Tennis Pros Get 'the Rush' at Matches in Coliseum," *Fort Worth Star-Telegram*, February 24, 1941.

47. Bob Smyser, "Marble and Budge Win in Professional Net Play," *Los Angeles Times*, March 3, 1941.

48. Harry M. Hayward, "Alice Back Home, Is Happy in New Role as Tennis Pro," *San Francisco Examiner*, March 4, 1941.

49. "Tennis Stars Arrive for Tomorrow's Big Show, Tilden Rides Alone; Miss Marble's Coach Is Also with Troupe," *Daily Dispatch* (Moline, IL), April 2, 1941.

50. "Queen of the Courts . . . Alice Marble," *Daily Dispatch* (Moline, IL), March 31, 1941.

51. "Moline Fans Anxious to See All-Time Champ Next Thursday," *Daily Dispatch* (Moline, IL), March 29, 1941.

52. "Heavy Advance Sale for Tennis Show Thursday, Quad-City Fans Are Anxious to See Net Queen Alice Marble," *Daily Dispatch* (Moline, IL), March 29, 1941.

53. Gene Lyons, "Record Crowd Sees Professional Tennis Show," *Daily Dispatch* (Moline, IL), April 4, 1941.

54. Advertisement, "Alice Marble Designs a New Sweater for Realsilk," *Life*, March 10, 1941.

55. "Alice Marble Gives Sweaters for Britain," *Indianapolis News*, April 14, 1941.

56. Deford, *Big Bill Tilden*, 170–71.

57. Ibid.

58. Zipp Newman, "Dusting 'Em Off," *Birmingham News* (Birmingham, AL), May 13, 1941.

59. "Wm. Du Pont, Jr., Gets Reno Divorce," *Philadelphia Inquirer*, February 26, 1941.

60. "Virginia Wolfenden Too Beautiful to Be Champ" *San Francisco Examiner*, March 4, 1941.

61. Belmar Gunderson, tennis champion, telephone interview by author, February 16, 2020.

62. Marble, with Leatherman, *Courting Danger*, 176.

63. "Alice Marble's Boyish Bob Proves a Versatile Hair-Do," *Daily Journal* (Vineland, NJ), January 24, 1941.

64. Betty Clarke, Associated Press, "Bleaching Tips of the Hair Is Newest Trick for Glamour," *Indianapolis News*, March 6, 1941.

65. Jean Pearson, "Alice's Dress Has Action Features; Ribbed Rayon Makes Trim Outfit," *Detroit Free Press*, January 20, 1941.

66. "Dressed for Defense," *Ithaca Journal* (Ithaca, NY), November 6, 1941.

67. "Fashion Preview," *Desert Sun* (Palm Springs, CA), November 14, 1941.

68. "Minute Woman" advertisement, *Boston Globe*, November 7, 1943.

69. Sheilah Graham, "Alice Marble to Aid Mayor La Guardia in Developing Women for National Defense," *Boston Globe*, September 22, 1941.
70. Dorothy Dunbar Bromley, "Keeping Fit the Alice Marble Way," *New York Times Magazine*, October 5, 1941.
71. Marie McGowan "Alice Marble Envisions Nation Turning Actively to 'Sports,'" *New York Herald Tribune*, September 29, 1941.
72. "Marble's Mission," *New Yorker*, January 3, 1942.
73. Marguerite Young, "Alice Marble's 'Hale America!' Rallies Women," *High Point Enterprise* (High Point, NC), October 23, 1941.
74. "Marble's Mission," *New Yorker*, January 3, 1942.
75. Lyn Tornabene, *Long Live the King: A Biography of Clark Gable* (New York: G. P. Putnam's Sons, 1976), 282.
76. "Very Sincerely Yours, Franklin D. Roosevelt," Dear Mr. Gable, accessed September 11, 2022, dearmrgable.com.
77. Tornabene, *Love Live the King*, 283.
78. Arthur P. Tiernan, "Indiana Pledges $2,000,000 for War Effort at Nation's First State-Wide Bond Rally," *Indianapolis Star*, January 16, 1942.
79. Associated Press, "All 22 Found Dead in Burned Wreckage of Lombard Airliner," *San Bernardino Sun* (San Bernardino, CA), January 18, 1942.
80. "Carole Lombard Dies in Crash after Aiding U.S. Defense Bond Campaign," *Life*, January 26, 1942.
81. Robert Matzen, *Fireball: Carol Lombard and the Mystery of Flight 3* (Pittsburgh: GoodKnight Books, 2017), 184–88.
82. *Report of the Civil Aeronautics Board*, July 20, 1942, in Investigations of Aircraft Accidents 1934–1965, accessed January 2, 2022, www.dotlibrary.specialcollection.net.
83. Tornabene, *Long Live the King*, 286.
84. Marble, with Leatherman, *Courting Danger*, 180.
85. Ibid., 179.
86. Sister Celluloid, "Joan Crawford Carries on for Carole Lombard in *They All Kissed the Bride*," Sister Celluloid: Where Old Movies Go to Live, September 20, 2015, accessed January 2, 2022, https://sistercelluloid.com.

21. Wonder Woman

1. "Gay Throngs Greet '42 in Times Square Undaunted by War," *New York Times*, January 1, 1942.
2. Marci Reaven, "Profile: New-York Historical Society," Thirteen, NYC-Arts, April 4, 2013, www.nyc-arts.org/showclips/57621/profile-new-york-historical-society.
3. Emily Yellin, "Lining Up for Wartime Weddings," *New York Times*, February 2, 2017.
4. Russ Symontowne, "Mayor Names 5 Days for City's Scrap Roundup," *Daily News* (New York), September 20, 1942.
5. "Letters to the Editor," John J. McKeogh, *Brooklyn Daily Eagle*, March 6, 1943.
6. Thomas A. Guglielmo, "Desegregating Blood: A Civil Rights Struggle to Remember," *Conversation*, February 12, 2015, updated January 30, 2018, theconversation.com/desegregating-blood-a-civil-rights-struggle-to-remember-37480.
7. "City Patrol Corps Gets Final Review," *New York Times*, August 20, 1945.
8. Emily Arbuckle, "The Civilian War Effort in New York City during World War I and World War II," *MCNY Blog: New York Stories*, Museum of the City of New York, Febru-

ary 3, 2015, blog.mcny.org/2015/02/03/the-civilian-war-effort-in-new-york-city-during -world-war-i-and-world-war-ii.

9. Kenneth T. Jackson, *WWII and NYC* (New York: New-York Historical Society and Museum; London: Scala, 2012), 27.

10. William du Pont Jr. papers, Manuscripts and Archives Department, Hagley Museum and Library, Wilmington, DE.

11. International News Service, "Tennis Queen Unable Stick in War Work," *Lincoln Star* (Lincoln, NE), April 15, 1942.

12. Associated Press, "Marble Resigns OCD Post; Begins Looking for a Job," *Salt Lake Tribune*, April 15, 1942.

13. "Marble in Exhibition," *Berkshire Evening Eagle* (Pittsfield, MA), May 8, 1942.

14. United Press, "N.Y. Army, Navy Relief Fund Show Draws 12,648," *Courier-Post* (Camden, NJ), June 15, 1942.

15. Associated Press, "Feller's Team Beat Army in All-Sports Show," *Star-Gazette* (Elmira, NY), June 15, 1942.

16. Alice Marble, with Dale Leatherman, *Courting Danger: My Adventures in World-Class Tennis, Golden Age Hollywood, and High-Stakes Spying* (New York: St. Martin's Press, 1991), 176.

17. William Moulton Marston, "Why 100,000,000 Americans Read Comics," *American Scholar* 13, no. 1 (Winter 1943–44), 35–44.

18. Jill Lepore, *The Secret History of Wonder Woman* (New York: Alfred A. Knopf, 2014), 223.

19. Howard Whitman, "City Opens Purses Wide as Big Bond Campaign Begins," *Daily News* (New York), June 16, 1942.

20. "Tunic Trend Finds Favor," *Miami Herald*, July 26, 1942.

21. Advertisement, "Tonight's the Night," *Brooklyn Eagle*, July 28, 1942.

22. Alice Hughes, "Tennis Pro Takes Game to Soldiers," *Akron Beacon Journal* (Akron, OH), June 13, 1943.

23. Marble, with Leatherman, *Courting Danger*, 190.

24. Advertisement, *St. Louis Post-Dispatch*, October 11, 1943.

25. "War Bond Tennis Show Is Most Successful," *American Lawn Tennis*, February 20, 1944.

26. Marble, with Leatherman, *Courting Danger*, 190.

27. Lt. (JG) Jack Miller, USNR, "Army-Navy Sponsors Tennis Tour," *American Lawn Tennis*, May 1944.

28. "Control, Rhythm Stressed by Mary Hardwick at Clinic," *Philadelphia Inquirer*, May 21, 1944.

29. Miller, "Army-Navy Sponsors Tennis Tour."

30. Caswell Adams, International News Service, "Army Camps Acclaim Hardwick Net Tour," *Minneapolis Morning Tribune*, July 6, 1943.

31. William D. Richardson, "Kramer Triumphs over Budge in Straight Sets," *New York Times*, March 15, 1944.

32. "Marble-Hardwick Play for Wacs," *American Lawn Tennis*, August 20, 1943.

33. Martha Summer, "Churchill's Daughter Belongs on Peachtree," *Atlanta Constitution*, September 1, 1943.

34. Marble, with Leatherman, *Courting Danger*, 190.

35. "Negro Net Tourney," *California Eagle*, August 10, 1944.

36. "The Politics of Creative Survival, 1915," *Breaking the Barriers: The ATA and Black Tennis Pioneers*, International Tennis Hall of Fame, accessed September 27, 2021, breaking barriers.tennisfame.com/exhibit.

37. "History," American Tennis Association, accessed September 27, 2021, www.yourata .org/history.
38. "Meet Hall of Famers, 2009 Inductees," Black Tennis Hall of Fame, accessed September 27, 2021, blacktennishalloffame.com.
39. Ed Hughes' Column, *The Brooklyn Daily Eagle*, July 30, 1940.
40. "Budge Plays in Harlem," *American Lawn Tennis*, August 5, 1940.
41. "1944: Alice Marble and Mary Hardwick Exhibition Event," *Breaking the Barriers: The ATA and Black Tennis Pioneers*, International Tennis Hall of Fame, accessed September 26, 2021, breakingbarriers.tennisfame.com/exhibit.
42. Cecil Harris and Larryette Kyle-DeBose, *Charging the Net: A History of Blacks in Tennis from Althea Gibson and Arthur Ashe to the Williams Sisters* (Chicago: Ivan R. Dee, 2007), 111.
43. "Meet Hall of Famers, 2009 Inductees, Robert Ryland," Black Tennis Hall of Fame, accessed September 26, 2021, blacktennishalloffame.com.
44. Harrison Smith, "Bob Ryland, First Black Tennis Player to Go Pro, Dies at 100," *Washington Post*, August 13, 2020.
45. "Galleries: Gallery of Champions #2," Black Tennis Hall of Fame, accessed September 26, 2021, blacktennishalloffame.com.
46. Associated Press, "Former Tennis Great Alice Marble Dies," *Montgomery Advertiser* (Montgomery, AL), December 14, 1990.
47. Harris and Kyle-DeBose, *Charging the Net*, 55.
48. "Girls Play for Servicemen," *American Lawn Tennis*, December 1944.
49. Alice Marble, As I See It, "Tennis and High Finances," *American Lawn Tennis*, September 1950.
50. Billie Jean King, with Johnette Howard and Maryanne Vollers, *All In: An Autobiography* (New York: Alfred A. Knopf, 2021), 15.
51. Du Pont to Marble, December 7, 1943, William du Pont Jr. papers, Manuscripts and Archives Department, Hagley Museum and Library, Wilmington, DE.
52. Du Pont to Marble, November 20, 1944, du Pont Jr. papers.
53. "U.P., Alice Marble to Wed When War Is Over," *Albany Democrat-Herald* (Albany, OR), January 24, 1944.
54. Alice Marble, interview by Courtney Gebhart, July 25, 1987, Prickly Pears: Portraits of Historical Palm Springs (local history project), vol. 48, Palm Springs Public Library, Palm Springs, CA.
55. Nancy Spain, *"Teach" Tennant: The Story of Eleanor Tennant, The Greatest Tennis Coach in the World* (London: Werner Laurie, 1953), 68.
56. Ted Tinling, with Rod Humphries, *Love and Faults: Personalities Who Have Changed the History of Tennis in My Lifetime* (New York: Crown, 1979), 171–72.
57. Marble, with Leatherman, *Courting Danger*, 237–38.
58. Marble, with Leatherman, *Courting Danger*, 238–39.
59. "'Softie' Sergeant Blames Stern Visage on Passion for Checkers," *Abilene Reporter-News* (Abilene, TX), February 14, 1943.
60. "Youngsters Frolic as Playground Season Is Opened in City," *Central New Jersey Home News* (New Brunswick, NJ), June 27, 1943.
61. Maureen Daly, author of *Seventeenth Summer*, "See Yourself as Others See You!" *The Chicago Tribune*, June 13, 1943.
62. "Try It," *West Point News* (West Point, GA), April 29, 1943.

22. A Good Address

1. Anatole Broyard, *Kafka Was the Rage: A Greenwich Village Memoir* (New York: Vintage Books, 1997), 7–8.
2. NYC: Landmarks Preservation Commission, Designations, Rockefeller Apartments, June 19, 1984, accessed January 2, 2022, https://www1.nyc.gov/site/lpc/index.page.
3. Alice Marble, interview by Lyn Tornabene, March 23, 1974, in Palm Desert, CA, Clark Gable collection compiled by Lyn Tornabene, Margaret Herrick Library, Academy of Motion Picture Arts and Sciences, Beverly Hills, CA.
4. "NY Bookstores in 1946," New York City April 1946, accessed January 5, 2022, https://sites.google.com/site/newyorkcityapril1946/books/ny-bookstores-in-1946.
5. "And Now a Book Machine, Automatic Vendor Offers 15 Titles at 25 Cents Each," *New York Times*, December 20, 1946.
6. Parul Sehgal, "May's Book Club Pick: Two Novels by Ann Petry, a Writer Who Believed in Art That Delivers a Message," *New York Times*, April 16, 2019.
7. After the war, Pardue continued to write books, including *Create and Make New*, *Korean Adventure*, and *The Eucharist and You*.
8. Christopher Lehmann-Haupt, quoted in Eric Pace, "Charles Scribner Jr., Who Headed Publishing Company, Dies at 74," *New York Times*, November 13, 1995.
9. A. Scott Berg, *Max Perkins: Editor of Genius* (New York: New American Library, 2016), 280.
10. Marble, Alice, 1913–. 1 folder: 35 letters about her book on her tennis career; Archives of Charles Scribner's Sons, C0101, Manuscripts Division, Department of Special Collections, Princeton University Library. The description of Marble's relationship with Scribner's and the correspondence that is cited are based on these archives. All references to Marble's relationship with Scribner's are covered by these archives unless otherwise noted.
11. W. L. Savage's other authors would eventually include "Reinhold Niebuhr and Paul Tillich, the theologians; Jacques Maritain, the philosopher; and Alan Paton, the novelist," according to his obituary, "William Lyttleton Savage, Editor, 91," *New York Times*, January 27, 1990.
12. Alice Marble, *The Road to Wimbledon* (London: W. H. Allen, 1947), 3.
13. This title was later discarded in favor of *The Road to Wimbledon*.
14. Letter on file in the Marble archives at the International Tennis Hall of Fame, Newport, RI.
15. Among the other discarded titles: "Forehand, Backhand and Serve," "Anybody Can Win," "Father Was a High Climber," "I Think I Can," and "Live, Breathe and Dream."
16. Marble, *The Road to Wimbledon*, 164.
17. S. Wallis Merrihew, "William M. Johnston," *American Lawn Tennis*, July 1, 1946.
18. Norman Plastow, in *Safe as Houses: Wimbledon 1930–1945* (London: John Evelyn Society, 1972), 89, writes, "The final figures for casualties were one hundred and fifty killed, four hundred and forty seriously injured and six hundred and thirty one requiring first aid treatment." John Olliff, "32 Nations at Wimbledon Reopening To-Day," *Daily Telegraph and Morning Post* (London), June 24, 1946.
19. "Alice Marble Tabs Kramer Man to Beat," *St. Joseph Gazette* (St. Joseph, MO), June 25, 1946.
20. Alice Marble, "Alice Tells Her Story," *American Lawn Tennis*, October 1946.
21. Mark Borkowski, "I'm Sorry Simon Cowell, You Are About 75 Years behind the Times," *Independent* (London), April 27, 2009.

22. "Alice Marble's Story," *The San Francisco Examiner*, October 4, 1946.
23. John Drohan, "Alice Marble's Saga Exciting," *Boston Traveler*, July 24, 1946.
24. Bill Newell, "Tennis Star's Fight," *Hartford Courant*, July 28, 1946.
25. Curley Grieve, "Sports Parade," *San Francisco Examiner*, July 12, 1951.
26. The scrapbooks are available for view by appointment at the International Tennis Hall of Fame, Newport, RI.
27. Filomena Gould, "Alice Marble Pits Competitive Spirit Against Shoppers Here," *Indianapolis News*, December 3, 1946.
28. Richard Hillway and Geoff Felder, "Stephen Wallis Merrihew and *American Lawn Tennis*," *Journal of the Tennis Collectors of America*, no. 29 (Autumn 2013), 452–456.
29. "A Whilom Sissy Game," *American Lawn Tennis*, August 5, 1932.
30. "History," American Tennis Association, accessed November 12, 2021, www.yourata.org /history.
31. Allen M. Hornblum, *American Colossus: Big Bill Tilden and the Creation of Modern Tennis* (Lincoln: University of Nebraska Press, 2018), 383.
32. Ibid., 383–90.
33. Alice Marble, As I See It, "My Mail and 'My Story,'" *American Lawn Tennis*, April 1948.
34. Advertisement, *American Lawn Tennis*, January 1949.
35. Walter Winchell, "Gossip of the Nation," *Philadelphia Inquirer*, September 21, 1949.
36. Alice Marble, with Dale Leatherman, *Courting Danger: My Adventures in World-Class Tennis, Golden Age Hollywood, and High-Stakes Spying* (New York: St. Martin's Press, 1991), 242.

23. A Vital Issue

1. Alice Marble, *The Road to Wimbledon* (London: W. H. Allen, 1947), 47.
2. Marble, *The Road to Wimbledon*, 8.
3. Althea Gibson, *I Always Wanted to Be Somebody*, ed. Ed Fitzgerald (New York: Harper and Row, 1958), 29.
4. Howard Cohn, "The Gibson Story," *American Lawn Tennis*, July 1, 1950.
5. Ibid.
6. Gibson, *I Always Wanted to Be Somebody*, 53.
7. Ibid., 46.
8. Ibid., 61–62.
9. Ibid., 62.
10. Bruce Schoenfeld, *The Match: Althea Gibson and a Portrait of a Friendship* (New York: Amistad, 2005), 22.
11. Gibson, *I Always Wanted to Be Somebody*, 31.
12. Schoenfeld, *The Match*, 64.
13. Ibid., 65.
14. From the *New York Herald Tribune*, "Alice Marble Calls a Turn," *Ventura County Star-Free Press* (Ventura, CA), July 11, 1950.
15. Gibson, *I Always Wanted to Be Somebody*, 140.
16. Ibid.
17. Ibid.

24. This Is Your Life

1. Kim Addonizio, daughter of Pauline Betz Addie, interview by author, April 2018.
2. Alice Marble, As I See It, "They're Off," *American Lawn Tennis*, December 1950.

3. Jeane Hoffman, "Alice Marble Believes Pro Future Dark for Gals," *Los Angeles Times*, January 11, 1953.

4. Letters to the Editor, *American Lawn Tennis*, January 1950.

5. Letters to the Editor, *American Lawn Tennis*, January 1951.

6. "Letters to the Editor, Reply from Alice Marble," *American Lawn Tennis*, January 1951.

7. Mark Hodgkinson, "In Memory of 'Gorgeous' Gussie Moran," Wimbledon.com, January 30, 2013, accessed September 9, 2022, https://www.wimbledon.com/en_GB/news/articles/2013-01-30.

8. Melissa Isaacs, "'Gorgeous Gussie': Holds On to Less-Than-Glamorous Life," *Orlando Sentinel*, June 19, 1988.

9. Letter from William du Pont Jr. to Alice Marble, August 10, 1951. William du Pont Jr. papers, Manuscripts and Archives Department, Hagley Museum & Library, Wilmington, Delaware.

10. Alice Marble, with Dale Leatherman, *Courting Danger: My Adventures in World-Class Tennis, Golden Age Hollywood, and High-Stakes Spying* (New York: St. Martin's Press, 1991), 244.

11. Du Pont to Marble, December 12, 1952, William du Pont Jr. papers, Manuscripts and Archives Department, Hagley Museum and Library, Wilmington, DE.

12. "Pat and Mike," *TimeOut*, August 17, 2012, www.timeout.com/movies/pat-and-mike.

13. Alice Marble, interview by Lyn Tornabene, March 23, 1974, in Palm Desert, CA, Clark Gable collection compiled by Lyn Tornabene, Margaret Herrick Library, Academy of Motion Picture Arts and Sciences, Beverly Hills, CA.

14. Alice Marble, interview by Patricia Young, January 28, 1980, at Palm Desert Country Club, Historical Society of Palm Desert, CA, Oral History Project.

15. Finding aid by Tanya Brun, William du Pont Jr. papers, Hagley Museum and Library.

16. Linda Marble McCrory, Alice Marble's grandniece, telephone interview by author, July 13, 2019.

25. The Homestretch

1. Alice Marble, "Gal Reactions: Tears for Branca, Shotton," *Brooklyn Daily Eagle*, October 1, 1947.

2. Whitney Martin, "Going to Town—That's Our Alice," *San Francisco Examiner*, November 14, 1940.

3. Alice Marble, "A Love Letter to Baseball," *New York Times Magazine*, August 28, 1955.

4. Alice Marble, interview by Patricia Young, January 28, 1980, at Palm Desert Country Club, oral history project, Historical Society of Palm Desert, CA.

5. Denise Goolsby, "Point Happy a Sweet Spot for Early Arrivals," *Desert Sun* (Palm Springs, CA), August 17, 2014.

6. Letter from Alice Marble to William du Pont Jr., March 13, 1956. William du Pont Jr. papers, Manuscripts and Archives Department, Hagley Museum & Library, Wilmington, Delaware.

7. Letter from Alice Marble to William du Pont Jr., April 23, 1956. William du Pont Jr. papers, Manuscripts and Archives Department, Hagley Museum & Library, Wilmington, Delaware.

8. Jeane Hoffman, "Alice Marble, Ex-Tennis Great, Changes into Nurse's Uniform," *Los Angeles Times*, August 25, 1957.

9. Alice Marble, with Dale Leatherman, *Courting Danger: My Adventures in World-Class Tennis, Golden Age Hollywood, and High-Stakes Spying* (New York: St. Martin's Press, 1991), 240.

10. Letter from Alice Marble to William du Pont Jr., July 31, 1956. William du Pont Jr. papers, Manuscripts and Archives Department, Hagley Museum & Library, Wilmington, Delaware.

11. Mildred Schroeder, "Alice Marble: Tennis Is Still Her Game," *San Francisco Examiner*, October 17, 1964.

12. Lynn Sherr, *Sally Ride: America's First Woman in Space* (New York: Simon and Schuster, 2014), 20.

13. Unless otherwise noted, details and quotations in this section are from: Billie Jean King, telephone interview by author, August 14, 2019.

14. The choice to refer to King largely by her first name in this text, as the choice to call Marble by hers, was influenced in part by King's own words in her autobiography, when she wrote: "By the way, let me say this here. You will notice that invariably I talk about 'Margaret', as I have in the paragraph above, or 'Chrissie' or 'Martina' or 'Tracy' and so on, but in another paragraph I refer to 'McEnroe', 'Borg' and 'Connors', etc. I know it's not proper or fair or equal. But it's just the way it is. People say: 'McEnroe will be playing Borg and Chrissie will be playing Hana.' Maybe some day we won't be saying that, but we do now, and so for the purposes of clarity, I'm just following the line of least resistance." Billie Jean King, with Frank Deford, *The Autobiography of Billie Jean King* (London: Granada, 1982), 60.

15. Ibid., 19.

16. Billie Jean King, with Johnette Howard and Maryanne Vollers, *All In: An Autobiography* (New York: Alfred A. Knopf, 2021), 63.

17. King, with Howard and Vollers, *All In*, 63.

18. King, with Howard and Vollers, *All In*, 66.

19. Billie Jean King, with Kim Chapin, *Billie Jean* (New York: Harper and Row, 1974), 36, 37.

20. King, with Deford, *The Autobiography of Billie Jean King*, 78.

21. King, with Howard and Vollers, *All In*, 64.

22. King, with Chapin, *Billie Jean*, 36.

23. King, with Deford, *The Autobiography of Billie Jean King*, 78.

24. King, with Chapin, *Billie Jean*, 37.

25. Jack Hawn, "Dethroned but Still Queen," *Los Angeles Evening Citizen News*, August 29, 1963.

26. Other sources give the spelling as "Elinore."

27. "Funeral Friday for Handball Ace Dan Marble," *San Francisco Examiner*, August 28, 1963.

28. Jack Hawn, "Hawn Your Mark . . . with Jack Hawn; Dethroned but Still Queen," *Los Angeles Evening Citizen News*, August 29, 1963.

29. Beverly Beyette, "Wimbledon Puts Alice Back in Wonderland," *Los Angeles Times*, June 24, 1983.

30. Marble, with Leatherman, *Courting Danger*, 242.

31. Marble, with Leatherman, *Courting Danger*, 242.

32. "Ex-Net Great Leaves to Join Hall of Fame," *Los Angeles Times*, August 5, 1964.

33. "Lawn Tennis at Newport," *Boston Post*, September 2, 1881.

34. "Ralston Forced to Default in Finals of Casino Tennis," and "Hall of Fame Inductees," photo caption, *Newport Daily News* (Newport, RI), August 17, 1964.

35. "Sports in the News," *Newport Daily News*, August 19, 1964.

36. Marble, interview by Young.
37. Letter from du Pont to Marble, October 26, 1965. William du Pont Jr. papers, Manuscripts and Archives Department, Hagley Museum & Library, Wilmington, Delaware.
38. Marble, interview by Young.
39. Belmar Gunderson, tennis champion, telephone interview by author, February 16, 2020.

26. Once a Champion

1. Marble, interview by Young.
2. Bucky Walter, "U.S. Tennis Needs Heroes," *San Francisco Examiner*, March 23, 1966.
3. Katherine Lowrie, "Alice Marble Still Defying the Odds," *Press-Enterprise* (Riverside, CA), February 5, 1978.
4. Ibid.
5. Beverly Beyette, "Wimbledon Puts Alice Back in Wonderland," *Los Angeles Times*, June 22, 1983.
6. "Alice Marble Appointed P.D.C.C. Social Head," *Desert Sun* (Palm Springs, CA), August 19, 1969.
7. Gene Lube, "Question and Answer: A Conversation with . . . Alice Marble," *Desert Sun* (Palm Springs, CA), July 27, 1981.
8. "Salute Due Alice Marble," *Desert Sun* (Palm Springs, CA), April 4, 1974.
9. "Lovers of Tennis Laud Living Legend Alice Marble," *Desert Sun* (Palm Springs, CA), April 22, 1974.
10. Alice Marble, interview by Lyn Tornabene, March 23, 1974, in Palm Desert, CA, Clark Gable collection compiled by Lyn Tornabene, Margaret Herrick Library, Academy of Motion Picture Arts and Sciences, Beverly Hills, CA.
11. Ted Tinling, *Tinling: Sixty Years in Tennis* (London: Sidgwick and Jackson, 1983), 141.
12. Tinling, *Sixty Years in Tennis*, 145.
13. Lowrie, " Alice Marble Still Defying the Odds."
14. Katherine Lowrie, "Alice Marble Still Defying the Odds," *Post-Enterprise* (Riverside, CA), February 5, 1978.
15. "CRTA to Hear Marble," *Desert Sun* (Palm Springs, CA), January 13, 1978.
16. Maybell Lyon, "Families Reunite," *Desert Sun* (Palm Springs, CA), September 26, 1979.
17. Ibid.
18. Linda Marble McCrory, telephone interview by author, July 13, 2019.
19. "Alice Marble on PD Resort Staff," *Desert Sun* (Palm Springs, CA), August 15, 1981.
20. Beyette, "Wimbledon Puts Alice Back in Wonderland."
21. Ibid.
22. Herb Pasik, "Portrait of a Legend," *Weekend Desert Post* (Palm Desert, CA), May 30, 1986.
23. Lowrie, " Alice Marble Still Defying the Odds."
24. Andrew Warshaw, Associated Press, "Alice Marble's Two Regrets: No Television, No Tiebreakers," *Desert Sun* (Palm Springs, CA), July 4, 1984.
25. Alice Marble, interview by Bud Lessor, March 11, 1975, Oral History Collection, International Tennis Hall of Fame, Newport, RI.
26. David Zaslawsky, "Alice Marble Looks Forward to Wimbledon Visit," *Desert Sun* (Palm Springs, CA), June 23, 1984.

27. Queen Alice

1. Julie Baumer, "Guess Where Jan Wasn't This Year," *Desert Sun* (Palm Springs CA), January 6, 1967.
2. Alice Marble, interview by Patricia Young, January 28, 1980, at Palm Desert Country Club, oral history project, Historical Society of Palm Desert, CA.
3. "Soroptimist Club Continues Tradition," *Desert Sun* (Palm Springs CA), May 5, 1984.
4. Bucky Walter, "A Night to Remember," *San Francisco Examiner*, February 19, 1984.
5. Jackie Story, "Good Food, Wine, Conversation, and Fond Memories," *Desert Sun* (Palm Springs, CA), March 13, 1985.
6. Walter, "A Night to Remember."
7. Bucky Walter, "A Night to Remember," *San Francisco Examiner*, February 19, 1984.
8. Beverly Beyette, "Wimbledon Puts Alice Back in Wonderland," *Los Angeles Times*, June 22, 1983.
9. Ibid.
10. Ibid.
11. Stan Hart, *Once a Champion: Legendary Tennis Stars Revisited* (New York: Dodd, Mead, 1985), 208.
12. Ibid., 21.
13. All quotes and observations about the Hart-Marble encounter are based on Hart, *Once a Champion*, chapter 13, "Alice Marble: Queen Bee," 207–21.
14. "Tiempo de los Niños Support Group Marks Pilot Pen Classic with Buffet," *Desert Sun* (Palm Springs, CA), February 9, 1985.
15. Jackie Story, "Tiempo de los Niños Pulls Off Successful Tourney Brunch," *Desert Sun* (Palm Springs, CA), March 15, 1985.
16. Jackie Story, "Rosen's Show Goes On," *Desert Sun* (Palm Springs, CA), March 27, 1985.
17. Kit Stier, "Marchetti, Nomellini, Three Others Enter Bay Sports Hall," *Oakland Tribune* (Oakland, CA), February 22, 1985.
18. "About: Our Mission," Bay Area Sports Hall of Fame, accessed June 27, 2022, Bashof.org.
19. Bucky Walter, "Morning Muse," *San Francisco Examiner*, February 24, 1985.
20. Herb Pasik, "Portrait of a Legend," *Weekend Desert Post* (Palm Desert, CA), May 30, 1986.
21. Ibid.
22. Fran Benes, "Retired Hero Shows Up at the Reinbolds," *Desert Sun* (Palm Springs, CA), November 21, 1986.

28. Taking a Chance on Love

1. Rita Mae Brown, *Rita Will: Memoir of a Literary Rabble-Rouser* (New York: Bantam Books, 1997), 145.
2. Rita Mae Brown, telephone interview by author, February 8, 2018.
3. Brown, *Rita Will*, 426.
4. Brown, telephone interview by author.
5. Brown, *Rita Will*, 427–28.
6. Except for contextualizing information about the Stage Door Canteen, the details of Marble's wedding and trip to Geneva are based on her version of the story as related to Dale Leatherman, in Alice Marble, with Dale Leatherman, *Courting Danger: My Adventures in World-Class Tennis, Golden Age Hollywood, and High-Stakes Spying* (New York:

St. Martin's Press, 1991) as well as information contained in the drafts of the screenplay by Rita Mae Brown.

7. Brooks Atkinson, "Curtain's Up at the Stage Door Canteen," *New York Times*, March 3, 1942.

8. Brock Pemberton, "The Canteen Grows Up," *New York Times*, February 25, 1945.

9. Marble, with Leatherman, *Courting Danger*, 183.

10. Ibid., 190.

11. Ibid., 187.

12. Ibid., 202.

13. Ibid., 212.

14. Ibid., 218.

15. Ibid., 219.

16. Ibid., 220.

17. Ibid., 220.

18. Ibid., 221.

19. Ibid., 222.

20. Ibid., 228.

21. Ibid., 232.

22. Rita Mae Brown papers, 1929–2001, MSS 12019, Small Special Collections Library, University of Virginia, Charlottesville.

23. All descriptions of and correspondence about the ABC movie project are based on the papers of Rita Mae Brown, 1929–2001, MSS 12019, Small Special Collections Library, University of Virginia.

24. Brown, telephone interview by author, February 8, 2018.

25. Brown, *Rita Will*, 428.

26. Alice Marble, *The Road to Wimbledon* (London: W. H. Allen, 1947), 34.

29. Lullaby at Night

1. Rita Mae Brown, *Rita Will: Memoir of a Literary Rabble-Rouser* (New York: Bantam Books, 1997), 427.

2. "Alice Marble Tennis Champion," Karl Gluesing, August 8, 2010, YouTube video, accessed January 15, 2022, https://www.youtube.com/watch?v=ufVT3_GaBXA. The account of the Alice Marble Center Court dedication is based on this video.

3. Fran Benes, "Women's Commission on Alcoholism Seeks to Establish Halfway House for Mothers," *Desert Sun* (Palm Springs, CA), May 14, 1987.

4. Alice Marble, interview by Courtney Gebhart, July 25, 1987, Prickly Pears: Portraits of Historical Palm Springs (local history project), vol. 48, Palm Springs Public Library, Palm Springs, CA.

5. She succeeded. Her movie credits include *My Name is Kahn* (2010), *Summer School* (1987), and *976-WISH* (1997). She also appeared on several television shows including *Thirty-something* and *Murphy Brown*. Currently, she is a life coach who helps people get "past their nervousness, work through their worries, fears and doubts, and succeed at what they have been born to do."

6. Gus Schirmer was named for an ancestor who started a music publishing company but he went into the theater as an agent, actor, and producer.

7. Herb Pasik "Portrait of a Legend," *Weekend Desert Post* (Palm Desert, CA), May 30, 1986.

8. Correspondence between Alice Marble and Rita Mae Brown can be found in the papers of Rita Mae Brown, 1929–2001, MSS 12019, Small Special Collections Library, University of Virginia.
9. Rita Mae Brown, telephone interview by author, February 8, 2018.
10. During the 1990s, memoir was the genre of the hour. By mid-decade the form held such sway that the *New York Times Magazine* published a cover story proclaiming, "Confessing for Voyeurs; The Age of the Literary Memoir Is Now," documenting the slew of new titles that outdid each other in exploring territory that used to be deemed private, as if there were some kind of bidding war over whose story was more eccentric or sodden or laden with grief, a contest with one aim: "Top this, top this, top this." James Atlas, "Confessing for Voyeurs; The Age of the Literary Memoir Is Now," *New York Times Magazine*, May 12, 1996.
11. Comments from Leatherman are based on in-person interviews by author, May 15–17, 2018, in West Virginia; and October 11, 2019, in Washington, DC, as well as numerous phone conversations and email exchanges.
12. Letter from Rita Mae Brown to Dale Leatherman, November 21, 1987, Papers of Rita Mae Brown, 1929–2001, MSS 12019, Small Special Collections Library, University of Virginia.
13. Unless ascribed to Alice Marble, with Dale Leatherman, *Courting Danger: My Adventures in World-Class Tennis, Golden Age Hollywood, and High-Stakes Spying* (New York: St. Martin's Press, 1991), quotations from Dale Leatherman are from interviews by author.
14. Several of these scrapbooks are currently available for view by appointment at the International Tennis Hall of Fame, Newport, RI.
15. Helena Frost, "Where Do Desert Residents Escape to in Summer?" *Palm Desert Post*, June 8, 1988.
16. Marble to Brown, December 12, 1988.
17. Marble, with Leatherman, *Courting Danger*, 250.

30. Iron Lady

1. Beverly Beyette, "Wimbledon Puts Alice Back in Wonderland," *Los Angeles Times*, June 22, 1983.
2. Comments from Leatherman are based on in-person interviews by author, May 15–17, 2018, in West Virginia; and October 11, 2019, in Washington, DC, as well as numerous phone conversations and email exchanges.
3. Thomas Rogers, "Alice Marble, 77, Top U.S. Tennis Star of the 1930's," *New York Times*, December 14, 1990.
4. Bill Plunkett, "Pioneer in Women's Tennis Dies," *Desert Sun* (Palm Springs, CA), December 14, 1990.
5. Fran Benes, "Top Hats and Tap Dances Add Dazzle to Club Affairs," *Desert Sun* (Palm Springs, CA), January 24, 1991.
6. Fran Benes, "Auxiliary Sends Board Off with 'Style,'" *Desert Sun* (Palm Springs, CA), May 2, 1991.
7. Jonathan Yardley, "Sizzling Serves," *Washington Post*, June 12, 1991.
8. Tim died on April 9, 1992, and Hazel on January 14, 1996.
9. Alice Marble, interview by Lyn Tornabene, March 23, 1974, in Palm Desert, CA, Clark Gable collection compiled by Lyn Tornabene, Margaret Herrick Library, Academy of Motion Picture Arts and Sciences, Beverly Hills, CA.

10. The description of Alice Marble Hall is based on the author's visit during January 2017. The exhibit may no longer be on display.

11. Rita Mae Brown, *Rita Will: Memoir of a Literary Rabble-Rouser* (New York: Bantam Books, 1997), 427.

12. Evelanne Heyman, "Birthdays Celebrated: Octogenarians Climb Pinnacle of Life," *Desert Sun* (Palm Springs, CA), February 1, 1980.

13. Courtney Gebhart, phone interview by author, February 27, 2019.

14. Linda Marble McCrory, telephone interview by author, July 13, 2019.

15. Billie Jean King, with Johnette Howard and Maryanne Vollers, *All In: An Autobiography* (New York: Alfred A. Knopf, 2021), 161.

16. Alice Marble, *The Road to Wimbledon* (London: W. H. Allen, 1947), 5.

17. Billie Jean King, telephone interview by author, August 14, 2019.

18. Brown, *Rita Will*, 428.

19. Ibid.

20. Ibid., 427.

31. Game, Set, Match . . . and Questions

1. Alice Marble, with Dale Leatherman, *Courting Danger: My Adventures in World-Class Tennis, Golden Age Hollywood, and High-Stakes Spying* (New York: St. Martin's Press, 1991), 3.

2. Ibid.

3. Ibid., 110.

4. "F. M. Warburg Dies at 66 in Home Here," *New York Times*, October 21, 1937.

5. Associated Press, "Felix Warburg, Banker, Dies," *Lancaster New Era* (Lancaster, PA), October 20, 1937.

6. Marble, with Leatherman, *Courting Danger*, 93.

7. "Senorita and Alice Marble in Semi-Final," *Daily Mirror* (London), May 28, 1937.

8. "LIZANA: 9–7, 9–7," *Star Green 'un* (Yorkshire, UK), May 29, 1937.

9. Sylva Weaver, "Hollywood's Fairest in Glamour Parade," *Los Angeles Times*, December 29, 1939.

10. Steph McColl, Information and Records Management, Office of the Registrar, Faculty of Arts and Sciences, Harvard University, confirmed on July 20, 2022 that the university has no record of a degree accorded to Marble. "Harvard Honorary Degree Recipients 1692–2008," Harvard University Archives, Research Guides, https://guides.library.harvard.edu/ld.php?content_id=14900437.

11. Gene Lube, "Question and Answer, A Conversation with . . . Alice Marble," *The Desert Sun* (Palm Springs, CA), July 27, 1981.

12. Joe Crowley's fate mirrors that of the spouse of another tennis star, Nancye Wynne, from Australia, who lost in the final match in the US National Championships to Alice in 1938. Wynne married George Bolton in 1940. An RAAF pilot, he was killed in 1942 during a raid in Germany, a tragedy that was widely reported.

13. Robin Finn, "Margaret Osborne duPont—Tennis Champion, Dies at 94," *New York Times*, October 25, 2012.

14. Conversations, Scout892, May 24, 2004, History & Events of World War Two (Moderated), soc.history.war.world-war-ii@googlegroups.com.

15. Fax provided to author by Leatherman.

16. George C. Chalou, ed., *The Secrets War: The Office of Strategic Services in World War II* (Washington, DC: National Archives and Records Administration, 2002), 20.

17. Elizabeth McIntosh, *Sisterhood of Spies: The Women of the OSS* (Annapolis, MD: Naval Institute Press, 1998), 14.
18. Ibid., 11.
19. Donald P. Steury, *The OSS and Project Safehaven: Tracking Nazi "Gold"* (Washington, DC: Center for the Study of Intelligence, 2007), www.cia.gov.
20. Jennifer Conant, *A Covert Affair: Julia Child and Paul Child in the OSS* (New York: Simon and Schuster, 2011), 60.
21. "Stories—Julia Child: Cooking Up Spy Ops for OSS," Central Intelligence Agency, March 30, 2020, accessed January 24, 2022, www.cia.gov.
22. Nicholas Dawidoff, *The Catcher Was a Spy: The Mysterious Life of Moe Berg* (New York: Pantheon Books, 1994), 72.
23. Serge Kovaleski, "The Most Dangerous Game," *Washington Post Magazine*, January 15, 2006.
24. Virginia Reynolds, "'15 Minutes a Day': Alice Marble Heeds Own Physical Fitness Advice," *Minneapolis Star-Journal*, April 20, 1945.
25. "1,000 Watch Alice Marble," *Minneapolis Morning Tribune*, April 20, 1945.
26. "Radio, Today's Aces," *Wisconsin State Journal*, April 22, 1945.
27. "Radio, Tonight's Aces, Variety," *Wisconsin State Journal*, April 23, 1945.
28. Perry E. Smith, "Tennis Queen Confesses—It's Fun to Be Fit, but Alice Admits She 'Slips,'" *Springfield Leader and Press* (Springfield, MO), April 26, 1945.
29. "India Holds National Chps.," *American Lawn Tennis*, May 1945.
30. "Jack Kramer in New Guinea," *American Lawn Tennis*, September 15, 1945.
31. Technology Collection, George Eastman Museum, Rochester, NY.
32. Marble, with Leatherman, *Courting Danger*, 90.
33. Ibid., 31.
34. Alice Marble, interview by Lyn Tornabene, March 23, 1974, in Palm Desert, CA, Clark Gable collection compiled by Lyn Tornabene, Margaret Herrick Library, Academy of Motion Picture Arts and Sciences, Beverly Hills, CA.
35. Billie Jean King, telephone interview by author, August 14, 2019.
36. Ibid.
37. Rita Mae Brown, *Rita Will: Memoir of a Literary Rabble-Rouser* (New York: Bantam Books, 1997), 428.
38. Rita Mae Brown, *Memoir of a Literary Rabble-Rouser*, 427.
39. Interview with the author.
40. Rita Mae Brown, *Memoir of a Literary Rabble-Rouser*, 427.

SELECTED BIBLIOGRAPHY

Agassi, Andre. *Open: An Autobiography.* New York: Alfred A. Knopf, 2009.

Altrocchi, Julia Cooley. *The Spectacular San Franciscans.* New York: E. P. Dutton, 1949.

Barry, John M. *The Great Influenza.* New York: Viking, 2004.

Beebe, Lucius. *The Overland Limited.* Berkeley, CA: Howell-North Books, 1963.

Benfey, Christopher. *If: The Untold Story of Kipling's American Years.* New York: Penguin Press, 2019.

Berg, A. Scott. *Max Perkins: Editor of Genius.* New York: New American Library, 2016.

Berry, David. *A People's History of Tennis.* London: Pluto Press, 2020.

Blair, Clay, Jr., and Joan Blair. *The Search for J.F.K.* New York: Berkley Publishing, 1976.

Boomer, Lucius M. *Hotel Management: Principles and Practice.* New York: Harper and Brothers, 1931.

Broyard, Anatole. *Kafka was the Rage: A Greenwich Village Memoir.* New York: Vintage Books, 1997.

Brown, Anthony Cave. *Wild Bill Donovan: The Last Hero.* New York: Times Books, 1982.

Brown, Ashley. *Serving Herself: The Life and Times of Althea Gibson.* Oxford University Press, 2023.

Brown, Rita Mae. *Rita Will: Memoir of a Literary Rabble-Rouser.* New York: Bantam Books, 1997.

———. *Rubyfruit Jungle.* New York: Bantam, 1988.

Browne, Mary K. *Design for Tennis.* New York: A. S. Barnes, 1949.

Budge, Don. *A Tennis Memoir.* New York: Viking Press, 1969.

Chaplin, Lita Grey. *My Life with Chaplin.* New York: Grove Press, 1966.

Collins, Bud. *The Bud Collins History of Tennis: An Authoritative Encyclopedia and Record Book.* Canada: New Chapter Press. Second edition, 2010.

———. *My Life with the Pros.* New York: E. P. Dutton, 1989.

Collis, Rose. *A Trouser-Wearing Character: The Life and Times of Nancy Spain.* London: Cassell, 1997.

Conant, Jennifer. *A Covert Affair: Julia Child and Paul Child in the OSS*. New York: Simon and Schuster, 2011.

Cooke, Sarah Palfrey. *Winning Tennis and How to Play It*. Garden City, NY: Doubleday, 1946.

Crosby, Alfred W. *America's Forgotten Pandemic: The Influenza of 1918*. New York: Cambridge University Press, 2003.

Crowninshield, Frank. *The Unofficial Palace of New York: A Tribute to the Waldorf-Astoria*. New York: Hotel Waldorf-Astoria Corporation, 1939.

Daniel, Thomas M. *Captain of Death: The Story of Tuberculosis*. Rochester, NY: University of Rochester Press, 1999.

Danzig, Allison, and Peter Brandwein, eds. *The Greatest Sports Stories from* The New York Times: *Sport Classics of a Century*. New York: A. S. Barnes, 1951.

Danzig, Allison, and Peter Schwed, eds. *The Fireside Book of Tennis*. New York: Simon and Schuster, 1972.

Davidson, Sue. *Changing the Game: The Story of Tennis Champions Alice Marble and Althea Gibson*. Seattle: Seal Press, 1997.

Davies, Marion. *The Times We Had: Life with William Randolph Hearst*. New York: Ballantine Books, 1979.

Dawidoff, Nicholas. *The Catcher Was a Spy: The Mysterious Life of Moe Berg*. New York: Pantheon Books, 1994.

Deford, Frank. *Big Bill Tilden: The Triumphs and the Tragedy*. New York: Simon and Schuster, 1976.

Eisenstaedt, Alfred. *Eisenstaedt on Eisenstaedt: A Self-Portrait*. New York: Abbeville Press, 1985.

Engelmann, Larry. *The Goddess and the American Girl: The Story of Suzanne Lenglen and Helen Wills*. New York: Oxford University Press, 1988.

Fadiman, Anne. *The Wine-Lover's Daughter*. New York: Farrar, Straus and Giroux, 2017.

Farrell, Frank. *The Greatest of Them All*. New York: K. S. Giniger, 1982.

Federal Writers Project of the Works Progress Administration. Introduction by David Kipen. *San Francisco in the 1930s: The WPA Guide to the City by the Bay*. Berkeley and Los Angeles: University of California Press, 2011.

Flamm, Jerry. *Good Life in Hard Times: San Francisco in the '20s and '30s*. San Francisco: Chronicle Books, 1999.

Gehring, Wes D. *Carole Lombard: The Hoosier Tornado*. Indianapolis: Indiana Historical Society Press, 2003.

Gibson, Althea. *I Always Wanted to Be Somebody*. Edited by Ed Fitzgerald. New York: Harper and Row, 1958.

Gillmeister, Heiner. *Tennis: A Cultural History*. New York: New York University Press, 1998.

Harris, Cecil, and Larryette Kyle-DeBose. *Charging the Net: A History of Blacks in Tennis from Althea Gibson and Arthur Ashe to the Williams Sisters.* Chicago: Ivan R. Dee, 2007.

Hart, Stan. *Once a Champion: Legendary Tennis Stars Revisited.* New York: Dodd, Mead, 1985.

Himber, Charlotte. *Famous in Their Twenties.* New York: Association Press, 1942.

Hornblum, Allen M. *American Colossus: Big Bill Tilden and the Creation of Modern Tennis.* Lincoln: University of Nebraska Press, 2018.

Hughes, Langston. *The Big Sea: An Autobiography.* New York: Hill and Wang, 1993.

Jackson, Kenneth T. *WWII and NYC.* New York: New-York Historical Society and Museum; London: Scala, 2012.

Jacobs, Helen Hull. *Gallery of Champions.* New York: A. S. Barnes, 1949.

Kastner, Victoria. *Hearst Castle: The Biography of a Country House.* New York: Harry N. Abrams, 2000.

Kimball, Warren F. *The United States Tennis Association: Raising the Game.* Lincoln: University of Nebraska Press, 2017

King, Billie Jean, with Johnette Howard and Maryanne Vollers. *All In: An Autobiography.* New York: Alfred A. Knopf, 2021.

King, Billie Jean, with Cynthia Starr. *We Have Come a Long Way: The Story of Women's Tennis.* New York: McGraw-Hill, 1988.

King, Billie Jean, with Frank Deford. *The Autobiography of Billie Jean King.* London: Granada, 1982.

King, Billie Jean, with Kim Chapin. *Billie Jean.* New York: Harper and Row, 1974.

Lannin, Joanne. *Billie Jean King: Tennis Trailblazer.* Minneapolis: Lerner, 1999.

Lepore, Jill. *The Secret History of Wonder Woman.* New York: Alfred A. Knopf, 2014.

Little, Alan. *Suzanne Lenglen: Tennis Idol of the Twenties.* Wimbledon, UK: Wimbledon Lawn Tennis Museum, 1988.

MacKay, Robert, Anthony K. Baker, and Carol A. Traynor. Foreword by Brendan Gill. *Long Island Country Houses and Their Architects, 1860–1940.* New York: Society for the Preservation of Long Island Antiquities and W. W. Norton, 1997.

Maidstone Club: The First Hundred Years, 1891–1991. West Kennebunk, ME: Phoenix Publishing, 1991.

Marble, Alice, with Dale Leatherman. *Courting Danger: My Adventures in World-Class Tennis, Golden-Age Hollywood, and High Stakes Spying.* New York: St. Martin's Press, 1991.

———. *The Road to Wimbledon.* London: W. H. Allen, [c. 1947].

Marshall, Jon Fisher. *A Terrible Splendor: Three Extraordinary Men, A World Poised for War, and the Greatest Tennis Match Ever Played.* New York: Crown, 2009.

Matzen, Robert. *Fireball: Carole Lombard and the Mystery of Flight 3.* Pittsburgh, PA: GoodKnight Books, 2017.

McIntosh, Elizabeth. *The Women of the OSS: Sisterhood of Spies*. Annapolis, MD: Naval Institute Press, 1998.

McPhee, John. *Levels of the Game*. New York: Farrar, Straus and Giroux, 1979.

McPhee, John. Photographs by Alfred Eisenstaedt. *Wimbledon: A Celebration*. New York Viking Press, 1972.

Mewshaw, Michael. *Short Circuit: The Shocking Exposé of Men's Professional Tennis*. New York: Penguin Books, 1984.

Miller, William H., Jr. *Picture History of the French Line*. Mineola, NY: Dover, 1997.

Morrison, William Alan. *Images of America: Waldorf Astoria*. Charleston, SC: Arcadia, 2014.

Nasaw, David. *The Chief: The Life of William Randolph Hearst*. Boston: Mariner Books, 2001.

Noel, Susan. *Tennis Without Tears*. London: Hutchinson's Library of Sports and Pastimes, 1947.

Parsons, Louella. *The Gay Illiterate*. Garden City, NY: Doubleday, Doran, 1944

Phillips, Caryl, ed. *The Right Set: A Tennis Anthology*. New York: Vintage, 1999.

Powers, John Robert, and Mary Sue Miller. *Secrets of Charm*. Philadelphia: John C. Winston, 1954.

Rae, John W. *Images of America: East Hampton*. Charleston, SC: Arcadia, 2001.

Robertson, Max, ed., with Jack Kramer, advisory ed. *The Encyclopedia of Tennis: 100 Years of Great Players and Events*. New York: Viking Press, 1974.

Randall, Monica. *The Mansions of Long Island's Gold Coast*. New York: Rizzoli, 1987.

Sander, Gordon F. *Serling: The Rise and Twilight of Television's Last Angry Man*. New York: Dutton: 1992.

Schoenfeld, Bruce. *The Match: Althea Gibson and a Portrait of a Friendship*. New York: Amistad 2005.

Sherr, Lynn. *Sally Ride: America's First Woman in Space*. New York: Simon and Schuster, 2014.

Snelling, Dennis. *Lefty O'Doul: Baseball's Forgotten Ambassador*. Lincoln: University of Nebraska Press, 2017.

Spain, Nancy. *"Teach" Tennant: The Story of Eleanor Tennant, the Greatest Tennis Coach in the World*. London: Werner Laurie, 1953.

Swift, Will. *The Kennedys Amidst the Gathering Storm: A Thousand Days in London, 1938–1940*. New York: Smithsonian Books and Collins, 2008.

Swindell, Larry. *Screwball: The Life of Carole Lombard*. Brattleboro, VT: Echo Point Books and Media, 2016.

Tinling, Ted, with Rod Humphries. *Love and Faults: Personalities Who Have Changed the History of Tennis in My Lifetime*. New York: Crown, 1979.

———. *Tinling: Sixty Years in Tennis*. London: Sidgwick and Jackson, 1983.

Tornabene, Lyn. *Long Live the King: A Biography of Clark Gable*. New York: G. P. Putnam's Sons, 1976.

Ungaretti, Lorri. Foreword by Harold Gilliam. *Stories in the Sand: San Francisco's Sunset District, 1847–1964*. San Francisco: Balangero Books, c. 2012.

Wade, Virginia, with Jean Rafferty. *Ladies of the Court: A Century of Women at Wimbledon*. London: Pavilion Books, Limited, 1984.

Walker, Nancy A. *Women's Magazines: Gender Roles and the Popular Press*. Boston: Bedford; St. Martin's, 1998.

Wall, Siobhan. *Quiet London*. London: Frances Lincoln, 2011.

Wallace, David Foster. *String Theory*. New York: Library of America and Little, Brown and Company, 2016.

Warner, Patricia Campbell. *When the Girls Came Out to Play: The Birth of American Sportswear*. Amherst and Boston: University of Massachusetts Press, 2006.

Wilson, Elizabeth. *Love Game: A History of Tennis, from Victorian Pastime to Global Phenomenon*. Chicago: University of Chicago Press, 2016.

INDEX

Alice Marble Center Court, 313–314, 315–316
Alice Marble Cup, 327
Alice Marble Tennis Courts, 326–327
Allen, Gracie, 220
All England Lawn Tennis and Croquet Club, 133–134, 174, 260
amateur status, rules regarding, 195
American Lawn Tennis
   Alice Marble with, 242–248, 253–256, 258–259
   overview of, 242–243
   prejudice within, 244
   quote within, 59, 148, 149, 157, 164, 165, 195–196, 221, 235, 253
American Red Cross, 8–9, 214, 218
American Tennis Association (ATA), 223, 243
Anderson, Margaret, 48
Anderson, Owen, 131
Anderson, Stanley, 48
Aquitania liner, 136
Arkell, Claire and Jimmy, 112
Arnold, Mary, 184, 185
Ashe, Arthur, 224
Associated Press, 164
Atlanta invitational championship, 183
Austin, Bunny, 195
Austin, Mary Therese, 35–36

Babcock, Carolin, 82, 94, 114, 115, 119, 137, 301–302
Bach, John, 271
Ball, Lucille, 128

Baltimore Country Club, 185
Bamboo Lounge (Racquet Club), 112
Bancroft, Mary, 340–341
baseball, 15–16, 22–23, 25
Bay Area Sports Hall of Fame, 295, 301–302
Bay Counties junior girls' championship, 36
Beckwourth, James, 4, 357n4
Bellamy, Ralph, 111–112
Berengaria liner, 132
Berg, Moe, 342
Berkeley Tennis Club, 28, 34–35, 113
Betz, Pauline, 71, 185, 186, 221, 235, 236, 260
Beverly Hills Hotel, 47–48
Beverly Hills Tennis Club, 139–140
Beyette, Beverly, 296, 334
Billboard magazine, 198–199
Birdwell, Russell, 237–238
Birmingham, Alabama, Alice Marble's tour stop within, 207–208
Bloomingdale, Alfred, 146
Bodie, Ping, 22, 23
Bogart, Humphrey, 246
Boomer, Lucius, 151
Boston, Massachusetts, Alice Marble's tour stop within, 202–203
Boston Traveler, 239
Bremen ocean liner, 94–95
Brisbane, Arthur, 91–92
British Columbia tennis championships, 43
Brooklyn Daily Eagle, 64, 141, 190

Brooklyn Times Union, 65
Brough, Louise, 236
Brown, Ashley, 327
Brown, Rita Mae, 303–304, 309, 311,
    318–319, 329, 331, 346
Browne, Mary K.
    advice from, 197–198
    at Civic Auditorium, 20
    at Coronado Hotel, 140
    home of, 282–283, 287
    military service of, 218
    overview of, 288–289
    pep talk from, 60
    personality of, 119
    professional status of, 19
    quote of, 339
    as spectator, 184
    on *This Is Your Life*, 266
    work of, 118
Broyard, Anatole, 231
Bruce, Virginia, 107
Budge, Don
    background of, 31
    on Bobby Riggs, 162
    at Cosmopolitan Tennis Club, 223
    Fourth War Loan Drive and, 221
    Hall of Fame and, 282
    at La Cienega courts, 140
    letters from, 141
    at Madison Square Garden, 200, 222
    marriage of, 202
    in Montreal, Canada, 206–207
    overview of, 193–194
    at Palm Sprints Racquet Club, 115
    on playing with Alice Marble, 296
    tour of, 192
    on turning professional, 168, 193–194
    victories of, 168
    wages of, 201
    at Wimbledon, 135, 136, 144
Bundles for Britain, 206
Bundy, Dorothy, 115, 116, 138, 140, 186,
    187

Bundy, May Sutton, 35, 66
Burns, George, 220
Burroughs, Edgar Rice, 271–272

California, tennis growth within, 27–28.
    See also specific locations
California Eagle, 222–223
California State Tennis Championships,
    28, 81, 113
California state tournaments, 52–53
California Tennis Club, 28, 35–36
Canada, Alice Marble's trip to, 41–42
Canadian championships, 42–44
Carnegie, Dale, 140
Chaffee, Nancy, 250
Champlain ocean liner, 169–170
Chaplin, Charlie, 50, 75
Child, Julia, 342
Christmas, memories of, 6–7
Coachella Valley, 111, 327
Coleman, Emil, 124–125, 138, 151
Collins, Bud, 90, 134–135, 187
Commons, Ernest, 105, 113
Connolly, Maureen, 71, 273, 289–290
Connor, Jimmy, 274
Considine, Bob, 176
Cooke, Elwood, 161–162, 174,
    189
Cosmopolitan Tennis Club, 223
costumes, tennis, 18–19, 33, 86–87,
    90, 145
Courting Danger (Marble), 38, 146–147,
    175, 222, 226, 280, 318–323, 325–326,
    329, 333–334, 335, 339, 344
Court Journal, 26
Coventry, England, 188
Cowen, Roz Schiffer Bloomingdale, 141,
    146, 175
Crawford, Joan, 50, 214
Crosby, Bing, 204–205
Cross, Ida, 34, 36
Crowley, Joseph Norman, 304–305,
    316–317, 337–338, 339

Cruickshank, Josephine, 81, 87, 94
Cukor, George, 263–264

Daily Alta California, 36
Daily Herald, 161–162
Daily Mail, 160
Daily Mirror, 142–143
Daily News, 136
Danzig, Allison, 57, 87, 148, 188,
    199–200, 221
Davenport, Iowa, Alice Marble's tour
    stop at, 117
Davies, Marion, 48, 72, 76, 77, 126, 131,
    367n26
Davis, Bette, 66
dead-ball era, 22–23
Delaware Oaks horse race, 182–183
*Diagnosis and Treatment of Pulmonary
    Tuberculosis, The*, 101
Dickenson, Harold, 43–44, 334
Didion, Joan, 101
Dietrich, Marlene, 112, 227, 336
Dietz, Howard, 156
DiMaggio, Joe, 141, 333
Doeg, May, 35
Donovan, William J., 311, 341
du Pont, Jean Ellen, 209, 284
du Pont, Jean Liseter, 180, 184,
    189, 208
du Pont, Will, Jr.
    actions of, 189
    Alice Marble's relationship with,
        180–183, 208–209, 218, 225
    background of, 179–180, 184
    death of, 284
    divorce of, 189, 280
    financial support from, 191, 225, 237,
        248, 270, 272, 273, 279–280
    illness of, 280–281, 283
    letter from, 216–217, 236, 263, 279–280,
        283
    marriage of, 241–242
    offer of, 191

    property of, 264–265, 270–273
DuPont de Nemours, Inc., 179

East Coast championships, 53, 54–60
Eastern Grass Court Championships,
    185
Eastern Indoor Championships, 251–252
Edwards, Ralph, 265–268
Edward VIII, 132, 160
Eisenhower, Dwight, 257
Eisenstaedt, Alfred, 170–171
Eldred, Brick, 24
Elizabeth II (queen), 257
Ennis, Al, 192, 202
Essex County Club tournament, 81, 129,
    148, 186
Evening Standard, 135
Evert, Chris, 294
Evert, Jimmy, 303–304

Fadiman, Clifton, 172, 203
Fales, Donna, 365–366n21
Farrell, Charles, 111–112
Flagstad, Kirsten, 157
Flippen, Jay C., 198–199
Flynn, Errol, 66, 112
Forest Hills, 57–58, 90, 119–120, 122–124,
    137–138, 148–149, 251. *See also* US
    National Championships
Fort Worth Star-Telegram, 186
Fourth War Loan Drive, 221–222
Fraser, Neale, 273
Fuller, Eddie, 160, 162
Fuller, William C. "Pop," 28, 30
Funato, Osamu, 328

Gable, Clark, 66, 112, 128, 139, 154, 159,
    176, 189, 212–214
Gaines, Max, 219
Gardner, Ava, 128
Gebhart, Courtney, 315, 329
George V (king), 160
George VI (king), 132, 160

Germantown Cricket Club, 58–59
Gibson, Althea, 224, 249–257, 267, 313,
    316, 336
Gill, Brendan, 73
Girls' Park Tennis Club, 36
Godfree, Kitty, 297
Golden Gate Park, San Francisco, 32,
    36–37, 38–39, 126
Gone with the Wind (film), 176, 189, 238,
    335–336
Gordon, Ruth, 264
Grand Central Station (New York), 54
Great American Women, 308–310
Great Depression, 54–55, 152
Greenwich Village, New York, 231–232
Grieve, Curley, 93, 98–99, 140, 149, 333

Hansell, Ellen, 27
Hardwick, Mary
    at Akron, Ohio tennis competition, 184
    on Althea Gibson, 250
    in Boston, Massachusetts, 202–203
    at Cosmopolitan Tennis Club, 223
    Fourth War Loan Drive and, 221–222
    at Madison Square Garden, 222
    military service of, 220
    at Seabright, 185
    tour of, 197, 224–225
    wages of, 201
    at Wightman Cup, 137
    at Wimbledon, 135, 161
Harlem, New York, 243–244
Harlow, Jean, 50, 78
Harris, Jack, 192, 194, 195, 199, 208
Hart, Stan, 297–302
Hartford Courant, 239
Hassler, William, 8, 9
Hearst, George, 73
Hearst, Millicent, 74
Hearst, William Randolph, 72, 73–74,
    75, 76–78, 126, 238–239, 366n9,
    367n26
Hearst Castle, 72–73, 74–79

heat wave, 83–89, 122–123
Henrotin, Sylvia, 96, 120, 224
Hepburn, Katharine, 263–264
Heston, Charlton, 279
Hoare, Samuel, 144, 166
Hope, Bob, 204, 301
Hopman, Harry, 96, 174
horse racing, 15, 149, 179–180
Hotel Huntington invitational
    tournament, 114–115
Hughes, Alice, 157, 220
Hughes, Langston, 54, 152–153
Hunter, Francis, 141
Hyde Park Hotel (London), 160

I. Magnin and Company, 20
Ince, Thomas, 73
influenza epidemic, 8–9, 12
Information Please radio show, 172–173
International Tennis Hall of Fame,
    281–282
Ireland, Alice Marble in, 168–169
Irish Lawn Tennis Championships, 169

Jacobs, Helen Hull
    background of, 30
    characteristics of, 123
    concern of, 95
    description of, 160
    at Eastern Grass Court
        Championships, 185
    at Essex County Club, 120
    at Forest Hills, 65
    Hall of Fame and, 295
    home of, 29
    homosexuality of, 30, 340
    injury of, 144
    military service of, 224
    patience of, 93
    personality of, 30–31
    quote of, 96
    ranking of, 129
    uniform choice of, 90

at US National Championships, 138, 173–174

at Wimbledon, 142, 143–144, 161, 165

James, Freda, 90, 91

Jedrzejowska, Jadwiga (Ja-Ja), 133, 136, 137, 138, 160, 161

Johnston, Billy, 19, 29, 40, 41, 192, 235, 246

Jones, Henry, 27

Junior Wightman Cup, 140

Kahn, Gilbert, 121, 132

Kahn, Otto, 121

Kahn Estate, 121

Kanin, Garson, 264

Kennedy, Joseph, 163

Kennedy, Rose, 163

Kilgallen, Dorothy, 176

King, Billie Jean, 66, 134, 194, 225, 274–277, 330–331, 346

Kinsey, Howard, 19, 52, 63–64

Kovaleski, Fred, 342

Kramer, Jack, 131, 187, 221, 222, 236, 259

Ladd, Cheryl, 316

La Guardia, Fiorello, 210, 215

lawn tennis, history of, 26

Leatherman, Dale, 191, 318–319, 323, 326, 340–341

Leigh, Vivien, 189

Lenglen, Suzanne, 18–21, 82, 118, 136, 143, 145–146, 194–195, 359n14

Library Journal, 326

Life magazine, 154, 170–171

Little, Alan, 19

Lizana, Anita, 133, 138, 142, 335

Loew, Arthur, 186

Lombard, Carole

  accident of, 103–104

  acting career of, 128

  advice from, 181–182

  background of, 105–107

  Clark Gable and, 128, 176

  coaching by, 130

  death of, 213–214

  in Hollywood, 50

  influence of, 115, 127

  at Los Angeles Tennis Club, 66

  marriage of, 159

  support from, 154

  war efforts of, 212–214

Longwood Cricket Club national doubles championship, 137, 148, 186

Longwood Cricket Club tournament, 81

Lorre, Peter, 50

Los Angeles Tennis Club, 66

Los Angeles Times, 140, 259

Lott, George, 282

Louis, Joe, 218

Madison Square Garden, 199–200, 222

Madrigal, Margarita "Tica," 175, 294, 310

Maidstone Club, 57, 81, 82, 83–89

Mako, Gene, 115, 136, 140

Mann, Thomas, 140

Marafioti, Mario, 196

Marble, Alice

  accident of, 182, 321–322, 338–339

  accolades to, 176

  acting career of, 130, 154, 169, 263–264

  aftermath of death of, 324–331

  anger of, 59, 90

  attacks from, 299–300

  baseball experience of, 15–16, 22–24, 25, 269–270

  birth of, 5

  book tour of, 240–241

  childhood of, 3, 4–5, 9–10, 15–17, 21–24

  child of, 345–346

  city life of, 12, 13

  criticism of, 157, 260

  death of, 324–325

  education of, 21–22, 43, 175

  family photo of, 10–11

  family reunion of, 291–292

  fashion sales of, 139, 149–150, 190, 209–210

Marble (cont.)
grief of, 12–13, 214, 278–279, 305, 339
home of, 4, 6, 7, 10–11, 271–272, 287, 328
homosexuality of, 175, 339–340, 346
illness of, 89, 93–94, 94–97, 101–104, 208, 247–248, 275, 277–278, 281, 294, 324, 336
inflation by, 332–347
injuries of, 42–43, 162, 163, 262–263, 314
last will and testament of, 326
living relatives of, 329
marriage of, 297, 305, 337–338
military service of, 210–212, 216–222, 340–344
miscarriage of, 338–339
as Miss Perpetual Motion, 10–11
movie love of, 14
nickname of, 10–11, 23, 65, 91–92
overstory of, 345
personal activities of, 296–297
personality of, 67, 293, 346–347
photograph description of, 171
photographic memory of, 296
physical features of, 25, 304
playing style of, 63, 163
popularity of, 41, 125–126, 289
portraiture of, 141–142, 225, 293, 322
professional status of, 190–191, 259–260
professional tour of, 192–214
as "Queen Alice," 298–302
radio work of, 190
ranking of, 91, 129
rape of, 37–38
recollections regarding, 292, 315–316, 321–322
romantic relationships of, 43–44, 132–133, 175–176, 208–209, 222, 225–226, 303–312
routine of, 69, 306–307
as secret agent, 306–308, 318–319, 340–344
as singer, 106, 151, 155–157, 166, 196, 198–199, 220–221
speculation regarding, 309–310
speech of, 170
sports broadcasting, Alice Marble's work within, 190
suicide attempt of, 339
as tennis coach, 273–277, 330
tennis introduction of, 17–21, 25, 32–39
on *This Is Your Life*, 265–268
training of, 33, 51, 63–64, 67–70, 114, 117, 156
wages of, 155–156, 168, 201, 216, 217–218, 240
on Wimbledon Centre Court, 133–134
work of, 33–34, 40–41, 60, 288, 345–346
as writer, 218–220, 232–248, 249–257, 258–259, 261, 262, 302, 318–323
Marble, Dan, 5, 6, 13, 17–18, 21, 24–25, 35, 40, 67, 92, 124, 278
Marble, George, 5, 6, 302
Marble, Harry, 3–4, 5–6, 10, 12, 301
Marble, Hazel, 5, 6, 12, 22, 98, 113, 326
Marble, Jessie, 4, 5, 7–8, 10, 13–14, 67, 72, 92, 98, 113, 124, 128–129
Marble, Mel, 12
Marble, Tim, 4, 5, 6, 14, 15–17, 91, 174–175, 273
March of Dimes, 203
Marston, William Moulton, 219
Mary (queen), 160, 163, 165
masking, influenza epidemic and, 8–9
Mathieu, Simonne, 136, 143, 144, 161
Mayer, Louis B., 214
McCormack, John, 168, 169
McCrory, Linda Marble, 292, 329–330
McLaren, John, 32–33
McLoughlin, Maurice, 28–29, 47
Merion Cricket Club, 184
Merrihew, Stephen Wallis, 54, 129, 193, 242, 244
Miller, Bonnie, 56, 58

Minneapolis, Minnesota, tennis
competition at, 183–184, 201–202
Minneapolis Star-Journal, 343
Model T, 10, 12
Moffitt, Willis Jefferson "Bill," 225
Moody, Helen Wills, 52, 83, 84–85, 91,
122, 142, 143, 144, 170, 185, 232,
288, 325
Moran, Gussie, 260, 261–262, 300
Murphy, Gerald and Sara, 82
Myrick, Julian, 82, 83–84, 85, 90, 94, 97,
113–114, 118–119, 157

Nassau, Bahamas, Alice Marble's tour
stop within, 204
National Clay Court Championships,
184
Navratilova, Martina, 313
New York City
Alice Marble in, 54–60, 231–232
as cultural capital, 231
description of, 152, 155
in the Great Depression, 54–55
Greenwich Village, 231–232
heat wave in, 85–86
Waldorf-Astoria hotel, 151–153, 156
during World War II, 215–216
New York Times, 54–55, 137, 138, 148,
154–155, 159, 169, 197
New York Times Book Review, 325–326
Northern California Championships, 93
Northern California Tennis Association,
64
Nuthall, Betty, 87–88, 90, 91, 142

O'Doul, Frank, 24, 333
O'Hara, Maureen, 203
Ojai Valley Tournament, 80
Olmsted, Frederick Law, 32
Orsatti, Frank, 169
Osborne, Margaret, 113, 235, 241–242,
273, 280
Osborne, Mr. and Mrs. L. G., 204

Pacific Coast championships, 34, 43, 184
Pacific Southwest Championships,
66, 139
Palfrey, Sarah
at Forest Hills, 64–66
at Longwood, 186
at Maidstone, 96
marriage of, 189
Paris travels of, 94
at Rye, New York, tournament, 137
at Seabright, 81
support from, 254
at US National Championships, 138,
148, 174, 187
at Wimbledon, 144, 161, 165
Palm Desert Country Club, 287–288,
292, 325
Palm Desert Resort and Country Club,
314–315
Palm Springs, California, 327–328
Palm Springs invitational tournament,
115, 131
Palm Springs Racquet Club, 111–113, 295
Panama-Pacific International
Exhibition, 8
Parker, Frank, 135
Parsons, Louella, 78, 128, 131
Pat and Mike (film), 263–264
peddlers, description of, 54–55
Pegler, Westbrook, 91
Perkins, Maxwell, 232–233, 236–237,
239–240
Perow, Dorothea, 41, 42
Petra, Yvon, 136, 236
Philadelphia Cricket Club, 27, 58
Pickford, Mary, 48, 279
Pittsburgh Press, 118
Plimpton, George, 297–298
Porter, Cole, 151, 152
Pottenger Sanitorium for Diseases of the
Lungs and Throat, 100–104, 336
Powell, William, 106–107, 112
Powers, John Robert, 127–128, 341

professional status, description of and challenges regarding, 192–194, 259–260
Publishers Weekly, 325

racism, 215–216, 249–257
Red Cross, 8–9, 214, 218
Reston, James "Scotty," 165–166, 187–188
Richards, Vincent, 19
Ride, Sally, 273–274
Riggs, Bobby, 50–51, 69, 115, 161–162, 165, 167, 184, 185, 186, 187, 246
Ritchie Coliseum, 203–204
Road to Wimbledon, The (Marble)
  confessions and recollections within, 25, 112, 297
  overview of, 357n1
  quote within, 3–4, 6, 41, 43, 44, 85, 103, 337–338
  sales of, 237, 239–240
  writing process of, 232–235
Robinson, Jackie, 223
Roland-Garros Stadium, 95–96, 172
Roosevelt, Eleanor, 170, 203, 210, 212
Roosevelt, Franklin D., 149, 203
Rossi, Angelo, Joseph, 125
Rubyfruit Jungle (Brown), 303
Russell, Jane, 238
Rye, New York, championships, 64–65, 137, 148
Ryland, Robert, 223–224

Salvation Army, 55
San Francisco, California, 7–9, 32, 205, 362–363n3
San Francisco Chronicle, 9
San Francisco Examiner, 18, 22, 23, 34, 36, 52, 65, 80, 113, 161
San Francisco News, 102–103
San Francisco Seals, 15–16, 17, 22–23
Scribner, Charles, Sr., 232, 239
Seabiscuit, 149

Seabright Lawn Tennis and Cricket Club, 56–57, 81, 119–120, 185
Seabright tournament, 147
Seames, Mary Ann, 223
Sears, Richard D., 27
Sedgman, Frank, 259
segregation, in tennis, 223
Serling, Rod, 271
Sert, Josep María, 156
Sert Room, Waldorf-Astoria hotel, 156
Shaw, George Bernard, 77–79, 334, 366n2
Shearer, Norma, 128
Shepherd, Cybill, 316
Sherr, Lynn, 274
Sherry-Netherland Hotel, 170
Shynook, Ike, 260, 262
Simpson, Wallis, 132
Skelton, Red, 203
Smith, Red, 179
Southern California championships, 80, 116
Sperling, Hilde, 135, 161
Spitz, Mark, 295
Sports Illustrated, 257
Stage Door Canteen, 304–305
Stammers, Kay, 121, 122, 138, 142, 160–161, 163, 164, 165, 174
Stanwyck, Barbara, 128, 205
Star Dust, 130
"Stardust" (Carmichael), 166
Steinmetz, Hans, 146–147, 306–308
Stevenson, Margaretta, 240–241
St. George's Hill Club, 133
St. Louis, Missouri, Alice Marble's tour stop at, 131, 140, 202
Sullivan, Ed, 220
Sunset District, San Francisco, 10
Swanson, Gloria, 156

Taylor, Robert, 112
Temple, Shirley, 296
Tennant, Eleanor (Teach)

accident of, 182
Alice Marble's breakup with, 226–227
as caregiver, 99, 102, 104–105, 133, 180
death of, 289
grief of, 214
influence of, 290–291
letter from, 192
letter to, 216–217
management by, 168
offer by, 66
overview of, 46–51
quote of, 63, 67, 69, 71, 88, 97–98, 104,
    114, 115, 117, 119, 139, 147, 159, 165,
    185, 226
reflections regarding, 290
tennis clinics, origin of, 49–50
on *This Is Your Life*, 267–268
training by, 69–71, 72, 131, 330
viewpoint of, 63
tennis
Alice Marble's early experience of,
    17–21, 25, 32–39
changes within, 293–294
history of, 26–31
surfaces for, 27, 28
tension within, 27
western versus eastern, 27–28
"This Can't Be Love," 166
This Is Your Life, 265–268
This Week magazine, 211–212
Thurber, James, 135
Tidball, Jack, 57, 115, 140
Tilden, Bill "Big Bill"
Bill Johnston and, 246
at Birmingham, Alabama, 207–208
at Chicago, Illinois, 200–201
controversy of, 244–246
at Germantown Cricket Club, 58
injuries of, 202
at Madison Square Garden, 200
My Story, 245–246
overview of, 192–193
personality of, 193

professional status of, 19
professional tour of, 192–193
quote of, 80, 93
ranking of, 29
wages of, 201
Time magazine, 30, 257
Tinling, Ted, 88, 119, 226, 261
Tracy, Spencer, 112, 263–264
Treadwell, Margaret, 233, 236
tuberculosis (TB), 100–101, 336
Turner, Lana, 203, 213

uniforms, tennis, 18–19, 33, 86–87, 90, 145
United States Lawn Tennis Association
    (United States Tennis Association),
    27, 53, 84, 118–119, 124, 252, 253
US National Championships, 137–138,
    148–149, 172–174, 181–183, 186–187
US National Indoor Championship,
    250, 252

Vancouver, British Columbia, Canada,
    Alice Marble's tour stop at, 41–42
Vancouver Sun, 41, 42
Van Ryn, Marjorie Gladman, 87, 90,
    186, 187
Variety magazine, 190, 199
Vicaji, Dorothy, 141–142, 322
Victoria, Helena (princess), 145
Vines, Ellsworth, 124
von Cramm, Baron Gottfried, 141

Waldorf-Astoria hotel, 151–153, 156
Wallace, David Foster, 134
Warburg, Felix Moritz, 138–139, 335
Warburg, Freddy, 132, 138
Warner, Pop, 295
Washington, Kenny, 223
Washington State tennis tournament, 43
WAVES, 210–212
Webb, Clifford, 161–162
Webb, Clifton, 50
weddings, during World War II, 215

Weir, Reginald, 223, 224
Weisel, Dorothy, 52, 57
Welles, Orson, 366n9
West Side Tennis Club, 29, 56
Wheeler, Gracyn, 115, 119, 122, 139, 183, 184
White, Harwood (Beese), 67–68
Wightman, George, 48–49
Wightman, Hazel Hotchkiss, 64, 81–82, 144, 158
Wightman Cup, 82, 90, 93, 115, 137
Williams, Serena, 224
Williams, Venus, 224
Wills, Helen, 19, 20, 29–30, 63–64
Wilson Sporting Goods, 50, 66
Wimbledon
   Alice Marble's performance at, 135–136, 143–145, 160–167
   Alice Marble's return to, 320–321
   All England Lawn Tennis and Croquet Club at, 133–134
   cancellation of, 183
   Centre Court of, 134
   as church, 134
   conditions of, 160, 162

   description of, 134–135
   Maurice McLoughlin as first American male finalist of, 29
   One hundredth anniversary of, 291–292, 297
   reopening of, 235–236
   television broadcast of, 135
   during World War II, 188, 235
Winchell, Walter, 247
Wingfield, Walter Clopton, 26
Wodehouse, P. G., 75
Wolfenden, Virginia, 183, 184
"Wonder Woman" stories, 219–220
Wood, Arthur (Uncle Woodie), 15–16, 41, 120
Wood, Marion, 37, 59
Wood, Sidney, 281–282
Workman, Dorothy, 37, 115, 131
World War I, 7, 16
World War II, 141, 154–155, 159, 171–172, 174, 187–189, 210–212, 215–216, 340–344
Wynne, Nancye, 148–149

Yorke, Adeline "Billie," 144, 165